THE FRONTIERS OF LANGUAGE AND NATIONALITY IN EUROPE

BY

LEON DOMINIAN

PUBLISHED FOR
THE AMERICAN GEOGRAPHICAL SOCIETY
OF NEW YORK
BY
HENRY HOLT AND COMPANY
1917

Copyright, 1917,

BY

THE AMERICAN GEOGRAPHICAL SOCIETY OF NEW YORK

THE QUINN & BODEN CO. PRESS
RAHWAY, N. J.

To my Alma Mater
Robert College of Constantinople

PREFACE

THIS book is submitted as a study in applied geography. Its preparation grew out of a desire to trace the connection existing between linguistic areas in Europe and the subdivision of the continent into nations. The endeavor has been made to show that language exerts a strong formative influence on nationality because words express thoughts and ideals. But underlying the currents of national feeling, or of speech, is found the persistent action of the land, or geography, which like the recurrent motif of an operatic composition prevails from beginning to end of the orchestration and endows it with unity of theme. Upon these foundations, linguistic frontiers deserve recognition as the symbol of the divide between distinct sets of economic and social conditions.

The attention bestowed on the Turkish area has been determined by the bearing of the Turkish situation on European international affairs and in the earnest belief that the application of geographical knowledge could provide an acceptable settlement of the Eastern Question. Never has it been realized better than at the present time that an ill-adjusted boundary is a hatching-oven for war. A scientific boundary, on the other hand, prepares the way for permanent goodwill between peoples.

My effort has been directed to confine the work to a presentation of facts, as I have felt that the solution of the boundary problems involved could not be reached satisfactorily by individual opinion. Should these pages afford a working basis, or prove suggestive, in the settlement of European boundary conflicts, I shall feel compensated for the time and labor bestowed on the collection of the material herein contained.

My thanks are due to the American Geographical Society for the liberal spirit displayed in promoting my efforts and particularly for the colored maps which illustrate the text. I am under special obligations to Councilor Madison Grant of the Society for new views and a better insight into the significance of race in European history. To Dr. Isaiah Bowman, Director of the Society, the extent of my debt would be difficult to estimate, as his interest in my work has been unfailing in spite of the pressure of his many duties. I owe him many alterations and suggestions which have greatly improved the text. Neither can I allow the volume to go to press without thanking the American Oriental Society and the Geographical Society of Philadelphia for the reproduction of portions of my articles printed in their publications. Acknowledgment of important criticism on two articles forming the nucleus of the present volume and published in Vol. 47 of the Bulletin of The American Geographical Society is also due to Professors Palmer, Le Compte and Seymour of Yale as well as to Professors Gottheil and Jordan of Columbia. Many friends, whose work has helped mine, I have never seen. To them also I extend thanks.

LEON DOMINIAN.

THE AMERICAN GEOGRAPHICAL SOCIETY,
New York.

SPECIAL ACKNOWLEDGMENTS FOR ILLUSTRATIONS

Figs. 1, 4, 23, 24, P. L. M. Railways of France.
Figs. 15, 16, 17, 19, 20, Swiss Federal Railroads.
Figs. 36, 37, American Scandinavian Review.
Figs. 40, 42, 46, Travel.
Figs. 45, 56, 58, Messrs. Sébah & Joaillier, Constantinople.
Figs. 52, 59, 60, 61, 62, 63, 64, 65, 66, Photos by Dr. E. Banks.

CONTENTS

LIST OF PLATES

INTRODUCTION

By Madison Grant

Mr. Dominian's book on "The Frontiers of Language and Nationality" is the logical outcome of the articles written by him in 1915 in the Bulletin of the American Geographical Society under the titles of "Linguistic Areas in Europe: Their Boundaries and Political Significance" and "The Peoples of Northern and Central Asiatic Turkey." In the present work the problems arising from the distribution of main European languages and from their relation to political boundaries are discussed with clearness and brilliancy. The text embodies a vast collection of facts and data laboriously collected by the author, who has applied to the subject his familiarity with Eastern languages, as well as an impartial vision which is hard to find in these days when our judgments are so warped by the tragedy of the Great War.

The difficulty of depicting conditions geographically in colors or with symbols is of necessity very great. The peasants who form the majority of the population of most European states often speak a different language or dialect from that of the educated upper classes, and such lines of linguistic cleavage frequently represent lines of race distinction as well. For example, in Transylvania the language of about sixty per cent of the inhabitants is Rumanian, while the literary, military and landowning classes speak either Magyar or German, and these Hungarians and Saxons, in addition to forming everywhere the ruling class, are gathered together in many places in compact communities. A similar condition of affairs exists along the eastern boundary of the German Empire, except that here the speech of the peasants is Polish and that of the dominant classes German.

The preparation of the maps which accompany this volume has been a task of peculiar difficulty. It is an easy matter to show by colors the language spoken by actual majorities, but such a delineation frequently fails to indicate the true literary language of the nation. Mr. Dominian's solution of these difficulties has been a very successful one, and the resultant maps are really of great value, especially where they deal with little-known frontiers and obscure lines of demarcation, such as the eastern and western frontiers of the German Empire.

In spite of exceptions, language gives us the best lines for the boundaries of political units whenever those frontiers conform to marked topographical features such as mountain systems. In many cases where the boundaries of language and nationality coincide they are found to lie along the crest of mountains or a well-defined watershed, often along the base of plateaus or elevated districts, and very seldom along rivers. But the boundaries of nationality and of language, when they do coincide, seldom correspond with those of race, and political boundaries are more transitory and shifting than those of either language or race.

There are a few nations in Europe, chiefly small states, which are composed of sharply contrasted languages and races, such as Belgium, where the lowlands are inhabited by Flemish-speaking Teutons, and the uplands by French-speaking Alpines. Belgium is an artificial political unit of modern creation, and consequently highly unstable. The Belgian upper classes are bilingual, a condition which precedes a change of language, and unless Flanders becomes united to Holland or Germany it is more than probable that French speech will ultimately predominate there also.

Among the Celtic-speaking peoples, we have in the highlands of Scotland, in the mountains of Wales, in western Ireland and in the interior of Brittany, remnants of two distinct forms of Celtic speech. These diverse populations have, in common, only their Celtic speech, and are not related, one to the other, by race. As a matter of fact, the Scotch, the Welsh and the Bretons are excellent representatives of the three most divergent races of Europe. The Armorican-speaking Bretons are Alpine by race, the Cymric-speaking Welshmen are Mediterranean, while the Gaelic-speaking Scots are Nordic. In short, there is today neither a Celtic race nor any recognizable remnant of it. If one of these three peoples be Celtic in bodily characters, the other two must of necessity not be Celtic, and furthermore, if we designate any one of the three as Celtic by race, we must include in that term other distant populations which by no stretch of the imagination can be so regarded.

The literary revival of some Celtic dialects may be interesting, but it will only serve to keep the Celtic-speaking populations still more out of touch with the march of modern progress. In the long run the fate of Erse, Gaelic, Cymric and Armorican is certain. They will be engulfed by the French language on the continent, and by the English speech in the British Isles, just as Cornish and Manx have become extinct within a century.

In eastern Europe, the Slavic tongue of Bohemia and Moravia, known as Czech, was fifty years ago on the point of utter collapse, but the literary revival of Bohemia has been successful because it had for support on the east a solid mass of Slavic speech and the political power of Pan-Slavism, and in consequence was able to hold its own against the encroaching German. These Slavic dialects all through eastern Europe and the minor tongues elsewhere are greatly handicapped by the lack of books, newspapers and good literary forms. In the case of Erse and Cymric the difficulties of the spelling are an almost insuperable obstacle. The French language in Quebec and the various languages spoken among newly arrived immigrants in the United States will ultimately meet the same fate, since a few million illiterate and poverty-stricken habitants of Canada and a few million laborers in the United States must in the long run inevitably succumb to the overwhelming power of the world language of the English people.

Although race taken in its modern scientific meaning—the actual physical character of man—originally implied a common origin, it has today little or nothing to do with either nationality or language, since nearly all the great nations of Europe are composed of various proportions of two and sometimes all three of the primary European races. The population of England owes its blood to the Mediterranean and to the more recent Nordic race. Germany is composed of a combination of Nordic and Alpine, Italy of a mixture of Alpine and Mediterranean, while France unites within her boundaries the Nordic in the north, the Mediterranean in the south and the Alpine in the center. Spain and Portugal, however, are overwhelmingly of Mediterranean blood, while the Scandinavian races are purely Nordic. Thus it is quite evident that nationality and language are independent of race, and in fact the meaning of the word "race" as used not only by the man in the street, but also by the historian, is based on the spoken language. So far as race is concerned in its scientific sense, there exists no such thing as a "Latin," a "Celtic," a "German," a "Slavic," or even an "Aryan" or "Caucasian" race. These are linguistic terms, and are not correlated to bodily characters.

Throughout Europe, as pointed out by Mr. Dominian, there is, however, a close correspondence between topographical and geological land features, on the one hand, and the extent and spread of language on the other. A similar close connection has been noted between geographical features and race. Man's topographical surroundings are among the most potent elements of environment, and have operated powerfully in the selection and development of man, but they do not transform or change one race into another. We have now discarded the old conception that blondness has anything to do with latitude, or altitude. Where two distinct races compete in a given environment, it generally happens that one or the other is better adapted to its surroundings, and that race tends to increase at the expense of its rival, with the result that one ultimately replaces the other. The races of Europe were originally adjusted to a certain fixed habitat, and when through conquest or commercial expansion they moved out of their native surroundings into unfamiliar ground, they tended to disappear. In short, race supplies the raw material, and environment is the molding force, or to use another simile, "the oak tree and the poplar tree are both wood, but the one can be polished by rubbing, while the other cannot." In other words, the Greek genius and Hellenic culture were not created by the irregularity and broken configuration of Greece, and if the Greeks had been transplanted at an early time to Arabia, it is hardly conceivable that the world would have seen classic civilization in its most typical form. On the other hand, we have no reason to believe that if the Arabs had settled in Greece, they would have produced either Homer or the Parthenon. If England had remained exclusively in the hands of its original Mediterranean inhabitants, and if the Teutonic Nordics had not conquered it, or even if the Nordic Normans had not reinforced the Saxon strain, it is more than probable that the British Empire would not have achieved its triumphs.

Geographical situation, conditions of soil and of climate, mountain barriers, navigable rivers and abundant seaports have a powerful, even a controlling environmental influence on the raw material supplied by heredity, but in the last analysis it is race that manifests itself by characteristic achievement.

The prevailing lack of race consciousness in Europe compels us to disregard it as a basis for nationality. In the existing nations, races are generally scattered unevenly throughout the map, and are nearly always grouped in classes, as originally race was the basis of all class, caste and social distinctions. Race therefore being not available as a test of nationality, we are compelled to resort to language. As a matter of fact, language is the essential factor in the creation of national unity, because national aspirations find their best expression through a national language.

At the close of the Great European War the question of national boundaries will undoubtedly come to the front and the data collected and set forth in this book will be useful to a thorough understanding of the problems involved. There is reason to believe that if, at the termination of the Franco-Prussian war, the international boundary in Alsace-Lorraine had been run in conformity with the linguistic facts, much of the bitter animosity of later years might have been avoided. Similar problems will press for solution during the next few years, and if a permanent peace is to be assured neither the Allies nor the Central Empires can afford to create new Alsace-Lorraine or Schleswig-Holstein problems by disregarding national aspirations as expressed and measured by a common language or literature.

In the Balkan states the difficulty of finding any political boundaries that in any way correspond to race or language has heretofore been insuperable, but when the Congress of the Nations convenes, whether this year or next, or the year after, every member of it should be familiar with all facts that bear on the case, and above all with the meaning of such facts, and there exists today no book which covers these questions so fully, so accurately and so impartially as Mr. Leon Dominian's "Frontiers of Language and Nationality."

THE FRONTIERS OF LANGUAGE AND NATIONALITY IN EUROPE

CHAPTER I

THE FOUNDATIONS

THE site of populous cities and of trim little towns was once wild waste or sunless woodland. Our rude forefathers, wandering upon uninhabited tracts, converted them into fair fields and domains which their descendants rounded out eventually into nations. Humanity has prospered and today we often think of countries in terms of their characteristic landscape and scenery. But the thought naturally suggested by the name France or England is that of a nation whose people speak French or English. To separate the idea of language from that of nationality is rarely possible.

To say that a man's accent betrays his nationality is another way of stating that every language has a home of its own upon the surface of the earth. A word or an accent will thrive or wither like a tree according to region. In the earliest forms of Aryan languages, words for fish or sea appear to be wanting— a want which points to inland origins. The natives of the scorching equatorial lowlands have no word for ice in their dialects. A further glimpse into the past is required for a proper estimate of these facts. Man's conquest of a region is achieved in two distinct stages. The first settlers rarely accomplish more than a material hold. Their task is exclusively that of exacting sustenance from the soil. Intellectual possession is taken at a later stage. The land then becomes a source of inspiration to its dwellers. Having provided for his material wants, man is now able to cultivate ideals and give free rein to his artistic propensities. Instead of brooding in gloomy anxiety over future support or becoming desperate through sheer want he is able to bestow a leisure hour on a favorite recreation. In both of these stages, his thoughts and the words used for their utterance are in harmony with their surroundings.

We therefore turn to the land for intimate acquaintance with man and his culture. His very character is shaped in the mold of his habitual haunt. And language is little more than the expression of his character. The earnest Scotchman and the steadfast Swede, both hardened by the schooling of a vigorous climate, contrast strikingly with the impulsive Andalusian or the fitful Sicilian trained to laxity and carelessness in the midst of plenty. The revengeful Corsican is the native of an unblest island, while the Russian, bred in the vast and monotonous steppe, cannot avoid injecting a strain of melancholy into the literary treasures which he contributes to the human brotherhood.

The emotional ties which bind man to his country or to his mother tongue are the same because they are rooted in the past. A citizen of any country is conscious of his nationality whenever he realizes that he has a common origin with his compatriots. Language is merely the outward form of this feeling. But without its unifying influence national solidarity cannot be perfected.

The growth of modern European nations and the spread of their languages have been parallel developments. This parallelism is founded on the material ties no less than on the spiritual affinity which bind men to the earth. To furnish evidence of this relationship lies within the province of geography. Historical testimony is also at hand to show that political and linguistic frontiers have tended to coincide during the past two centuries, except where artificial measures have been brought into play. Broadly it may be submitted that the advance of civilization in most countries has been marked by the progress of nationality, while nationality itself has been consolidated by identity of speech.

Language areas, in common with many other facts of geography, have been largely determined by the character of the surface or climate. Occurrences such as the extension of Polish speech to the Carpathian barrier or the restriction of Flemish to the lowland of northwestern central Europe, are not the work of mere chance. An investigation of linguistic boundaries, therefore, implies recognition of the selective influence of surface features. But the influence of region upon expansion or confinement of language is far from absolute. The part played by economic factors will be shown in the following pages to have been of prime importance.

Considered as political boundaries, linguistic lines of cleavage have twofold importance. They are sanctioned by national aspirations and they conform to a notable degree with physical features. Every linguistic area considered in these pages bears evidence of relation between language and its natural environment. A basis of delimitation is therefore provided by nature. Eastern extension of French to the Vosges, confinement of Czech to a plateau inclosed by mountains, uniformity of language in open plains and river basins, all are examples of the evidence provided by geography for statesmen engaged in the task of revising boundaries.

Europe may be aptly regarded as a vast field of settlement where the native element has, again and again, been swamped by successive flows of immigrants proceeding from every point of the compass. The wanderings of these invaders have been directed, in part, into channels provided by the main mountain ranges of Eurasia. Valleys or plains which favored expansion of nationality were, at the same time, the avenues through which languages spread. The barrier boundary of the Mediterranean basin contains a number of important breaches on the north [1] which facilitated the mingling of the Nordic race with Mediterranean men after it had mixed with Alpine peoples. Within historic times men of Celtic speech have been driven westward by Teutons, who also pressed Slavs in the opposite direction. The consequence is that few Frenchmen or Germans of our day can lay claim to racial purity. Northern France is perhaps more

---

[1] E. C. Semple: The Barrier Boundary of the Mediterranean Basin and Its Northern Breaches as Factors in History, *Ann. Assoc. Amer. Geogr.*, Vol. 5, 1915, pp. 27-59.

Teutonic than southern Germany, while eastern Germany is, in many places, more Slavic than Russia. To ascribe political significance to race is therefore as difficult today as it was when Roman citizenship meant infinitely more in comparison.

Nationality, however, an artificial product derived from racial raw material, confers distinctiveness based on history. It is the cultivated plant, blossoming on racial soil and fertilized by historical association. In the words of Ossian: "It is the voice of years that have gone; they roll before me with all their deeds." Men alone cannot constitute nationality. A nation is the joint product of men and ideas. A heritage of ideals and traditions held in common and accumulated during centuries becomes, in time, the creation of the land to which it is confined.

Language, the medium in which is expressed successful achievement or hardship shared in common, acquires therefore cementing qualities. It is the bridge between the past and the present. Its value as the cohesive power of nationality is superseded, in rare instances, by ideals similarly based on community of tradition, hope, or in some cases religion. In speech or writing, words give life to the emotion which nationality stirs in the heart or to the reasoning which it awakens in the mind.

The distinction between the conceptions of race, language and nationality should, at the very outset, be clearly established. Race deals with man both as a physical creature and as a being endowed with spiritual qualities. Tall, blond men constitute a race distinct from their fellows who combine stockiness and brunetness. The basis of differentiation in this case is anatomical. Hence, to talk of an English or Persian race is erroneous. Every nation contains people endowed with widely different physiques, owing to the extensive intermingling of races which has taken place in the course of the million years during which the earth has been inhabited. To be precise, our conception of racial differences must conform to classifications recognized by modern anthropologists. We shall therefore consider the Mediterranean, Alpine and Nordic races—to mention only those com-

FIG. 1—View of the "route d'Italie" or road to Italy at the extreme southeastern border of France and well inside the small area of Italian language lying
within the French political boundary.

posed of white men—and we shall find that they all blend in European nationalities.

Take, as an example, the racial elements entering into the composition of French nationality. The dominating type, in northern France, belongs to the tall, narrow-headed Nordic race, with blue eyes and fair hair. Frenchmen with these characteristics are descendants of Franks and Gauls who settled in the northern plains of the Paris basin. In Brittany and the Massif Central, however, a round-headed and dark type, short and stockily built, is scattered over the two main piles of Archean mountains which still remain exposed to view. In the Aquitaine basin, as well as in the Lower Rhone valley, the narrow-headed Mediterranean race, with dark eyes and hair, is everywhere evident in the short, brunet inhabitants.

Ripley adheres to the racial segregation of European man in the three groups enumerated above. But a further reduction can be established on a purely geographical basis, with the result that Europeans may be classed primarily either as highlanders or lowlanders. Anthropological classification fits admirably in this dual distinction, since the inhabitants of European mountain lands belong to the round-head type while the dwellers of the depressions north and south of the central uplifts have long heads.

From the conception of race we attain that of people by considering the second as derived from the mingling of the first. Intercourse between the three great races of Europe has always existed as a result of migratory movements. The impulse to wander, however much it differed in each known instance, can usually be traced to a single determining cause, definable as the quest after comfort. This was the motive which led men of the Nordic race to abandon their uncomfortable habitat in the north. The same feeling was experienced by Alpine mountaineers as they descended towards attractive lowlands north and south of their rough mountain homes.

Nordics moving to the south and Alpines crowding toward the lowland converged upon one another. No meeting of human beings, in the entire history of mankind, has been fraught with consequences of wider reach than the contact between members of these, the two hardiest races which the world has produced. European nationalities and Aryan languages were born in those momentous meetings. The zone of contact extended from the northwestern, lowland fringe of continental Europe to the saucer-shaped land of Polesia. Along the depressed margin of western Europe a heavy flow of Mediterranean men, moving constantly northward, introduced a third element in the racial constituents of French and British populations. Each of the three races contributed a characteristic share of physical and moral traits to the spirit of nationality in Europe. The Nordics left the impress of their northern vigor wherever they passed. Their native restlessness, the joint product of cold weather and a hard life, became converted into a magnificent spirit of enterprise when-ever it blended with Alpine hardiness or Mediterranean ambition. The Alpines, often considered as the intellectual type, also imparted the virility of highland physiques as they migrated to the lowland. Last, but not least, Mediterranean men contributed the softness of their native character as well as the fine qualities due to a keen artistic sense. The fusion of the three races was accompanied by the creation of the three great groups of European peoples, known as Celts, Teutons and Slavs. The differentiation of these peoples from the fused group occurred at an early period and was probably in full swing towards the close of the Neolithic.

We are thus led to picture the early home of Celtic dialects on territory now falling under French, Dutch and German rule. It is not unlikely that England and Ireland are areas of expan-sion of this language. Eastward, it is known that the Celtic territory extended at least as far as the Elbe. Beyond, in the same direction, an ever widening wedge of Teutonic area inter-posed itself between Celts and Slavs. The prehistoric home of the Teutons will be found in the region around the western extremity of the Baltic Sea. It comprised southern Sweden, Jutland, the German Baltic coast to the Oder and the Baltic islands as far as

FIG. 2—Schwarzwald scenery. A region of transitional dialects between High and Low German.

Gothland. The Slav's original homeland had its site on an imperfectly drained lake-bed extending westward from the middle Dnieper valley to the Niemen and Priepet marshland.

From east to west on the Eurasian land mass the three main forms of language occupy strictly geographical settings. Mono-syllabic Chinese lies rigid and lifeless within its barriers of high mountains and vast seas. The static condition of Chinese civili-zation is reflected in the changeless form of its language. A new idea requires a new word and a corresponding symbol. In the wild and wide-stretching steppes of Siberia, communication of thought or feeling is maintained through the medium of agglu-tinative forms of speech. Grammatically, this marks an improve-ment over the monosyllabic language. In the case considered here it expresses the restlessness and mobility of steppe life. At the same time inferiority of civilization is revealed by poverty of ideas and consequently of words. In the west, however, whether we consider western Asia or Europe, we deal with the world's best nursery of civilization. In those regions are found the highly inflected and flexible languages of the Aryan and Semitic families. The grammar of these languages—a mere adaptation to superior requirements of order and method—ren-ders them particularly responsive to the constant improvement in thought which characterizes western countries.

Aryan languages are spoken all the way from northern India to Europe's westernmost confines. This territory comprises the western extension of the central belt of high Eurasian mountains together with its fringing lowlands. In its elevated portion it is the domain of the Alpine race and of the Nordic in its depressed northern border. On the other hand, that portion of the northern Eurasian grasslands which extends into Europe forms part of the area of Uralo-Altaic languages. It is sometimes contended that the original home of Aryan languages was situated in north-ern Europe, where full-blooded northerners now speak languages belonging to this family. But the weight of evidence in favor of a central European origin will seem almost decisive when we remember that culture and civilization have invariably proceeded from temperate regions. The Aryans issued at first from the contact of northern European lowlanders with the highlanders of central Europe, subsequently mingled with the inhabitants of the Mediterranean basin. As they migrated southward they must have changed continually in race. Every absorption of southern elements tended to modify their racial characteristics. A given type therefore corresponds to a definite period and place. The vagueness conveyed by the term Aryan, whether applied to language or people, is to be explained by the inherent instability of the subject.

A theoretical representation of the operation of this change may be offered by assuming that NA is the offspring of the first Nordic N having come in contact with an Alpine A. The tendency for NA is to migrate southwards. His offspring may be represented as NAA as the likelihood is that NA will have taken an Alpine wife to himself. This is the prelude to a long series of generations to each of which an A strain is added. At the same time the steadily maintained migration of Nordics in a southerly direction towards and beyond the territory occupied by the Alpines tends to bring new N strains to the mixed product. At a given stage contact with Mediterranean races becomes established and the process of obliterating Nordic traits is intensified.

We thus see that as the northern invaders pressed southward they became more or less absorbed in the indigenous populations. Their physique changed and their individuality vanished. However great the strength of the invaders, they could bring relatively few women in their train. This was especially true whenever they operated in a mountainous country. The passes through which their advance was made were open only to the more vigorous in the bands of fighting men or adventurers.

At the end of the Neolithic, about 5,000 years ago,[2] Europe was the home of a type of man physically similar to any average European of our day. This type is the product of long-continued contact between the original human product of Europe, Asia and Africa. The dawn of history finds him speaking Celtic in western

---

[2] The Neolithic lasted longer north of the Alps.

central Europe.   An immense variety of dialects must then have been spoken on the continent, since intercourse was slight.   Their fusion into modern languages has been the work of centuries. Out of the linguistic sifting of the past two millenniums, three great groups of languages have emerged: the Romanic, Germanic and Slavic, distributed over Europe from west to east.   In these three groups French, German and Russian occupy respectively the leading rank.

The distinction between the languages spoken in northern and southern France was highly marked in early medieval days.   The langue d'oïl in use north of a line starting at the mouth of the Gironde River and passing through Angoulême, L'Isle-Jourdain and Roanne eventually acquired ascendancy over the langue d'oc spoken to the south.[3]   The dialect of this northern language which prevailed in Ile-de-France was the precursor of modern French.   It spread rapidly throughout the country after the acquisition of Aquitaine by French kings and the consolidation of France by the annexation of Burgundian lands.   The French of Paris thus became a national language whose linguistic and literary prestige is still strongly felt over the rest of the country.

---

[3] The dialects or patois spoken today in France all fall under one of these two languages. They can be classified as follows:

Langue d'Oc

Patois	Spoken in the Departments of
Languedocian	Gard, Hérault, Pyrénées-Orientales, Aude, Ariège, Haute-Garonne, Lot-et-Garonne, Tarn, Aveyron, Lot, Tarn-et-Garonne.
Provençal	Drôme, Vaucluse, Bouches-du-Rhône, Hautes- and Basses-Alpes, Var.
Dauphinois	Isère.
Lyonnais	Rhône, Ain, Saône-et-Loire.
Auvergnat	Allier, Loire, Haute-Loire, Ardèche, Lozère, Puy-de-Dôme, Cantal.
Limousin	Corrèze, Haute-Vienne, Creuse, Indre, Cher, Vienne, Dordogne, Charente, Charente-Inférieure, Indre-et-Loire.
Gascon	Gironde, Landes, Hautes-Pyrénées, Basses-Pyrénées, Gers.

Langue d'Oïl

Norman	Normandie, Bretagne, Perche, Maine, Anjou, Poitou, Saintonge.
Picard	Picardie, Ile-de-France, Artois, Flandre, Hainaut, Lower Maine, Thiérache, Rethelois.
Burgundian	Nivernais, Berry, Orléanais, Lower Bourbonnais, part of Ile-de-France, Champagne, Lorraine, Franche-Comté.

The Roman conquest of Gaul brought Latin to the country because the civilization of the south was superior. At the time of the coming of the Franks, the Latinized Gaulish language was taken up by the conquerors because it also was the symbol of

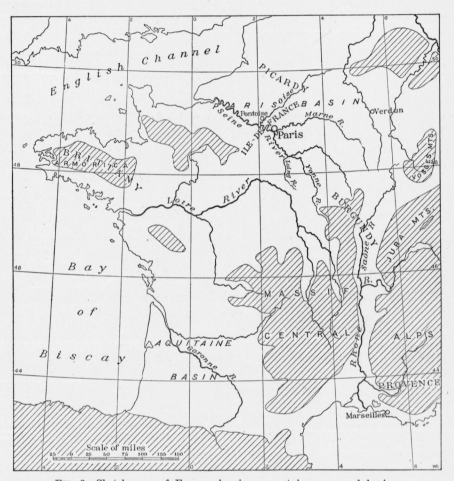

FIG. 3—Sketch map of France showing mountain areas and basins.

superior intellectual development. The conversion of barbarian invaders to Christianity helped to maintain Latinized forms of speech. The Latin of the Romans was modified, however, by the different local dialects. Thus the patois of langue d'oc and of langue d'oïl acquired resemblance through the leavening influence of Latin.

As long as southern France exercised a preponderating influ-

FIG. 4—St. Seine l'Abbaye near Dijon lies in the area of langue d'oil. The fair land of Burgundy, of which the view is typical, has been open to northern invasions on the northwest and the northeast.

FIG. 5—A farmhouse in the Black Forest, a typical habitation in districts in which High German is spoken.

ence in national affairs, the langue d'oc occupied the first place in the country. In the eleventh century it was spoken by the leading classes in the north, as well as by the masses in the south. Such, at least, is the testimony of manuscripts of this period. But with the passing of power into the hands of northern Frenchmen, the langue d'oïl came into wider use, until one of its patois gave rise to the French which was subsequently to become the medium of expression for the genius of Molière and the notable host of his literary countrymen.

Between the langue d'oc and the langue d'oïl the difference was that of north and south. The southern idioms expressed feeling and harmony, hence they were preferred by poets. The troubadours favored them exclusively during the Middle Ages. The "parlers" of the north, on the other hand, were endowed with the staying qualities of lucidity, order and precision. The beauty of modern French, as well as the attraction it exerts on cultivated minds, is due to its well-balanced blend of northern and southern elements. French of our day is the shrine in which the treasured remains of earlier centuries are still preserved. In it the sunshine of the south pierces with its warm rays the severity of northern earnestness. No other European language can boast of an equally happy composition. In this respect it is a true mirror of the French mind as well as of French nationality.

As spoken at present, French is derived in direct line from a sub-dialect of the Picard patois formerly spoken in Paris and Pontoise and which spread throughout all Ile-de-France. This province may be aptly described as the bottom of the bowl-shaped area of northern France. It owes its geographical distinctiveness to the convergence of a number of important valleys which empty the products of their fertility into the Paris basin lying in its very center. Five of these irregular furrows, the Seine, Loing, Yonne, Marne and Oise, radiate outwardly from the low-lying Paris center. The ebb and flow of national power and language sped its alternate course along their channels until, from being the heart, Paris, always inseparable from its language, became also the head of France.

The Frankish dukedom founded on such a site grew naturally into a kingdom. And along with the establishment of a royal court, the language of the region acquired part of the kingly prestige. Herein we find the explanation of the derivation of the name French from that of Frankish as well as of the language from the local sub-dialect of the Picard patois. Already in the thirteenth century, from this magnificently situated base as a

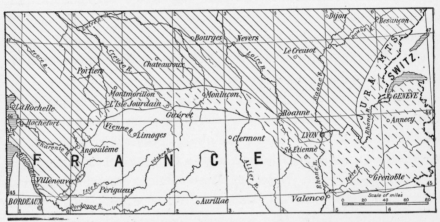

FIG. 6—Part of France showing the contact between "langue d'oc" and "langue d'oïl" countries. The shaded area represents the "langue d'oïl" or northern language. "Langue d'oc" prevailed in the unruled area. Between these two regions a transitional zone, shown by broken ruling, intervened, in which a mixture of the two languages was spoken.

center, both language and nation had absorbed additional territory by a process of steady outward growth. It was French unity in the early making. As early as the twelfth century, no northern nobleman dared appear at the French court without having previously acquired familiarity with its language and manners. The precious literary monuments of this century show that this court language was already known as "François." A hundred years later, about 1260, French had acquired so much polish and importance that we find Italian writers using it in preference to their own dialects. So in 1298, Marco Polo, a Venetian, gives out the first account of his eastern travels in French, while Brunetto Latini, who was Dante's tutor, writes his Tesoreto in the same language, explaining his preference by remarking that French "est plus délitaubles languages et plus communs que moult d'autres."[4]

German was to become the language of central Europe. Interposed between the territories of Romanic and Slavic languages, the area of German speech occupies a magnificently commanding position. Originally the language spoken west of the Elbe and Saale rivers, it had advanced considerably to the east in the first century of the Christian era. The imposition of Teutonic language on Slavic populations is one of the results of this ancient expansion of Germanic peoples. During the past thousand years very little change in the distribution of the main German dialects is believed to have taken place.

Modern German is generally divided into three sub-branches, Low, High and Middle German. Low German, Niederdeutsch or Plattdeutsch,[5] the language of the plain, is restricted to the extensive northern lowland. Dialects spoken in the northeastern corner of Rhenish Prussia, Holstein, Mecklenburg, Brandenburg and Prussia enter into its composition. High German, Oberdeutsch or Hochdeutsch, is the German of the highland. It comprises the Bavarian, Swabian and Alemannic dialects of Bavaria, Württemberg and Baden. Its use as the literary language of all German-speaking people became well established in the Middle Ages. Luther's translation of the Bible written in Saxonian dialect, a combination of High and Middle German, contributed no mean share to the diffusion of the language. Its use has been favored by Germany's most noted writers since the seventeenth century. Schools and newspapers tend to convert it eventually into the only speech that will survive within German boundaries.

A fact of special importance can be traced among the causes leading to the supplanting of Low German, the language of the German plain, by High German as the national tongue. The superiority of the highland dialect is due to its greater assimila-

---

[4] The terminal *s*, a distinctly Latin form, is seen to persist in this early stage of the language.

[5] Niederdeutsch is derived directly from Old Saxon, the language which enters into the composition of the Anglo-Saxon current in England at the time of the Norman Conquest.

tion of Celtic words. This civilizing influence of Celtic culture
is by no means a modern development in Germany. In the protohistoric period it was mainly through contact with the Celts that
the Teutons became civilized. This intellectual dependence of the
Germans is revealed for the period about 300 B.C. by the then
existing civilization, which was entirely Celtic. The history that
spans the intervening years naturally brings to mind the influence
which French language has always had in Germany. Voltaire's
sojourn at the Prussian court does not rank among forgotten
episodes and it was not so long ago that Leibnitz had to resort to
French or Latin as the medium of his written expression.

The transition from the northern plain of Germany to the
high central regions is represented, on the surface, by a zone of
intermediate uplands in Saxony, Lusatia and Silesia. This area
is characterized linguistically by a transitional form of speech
between Low and High German.[6] The similarity, however, of
this midland German to High German is observable to the extent
to which the rising land over which it is distributed presents
analogy to the mountainous region towards which it trends. The
transitional dialects include East, Middle and Rheno-Franconian,
as well as Thuringian. They occur in the middle Rhineland, the
banks of the Moselle, Hesse, Thuringia and Saxony.

A bird's-eye view of the area of German speech shows that
the language prevails wherever a well-defined type of dwelling is
found. This representative habitation consists of a frame house
with an entrance in the middle of one of its long sides. The
hearth generally faces the threshold. Barns and outlying buildings do not connect with the main house, but form with it the
sides of an open inner yard. German houses can furthermore
be subdivided into three distinct sub-types which correspond to
the linguistic divisions of Low, Middle and High German. The
Saxon sub-type, which rarely rises above a single story, prevails
in the northern lowlands, while the Bavarian sub-type dots the
mountain districts which resound to High German. Between the

---

[6] Cf. Sheets 12a, Europe, Flusz-Gebirgskarte, and 12c, Europa, Sprachen- und
Völkerkarte, both 1:12,000,000, in Debes: Handatlas.

two an intermediate sub-type of construction exists in the zone of Middle German.

Russian language while Slavic, and as such Indo-European, is at the same time the transition speech between the Indo-European and Uralo-Altaic groups. Its inflections connect it with the western group. But the dominant use of vowels bears impress of the strong influence exerted by Asia in the formation of the

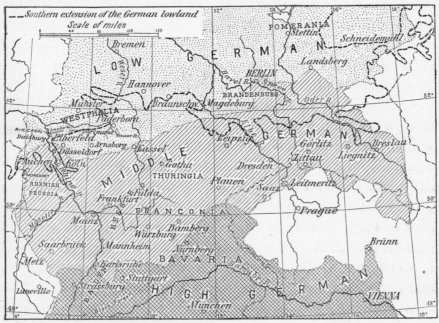

FIG. 7—Sketch map showing relative position of the three main areas in which the dialects of German language are grouped.

language. The very consonants in Russian are liquid and softened so as to shade insensibly into vowels. These are characteristics of Turkish and Finnish. The singular charm with which the melodious sounds of the Russian language greet a stranger's ears is derived from this Asiatic strain. In spirit also the fundamental fatalism of Russians increases in the eastern sections of the country. The trait can hardly be characterized as Slavic. In the case of the Poles or Bohemians, it gives place to buoyant hopefulness which helps to color life and the world in roseate hues. The fatalism of the Russian is a relic of past habitat in the interminable steppes of central Eurasia. The Turks whose former roaming ground was the same are also imbued with this spirit. It is the sophism of the level land. No matter how far the horseman urged his mount, the same monotony met his gaze. No effort on his part could ever change the prospect.

As late as the twelfth century the peoples of the basin of the Volga spoke purely Tatar dialects. The wide and open steppes of Siberia, extending without break into eastern Europe, poured the overflow of their populations into the valleys of the Russian rivers which flow into the Black Sea. The great Russian cities of the borderland between Europe and Asia were either founded or Slavicized after the eleventh century. About that time the Slavic dialects of the Vistula and the Dnieper began to blend with the Asiatic languages of the Oka, Kliasma and Volga valleys. Modern Russian, a mixture of Slavic and Tatar or Mongolian words, was born of this blending. In a broader sense it is the expression of the union of Europe and Asia to create a Russian nation, for Russia is the product of the ancient Russ or Ruthenian principalities and the old Muscovite states. The former were Slav and lay in Europe. The latter were Tatar and belonged physically to Asia. As a nation the Russia of our time sprang into existence at the end of the seventeenth century. Prior to that period, its western section is known to history as the land of Russ or Ruthenia. Its eastern part was Muscovy. Through the union of the eastern and western sections the Russian Empire of modern times came into being. No literary monuments antedate the birth of its nationality.

In Russia the Slav who is free from Asiatic contamination is rarely met east of the 35th meridian. A line from Lake Ladoga to Lake Ilmen and along this meridian to the mouth of the Dnieper forms the divide between the Russians of Europe and of Asia. The parting of the waters belonging respectively to the Don and the Dnieper is, from a racial standpoint, the boundary between the two groups. The Tatar in the Russian appears east of this frontier. The Oriental customs which permeate Russian life, the Tatar words of the Russian language, all begin to assume intensity east of this dividing line, while to the west

FIG. 8.

FIG. 9.

FIG. 8—This group of Russian officers conveys an idea of the excessive racial mingling in Russia. Alpine and Tatar features can be recognized as dominant.

FIG. 9—The heart of Moscow with the buildings of the Kremlin in the background.

the spirit of the vast stretch of north Asiatic steppes disappears. Thus the commonly accepted Ural frontier of European and Asiatic Russia is unwarranted in the light of ethnic facts. The inhabitants of the Volga lands are essentially Asiatics among whom the numerically inferior Slav element has become dominant.

Asia's linguistic contribution to Europe is the gift of its unwooded steppelands. The immense tract of monotonous country extending west of the Altai Mountains to Europe is the home of a family of languages known as the Uralo-Altaic. Among these the highly vocalic branch of Finno-Ugrian traveled west with the nomadic herdsmen who used it. In Europe it acquired the polish which brought it to the forms recognized respectively as Finnish or Suomi and Hungarian. Both enjoy the distinction of being the most cultivated of the great northern Asiatic family of languages. The case of Finnish is especially remarkable owing to its high development without loss of its original agglutinative character.

The picture of this linguistic evolution can be painted only with the colors of geography. The well-defined individuality of the Hungarian Puszta has its counterpart in the Siberian steppe region. The one is the reproduction of the other in small—a miniature. Both consist of undulating land, devoid of mountains or hills, and covered by deep sand. In Finland too a remarkably level stretch of granite land, marked by gentle swelling, lies under a sandy glacial mantle. The two European regions have only one advantage over their Asiatic type. They are better watered. The furthest penetration of Eurasian lowlands into Europe is obtained through them. The approach to Hungary is made without a break, through the valley of the Danube. To Finland access is equally easy once the Urals are crossed. That this range proved no obstacle to the westerly spread of central Asiatic peoples is indicated by their presence west of its axis and their settlement in the Volga valley prior to Slav inroads. But neither in lake-dotted Finnish lands nor within the limited and mountain-hedged area of Hungary could the Asiatic invaders find room for expansion or nomadism. From herdsmen they became farmers. The change is the dawn of their history as a European nation, and of the development of every manifestation of their culture. A more advanced language became the measure of the increasingly complex character of their needs—that is to say, of higher civilization. The whole story, traced from its origin, illustrates the superior civilizing power vested in European geography. In the sterile steppes of the northern half of Asia man led an easier life than in the cramped regions of diversified Europe. On the broad flatlands of the east he roamed with little thought of the morrow and without incentive to improve his condition. In the west he was spurred to activity by the very limitations of his homeland.

In our day about seventy different languages are spoken in Russia. In this fact is found a serious drawback to effective national unity. Fortunately the spread of the dialects belonging to the Slavic group of languages is steady. The thorough Slavicization of the peoples of the basin of the Volga is not yet ended, but Great Russian is gradually uprooting the native Uralo-Altaic tongues. It is also imposing itself upon Asiatic languages in Caucasia and Transcaspian territory. Wherever there has been a thorough blending of dialects into Russian, nationality has sprung into existence. Elsewhere unity is in process of formation. The problem before the governing class consists in hastening the assimilation of the different elements to the original Slavic nucleus. Not until this consummation has taken place will the country have developed its full strength. And the measure of progress will be indicated by the growing replacement of the numerous dialects by a single national language.

Looking back over the stormy centuries during which French, German and Russian nationalities were elaborated, we behold the formative influence of language everywhere. Aspirations which precede the period of free and unfettered national life give way to achievement when national hopes are crowned. This we shall find in greater detail in the succeeding chapters.

Fig. 11—Plain of the Dnieper at Kiev.

Fig. 10—View of Nizhni-Novgorod and the Fair across
the Oka River.

CHAPTER II

THE BOUNDARIES OF FRENCH AND GERMANIC LANGUAGES IN BELGIUM AND LUXEMBURG

THE western section of the Franco-German linguistic boundary extends over Belgian territory through a country in which the formation of nationality has been exceedingly laborious. Flemish and Walloon, two languages within a single political boundary, represent the obstacles which stood in the way of national growth. Physically Belgium also consists of diversified regions. Its history is the long drawn-out struggle between two powerful neighbors. Over and over again its inhabitants have found themselves drawn into foreign quarrels against their will.

The country is a marshland in which the mountains and plains of Europe meet. The main divisions which correspond to this background have inherited the names of Flanders and Wallonia. The clashing-ground of men of the Alpine and Nordic races, Belgium received wave after wave of northerners who came to colonize its broad flatlands. At the time of the conquest, the Romans came upon long-established colonies, but found to their cost that Teuton invasions were not ended. In the fifth century of our era the northern lowland was cleared of Romans by the Franks; but to this day the dualism of its people has not been obliterated. To whatever extent inbreeding has destroyed racial purity, the Fleming of our day represents the Nordic race, while the Walloon is mainly Alpine. Of the two, the fair-complexioned product of the north speaks a Teutonic language, whereas the swarthy highlander is both the user and disseminator of French.

At the partition of the Carolingian Empire in 843,[1] the Schelde became the dividing line between Lotharingia and France.

---

[1] The importance of the treaty of Verdun of this date with regard to the conflict between the French and the German languages is pointed out in the next chapter.

Flemings and Walloons, who had been thrown together for centuries, were separated into an eastern and a western group. Nevertheless their struggle for unity and independence continued to fill Belgium's history. In the ensuing period of national trials, the political disruption of the country is manifested by the growth of civic communities. Belgium became in turn a Burgundian, an Austrian and a Spanish province. The golden age of the Burgundian period brought prosperity to the land, but economic decadence accompanied the prolonged strife between Hapsburgs and Bourbons. It was Belgium's misfortune to be the scene on which the rivalry was fought out. With a population reduced by the horrors of war, Belgium emerged from under the heel of Spanish oppression only to fall successively under Austrian, French and Dutch domination. But the seed of nationality, planted upon its uncertain soil when the valley of the Schelde became part of Burgundy, sheltered a smouldering vitality which, finally, in the nineteenth century was fanned to independence.

The line of contact between French and the languages belonging to the Germanic group begins at the sea on French soil. Starting a few miles west of Dunkirk,[2] the linguistic divide follows a direction which is generally parallel to the political boundary between France and Belgium until, a few miles east of Aire, it strikes northeast to Halluin, which remains within the area of French speech. From this point on to Sicken-Sussen, near the German border, the line assumes an almost due east trend.

This division corresponds broadly to the mountainous and depressed areas into which Belgium is divided. The upland has always been the home of French. Walloon is but a modified form of the old langue d'oïl.[3] Flemish, on the other hand, is a Germanic language which spread over Belgian lowlands as naturally as the Low German dialects to which it is related had invaded

---

[2] G. Kurth: La frontière linguistique en Belgique et dans le nord de la France, *Mém. couronnés, Acad. R. Sci. Let. et Beaux-Arts de Belg.*, XLVIII, Vol. 1, 1895, Vol. 2, 1898, Brussels.

[3] Cf. Map, "Ausbreitung der Romanischen Sprachen in Europa," 1:8,000,000, in Gröber: Grundriss der Romanischen Philologie, Trübner, Strassburg, 1904-1906.

the plains of northern Europe. This east-west line also marks the separation of the tall, blond, long-skulled Flemings from the short, dark, round-skull Alpine Walloons.

The remarkably straight course of the linguistic divide, in Belgian territory, is generally regarded as an effect of the plain over which it extends. Whatever ruggedness it may have once possessed has been smoothed away in the course of centuries by the ease with which either Flemish or French could spread in the low-lying flatland. The two languages have now been facing each other for about four centuries. Place names indicate that the variations of the line have been slight. It is a rare occurrence to find Roman village names north of its present extension. Teutonic roots, in locality names to the south, are likewise unusual. A few can be traced. Waterloo, Tubize, Clabecq, Ohain were once Flemish settlements. Tubize was originally known as Tweebeek and became a Walloon center in the fifteenth century. Ohain likewise is known in the form of Olhem in twelfth century documents.

Belgium's linguistic dualism prevailed throughout the five centuries of the Roman occupation. Intercourse at that time between the Belgae dwelling south of the Via Agrippa, and the Romans who were pushing steadily northwards was frequent and intimate. The Latin of the Roman invaders, modified by the Celtic and Germanic of native populations, gave birth eventually to the Walloon of subsequent times.[4] The Belgae of the lowlands farther north, however, successfully resisted the efforts made by the Romans to conquer them. The marshes of their nether country, and the forested area which was to be laid bare by the monks of the Middle Ages, constituted a stronghold in the shelter of which Germanic dialects took root. This forested area—the Sylva Carbonaria of the Romans—was the chief geographical feature which prevented thorough fusion of Flemings and Walloons. It was the westernmost extension of the Ardennes forests and its

---

[4] The Belgae of Caesar are probably represented by the Teutonic populations of northern France—Flanders and Batavia—rather than by the Walloon. They are a Germanic tribe who made their appearance in Belgium about the third century, B.C.

gloomy solitudes covered the largest part of the territory which has since become the province of Hainaut. Beyond its northern boundary lay the lands of Teutonic culture and language. To the Flemings, living north of the wooded curtain, the Gallo-Romans, who became known as Walloons, were the Walas or "foreigners" who dwelt south of the tree-studded barrier. A sharply defined line of separation intensified, in this manner, all pre-existing racial differences.

At a later date, the growth of the temporal power of the Roman Church resulted in the establishment of a number of bishoprics over districts segregated irrespectively of linguistic differences. Perhaps one of the most striking features of Belgian history is found in the fact that its linguistic and political boundaries have never coincided. Every century is marked by renewal of the age-long clashes between the northern and southern races which have been thrown in contact along the western end of the line which separates the plains of northern Europe from the mountainous southland of the continent.

It may be gathered from all this that the linguistic line of cleavage has undergone very little modification in the course of centuries.[5] It now divides the country into a northern section, the inhabitants of which consider Flemish as their vernacular, but who also generally understand French, and a southern section peopled by French-speaking inhabitants, who adhere to the use of Walloon dialects in the intimacy of their home life. To the east, the political frontier between Belgium and Germany does not divide the two countries linguistically. Within Prussian territory, Malmedy and a group of fifteen villages are inhabited by a French-speaking folk. As though to offset this intrusion of French speech on Prussian soil, a corresponding area of German speech is found in the Belgian province of Luxemburg around Arlon.[6] Altogether about 31,500 Belgians employ German as a vernacular.

[5] G. Touchard: Les langues parlées en Belgique, *Le Mouv. Géogr.*, May 11, 1913, pp. 226-229.

[6] N. Warker: Die deutsche Orts- und Gewässernamen der Belgischen Provinz Luxemburg, *Deutsche Erde*, Vol. 8, 1909, pp. 99, 139.

The figures of the last (Dec. 31, 1910) Belgian census [7] show that the Flemish provinces are bilingual, whereas the Walloon region is altogether French. Knowledge of French as an educational and business requirement accounts for its occurrence in Flanders. The Romance language, therefore, tends to supersede the Germanic idiom as a national vernacular. The utter absence of Flemish in the Belgian Congo constitutes perhaps the strongest evidence in favor of French as Belgium's national language.

In northwestern France, the language of the plain has, since the thirteenth century, steadily receded before the uplander's speech. At that time Flemish was spoken as far south as the region between Boulogne and Aire.[8] The area spreading east of the Atlantic, between the present linguistic boundary and a line connecting these two cities, is now bilingual with French predominating. It might be noted here, however, that Boulogne has been a French-speaking city since Frankish days.

The use of Flemish in France is restricted to the two arrondissements of Dunkirk and Hazebrouck as well as to a few communes of Lille. Dewachter's studies [9] in this locality have been summarized by Blanchard.[10] According to these investigations, the arrondissement of Dunkirk contains 41 Flemish-speaking communes, four of purely French language and 20 of dual speech. Of the last, only five reveal a majority of Flemish speakers. In Hazebrouck there are 36 Flemish communes, eight French and nine bilingual. Five of the latter show French predominance. In the arrondissement of Lille, Flemish is spoken only in six bilingual communes, four of which have a majority of French-speaking residents. Furthermore a few Flemish-speaking families are found in the suburbs of St. Omer as well as in a commune near by. About one-third of the inhabitants

---

[7] Statistique de la Belgique, Recensement Général de 1910, Vol. 2, 1912, Vol. 3, 1913, Brussels.

[8] G. Kurth: op. cit. Kurth's work is based partly on place names. See also L. De Backer: La langue flamande en France, Samyn, Ghent, 1893.

[9] Le flamand et le français dans le nord de la France, 2me Congrès international pour l'extension et la culture de la langue française, Weissenbruch, Brussels, 1908.

[10] Le flamand dans le nord de la France, Ann. de Géogr., Vol. 20, Dec. 15, 1909, pp. 374-375.

of Tourcoing understand Flemish. This is also true of one-half the population of Roubaix. In each of the cities of Lille and Armentières, the ratio falls to one-quarter. Outside of the Flemish-tainted communes of the arrondissement of Lille, the boundary of this language is indicated by the course of the Aa, the canal of Neuffossé and the Lys.

The progress of French, in the Flemish-speaking districts of France, may be followed through the growing invasion of French words in the local vernaculars. The Flemish spoken in Dunkirk or Hazebrouck is an archaic dialect which is growing further and further away from the Flemish of Belgium, as this language tends to identify itself with Dutch in order to acquire literary form. As a rule, French is gradually replacing the Germanic idiom throughout the line of linguistic contact. The Frenchifying of the communes between the Aa and Dunkirk has taken place within the last fifty years. In the same period, Flemish has almost entirely disappeared from the suburbs of St. Omer, and the progress of French towards Cassel and Hazebrouck becomes yearly more apparent. The bilingual aptitude of the inhabitants in all of these localities is on the increase in the sense that many of the Flemings are acquiring proficiency in French. Business requirements in a large degree account for the change.

The only opposition to the advance of French is found in the Flemish immigration which brings fresh linguistic energy in its train. Fortunately for the Romance language, the tide of this immigration is weak and the newcomers are easily assimilated by the French-speaking element. A locality in which the decline of French is noticeable is found in the vicinity of Menin on the Lys river. The number of Flemish immigrants is particularly heavy in this region. Communes which have been French since immemorial times are fast becoming Flemish. Everywhere else, however, French is steadily encroaching upon the domain of Germanic speech.

Brussels typifies the bilingual character of the country of which it is the capital. French and Flemish are spoken both in its precincts and suburbs. The distribution of inhabitants,

FIG. 12.

FIG. 13.

FIG. 12 is a view of the lowlying plain of Flanders in the vicinity of Waterloo.

FIG. 13—Shows the environs of Chaudfontaine and gives an excellent glimpse of the hilly country in which Walloon language has held its own. These two photographs show the contrast between the areas of Walloon and Flemish in Belgium.

according to communes or wards, showed French predominance on December 31, 1910, as follows:

COMMUNES (wards)	Number of inhabitants	French-speaking	Flemish-speaking	Speaking French and Flemish
Bruxelles	177,078	47,385	29,081	85,414
Anderlecht	64,157	11,211	24,320	23,486
Etterbeck	33,227	11,107	6,596	13,166
Forest	24,228	7,975	5,247	8,756
Ixelles	72,991	39,473	6,733	19,799
Jette	14,782	1,811	7,775	4,191
Koekelberg	12,750	1,770	5,702	4,378
Laeken	35,024	4,720	12,702	15,230
Molenbeek-St. Jean	72,783	11,663	24,910	31,331
Saint-Gilles	63,140	24,376	5,928	27,497
Saint-Josseten-Noode ...	31,865	10,547	3,349	14,859
Schaerbeek	82,480	20,975	13,677	40,525
Uccle	26,979	5,818	9,074	10,169
Woluwe—St. Lambert ...	8,883	2,035	3,839	2,262
Totals	720,367	200,866	158,933	301,063

Although Brussels is generally placed on the Flemish side of the linguistic divide, it is interesting to note that the city may appropriately be considered as the northernmost extension of the area of Romance languages in Belgium. Only two villages of Flemish speech intervene between the capital and the Walloon area. They are Rhode-Saint-Genèse and Hoeylaert. Were it not for these two small communities, Brussels would not be an enclave of French speech in Flemish territory. But the two villages are separated by the forest of Soignes which extends in an elongated band, all the way south of Uccle and Boitsfort, to within reach of Waterloo. This wooded area acts as a link which connects Brussels with the ancient area of Romance speech. It tends to restrict Flemish in this section to the lowland to which it really belongs.

Within the city limits the canal, which now replaces the natural water course flowing on the site, divides Brussels into Flemish-speaking quarters and districts entirely given up to French language. West of the waterway, the native vernacular prevails predominantly. This section of the Belgian capital is the site of its industries. Its population consists mainly of laborers. As

early as the twelfth century, the members of the city's guilds
found it convenient to reside along the banks of the stream which
watered the heart of their settlement.   In our day, this part of

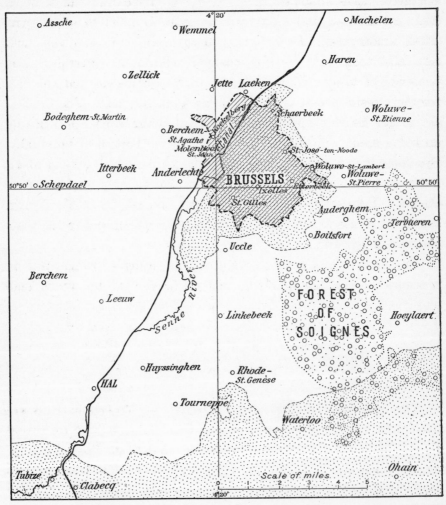

Fig. 14—Sketch map of the environs of Brussels showing the forested patch of
Soignes intervening between the Brussels area of French language (shown by dots)
and the adjacent part of the area of the French language in Belgium (also shown
by dots).   The blank area is territory of Flemish speech.   (Based on a map by P.
Reclus in *La Géographie,* Vol. 28, 1913, p. 312.)

Brussels presents similar advantages to factory owners and
operators of industrial plants.

The rising ground east of the canal has always been favored
as a residential site by the leaders of the community.   In the

Middle Ages the counts of Brabant erected their palace on the summit of this eminence. Since then the well-to-do residents of Brussels have built their homes on this side of the canal. The bourgeois class followed the lead of the aristocracy as soon as their commercial and industrial revenues equaled those of their titled countrymen. French, the language of culture in the land, naturally took root in this eastern section of Brussels. The tendency of the privileged classes to select this part of the city for their residence is as strong today as in the past. The bracing air of the heights and of the forest of Soignes near by affords an inducement which cannot be found in the bottom of the valley. Spacious avenues enlivened by elaborate residences extend along the crest lines. The intervening blocks are tenanted by the middle classes. Educational institutions also flourish in these eastern wards of Brussels. French prevails overwhelmingly in all their nooks and bypaths.

The growth of French in Brussels is strongly brought out by a comparison of the following census figures for the years 1846 and 1910:

	1846	1910
French-speaking inhabitants	70,000	480,000
Flemish " "	130,000	280,000
Totals	200,000	760,000

The gradual replacement of Flemish by French in Brussels may often be traced to recent changes in the growth of the city.[11] In the faubourgs of Woluwe, Boitsfort and Uccle the number of users of French is on the increase each year. The growth proceeds with sufficient regularity to forecast a thorough spread of the language by 1935. In some cases it is easy to foresee that some of the outlying villages will be Frenchified sooner than certain wards of the western part of the city. Tervueren and Linkebeek, for instance, are both noted for the charm of their scenery. Both are centers of attraction for the well-to-do Belgians and as a result tend to lose their Flemish character.

---

[11] P. Reclus: Les progrès du Français dans l'agglomération Bruxelloise, *La Géogr.*, Vol. 28, No. 5, Nov. 15, 1913, pp. 308-318.

In recent years a keen struggle for predominance between Flemings and Walloons has been observed in every province of the country. Each element aspires to impose its racial traits, customs and ideals on its rival. The contest sometimes degenerates into extreme bitterness. The university, the street, the theater, even the government offices are converted into scenes of polemical wrangling. News items in the dailies reveal a constant state of tension between "Flammigants" and "Fransquillons." In this racial struggle, language has been adopted as the rallying standard of both parties. Each faction consistently aims to eliminate the study of the rival tongue in the primary schools of its territory.

The Walloons now represent a true blend of northern, central and southern European types. The mingling was attended by the clash and contest which has always marked racial fusion. As a language Walloon forced itself into existence out of the confusion which followed a long bilingual period and by the sheer obstinacy of an humble Belgo-Roman people whose ears had been attuned to vernacular speech at church and school. It was no mean feat for the inhabitants of the principality of Liége to have retained their language, surrounded as they were by Germanic peoples on all sides but one. The ancient state had the shape of a triangle whose base abutted against a land of French speech. Its sides, however, on the north and the east penetrated like a wedge into districts of Flemish and German.

The language became prevalent in the principality of Wallonia after the tenth century. It was then still in a state of infancy and the literature of its early period is relatively poor.[12] Contrasted with official and aristocratic French the Walloon was a dialect of little account prior to the eighteenth century. Since that time, however, genuine interest has been manifested in its folk-tales and literature by educated Frenchmen. But it remained for Dutch presumption to give a final impetus to the revival of

---

[12] M. Wilmotte: Le Wallon, histoire, littérature des origines à la fin du XVIIᵉ siècle, Rosez, Brussels, 1893. J. Demarteau: Le Wallon, son histoire et sa littérature, Liége, 1889.

Walloon. By the terms of the treaty of Vienna, Belgium and
Holland had been assembled into a single state known as the
Netherlands. The Dutch represented the dominant element in the
union. Their endeavor to impose their language on the Flemings
and Walloons was vigorously resisted by the latter. The streets
of Belgian towns resounded with the hatred of the Dutch
expressed in Walloon words.[13] The separation of Belgium from
Holland in 1830 was in a sense the expression of the linguistic
diversity which had characterized the kingdom of the Netherlands.

Fusion of the two elements of the Belgian population is
observable in the Brabant country, in the vicinity of the linguistic
frontier. Flemish laborers tend to invade Walloon settlements
with the result that the number of inhabitants of Flemish speech
is on the increase. A counter immigration of Walloons into
Flemish villages also exists, with a corresponding addition to the
number of French-speaking inhabitants wherever it takes place.
The fact remains, however, that while Flemings acquire the
French spoken by Walloons, it is an extremely rare occurrence
for the latter to take up Flemish. In the course of time the
Flemish immigrant in Walloon villages learns French, while the
Walloon newcomer in Flemish villages manages to impose his
language on his new neighbors. The net result is a gain for the
French language.

Today, after almost a hundred years' quiescence, the Belgian
question enters upon another critical stage. The problem is one
of language in so far as the two languages spoken in the country
represent the aims and interests of two different peoples. The
Belgian question dates, in reality, from the treaty of Verdun of
843 and the partition of Charlemagne's empire. Belgium then
became the westernmost province of the transition state known
as Lothringia. It was the hedge-country artificially created to
act as a barrier between the peoples of Romanic and Teutonic
speech. Its population, drawn from both elements, has been the
alternate prey of French and German powers. But all of Bel-

---

[13] J. Demarteau: op. cit., p. 134.

gium's troubled history has been affected by the shape of the land. The only frontier with which the nation has been supplied by nature is the sea on the west. On the other three sides land features merge gradually with the main types in their neighborhood. Within Belgian territory, the lowlands of northern Europe join with the outliers of the uplifts of central Europe and their extension into France. Nowhere is the break sharp. The basin of the Schelde itself trespasses on the neighboring basins of the Rhine, the Meuse and the Somme.

Aggravation of the feud between Walloons and Flemings may lead to secession. The Flemish provinces might then cast their political lot with the Dutch, with whom their intercourse has been marked by a degree of friendliness which has never characterized their relations with other neighbors. This extreme course might not unreasonably be adopted as a measure of self-preservation.[14] The languages spoken in Holland and Flanders are practically identical. Religious differences alone have stood in the way of political fusion in the past. Flemish princes, swayed by religious scruples, had refused to side with the Protestant communities whose political connection had been established by the Union of Utrecht in 1597. The menace of absorption by Germany may yet drive the Flemings to union with their close kinsmen of the lowlands on the north. Walloons would then naturally revert to French allegiance. The coincidence of political and linguistic boundaries in the westernmost section of central Europe would then become an accomplished fact.

The language of the Duchy of Luxemburg is a Low German dialect in which a strong proportion of Walloon French words is found. French is taught in schools and is the language of the educated classes. It is also used in tribunals, and in many places as the official language of governing and administrative bodies. The use of French is largely due to intimate intellectual ties which bind Luxemburgers and Frenchmen. It is estimated that at least

---

[14] Germany's violation of Belgian neutrality in 1914 has been followed by systematic endeavors to induce Flemings to favor annexation of their land to Germany on the plea of ancestral kinship.

30,000 natives of the Grand Duchy, or about one-eighth of its population, emigrate to France for business reasons. Many marry French women. Maternal influences prevail with the children born of these unions with the result that, upon returning to their native land, the families bring French speech along.

But French as a commercial language is on the wane throughout the Grand Duchy. German has been replacing it gradually since 1870. This is one of the results of the small state's admission into the ring of German customs. Prior to that period business was transacted mainly in the French dialect of Lorraine. The spread of German is furthermore the result of a systematically conducted propaganda carried on with well-sustained determination. German "school associations" and "Volksvereine," established in every city of importance, help to spread German speech and thought. Lectures of the type entitled "The beauty of Schiller's and Goethe's speech" are delivered by orators who are in reality skilled pioneers of empire engaged in the work of reclaiming populations to Germanism. The efficiency of their methods is proved by the results they have obtained. Out of a population of about 21,000 inhabitants, hardly 4,000 natives of Luxemburg speak French exclusively, while of the six or seven papers published in the capital, two alone are issued in French.

This closing of the German grip over the land stimulated the growth of national feeling among the inhabitants. They were reminded by their leaders that, from having formerly been one of the seventeen provinces of the Netherlands, the duchy acquired the status of a sovereign state in 1890, on the accession of Queen Wilhelmina to the throne. Henceforth the maintenance of Luxemburg's independence rests on the European powers' observance of the pledges by which they guaranteed national freedom for this little state.[15] The natives are free from the burden of onerous taxation imposed on inhabitants of the neighboring powerful countries. Peaceful development of their commerce and

---

[15] Luxemburg's neutrality was guaranteed by the treaty of London, May 11, 1867, to which Britain, Austria, Prussia, France, Belgium, Holland, Italy and Russia were signatories.

industry is thus facilitated. Their land is richly endowed by nature. The wine produced in the Moselle valley and the extensive deposits of high grade iron ore found around Etsch make the community one of the most prosperous on the European continent.

Nevertheless the country seemed predestined by nature itself to form a part of Germany. The broken surface of the Ardenne hilly region and the extension of the plateau of Lorraine are drained by the Sauer and Moselle into German territory. The life of the inhabitants of the entire state is influenced by this easterly drift and tends yearly to greater dispersal in the same direction. This is the danger which prompts them to cling to their independence with patriotic tenacity. Their feelings are reflected in their national hymn, which begins with the words "Mir welle bleiwe wat mer sin" (We wish to remain what we are). These are the words of the tune rendered daily at noon by the chimes of the Cathedral of Luxemburg.

Some fifty miles north of Luxemburg, and at the point of contact of the French, German and Dutch languages, lies the neutral territory of Moresnet, barely three and a quarter square miles in area. This forgotten bit of independent land is claimed by both Prussia and Belgium on account of the exceedingly valuable zinc deposits which it contains. It has a population of some 3,000 inhabitants who, alone among Europeans, enjoy the inestimable privilege of not paying taxes to any government. A Burgomaster, selected alternately from among Prussian and Belgian subjects, rules this diminutive state in conjunction with a Communal Council.

The survival of such a relic of medieval political disorders was due to the impossibility of making a settlement between the two claimants of its territory. In the fifteenth century its mines were the property of the Dukes of Limburg, who had leased them to Philip the Good, Duke of Burgundy. Shortly after the French Revolution, they were declared national property by the French Republic and were operated by the government.[16] With the fall

---

[16] The Neutral Territory of Moresnet, Riverside Press, Cambridge, 1882, p. 14.

of Napoleon, the estate passed under the management of both Prussia and Holland. After the Belgian revolution of 1830, however, the entire property became part of Belgium's share. A demand for rents in arrears from the lessee by Prussia, although recognized as valid by the courts of Liége, was not approved by the new Belgian state and the only compromise that could be reached was a declaration of the neutrality of the territory.

The Belgian question as well as the related Luxemburg and Moresnet problems, the latter being of slight significance, present themselves today as economic settlements no less than political adjustments. The inner reason which had led German hope to dwell on the annexation of Belgium is the knowledge that such an addition in territory would convert Germany into the dominating industrial nation of Europe. This position of superiority would be firmly established if, in addition, the French basins of Longwy and Briey could be turned into Reichslands, as had been done with Alsace-Lorraine in 1870. Fortunately for Europe, the developments of the armed contest begun in 1914 proved that the threat of this economic vassalage is no longer to be feared. Incidentally it is worth remembering that its realization would obviously have been followed by the loss of Holland's independence.

Belgium's political independence is therefore a necessity for the fine adjustment of the balance of European industrial life. And there are quarters where such economic considerations carry greater weight than national sentiments. The main point to be made, however, is that Belgian nationality is entitled to survival, whether it be examined from a material or a moral standpoint. Changes, if any, of its frontiers are indicated in the east, where Malmedy and its environs in Rhenish Prussia constitute a domain of French language. The exchange of this territory for districts of German speech in Belgian Luxemburg and the strategic reinforcement of this eastern frontier, as a safeguard against future aggression, are desirable for Belgians as well as for Germans.

TABLE I

FRENCH- AND FLEMISH-SPEAKING INHABITANTS OF BELGIUM

Census of December 31, 1910

PROVINCES	Number of inhabitants	French-speaking	Flemish-speaking	Speaking French and Flemish
Antwerp	968,677	12,289	762,414	113,606
Brabant	1,469,677	382,947	603,507	381,997
E. Flanders	1,120,335	9,311	934,143	116,889
W. Flanders	874,135	31,825	669,081	123,938
Hainaut	1,232,867	1,113,738	17,283	49,575
Liége	888,341	748,504	14,726	50,068
Limbourg	275,691	9,123	218,622	29,386
Luxemburg	231,215	183,218	153	1,393
Namur	362,846	342,379	733	4,436
Totals	7,423,784	2,833,334	3,220,662	871,288

This table shows French predominance for the entire country. The arrangement given immediately below brings out this fact more clearly.

Inhabitants speaking	French only	2,833,334
"	"	French and Flemish	871,288
"	"	French and German	74,993
"	"	French, German and Flemish ..	52,547
"	"	German only	31,415
"	"	German and Flemish	8,652
"	"	Flemish only	3,220,662
"	"	None [17] of the three languages	330,893
			7,423,784

[17] Children under two and foreigners are included under this heading.

CHAPTER III

THE FRANCO-GERMAN LINGUISTIC BOUNDARY IN ALSACE-LORRAINE AND SWITZERLAND

WITH the exception of a few districts in Alsace-Lorraine, the political boundary between France and Germany is also the linguistic line between French and German languages. This condition is a result of the modifications which French frontiers have undergone since the treaty of Utrecht in 1714. Unfortunately the Napoleonic period and its disorderly train of political disturbances brought about an unnatural extension of the northern and eastern lines. France departed for a time from the self-appointed task of attracting French-speaking provinces to itself. Between 1792 and 1814 almost all of the territory of Belgium and Holland was annexed and the eastern frontier extended to the Rhine. Teutonic peoples in Holland, Flanders, Rhenish Prussia and the western sections of Hesse and Baden passed under French control. But their subjection to Napoleon's artificial empire was of relatively short duration. The German-speaking people in 1813 united in a great effort to drive the French across the Rhine. They were merely repeating the feat of their ancestors who, at an interval of eighteen centuries, had defeated the Latin-speaking invaders of their country led by Varus. Success in both movements was largely the result of the feeling of kinship based on language. In 9 A.D. the Romans were forced back to the Rhine from the line they occupied on the Weser. The treaty of Vienna restored French boundaries to the lines existing in 1790. French territory was once more confined to the normal boundaries which inclose members of the French-speaking family. A natural frontier thus became determined for the country. The union of Frenchmen into a compact political body was shattered, however, by the treaty of Frankfort in 1871, when France was obliged to cede the provinces of Alsace and Lorraine to Germany.

The part to be played by the province of Lorraine in the history of Franco-German relations was laid out by nature itself. The province had always been a wide pathway connecting highly attractive regions of settlement. It lies midway between the fertile plains of the Rhine and the hospitable Paris basin. It is also placed squarely in the center of the natural route leading from Flanders to Burgundy. Physically the region was part of France; its inhabitants have therefore always been Frenchmen, but the lack of a natural barrier on the east provided a constantly open door for Teutonic invasion. In particular, the Moselle valley has always facilitated access into Lorraine. The province was thus a borderland disputed first by two adjoining peoples and, subsequently, by two neighboring nations.

As a duchy, Lorraine had attained a state of semi-independence in the tenth century. It then included the three bishoprics of Metz, Toul and Verdun. From the eleventh to the eighteenth century, the house of Lorraine furthermore exerted sovereign power over Nancy and Lunéville. The loosening of the ties of vassalage which united it to the German Empire grew as centuries passed.

This long period of conflict was necessarily accompanied by modifications of linguistic boundaries. Glancing back to the end of the Middle Ages, a slight westerly advance of the area of German speech may be ascertained for the period between the tenth and sixteenth centuries.[1] From that time on, however, the regional gain of French has been in excess of previous German advances. Toponymic data afford valuable clues to early distribution of languages in the region. Occurrences of the suffix "ange" which is the Frenchified form of the German "ingen," in names lying west of the present line, show the extent of territory reclaimed by the French language.[2]

---

[1] H. Witte: *Forsch. z. deut. Landes- u. Volkskunde*, Vol. 10, 1897, No. 4, pp. 299-424.

[2] L. Gallois: Les limites linguistiques du Français, *Ann. de Géogr.*, Vol. 9, 1900, p. 215.

The linguistic boundary in Lorraine assumes a general north-west-southeast direction as it winds onward according to the predominance of German and French. About 65 per cent of the area of Lorraine, at present under German rule, contains a French-speaking majority.[3] From Deutsche-Oth, the line crosses the Moselle south of Diedenhofen and extends towards Bolchen and Morhange. The entire lake district farther south is in French-speaking territory. About two miles southwest of Sarrebourg the line traverses the Saar. The Lorraine boundary is attained close to the headwaters of the same river. A German enclave occurring at Metz is the only break in the unity of the area of the French language. A large frontier garrison and a host of civilian officials account for the numerical superiority of German in this provincial capital.

The fluctuations of French in Lorraine since the eleventh century have been studied with great minuteness by Witte.[4] Basing himself on the text of documents examined in the archives of Strassburg, Metz, Nancy and Bar-le-Duc this scholar succeeded in plotting the linguistic divide for the years 1000 and 1500. To these two lines he added the present language boundary as determined from his own field observations. His method consisted in traveling from village to village, usually on foot, and ascertaining personally the predominance of French and German in each locality he visited.

Between the eleventh and sixteenth centuries changes along this linguistic boundary appear to have been unimportant. The five intervening centuries are characterized by a slight westerly advance of German. From the sixteenth century to our time, however, the easterly spread of French has been considerable. This change is particularly noticeable in southern Lorraine, as if to show that the gap between the heights of the Moselle and the northern Middle Vosges had provided an outlet for the overflow of the language on German soil.

---

[3] P. Langhans: Sprachen Karte von Deutsch-Lothringen, 1:2,000,000, *Deutsche Erde*, 1909, Pl. 3.

[4] Das deutsche Sprachgebiet Lothringen und seine Wandelungen, etc., *Forsch. z. deut. Landes- u. Volksk.*, Vol. 8, 1894, pp. 407-535.

Compared with Lorraine, Alsace has the advantage of greater definiteness as a geographical unit. It is the region of the valley of the Ill which ends at the wall of the Vosges Mountains on the west. Its easterly extension attains the banks of the Rhine. This elongated plain appears throughout history as a corridor through which races of men marched and countermarched. The Alpine race provided it with early inhabitants. Barbarians of northern lineage also swarmed into its fields. Romans subjugated the land in the course of imperial colonization. The province subsequently passed under Germanic and Frankish sway.

The entry of Alsace into linguistic history may be reckoned from the year 842, when the celebrated oaths of Strassburg were exchanged in Romance and Teutonic languages by Louis the German and Charles the Bald, respectively. This solemn function was a precautionary measure taken by the two brothers to safeguard their territory against the coveting of their senior, Lothaire, to whom Charlemagne had bequeathed the area which, for a time, was known as *Lotharii Regnum,* and which comprised modern Lorraine, Alsace, Burgundy, Provence and a portion of Italy. The main point of interest in the territorial division which marked the passing of Charlemagne, lies in the fact that the future division of central Europe into nations of French, German and Italian speech was outlined at this period. Strassburg, the chief city of the borderland between areas of French and German speech, was a bilingual center at this early date. The versions of the oaths taken on February 18, 842, by the royal brothers, as handed down by Nithard, Charlemagne's grandson and a contemporary historian, show a formative stage in French and German. The document has been aptly called the birth certificate of French. Louis the German spoke the following words in the *lingua romana,* which was then the speech of Romanized Gaul:

Pro Deo amur et pro christian poblo et nostro commun salvament, dist di in avant, in quant Deus savir et podir me dunat, si salvarai io cist meon fradre Karlo, et in adjudha, et in cadhuna cosa, si cum om, per dreit, son

fradre salvar dist, in o quid il mi altresi fazet; et ab
Ludher nul plaid numquam prindrai qui, meon vol, cist
meon fradre Karlo in damno sit.[5]

Charles the Bald used the *lingua teudisca* as follows:

In Godes minna ind in thes christianes folches ind unser
bedhero gealtnissi, fon thesemo dage frammordes, so fram
so mir Got gewizci indi madh furgibit, so haldih tesan
minan bruodher, soso man mit rehtu sinan bruodher scal,
in thiu, thaz er mig sosoma duo; indi mit Ludheren in non-
heiniu thing ne gegango the minan willon imo ce scadhen
werhen.

Ever since this event Alsace has occupied the European
historical stage as a bone of contention between German-speaking
peoples and their rivals of French speech. A year had hardly
elapsed after this exchange of pledges, when the division of the
Frankish Empire between the grandsons of Charles the Great
was formally settled by the treaty of Verdun. Lothaire, the
eldest brother, was awarded Alsace and Lorraine. From this
time on, Alsace became a part of the lands of German speech
which form a compact block in central Europe. In 1469, however,
Sigismund of Austria mortgaged his land holdings in Upper
Alsace to Charles of Burgundy who thereby assumed jurisdiction
over the districts affected by the mortgage. The treaty of St.
Omer which contains the terms of this transaction paved the way
for subsequent French intervention in both Alsace and Lorraine.
Accordingly, a few years later, by the treaty of Nancy (1473),
Charles of Burgundy was recognized by René II of Lorraine as
the "protector" of Lorraine.

It was only in the seventeenth century, however, that France

---

[5] Translation: By the love of God and that of Christian people and of our common
salvation, from this day on, in so far as God shall grant me knowledge and power,
I will support my brother Karl, here present, by every manner of help, as one must,
in duty bound, support one's brother, provided he acts in the same manner with me;
neither will I ever make agreements with Lothaire which, through my own will, shall
prejudice my brother Karl here present.

obtained a definite foothold in Alsace and Lorraine. In 1648, the country won by treaty settlement her long contested rights in Alsace. The treaties of Nimwegen (1679) and Ryswick (1697) confirmed Louis XIV in his possession of the major portion of Alsace. By that time French influence had acquired a paramount share in both of the border provinces. Lorraine, however, was not formally ceded to France until the treaty of Vienna was signed in 1738. French sovereignty over Alsace was confirmed again by the treaty of Lunéville, in 1801, and by the Congress of Vienna in 1815. It was to last until 1871. In that year Alsace and Lorraine became part of the newly constituted German Empire, the cession being determined by Arts. I to IV of the treaty of Frankfort.

The preceding paragraphs show that the earliest form of French and German nationality assumed shape immediately after the treaty of Verdun and at about the time when the language spoken in these countries began to present similarity to the forms used at present. In the partition of Charlemagne's empire only two of the three divisions were to survive. The western evolved finally into modern France. The easternmost became Germany. Lying between the two, Lothringia naturally became the coveted morsel which crumbled to pieces in the struggle waged for its possession.

A highway of migration cannot be the abode of a pure race. Its inhabitants necessarily represent the successive human groups by which it has been overrun.[6] The Alsatian of the present day is, accordingly, a product of racial mingling. But the blending has conferred distinctiveness, and Alsatians, claiming a nationality of their own, find valid arguments in racial antecedents no less than in geographical habitation. The uniform appearance of the Alsatian region strikes the traveler at every point of the fertile Ill valley, where the soil is colored by a reddish tinge which contrasts strongly with the greens and grays of surround-

---

[6] Anthropologic data for the southwestern section of Alsace are instructive. The generation of a transition type between the short and sturdy Alpine type and the "sesquipedal" Teuton is observable. Cf. Ripley: The Races of Europe, New York, 1899, pp. 225-226.

ing regions. By race also the Alsatian represents a distinct group
in which the basal Alpine strain has been permeated by strong
admixtures of Nordic blood. The confusion of dark and fair
types represent the two elements in the population. In
a broader sense the Alsatians are identical with the Swiss
population to the south and the Lorrains and Walloons to
the north—in fact, they are related to the peoples of all the
districts which once constituted the Middle Kingdom of Burgundy.

Although sharply defined by nature, Alsace never acquired
independence. Its situation between the areas peopled by two
powerful continental races was fatal to such a development. But
the influence of its physical setting always prevailed, for, despite
its political union with Frenchmen or Germans, the region has
always been recognized as an administrative unit defined by the
surface features which mark it off from surrounding regions.
The influence of topographic agencies has even been felt within
the province. The separation of Lower from Higher Alsace
originated in a natural boundary, formed by a marshy and forest-
clad zone extending from the Tännchal and Hohkönigsberg mountains to the point of nearest convergence between the Rhine and
the Vosges. This inhospitable tract first separated the two Celtic
tribes known as the Sequani and the Mediomatrici. Later, it
afforded a convenient demarcation for the Roman provinces of
Maxima Sequanorum and Tractus Mediomatricorum. The two
archbishoprics of Besançon and Mayence, both of Middle-Age
fame, were similarly divided. The coins of Basel and of Strassburg point to the subsistence of this line during the Renaissance,
when two distinct territories of economic importance extended
over the region. In the administrative France of modern days,
the departments of Bas-Rhin and Haut-Rhin again reveal adherence to the dividing line provided originally by nature. Finally
after the German annexation of 1871 the "districts" constituted
under German authority, with Colmar and Strassburg as their
chief towns, conformed once more with the historical line of
division.

The Vosges[7] uplift has been until recent times the means of barring intercourse between the plains facing its eastern and western slope. The chain has prevented communication on account of the height of its passes, its thickly forested slopes and the sterility of its soil. The influence of these mountains on European history deserves contrast with that of the Alps where nature's provision of passes and defiles has at all times facilitated land travel in and out of the Italian peninsula. Primitive wandering tribes found but scant inducement to settle in the mountainous area of the Vosges. Pastoral Celts settled in its environing plains long before they attempted to occupy the rocky mass itself. The Teutonic tribes which followed the Celts likewise found little to attract them to the Vosges, and generally migrated southward around its northern and southern extremity, the former route being that of the Franks while the Goths, Burgundians and Alemanni invaded France through the Belfort gap.

Alsace was a province of German speech throughout the Middle Ages as well as after Louis XIV's conquest of the land. French took a solid foothold mainly after the revolution and during the nineteenth century. An enlightened policy of tolerance towards Alsatian institutions cemented strong ties of friendship between the inhabitants and their French rulers. Alsatian leanings towards France were regarded with suspicion by the victors of 1870, who proceeded to pass prohibitory laws regarding the use of French in primary schools, churches and law courts. These measures of Germanization were attended by a notable emigration to France. In 1871 there were 1,517,494 inhabitants in Alsace-Lorraine. The number had decreased to 1,499,020 in 1875 in spite of 52.12 per cent excess of births over deaths.

Nancy, by its situation, was destined to welcome Alsatians who had decided to remain faithful to France. The number of immigrants to this city after the Franco-Prussian war was esti-

---

[7] The name has been traced to the generic meaning of forest through its consonants v-s-g, which are convertible into b-s-k, the latter corresponding to bosquet, busch, bush, etc. Cf. J. C. Gerock: Die Benennung und Gliederung des linksrheinischen Gebirges, *M. Philomath. Ges. Elsass-Loth.*, Vol. 4, 1910, pp. 251-274.

mated at 15,000.[8] Pressing need of workingmen in the city's growing industrial plants intensified this movement. Alsatian dialects were the only languages heard in entire sections of the urban area. Peopled by about 50,000 inhabitants in 1866, Nancy's population jumped to 66,303 in 1876. Metz, on the other hand, with a population of 54,820 inhabitants in 1866, could not boast of more than 45,675 in 1875. The census taken in 1910 raised this figure to 68,598 by the addition of the garrison maintained at this point. Altogether it was estimated that, in 1910, French was spoken by 204,262 inhabitants of Alsace-Lorraine, out of a total population of 1,814,564.[9]

The present line of linguistic demarcation in Alsace-Lorraine rarely coincides with the political boundary. Conformity between the two lines is observable only in stretches of their southernmost extension. East and southeast of Belfort, however, two well-defined areas of French speech spread into German territory at Courtavon and Montreux. In the elevated southern section of the Vosges, the line runs from peak to peak with a general tendency to sway east of the crest line and to reveal conspicuous deflections in certain high valleys of the eastern slope. Its irregularity with respect to topography may be regarded as an indication of the fluctuations of protohistoric colonization.

From Bären Kopf to about 10 miles beyond Schlucht Pass, the mountainous divide and the linguistic line coincide. Farther north, however, French prevails in many of the upper valleys of the Alsatian slope. This is true of the higher sections of the Weiss basin, as well as of the upper reaches of the Bruche. At a short distance south of the sources of the Liepvre, parts of the valley of Markirch (Sainte-Marie-aux-Mines) are likewise French. Here, however, the influx of German miners, who founded settlements as far back as the seventeenth century, converted the district into an area linguistically reclaimed by Germans.

The linguistic boundary in the valley of the Bruche corre-

---

[8] R. Blanchard: Deux grandes villes françaises, *La Géogr.*, Vol. 30, Nos. 2-6, 1914, pp. 120-121.

[9] The Statesman's Yearbook, 1915, p. 972.

sponds to the dividing line between houses of the Frank-Alemannic style and those of the purely Alemannic.[10]   Villages of the Frank-Lorrainer style, in which narrow façades, flat roofs and close lining-up of houses are observable, belong to the period of French influence which followed the Thirty Years' war and should not be confused with the former types.   In Lorraine the houses are built with their longest sides parallel to the street.   The entrance leads into the kitchen; rooms occupy the left wing of the building, the right providing stable space.   In some respects this structure recalls the Saxon houses met east of the Elbe valley.   The characteristic feature of the Lorraine dwelling, however, is found in the construction of the entrance on the long side, whereas in the German type of house it lies under a gable on the short side.   As a rule the Alemannic type of house prevails in the mountainous sections and attains the valleys of the Meurthe.   In the Vosges, Black Forest and Swabia these dwellings are distinguishable by their characteristic inclusion of all outhouses and barns under a single roof.   In the densely peopled valley of the Bruche the most important settlements rest on the alluvial terraces of its affluents.   In the upper valley the villages are scattered on rocky amphitheaters, and here the Celtic type of settlement is oftener met.

Witte's studies show that, in Alsace,[11] the delimitation of the Germanic and Romanic domain is somewhat more complicated than in Lorraine.   Valuable clues are generally afforded by toponymic data.   The Alemanni are responsible for the suffix "heim."   Towns and villages with names bearing this suffix are restricted to the plain.   The dividing line extends on the west to the sub-Vosgian foreland and attains the forest of the Haguenau on the north.   This last section corresponds to the beginning of an area of Frankish colonization having its center at Weissenburg.   The suffix "ingen," which occurs in place names of southern Alsace, is likewise Alemannic.   It is supposed to corre-

---

[10] J. B. Masson: Die Siedelungen des Breuschtals Elsass, *Monatschrift Gesch. u. Volksk.*, 1910, pp. 350-373 and 479-498.

[11] Zur Geschichte des Deutschtums in Elsass und im Vogesengebiet, *Forsch. z. deut. Landes- u. Volksk.*, Vol. 10, No. 4, 1897.

spond, however, to a later period of settlement. The ending "weiler" accompanies the names of villages found on the heights.

These data led Witte to assume that the Celto-Roman natives of the plains were thrust back towards the mountains by the Alemannic invasion proceeding from the east. The designation "weiler," which is also spelled "weyer," "weyr" and "wir," indicates the mountain sites to which the population of the plain was repelled by the Germanic flow. The Vosges mountains have thus been a place of refuge against Germanic aggression. Witte's researches point to the probable peopling of the Alsatian slopes of the Vosges by tribes speaking a Romanic language during the invasions of Teutonic barbarians. The so-called Welsh element appears to be a Celto-Roman remnant of the population of the locality.[12]

The character of Alsace-Lorraine as a connecting region between two great European nations is shown also by demographic studies.[13] Life in the provinces is accompanied by conditions which prevail in Germany or France. The excess of births over deaths, which maintains itself on an average at about 10 per 1,000, is lower than in any other part of the German Empire. The rate of birth has decreased from 36 to 28 per 1,000 in spite of an increase in the population. The tendency of the inhabitants to emigrate is evinced by the large number of uninhabited houses. The decrease in the native population is largely due to the desire of many of the inhabitants to emigrate to French soil. In 1875 the proportion of native-born inhabitants amounted to 93 per cent of the total population. In 1905 it did not exceed 81 per cent. The strictly German element had grown from 38,000 in 1875 to 176,000 in 1905. Fully 90 per cent of these are native-born Prussians. Among them the teaching of French to children has increased. Molsheim, in Lower Alsace, and Ribeauvillé, in Upper Alsace, are centers for the study of French. In recent

---

[12] H. Witte: Romanische Bevölkerungsrückstände in deutschen Vogesentälern, *Deutsche Erde*, Vol. 6, 1907, pp. 8-14, 49-54, 87-91.

[13] DuMont Schanberg: Die Bevölkerung Elsass-Lothringen nach den Ergebnissen der Volkszählung vom 1 Dezember 1905 an der Früheren Zählungen. *Stat. M. über Elsass-Lothringen*, Vol. 31, Stat. Bur. f. Elsass-Lothringen, Strassburg, 1908.

years German immigrants have become the preponderant element of the province.

Two methods of indicating the presence of a French element in Alsace-Lorraine are given in the accompanying map (Pl. II) of this region. The method of showing percentages according to administrative districts [14] has been contrasted with the plan of representing the actual extension of French predominance.[15] In one respect the map is illuminating. It shows the concordance of French and German authorities regarding the German character of the language spoken in Alsace, as well as the French nature of a substantial portion of Lorraine. The Rhine valley, a natural region, appears throughout as an area of German speech. The startling preference of Alsatians for French nationality cannot therefore be substantiated by geographical evidence. It suggests the persistent influence of the human will swayed by feelings of justice and moral affinity rather than by material considerations.

To primitive societies, a river as large as the Rhine provided almost as impassable a frontier as the sea itself. It had the advantage of being defined by nature. The boundary was actually marked on the ground. As frontiers of the Roman Empire, the Rhine and the Danube proved their practical value by the long period during which they marked the extent of imperial or republican domain. The history of oversea colonization indicates the partiality of colonial powers for rivers as boundaries. It is likely that in the very early period of man's habitation of the earth, the tribes settled on either side of watercourses had little or no intercourse. As they advanced in civilization relations were developed. The divisive influence of running waters was therefore exerted most strongly at the dawn of human history. Later the river may become a link and finally may attain the stage when it is a rallying line for the activity and thought of the inhabitants of its entire valley.

The Gallo-Teutonic line of the Rhine was the scene of many

---

[14] After the language map of Alsace-Lorraine in Andrée's Handatlas, pp. 67-68, 6th ed.

[15] After Gallois' map, *Ann. de Géogr.*, Vol. 9, 1900, Pl. 4.

a struggle during the reign of Clovis. In the days of Charlemagne the dwellers on the right bank of the Rhine were the "gens atroces et féroces" of French chroniclers. They represented northern barbarians, the foes of Christianity and of the civilization which Rome had given to the world. Before becoming a German river the Rhine flowed in a valley peopled by inhabitants of Celtic speech. The name it bears is of Celtic origin. When men of Teutonic speech began to press westward, the river supplied a natural moat which, for a long period, had formed part of the system of defense devised by the earlier inhabitants of the land. The strength of the position is attested by the slowness of Germanic infiltration on the left bank of the river. To this day the valley province owes more to France in thought and ideals than to any other country. The Alsatian temperament has much of that mental sunshine which Mirabeau calls the "fond gaillard." This is assuredly not derived from Germany. His wit is of the true Gallic type—mocking, and tending to the Rabelaisian; its geniality is reserved for France and French institutions, its caustic side for Germany and Germans. It could never have proceeded from the ponderous Teutonic mentality. Alsatians are French in spirit because they know how to laugh well, to laugh as civilized men with the cheer that brightens the good and the irony that draws out in full relief the ugliness of evil.

The spread of the French language in Alsace after the conquest of Strassburg by the soldiers of Louis XIV was slow. The French governors of the province never compelled the Alsatians to study their language. Up to the time of the French Revolution, French served as the medium of intercourse in official circles and among the nobility. The mass of the people, however, retained their vernacular. Freedom, granted by the French civil administration, was equally maintained by the official representatives of French ecclesiastical authority. Religious tolerance in Alsace was felt notably at the time of the Revocation of the Edict of Nantes, the province being probably the only one in which Protestant Frenchmen were unmolested. Moral ties with France were thus cemented by the extremely liberal character of French rule.

The French Revolution was enthusiastically welcomed by the democratically inclined Alsatians. This event in fact consolidated Alsace's union with France. French military annals of the period contain a high proportion of Alsatian names. A community of ideas and interests had come into being. The study of French was taken up with renewed enthusiasm in Alsace because the language was the agency by which the new spirit of the time was propagated. It became the medium of communication among thinkers. The revolution of 1848 accentuated this tendency. By that time every Alsatian who could boast of any schooling knew French. This linguistic conquest of Alsace was the result of sympathy with French thought and ideals.

The German method of imposing the rival tongue was distinctly different. All the brutality which attends misconceptions of efficiency among petty officials was given free rein in the process of replacing French by German. A stroke of the pen on April 14, 1871, suppressed teaching of French in the primary schools of the annexed territory. In other educational establishments the study of the language was relegated to the position of minor courses. It is worth mentioning that Alsace and Lorraine are the only territorial units of the German Empire in which the study of French has met opposition on the part of the government. The interest shown for the Romance language elsewhere in the Kaiser's land contrasts with the efforts made to root it out of Alsatian soil.

The unrelenting activity of the Prussian officials stationed in Alsace-Lorraine has borne fruit, for the use of French by the inhabitants is on the wane. This is partly due, however, to the emigration of a large number of native-born Alsatians and the swarm of settlers brought from other sections of Germany. In one respect the results of the Germanizing propaganda have differed from expectations. They have tended to foster the development of Alsatian dialects as well as the spirit of nationality among the people. Alsatians preferred to become proficient in their own tongue rather than in German. At the same time, if Alsace is to be German, they are united in the desire to see their native province form part of the Empire on a footing similar to that of other German states. They apprehend eventual absorption by Prussia as much as the prolongation of the present "Reichsland" status of their native land.

The European war brought its train of trials to Alsatians no less than to other European peoples. French papers contain the complaints of natives of Alsace and Lorraine serving in German regiments to the effect that their officers exposed them to the worst dangers of war with undue harshness. It is not unlikely that at the cessation of hostilities the number of native-born Alsatians will have dwindled to insignificant proportion. A plebiscite on the fate of the province, taken then, might help German designs. But since a revision of the Franco-German boundary seems inevitable, a preliminary solution might be found in the abrogation of the treaty of Frankfort. The final settlement of the problem will be equitable only when the desires of native-born Alsatians shall have been taken into consideration.

Beyond Alsace, French and German languages meet along a line which extends across western Swiss territory to the Italian frontier.[16] Its present course has been maintained since the fifteenth century.[17] Beginning at Charmoille, north of the Bernese Jura, the linguistic frontier strikes east towards Montsevilier,[18] after which it makes a sharp turn to the southwest as it follows the strike of the Jura mountains. In this region the historical division between Teutonic and Latin civilization occurs in the valley of Delémont through which the Sorne flows. Teutonic invaders never succeeded in penetrating beyond the Vorburg barrier. East of the Jura, the line passes through Bienne, Douane and Gléresse. At Neuveville the valley is French. The line follows thence the course of the Thièle. With the exception of its northeastern shore all Lake Neuchâtel is surrounded by French-

---

[16] P. Langhans: Die Westschweiz mit deutschen Ortsbenennung, 1:500,000, *Deutsche Erde*, Vol. 5, 1906, Pl. 5.

[17] E. Gallois: Les limites linguistiques du Français, *Ann. de Géogr.*, Vol. 9, 1900, p. 218.

[18] P. Clerget: La Suisse au XXme siècle, Paris, 1908, p. 55.

speaking communities. The parting next coincides with the line
of the Broye river and extends across the waters of lake Morat.
The western and southern shores of the lake are likewise French.
It then skirts the banks of the Sarine until it reaches Fribourg,
which it cuts into two portions. A strenuous struggle for linguistic supremacy is maintained at this urban edge of French-
speaking territory. Inside the city's line, German is spoken
principally in the quarters tenanted by the laboring classes.
With the middle classes both language and tradition are largely
French.

In the twelfth century Fribourg had been turned into a fortified outpost of German power by the Dukes of Zähringen.[19] The
city's position between the Alps and the Jura favored its selection
for this aggressive purpose. German language flourished under
the shadow of its castles and probably would have taken deeper
root among its citizens but for one fact. At the time of the
Reformation, the Fribourgers decided to stand with the Roman
Church. This decision converted the city into a haven to which
the Catholic clergy of French-speaking Switzerland repaired; and
the Bishopric of Lausanne was transferred to Fribourg, where
it became the headquarters of active French propaganda.

It should not be taken for granted from what has been said
that the cause of French in Switzerland is related to Catholicism.
The case of Fribourg is an isolated one. At Bienne, another of
the cities on the linguistic divide, the growth of French has an
entirely different origin. This city is the center of an important
watch-making district. The growth of its native industry favored
rapid increase in its population. But the new citizens were drawn
principally from the mountainous region of which Bienne is the
outlet. The French-speaking highlanders swelled the ranks of the
city's French contingent to such an extent that, from numbering
one-fourth of the population in 1888, it had grown to one-third
in 1900. The German-speaking farmers of the plains surrounding
Bienne, however, were never attracted by the prospect of factory

---

[19] L. Courthion: Le front des langues en Suisse, *Mercure de France*, Vol. 112, No.
420, Dec. 1, 1915, pp. 636-646.

FIG. 15.

FIG. 16.

FIG. 15—The shady arcades and sunny streets of Lugano in the Swiss area of Italian languages recall the typical aspects of Italian cities.

FIG. 16—The basin of Lake Geneva is an ancient domain of French language in Switzerland.

Fig. 17—Basel in German Switzerland recalls German cities. The Marketplace and the Government House (on left) are seen in this view.

work. At present Bienne's population is believed to be equally divided between the two tongues.

From Fribourg the line takes a straight course to the Olden-

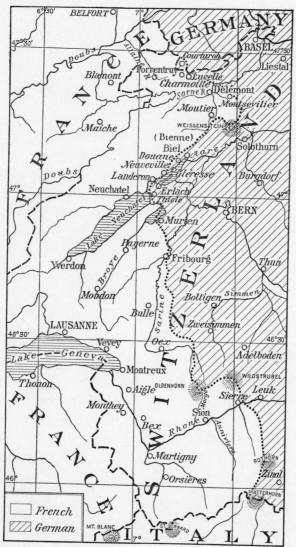

FIG. 18—The boundary between French and German in Switzerland.   Scale, 1:1,435,000.

horn. Here it elbows eastward to Wildstrubel and attains the Valais country. In the upper valley of the Rhone, the line becomes well defined as it coincides with the divide between the

Val d'Anniviers and Turtman Thal. In the Haut Valais the construction of the Simplon tunnel appears to have affected German adversely and to have caused an extension of French speech in the region. The recession of German from the Morge valley to the east of Sierre lies within the memory of living natives. The linguistic line finally cuts across the Rhone valley above Sierre and strikes the Dent d'Hérens on the Italian frontier. In southeastern Switzerland, French surrounds the uninhabited massif Mont Blanc. One would naturally expect to find this language confined to the western slopes of the uplift only. But the inhabitants of Bas-Valais districts and of the Aosta valley speak French as fluently as the population of the elevated valleys of Savoy.

The prevalence of French has been shown to be due to the direction of travel in this mountainous region. The two St. Bernard Passes, the "Col du Grand St. Bernard" and the "Col du Petit St. Bernard," have determined the route along which human displacements could be undertaken with a minimum of effort.[20] The road encircles that famous Alpine peak. It has acted as a channel through which French has flowed into areas of Italian and German speech. This instance may well be adopted as a classical example of the influence of geography in the distribution of linguistic areas.

The origin of linguistic differences in Switzerland may be traced to the dawn of the period that followed Roman conquest. At the time of Caesar's invasion of Helvetia, the mountainous land was peopled by men of Celtic speech. Barbarian invasions put an end to the uniformity of language prevailing in the country. Romance language survived in the highlands of the Jura and throughout the western sections of Switzerland. The Celtic and Latin languages spoken in the first five centuries of our era gave birth to French. The Burgundian conquerors themselves adopted this language at the time of the foundation of the first kingdom of Burgundy. German, on the other hand, is a relic of Teutonic invasion of eastern and central Switzerland. In the

[20] J. Brunhes: La géographie humaine, Paris, 1912, pp. 599-601.

sixth century, the Alemanni took advantage of the weakening of the Burgundian Kingdom to spread beyond the Aar and overrun the attractive lake district. By the eleventh century they had succeeded in imposing their language on the native populations of the Fribourg and Valais country. The reunion of the two states under the reign of Clovis failed to unify the language of Switzerland. A split occurred again after the partition of Charlemagne's dominions, followed by another period of joint political life until the death of Berthold V of Zähringen. After this event the consolidation of languages became impossible in Switzerland. The rivalry of the Alemanni and Burgundian kingdoms was maintained among Swiss populations. In feudal days, German Switzerland acknowledged the suzerainty of Hapsburg counts. Romanic Switzerland, on the other hand, leaned towards the House of Savoy.

That the area of French speech has receded during our era cannot be doubted. There was a time when French was spoken on the left bank of the Aar, from its headwaters to below Berne. At three different periods of history the German language made notable strides in Switzerland. Its earliest forward move occurred between the fifth and ninth centuries. Another advance took place between the eleventh and the thirteenth. The language made further progress during the religious struggles of the Reformation. Each of these periods was followed by partial regain of lost territory by French language. But the French gains fell short of the Germanic advances. Since the eighteenth century very little variation in the line has been recorded. A slight advance of French in the nineteenth century can be traced.

In the minds of Pan-Germanists a significant proof of the progress of French is seen in cases of the replacement of the word "Bahnhof" by "gare" at railroad stations—as for example along the mountainous tract between Viège and Zermatt. They also complain of the introduction of French words and expressions in the German spoken by Swiss citizens. To the tourist's eye the advance of German in the Swiss villages of the Grisons Alps is indicated by the red-tiled roofs in the midst of gray shingled roofs. This is noticeable in the Albula valley where Romansh was formerly the only language of the natives. Now the old Romansh dwellings with their low roofs, white walls and narrow windows are disappearing before the wooden houses of the German settlers.

According to the census of 1910 there were 796,244 inhabitants of Switzerland who spoke French. This was about one-third of the country's total population. Of this number, 765,373 were dwellers in French Switzerland, which comprises the cantons of Geneva, Vaud, Neuchâtel, a portion of the cantons of Valais and Fribourg and the Bernese Jura. The remainder were scattered in the German and Italian districts of the Republic. Notable colonies of French-speaking Swiss in the midst of the area of German speech are found at Berne and Basel. In all, three of the twenty-two cantons are of French speech. Fribourg and Valais contain French-speaking majorities.[21] The canton of Tessin with its 140,000 inhabitants is Italian in language. In Berne the majority of the city's population speak German, only 120,000 inhabitants out of a total of 600,000 using French.

The history of Switzerland shows that at bottom neither language nor physical or racial barriers suffice to constitute nationality. Human desire to achieve and maintain national independence, or to establish liberal institutions, depends on will or purpose far more than on physical facts. Diversity of language never impaired Switzerland's existence as a sovereign nation. Racial heterogeneity in its population likewise failed to weaken national feeling. Over such natural drawbacks the indomitable determination of free-born Helvetians to maintain their country's sovereignty has prevailed. Frenchmen and Germans have always been warring elements in Switzerland, but animosity bred by racial differences invariably disappeared in matters where national existence was at stake. A bond of patriotism based on common religious and democratic ideals proved strong enough to overcome divergencies due to natural causes.

---

[21] The French-speaking population of the Valais is estimated at 70 per cent of the inhabitants of the canton.

FIG. 19—View of Dissentis in the section of Switzerland where Romansh is spoken. This view is taken looking toward the Oberalp Road. The famous Benedictine Abbey stands out conspicuously on the right.

Fig. 20—The town of Zermatt, which lies within the area of French language in Switzerland. The Matterhorn appears in the background.

The Swiss Confederation originally consisted of the three German-speaking cantons of Uri, Schwyz and Unterwalden,[22] clustering round Lake Lucerne, in the very heart of the mountain state. The desire to rid their land of Hapsburg tyranny had drawn together the inhabitants of this region as early as in 1291. In the ensuing twenty-five years, these mountaineers succeeded in making their democratic ideas dominant in their home districts. This led to the gradual adherence of adjoining territories. By the middle of the fourteenth century an "Everlasting League" had been securely established in this orographic center of the European continent. At the Congress of Vienna, in 1815, twenty cantons of the present confederation were finally rounded out. Of these, fifteen are now predominantly German.

French Switzerland receives a large number of German immigrants. In 1900 the number of Germans, both from German cantons and from the German Empire, was estimated at 164,379. In 1910 this foreign element had grown to a community of 186,135. The tendency of these newcomers is to become assimilated. Intermarriage and social intercourse favor French influence. As a rule the second generation of these Germans cannot speak the paternal vernacular and become lost in the mass of its French-speaking neighbors. The assimilating power of the French Swiss is also observable at Delémont and Moutier, in the Bernese Jura, where the piercing of the Weissenstein has brought a heavy flow of German immigrants.

The only localities in which German gains were recorded in the census of 1910 were Porentruy and the northern part of the canton of Fribourg. A counter advance of French at Bienne tends to maintain the balance even. This city had 8,700 inhabitants of French speech in 1910, as against 7,820 in 1900. In Fribourg itself the stronghold of Swiss Germanism is found in the university. The cultural influence of this institution radiates far into the mountain villages of Switzerland, but its work is offset by the campaign carried on in favor of French at the universities of Geneva, Lausanne and Neuchâtel.

---

[22] M. L. Poole: Historical Atlas of Modern Europe, Oxford, 1902, Pl. 44.

NOTE ON CELTIC LANGUAGE IN FRANCE AND ITS RELATION TO ITALIC

A parent language for Celtic and Italic may have flourished at a yet undetermined point in the Western Alps. Meillet [23] points to the possibility of a period of common development of their dialects in view of similarities in the highly ancient forms of the two groups. In that case, westerly and southerly divergences eventually led to modern French and Italian. Of the two branches in which Italic dialects are represented at the dawn of history, namely, Latin-Faliscan and Oscan-Umbrian, the former alone survived in noteworthy degree, under the guise of Latin. Oscan-Umbrian dialects, known by inscriptional remains, gave way before Latin at the beginning of the Christian era.

Celtic, at that period, had been supplanted by two important derived languages: Gaelic and Breton, which prevailed for many centuries. Gaulish, the gaulois language of French writers, was disappearing fast. The case of Breton deserves particular mention in the study of the migrations of languages. This form of Celtic belongs to the British subdivision of its linguistic family. Its persistence in Armorica is due to immigration from British soil which intensified the preëxisting Celtic character of the mountain speech. The inflow of emigrants to France was particularly strong during the period of Saxon invasions.

Celtic, the earliest language of Gaul, was spoken by the Celts, whose original home was in northwestern Europe. The British Isles and continental Europe from Hanover southward to the Pyrenees and the basin of the Po were colonization areas of the Celts. The fact that Celtic stands linguistically in the closest relation with Italic and Germanic may be taken as a proof of its intermediate geographical position between the two. In the middle of the first pre-Christian millennium the Teutons' nearest neighbors to the south were the Celts. In 400 B.C. Bohemia was probably occupied by a Celtic people. This country is the easternmost colony of this group. In these early periods the Elbe marked the boundary between Teutons and Celts. About 200 B.C. Teutonic speech first attained the Rhine, having reached the river from the northeast.

Celtic became Romanized after the Roman conquest in the first century of our era. The *lingua vulgaris* used by the soldiers and traders sent to colonize the country gradually displaced native vernaculars. By the end of the fourth century Celtic as a language had practically disappeared from the entire country. The new Romance language had taken such strong root in the land that successful invaders of French soil were henceforth to adopt it and abandon their native tongue. Thus Visigoths, Burgundians and Franks who invaded Gaul in the fifth century forsook their own language and employed the speech of the people they had conquered. This was a result of the superior intellectual qualities of the conquered race. The Franks in particular, a Teutonic people, established themselves firmly enough in northern Gallo-Roman territory to confer the name of France to the whole region, although their endeavors to settle in southern France had been unsuccessful. It required fully six centuries for the language of the Roman colony of Gaul to become definitely differentiated from Latin. By the seventh century the idiom spoken in France was known as Romance or Romanic.

---

[23] Introduction à l'étude comparative des langues indo-européennes, Paris, 1915.

TABLE I

DISTRIBUTION OF LANGUAGES IN SWITZERLAND ACCORDING TO THE CENSUS OF 1910

CANTON	German	French	Italian	Romansh	Others
Aargau	222,571	1,532	6,197	72	389
Appenzell A/R	56,505	134	1,285	27	68
Appenzell I/R	14,469	32	97	4	6
Basel City	127,491	3,601	4,021	138	1,062
Basel	72,809	1,124	2,548	27	114
Berne	528,554	104,412	12,247	172	2,198
Fribourg	42,634	94,378	1,911	42	586
Geneva	17,456	120,413	12,641	196	5,058
Glarus	31,733	66	1,306	69	120
Graubünden	58,465	838	20,963	37,147	2,441
Lucerne	161,083	1,316	4,808	126	365
Neuchâtel	17,305	111,597	3,747	50	816
Nidwalden	13,329	31	319	5	6
Obwalden	16,738	66	330	28	23
St. Gall	282,722	1,099	17,584	456	967
Schaffhausen	43,795	379	1,712	18	193
Schwyz	56,311	258	1,612	64	60
Soleurne	111,373	2,818	2,570	21	179
Tessin	5,829	1,008	147,790	131	457
Thurgau	125,876	593	8,328	89	291
Uri	20,937	80	1,053	56	15
Valais	37,351	80,316	10,412	16	165
Vaud	34,422	264,222	16,694	220	8,194
Zug	26,406	217	1,454	26	71
Zürich	472,990	5,714	19,696	634	4,601
SWITZERLAND	2,599,154	796,244	301,325	39,834	28,445

TABLE II

PERCENTAGE OF LANGUAGES SPOKEN IN SWISS CANTONS [1]

CANTON	French	German	Italian	Romansh	Others
Aargau	0.7	96.4	2.7		0.2
Appenzell A/R	0.2	97.4	2.2	0.1	0.1
Appenzell I/R	0.2	99.0	0.7		0.1
Basel City	2.6	93.5	3.0	0.1	0.8
Basel	1.5	95.0	3.3		0.2
Berne	16.1	81.6	1.9		0.4
Fribourg	67.6	30.6	1.4		0.4
Geneva	77.3	11.2	8.1	0.1	3.3
Glarus	0.2	95.3	3.9	0.2	0.4
Graubünden	0.7	48.8	17.5	31.0	2.0
Lucerne	0.8	96.0	2.9	0.1	0.2
Neuchâtel	83.6	13.0	2.8		0.6
Nidwalden	0.2	97.3	2.3	0.1	0.1
Obwalden	0.4	97.4	1.9	0.2	0.1
St. Gall	0.4	93.3	5.8	0.2	0.3
Schaffhausen	0.8	95.0	3.7	0.1	0.4
Schwyz	0.4	96.6	2.8	0.1	0.1
Soleurne	2.4	95.2		2.2	0.2
Tessin	0.6	3.8	95.2	0.1	0.3
Thurgau	0.4	93.1	6.2	0.1	0.2
Uri	0.4	94.6	4.7	0.2	0.1
Valais	62.6	29.1	8.1		0.2
Vaud	81.6	10.6	0.1	0.1	2.5
Zug	0.8	93.7	5.2	0.1	0.2
Zürich	1.2	93.9	3.9	0.1	0.9
SWITZERLAND	21.1	69.0	8.0	1.1	0.8

[1] Graphisch-statistischer Atlas der Schweiz, Bureau des eidgen. Departements des Innern, Berne, 1914, Taf. 7.

CHAPTER IV

BORDERLANDS OF ITALIAN LANGUAGE

Italy's early history is molded by the shape of the land and its natural divisions. In the beginning, each valley was a tribal seat. The basin of the Po was the home of Celtic-speaking Gauls. Etruscans, whose early language cannot fit into the Indo-European group, peopled Tuscany. Greeks settled in southern Italy in numbers sufficiently large to bestow the name of Magna Graecia on the districts they occupied. The welding of these territorial elements into the Roman state was attended by the spread of the Latin language within the land. Rome's Latin eventually reached far beyond peninsular frontiers.

Modern Italian nationality did not, however, acquire concrete expression before the nineteenth century. For fully two hundred years prior to that time the Hapsburgs had steadily encroached on Italian territory. It remained for the democratic ideals of the French Revolution to become the moving force in the shaping of Italian nationality. Unity of language favored its rapid development. Beginning with Piedmont in the first half of the nineteenth century Italy grew to its present extent by the addition of territory to the south. Lombardy was added in 1859, Tuscany and the kingdom of Two Sicilies in 1860, Venetia in 1866 and the Papal States in 1870. Prior to these years Italian national aspirations had found solace in a Venetian saying, expressive of Austrian covetings, "Carta tua, montagna mia," which may be rendered as "Yours is the map, but mine the land." Since then, a people speaking the same language has become united into a single nation on the Italian peninsula. The land frontier of Italy, however, has remained to this day a zone of linguistic mingling.

Districts of non-Italian languages are occupied by populations made up of descendants of immigrants from beyond the Alps or from beyond the seas. Six foreign linguistic groups can be distinguished, to wit: (1) Franco-Provençal, (2) German, (3) Slovene, (4) Albanian, (5) Greek, (6) Catalan.[1] The political significance to be attached to these settlements is slight, as they contain a negligible proportion of the kingdom's population. The foreign languages are used only in the home. Beyond the threshold Italian prevails everywhere.

Franco-Provençal dialects are in current use among the dwellers of the Stura, Orco and Doire Baltée valleys. In the province (*circondario*) of Aosta the foreign language was current in over 70 villages (*communi*) at the time of the census of 1901. The province of Pignerol boasted of the two communi of Praly and San Martino di Perrero in which the same French dialects prevailed. The names of the communi of Beaulard, Bousson, Champlas du Col, Clavières, Fenils, Mollières, Rochemolles, Salbertrand, Sauze d'Oulx, Solomiac and Thures, all in the circondario of Suse, likewise indicate the presence of French-speaking inhabitants. It was computed that the language was used in the daily life of 18,958 families out of the 30,401 recorded in the census of that year. The average number of individuals to a family being 4.22 in those districts, it follows that about 80,000 subjects of the king of Italy speak a French dialect. In 1862, French was spoken by 76,736 inhabitants of the valley of Aosta. The importance of the language has hardly changed since then, as it has remained the medium of church, school and general culture. Nevertheless the use of French dialects is on the wane in the circondarii of Pignerol and Suse since the reconstitution of Italy.

Planted between France and Italy, Piedmont became a connecting province in which the transition from one country to the other can be followed. Its rôle is analogous to that of Alsace-Lorraine on the confines of the French and the German languages. French taste and mode of living prevail in many sections of Piedmont. Turin strikes travelers proceeding from southern

---

[1] Colonie straniere nel territorio politico. *La Geogr.*, Vol. 3, 1915, May-June, pp. 222-224.

Italy as being in many respects a city of French customs. The French spoken in Italy also represents a transition speech between the langue d'oïl and the langue d'oc. It has close analogy with the patois spoken in French Switzerland, the Dauphiné, the Lyonnais and the valley of Aosta. All these regions once formed part of the kingdom of Burgundy.

The French vernacular of thousands of Piedmontese is fur-

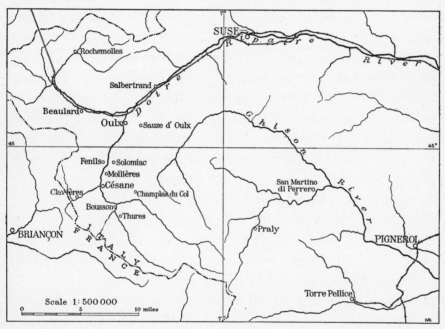

Fig. 21—Map showing some of the important localities of French speech in Northwestern Italy.

thermore related to the cause of Protestantism, which has taken solid root in this mountain land in spite of the persecutions to which it had been formerly subjected. As used by the natives of the region the local dialect consists, more properly, of a modern form of an old langue d'oc dialect similar to the patois of various districts in the French High Alps. To the Protestant inhabitants of these mountain communities French has served as the only medium of intercourse with their co-religionists in Switzerland and France.

The little village of Torre Pellice, on a small mountain railway leading into one of the main valleys of Piedmont, offers the strange contrast of being peopled by inhabitants whose language is French, while their customs are Italian, and their religion Protestant. The austerity of their manners recalls at first impression the natural gravity of mind observable among French-speaking Swiss who belong to the same faith. Ampler acquaintance with the simple mountaineers will draw out their pride of being descendants of Protestants whose religious views antedate Luther's preaching by fully three centuries.

History and geography have concurred in the preservation of religious and linguistic individuality in the three Valdese valleys. Their inhabitants are sons of twelfth and thirteenth century heretics known by the names of Albigenses, Lollards, Cathars or Vaudois, against all of whom the persecution of the Roman church was directed. Massacres and forced conversions uprooted heresies everywhere in Europe except in the high valleys of Piedmont. Here the arduous character of the region afforded defense against the organized bands sent to conquer early adherents of reformed doctrines. The narrow gorges became the theater of bloody affrays in which victory would sometimes favor the attacking foreigners and sometimes the besieged. No definite conquest of the mountain zone was ever made by the Catholic armies. The surname of Israel of the Alps, bestowed locally on the village of Torre Pellice, is a memorial of this period of religious struggle.

An episode in this long contest, which is not unrelated to the current prevalence of French, took place in 1630. The operations of the army sent by Richelieu in that year were followed by an epidemic of plague to which thousands of natives succumbed. Many of the community's religious leaders were carried off by the dread disease. Their places were taken by pastors and preachers who came from Geneva or the Protestant towns of France. From this period on religious services were carried on in French. The influence of the language spread beyond the rough mountain sanctuaries to which it was at first confined. In such retired valleys cultural influences generally emanate from the church, a fact observable particularly in the mountainous portions of Asia. Today along with the memory of former struggles the language, which was partly a result of their bitterness, has survived. To the highlander of western Piedmont, French is the symbol of successful resistance against religious oppression. He clings to it and will not tolerate Italian in its place. His mountain villages are in fact the nursery of hundreds of teachers of French employed in Italian schools.

The Franco-Italian linguistic boundary starts at Monte Rosa and extends south, past Gressoney, into the valley of the Doire Baltée, to the town of Settimo Vitone. French has always predominated in this region. It is at present the vernacular of the well-to-do inhabitants and is taught in schools concurrently with Italian. Thence to the west the linguistic boundary passes south of Grand Paradis Peak and attains the political boundary at the sources of the Orco river. Linguistic and political boundaries coincide in the next 27 miles, the line passing through a mountainous and scantily settled region.

North of Suse, linguistic and political lines diverge from each other. The former crosses the Doire Ripaire at about five miles east of the town. It then extends in a southerly direction to Pérouse on the Ghison river and traverses the Pellice where the river leaves the highland. The Po is attained near Monte Viso and the political frontier. From the latter peak the line reaches Sampeyre, beyond which it crosses the Stura at Vinadio. The Franco-Italian boundary is reached once more at a few miles east of Lantosque. From here on to the sea Italian speech invades French territory.

The structure of the Alps has contributed powerfully to the peopling of a part of the basin of the Po by a Celtic-speaking race. In Turin the name of the Taurins, a Celto-Ligurian tribe, has been preserved to this day. Alpine valleys converge towards the east and diverge towards the west. Human migrations have, therefore, been more intense from west to east than in the opposite direction. Western Piedmont thus passed under French influence after the Middle Ages. At that time the counts of

Savoy obtained possession of the country around Suse and Turin. Later they added all of Piedmont to their domain. The upper valley of the Doire Ripaire was part of the French kingdom until the treaty of Utrecht in 1715.

From the Mediterranean northward, the last section of the Franco-Italian linguistic boundary traverses French soil and coincides roughly with the crest of the eastern watershed of the Var. This region is known administratively as the Département des Alpes-Maritimes. Linguistic unity within its boundaries has been determined mainly by the relief of the land.[2] Practically every one of the high Alpine valleys debouches into the Var. Connection between the sea and the mountain districts is obtained through the channels of this basin. Intercourse among the inhabitants of the département has thus been reflected towards France rather than Italy. The langue d'oc prevails in the entire Var system, but Genoese dialects of Italy, or the "si" languages, appear immediately to the west. The linguistic divide can, therefore, be located between the valley of the Var on the one side and those of the Roya and Bévéra on the other. It should be made to pass, according to Funel,[3] at the very point in La Turbie where Augustus, a Roman emperor, erected a monument to mark the boundary between his domain and Gaul. The inhabitants of the eastern section of this line appear, however, to be content with French nationality in spite of their Ligurian dialects. At the time of the rectification of this frontier in 1860, their French leanings were proclaimed in a referendum which set forth their desire to acquire citizenship under the French tricolor.

The city of Alghero and its environs in the island of Sardinia contain a colony of Catalonians whose language is identical with the vernacular in use on the Balearic islands. This group consists of 9,800 individuals out of a total of 10,741 inhabitants of the commune of Alghero. In 1862 this small community comprised 7,036 individuals. This rooting of a Spanish dialect on an

---

[2] L. Funel: Les parlers populaires du Département des Alpes-Maritimes, *Bull. Géogr. Hist. et Descrip.*, 1897, No. 2, pp. 298-303.

[3] Op. cit.

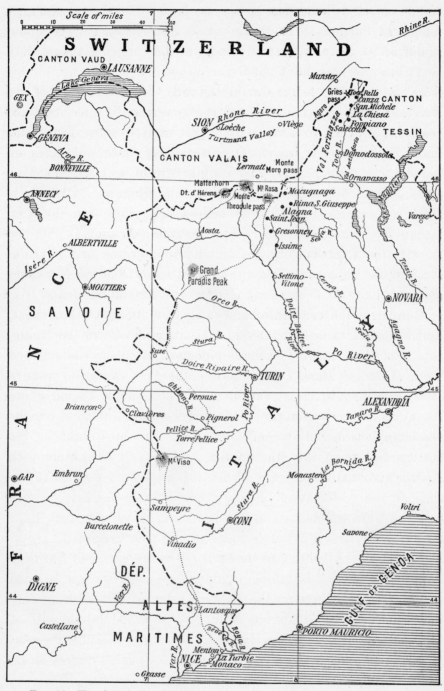

FIG. 22—The dotted line indicates the divide between the areas of French and Italian language. Black dots near the Swiss border show Italian villages where German is the vernacular of the natives.

Italian island is traced to the year 1354 when the Aragonians conquered Sardinia. The long period of Spanish rule over the island accounts for the survival of the language to this day.

The southern boundary of German speech abuts against Italian from Switzerland [4] to the Carinthian hills.[5] The intrusion of the Romanic tongue within the Austrian political line lacks homogeneity, however, for it is Italian proper in western Tyrol and Ladin in its western extension. But of the 400 odd miles of boundary between Austria and Italy a bare 60 will coincide with the linguistic divide between German and Italian. Moreover a number of enclaves of German speech exist within the area of Italian language spreading over Austrian territory. Some of these German settlements are found near Pergine and Fersina. Close to the Italian frontier, the town of Casotto in the Lavarone region is likewise peopled by German-speaking inhabitants.[6]

German is the vernacular of two small districts within Italian boundaries which adjoin the Swiss frontier and lie in the Alpine valleys of Piedmont. The most important of the two is situated south of Monte Rosa. It comprises the three adjacent valleys of Gressoney, Sesia and Macugnaga. The other is found in the Val Formazza or upper valley of the Toce. Both of these groups are extensions of the area of German speech which spreads over the eastern portion of the canton of Valais. This section of Switzerland was swamped between the ninth and sixteenth cen-

---

[4] Blocher u. Garraux: Die deut. Ortsnamenformen in Westschweiz, *Deutsche Erde*, Vol. 5, 1906, p. 170.

[5] The Italian population of Austria-Hungary is estimated at 768,422 according to the Austrian census of 1910. Italian computations set the total number of Italians living in Austria at 837,000, distributed as follows (*Boll. Real. Soc. Geogr.*, Aug. 1, 1915, p. 897):

Upper Adige Valley	25,000
Trentino	373,000
Triest	142,000
Austrian Friuliland	93,000
Istria	148,000
Dalmatia	30,000
Fiume	26,000
Total	837,000

[6] G. de Lucchi: Trentino e Tirolo, *Boll. 16, Minist. Aff. Esteri*, Rome, 1915, p. 70.

FIG. 23—The rearland of Nice as typified by this view of the Mediterranean Alps contains numerous bilingual settlements. The bridge in the photograph is the Pont du Loup.

FIG. 24—Nice with its pleasant approach and its Alpine background is built on the transition area between French and Italian language.

turies by a flood of Teutonic invaders consisting mainly of Alemannic tribes [7] proceeding from the Bernese Oberland. All of the upper Valais, from Münster as far as Loeche and Zermatt, became Germanized during that period. The easterly spread of this movement led a number of German-speaking colonists to cross Gries Pass into the Formazza valley, while others went through the passes of Monte Moro and Monte Theodule to the upper valleys of Piedmont. According to historical documents the German settlers reached the shores of Lake Maggiore. But their language became lost in the midst of Italian speech and held its own only in the valleys already mentioned.

The Piedmontese group of German dialects occurs in small settlements distributed on the southern slopes of Monte Rosa. The most noteworthy localities of Teutonic speech are Gressoney, Saint Jean, Gressoney-La Trinité and Issime. Dialects belonging to the same group occur in the Alagna and Rima S. Giuseppe villages, in Valsesia as well as in the Agaro, Formazza, Macugnaga and Salecchio localities of the Ossola valley. Altogether these settlements contain about 5,000 German-speaking inhabitants. Occupation of the region by Germans dates from the twelfth and thirteenth centuries when emigration into upper Valais took place. The language once extended as far south as the Ornavasso. Its progress during the past half century has been insignificant.

Val Formazza comprises the entire upper valley of the Toce, north of Foppiano. The region is locally known as Val d'Antigorio in its southern stretch. To the north, from Domodossola onward, it acquires the name of Val d'Ossola. It has seven settlements scattered along the banks of the river and contains a population of about 800 inhabitants engaged chiefly in cattle-raising. La Chiesa is its most important village. The region is noted in the list of scenic spots of northern Italy on account of the Toce falls, which attract a large number of tourists. The dual character of its human institutions is reflected in the names of

---

[7] A. Dauzat: Les valées italiennes de langue allemande, *A Travers le Monde*, 1913, Sept. 6, pp. 285-286.

its villages, which are both Italian and German. Foppiano is also known as Unterwald; La Chiesa as Andermatten; San Michele as Pommat; Canza as Fruttwald. German names are gradually being dropped, however, concurrently with the steady replacement of the Teutonic language by Italian.

All these valleys are bridges which connect the areas of Italian and German. Travelers are struck by the transitional character of every human manifestation within their boundaries. As one proceeds northwards from the main Italian area, the type of stone habitation characteristic of Italian villages gives way to the wooden house of German villages. Examples of both styles are in evidence throughout the settlements of German speech on Italian soil. The native costume of the women also recalls the intermediary character of the region. Black skirts as well as high and tight waists, of the same color, are characteristic of the canton of Valais. The headdress—an ample foulard of black interspersed with green and red—worn close, is of unmistakable Italian origin. The style in which middle-aged native women comb their hair is also Italian. They part it into a number of small plaits held together by metallic combs after a fashion seen among elderly dames in Lombardy.

The eastern borderland of Italian language contains German-speaking inhabitants in the provinces of Verona, Vicenza, Belluno and Udine, who are living witnesses of the early German settlements founded as trading posts on the way to the Adriatic coast. Bavaria provided many of these emigrants in the beginning of the thirteenth century. The language spoken by their descendants is known locally as Cimbro. It has practically disappeared from the Veronese district, where its survival is traced in the forested areas of the "commune" of Progno through some 50 inhabitants. The inhabitants of the communes of Sappada and Sauris and of the Timau district in the Paluzza commune also employ German. It is estimated that 1,170 families, representing about 5,500 inhabitants, speak Teutonic dialects in these Venetian districts of Italy.

South of the Dolomite Alps the tableland of the Sette Communi is also inhabited by German-speaking subjects of the king of Italy. Teutonic dialects have survived in seven villages scattered in the adjoining valleys of the Upper Astico and the middle Brenta. These communities formed the regency of the Sette Communi, which from 1259 to 1807 was an independent state. Rotzo, the westernmost and oldest, has a splendid location in the wooded area at the outlet of Val Martello. In Roana to the east

FIG. 25—The localities of German speech in the Sette Communi districts of Italy are underlined. The broken line indicates the Austro-Italian frontier.

over five hundred families still employ the German dialect as their vernacular. At Asiago, however, the German element has almost disappeared, although during the Middle Ages the town was an important center of Teutonism, as is testified by the historical collections deposited in its museums. Gallio is known in history as a trading center of local magnitude. Enego, the last settlement towards the east, was founded before its Teutonization, for it was a Roman colony. San Giacomo di Lusiana is the only settlement of German speech beyond the plateau borders. Its situation on the southern slope brought it within the sphere of Venetian influence to a degree never felt by its sister communities.

Past the Italian frontier, traveling towards Trent, every town and village of the valley of the Adige bears an Italian name and is peopled by Italians. Ala, Mori, Rovereto and Calliano are types of these Italian communities within Austrian territory. These small towns, scattered along the banks of the river which brought life to the region, are peopled mainly by farmers. The valley in which they are found has played an important part in Italian history. In ancient times barbarian invaders marched to the conquest of the peninsula through its conveniently situated gap. During three centuries the armor-clad troops sent by German emperors to crush revolts in Cisalpine cities crossed the Alps at the Brenner Pass and followed the channel of the Adige as it broadened towards the south. Down the same valley Austrian regiments poured into Lombardy in 1860, when the plainsmen gave signs of readiness to revolt from foreign rule. Modern changes have failed to detract from the importance of this ancient highway, for the shortest railroad route connecting Italy with central Germany is constructed along the natural groove carved by the southward flowing waters of the Adige, and the transit trade between the two countries follows its channel.

The most important Germanic invasion of the Trentino in historical times began in 375 A.D. and lasted two centuries. This movement was repeated in the last half of the tenth century. Under the rule of the bishop-prince Frederick of Vanga, a considerable number of German settlers established themselves on his territory between the years 1207 and 1218. The actual Germanization of the highlanders of the southern Tyrol had its start in this period, the records of the time showing changes from Italian to German in the names of localities as lands and estates were acquired by Germans. But throughout medieval times and to the end of the eighteenth century, historical records make mention of the Florentine character of its industrial and commercial life.

The southerly advance of the German language in the moun-

Fig. 26.

Fig. 27.

FIG. 26—View of the historic Brenner Pass. Through this mountain gap Teutonic invaders have poured into Italy since the dawn of history.

FIG. 27—The mountain settlement of Cortina in the Ampezzo district in the Trentino is inhabited mainly by Italians.

FIG. 28.

FIG. 29.

FIG. 28—The approach to Meran in the Austrian Tyrol and at the Italo-Germanic language border.

FIG. 29—Stelvio Pass at the eastern edge of the area of Romansh dialects, showing the mountainous character of the country in which this language has survived.

tainous province has followed the valleys of the Etsch and
Eisack, for the channels through which mountain waters flowed

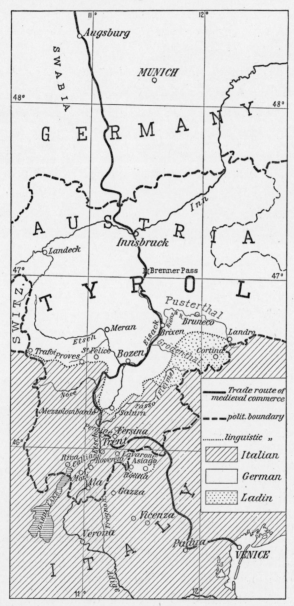

Fig. 30—Sketch map of the Trentino showing languages spoken.   Scale, 1:2,400,000.

towards the Adriatic also facilitated the transportation of goods
from the German highlands of central Europe to the Mediterranean.   A steady current of freight has been maintained in a

southerly course along this route since the beginning of continental commerce in Europe. In the Middle Ages numerous colonies of German traders had acquired solid footing along the much traveled road over the Brenner Pass which connected Augsburg and Venice.[8]

Early activity of German traders stamped its imprint on the linguistic map by a wedge of Teutonic speech thrust towards the Trentino, between Italian on the west and Ladin on the east. This linguistic protuberance occupies the valley of the Etsch south of its confluence with the Eisack. The divide between the two languages has its westernmost reach near Trafoi,[9] known also as Travis. The junction of Swiss and Austrian political boundaries at this point corresponds to the contact between the German of the Tyrol and the Romanic idioms of Engadine. Thence, the linguistic line of separation skirts the base of the Ortler massif and subsequently coincides with the watershed of the Etsch and Noce rivers. Ladin settlements begin north of the Fleims valley[10] and spread beyond the Gradena basin (Grödenthal) to Pontebba (Pontafel) and Malborghet where the meeting of Europe's three most important linguistic stocks, the Romanic, Germanic and Slavic, occurs.

The language spoken by the Italians of the Trentino consists of Lombard and Venetian dialects. Ladin dialects are spoken in some of the small valleys east of the Adige. In the valley of Monastero, near the Swiss frontier, the inhabitants speak a dialect of Ladin or Romansh which is akin to Friulian. This patois was in greater use during the Middle Ages. The Ladins, both in Austria and Italy, are Italians in every respect save that of language, although here also the two peoples are closely related. Ladin language is a slightly altered form of Latin containing words of non-Romanic stock which differ according to the locality overrun by the Romans. The same definition applies to the Romansh language of Switzerland. Romansh and Ladin are

---

[8] O. Noel, Histoire du commerce du monde, Paris, 1891, Vol. 2, pp. 148-168.

[9] B. Auerbach: Races et nationalités en Autriche-Hongrie, Paris, 1898, p. 86.

[10] Scheller, Deutsche u. Romanen in Südtirol u. Venetien, *Pet. Mitt.*, 1877, pp. 365-385.

therefore basically Latin languages which did not develop to the stage of Italian or French and which differ from each other in the number of pre-Roman words they contain. Friulian belongs to the same category of Romance languages and differs from Ladin merely in having a larger proportion of Italian words. Like Ladin it is not a literary language and is therefore being superseded by Italian. Romansh dialects of Switzerland will probably survive longer since in the canton of Grisons they are recognized as official together with German and Italian, and in Engadine Romansh is still a literary dialect.

The claims of Italy in the Trentino include [11] the Bolzano district lying at the confluence of the Isarco and the Adige. This locality is peopled by 16,000 Germans and 4,000 Italians. Meran, the upper valleys of the Adige and Isarco together with their affluents, Bressanone on the Isarco, and Bruneco on the Rienza likewise fall within the territory claimed by Italy. A return to the Italian fold of the small groups of Italians scattered between Salorno and Bolzano, between Bolzano and Meran and between Bruneco and Bressanone is shown in this manner to lie within the realm of possibility. As early as 774 Charlemagne's division of the region between the kingdoms of Bavaria and Italy had implied recognition of linguistic variations. But the importance of maintaining German control over natural lines of access to southern seas determined his successors to award temporal rights in the southeastern Alps to bishops upon whose adherence to Germanic interests reliance could be placed. The bishopric of Trentino thus passed under the Teutonic sphere of influence. The present political union of the territory of the old see with the Austrian Empire is hence a relic of medieval German politics.

Historically the Trentino's connection with Italy rests on ancient foundations. At the height of Roman power Tridentium was an important city. It was situated in the tenth Italian region, known as Venetia et Histria. After the fall of the western Empire it was included in the Italian districts conquered by the

---

[11] A. Galanti: I diritti storici ed etnici dell' Italia sulle terre irredente, *La Geogr.*, Vol. 3, Nos. 3-4, March-April 1915, p. 88.

Ostrogoths and Byzantines. Under the Lombards Trent became the capital of a dukedom. In the Romano-Germanic feudal period it was part of the kingdom of Italy constituted by Charles the Great, and later, of the Marches of Verona established by Otto I. Conrad II in 1027 turned the region over to religious ownership. From this date on it is known as the princely bishopric of Trent. The bishop-princes who ruled in the Trentino, however, were constantly at war with the feudal lords who had authority over the lands north and south of the Trentino. In the sixteenth century the court of Bernardo Clesio, one of the most famous of these religious rulers, was distinctly Italian in thought and customs.

The Trentino bishopric was abolished in 1805 by Napoleon and the region then became part of the kingdom of Bavaria. From 1809 to 1814, however, the Trentino, together with a part of the upper Adige valley, was converted into an Italian administrative district under the name of Dipartimento dell' Alto Adige. In 1815 the region was assigned to Austria together with Lombardo-Venetia and the Tyrol.

Throughout the eventful history of the present millennium the Tyrol has been the cockpit of Germano-Romance clashes. A lively competition between German and Italian traders has always been maintained within its borders. During the era of religious upheavals, the Germans rallied to the cause of the Reformation while the Italian element remained faithful to the authority of the Vatican. Contact with the Teutonic element appears to have failed, however, to eradicate or modify the Italian character of the region's life and institutions.[12]

The splendor of the Italian Renaissance stamped its mark on all the Tyrolese districts drained by waters flowing southwards. Castles and churches of the Trentino show the influence of Italian architectural styles. Their interior ornamentation derived its inspiration from the same source. In painting, the Bressanone and Bolzano schools of the fifteenth century likewise maintained Italian traditions in the valley of the upper Adige. Statues and

---

[12] A. Galanti: I Tedeschi sul versante meridionale delle Alpi, Typ. Acad. Lincei, Rome, 1885, p. 185.

bas-reliefs in the towns of this region also bear witness to the Italian taste of its inhabitants.

All these artistic leanings towards Italy are best observed in Trent itself. The celebrated castle of the "Buen Consiglio" is a blend of Venetian and Veronese styles. Bramante was the architect of the Tabarelli palace, and a disciple of Tullio Lombardo built that of Moar. The Duomo di Trento owes its beauty mainly to the artistic conceptions of the Comacini masters. Some of its frescoes dating from the fourteenth and fifteenth centuries are the handicraft of Veronese artists. This Italian influence has been maintained to the present day. A tourist reaching the city will behold Dante's symbolic statue—the work of Zocchi, a Florentine—immediately upon leaving the main station.[13] Roaming through the city his attention will be attracted by innumerable reminders of modern Italian work of the type seen in the façade of St. Peter's church. These are concrete manifestations of an intellectual and artistic outflow from the Italian border northward.

Reports on the German propaganda carried on in the Trentino have been made on several occasions to their governments by Italian consular agents.[14] This movement is prosecuted with untiring perseverance by the members of the Tiroler Volksbund, an organization founded in 1905, for the purpose of diffusing German language and customs in southern Tyrol. Schools and other institutions managed by German staffs provide Teutonic education free of cost to the natives. Periodicals and pamphlets are distributed profusely to this end. Lectures setting forth the Germanic origins of Trentino settlements are delivered. A more aggressive method of action consists in sending out "Wanderlehrers" or traveling teachers to give elementary courses from village to village.

Descendants of Rheto-Romans settled in eastern Tyrol speak a language of Latin stock which, in common with other moun-

---

[13] According to press reports in 1915 Dante's monument was destroyed by the Austrians.

[14] G. de Lucchi: Trentino e Tirolo, *Boll. 16, Minist. Aff. Esteri*, Rome, 1915.

tain languages, failed to blossom into literature mainly on account of the secluded life of its highland users. The dialect is closely allied to the Friulian. The two form together the western border of the Slovene linguistic area and attain Triest on the south. Lack of written masterpieces tends to weaken the life of the language and it is being replaced by Italian. Concurrently with the growth of the region's foreign intercourse in modern times invasion of German words can also be detected, though not to the extent of impairing the fundamental Romanic strain.

The Adriatic provinces of the Austro-Hungarian Empire are peopled mainly by Italians and Slavs. German and Hungarian elements in the population consist of civil and military officials and of merchants. From an ethnological and linguistic standpoint the maritime district is Italian or Slav according to its elevation. The Romanic stock forms the piedmont populations while the dwellers of the hilly coast chains are of Slavic issue and speech. The western coast of the Istrian peninsula, however, is an area of Italian speech, which is generally confined to urban centers.

The following figures for the population of the Dalmatian islands show the numerical inferiority of the Italians: [15]

LOCALITY	Population according to census of 1910	Inhabitants speaking Serbo-Croatian dialects		Inhabitants speaking Italian	
		Number	Per cent	Number	Per cent
Lissa, St. Andrea and Busi	10,041	9,939	98.98	92	0.92
Lesina, Spalmadori and Torcola	16,861	16,340	96.91	494	2.92
Curzola, Cazza, Lagosta and adjoining reefs	21,628	21,186	97.95	436	2.01
Stagno district, including Meleda island [16]	9,424	9,393	99.67	9	0.1

[15] O. Keude: Italien und die Dalmatienische Inselfrage, *Kartogr. Zeits.*, Vienna, Nov. 15, 1915.

[16] Austrian census returns have been the object of frequent criticism in non-Germanic countries. The political interests of the Austrian government may have led its officials to minimize the importance of the language spoken by dissenting peoples. A tendency to overestimate the spread of German has always been suspected. A common practice consists in forming artificial administrative districts so as to create German numerical superiority within their borders. As a rule an increase of 10 per cent in the number of Slavs, Rumanians and Italians can be safely added to the figures set forth in government statistics. Conversely the same percentage may be subtracted with safety from the totals for Germans and Hungarians.

Zara, Spalato, Sebenico, Ragusa and Cattaro,[17] however, contain flourishing colonies of Italians whose commercial enterprise has helped their mother tongue to prevail if not predominate in their region. Outside of these cities, the Italian element, wherever present, is restricted to littoral strips. The Slavs invariably occupy the plateau and the slopes extending seaward.

The Istrian region of predominant Italian speech consists of the western peninsular lowland extending south of Triest [18] to the tip of the promontory beyond Pola.[19] Istrians to whom Italian is vernacular number 147,420 individuals according to the census of 1910. The Slavs of the Karst and terraced sections constituting the rest of the population belong to the Roman faith, but have no other common bond with their Italian countrymen.

Istria is a triangle about 60 miles long with a maximum breadth of 46 miles. It rises from the southwestern coast gradually up to the Dinaric Alps. Owing to its undulating surface and the absence of coastal plains, it may be regarded as a part of this range, jutting out into the sea. On the whole, Istria may be called a Karst land, for three-fourths of its surface consists of Karst-forming limestone and only one-fourth of sandstone and marl. With few exceptions its natural waterways are confined to the sandstone districts. The peninsula is also a transition region between the mild Mediterranean and central European climates. The summers are dry and in autumn heavy rains fall. Almost all the land is productive and 67 per cent of its population live by agriculture and forestry.

Settlement by Slavs of the hills dominating the Adriatic appears to have taken place continuously from the ninth to the seventeenth century. Feudatory chiefs of medieval ages first

---

[17] Italian predominates in both Zara and Spalato, the latter city being second in commercial importance along the Dalmatian coast. It is estimated that, in all, more than 18,000 Italians inhabit Dalmatia.

[18] Triest and its environs are peopled mainly by Italians. The suburbs are inhabited by crowded Slavic settlements. The census of 1910 shows 118,960 Italians, 57,920 Slovenes, 11,860 Germans and 2,400 Croats. For Istria returns of the same date give: Italians 147,417, Serbo-Croatians 168,184, Slovenes 55,134.

[19] M. Wutte: Das Deutschtum in Österreichischen Küstenland, *Deutsche Erde,* Vol. 8, 1909, p. 202.

resorted to this method of developing the uncultivated slopes and highlands of the eastern coast. The Venetian republic and the Austrian government adopted similar measures of colonization. Slavic tribes, hard pressed by their kinsmen or by Tatars from the east, thus found refuge in the mountainous Dalmatian coastland under the ægis of western nations. A traveler taking ship today and sailing from harbor to harbor along the shores of the eastern Adriatic would readily notice the numerical superiority of these descendants of Slavs. They constitute the mass of toilers in every walk of life, and sooner or later probably will erect a political fabric on the foundations of their linguistic preponderance.

Slavic dialects are found in the Friulian sections of eastern Italy as well as in the Abruzzi and Molise regions. The Slavic population of Friuli was estimated in 1851 at 26,676. The census of 1901 records the existence of 5,734 Slavic-speaking families scattered in 16 communi and consisting of about 36,000 individuals.

The Slavs of Italy may be divided into four dialectical groups as follows:[20]

Natisone	group	composed	of	17,291	individuals
Torre	"	"	"	12,986	"
Judrio	"	"	"	1,230	"
Resia	"	"	"	4,671	"

The Molise group is the remnant of a once extensive Slav colony which had reached the province of Chieti. Round-headedness, accompanied by high stature and blondness, among inhabitants of the communes of Vasto, Cupello, Monteoderisio, Abbateggio, Lanciano, San Giovanni Teatino, Cascanditella and San Vito Chietino betrays Slavic ancestry. And yet Slavic dialects are hardly heard any longer in these country districts. The communes of Acquaviva Collecroce and San Felice Slavo alone boast of some 4,500 inhabitants who speak Slovene.

The Karst or Carso formation on which Slovene life developed

---

[20] G. Canastrelli: Il numero degli Slavi in Friuli, *Riv. Geogr. It.*, Vol. 21, Nos. 1-2, Jan.-Feb. 1914, pp. 96-102.

is the western section of a long calcareous plateau which extends from the Julian Alps, along the border of the ancient Friulian gulf and attains Balkan ranges. It separates the valley of the Save from the Adriatic. A characteristic aspect is noticeable over all its extent in the thickness of its limestone beds and their deep fissures. Surface water cannot collect and flow for any distance without disappearing into a fissure. The erosion forms of the plateau are of the Karst type and differ radically from those of the average humid climate. Chambers of marvelous dimensions are formed; funnel-shaped sink-holes dot the surface; and the rivers run underground.

The Slovenes settled on the calcareous plateau of Carniola cluster around Laibach and attain the area of German speech on the north, along the Drave between Marburg and Klagenfurth. Eastward they march with Hungarians and the Serbo-Croat group of southern Slavs. Their southern linguistic boundary also coincides with that of the latter. Around Gottschee, however, a zone of German intervenes between Slovene and Croatian dialects. Practically the entire eastern coast of the Gulf of Triest lies in the area of Slovene speech. The group thereby acquires the advantage of direct access to the sea, a fact of no mean importance among the causes that contributed to its survival to the present day in spite of its being surrounded by Germans, Hungarians, Croats and Italians.

The Slovenes may be considered as laggards among the Slavic immigrants who followed Avar invasions. They would probably have occupied the fertile plains of Hungary had they not been driven to their elevated home by the pressure of Magyar and Turkish advances. Confinement in the upland prevented their fusion with any of the successive occupants of the eastern plains below their mountain habitations. Racial distinctiveness, characterized by language no less than by a highly developed attachment to tradition, resulted from this seclusion.

Starting from the Adriatic Sea in the vicinity of Triest the boundary of Slovene territory, according to Niederle, extends to Duino, Montefalcone, Gradisca and Cormons. From the last locality it heads for Italian territory, within which it cuts off the districts east of Tarcento and Resia from the area of Italian speech. At Kanin the line is once more on Austrian soil. It now proceeds to Pontafel, Saint-Hermagoras, Dobrac and Villach, the latter city being mainly German. Beyond the Drave, the linguistic frontier passes close to Woerther Lake and thence by Kostenberg and Moosburg. From this town the divide is prolonged to Gurk and extends towards Diex, Greutschach, Griffen and St. Pancrace. It next attains Arnfels. Fifty years ago, according to the same authority, the environs of this village were inhabited by Slovene populations. The district has since then been reclaimed by German speech. The same is true of the right bank of the Mur in the vicinity of Radkersburg.

At Radgona, the Slovene boundary crosses the Mur once more and extends northward into Hungary as far as the German village of St. Gotthard, which it leaves to the north. Thence it turns southward at the Raab and heads for the Mur, which it crosses at Gornia Bistrica. The line then runs close to the provincial boundaries of Croatia and Carniola before attaining the sea again in Istria. The Slovene area thus delimited comprises the duchy of Carniola, excepting the Gottschee enclave, northern Istria, the Udine region, southeastern Karinthia, southern Styria and part of the Hungarian "comitats" of Vas and Zala. This Slovene land is now but a dwindled remnant of its former extension. At one time the Slovenes extended as far west as the Pusterthal in Tyrol, while their settlements even reached the Danube (at Linz and Vienna).

Contact between languages on the Italo-Austrian frontier has influenced the political relations between the two countries. The whole foreign policy of the Austrian Empire, in fact, may be said to have been stimulated mainly by the necessity of keeping its mixed population in subjection. The central position of Austria-Hungary had made it the meeting-place of every important race in Europe. The mountain-girt monarchy is a seething reservoir of nationalities. Germans from the west flow into it. Czechs and Slovaks press in from the northwest, Poles and Ruthenians from the north and northeast. A Rumanian drive proceeds from the southeast. Croats, Serbians and Slovenes are steadily pushing northward. Italians, advancing from the southwest, complete the

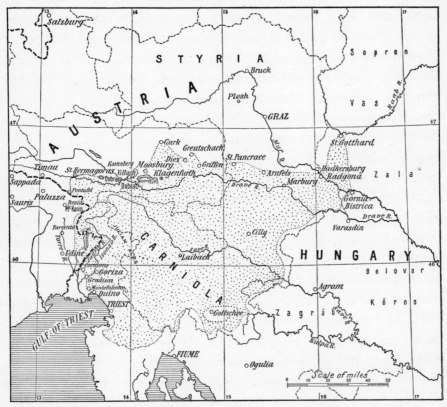

FIG. 31—The area of Slovene speech in Austria and adjacent parts of Italy.

ring. Facing these racial swarms a central mass of Hungarians are striving to expand against them.

For more than twelve centuries Austria's geographical position has made her the protectress of Europe from successive onslaughts of barbarian hordes pressing from the east. The German-speaking nucleus of the present Dual Monarchy was founded, at the end of the eighth century, by Charles the Great as a bulwark against the Avars. A little later the rôle of stemming the tide of Hungarian attacks also devolved upon it. Fighting incessantly and on the whole successfully against eastern invaders, the Austrians gradually extended their territory towards the Orient. The valley of the Danube provided them with settling-land and passage-way. War and marriages brought their share of added territory to the Hapsburg reigning family. By 1526 Moravia, Bohemia, Silesia and Hungary had been added to the Empire. Transylvania was conquered in the seventeenth century, Galicia and Bukovina in the eighteenth. At the beginning of the nineteenth century, Austria was the leader among German-speaking states. Prussian shot and shell ousted her from this position at the battle of Sadowa in 1866. But the task undertaken over a thousand years ago is still being performed. Austrians today are engaged in another effort to check the westward Slavic flow.

The country is ill-prepared to meet its hereditary foe. The sovereign existence of Austria-Hungary to this day can be regarded only as an exceedingly marvelous feat of political jugglery. Its weakness lies in the presence of strong contingents of dissimilar races in its population. Struggle between the component masses is as unending as it is passionate. To the lack of linguistic or racial affinity must be added the want of a liberal form of government in the strictly representative or federative sense. Representative government, in the absence of everything else, might have provided the required bond of political cohesion. Of the total population of Austria only 11,000,000, or 24 per cent, are Germans. These Teutons pay allegiance to the Hapsburg emperor along with 9,000,000 Hungarians, 3,000,000 Rumanians and about 1,000,000 Italians. The Slavic race, however, outnumbers every other element in the Empire. Its 21,000,000 members constitute 44 per cent of the subjects of Charles I.

In one sense Austria's mission of protecting Europe ended as soon as the Ottoman Empire ceased to be a source of danger. To consolidate Danubian nationalities in a single group capable of withstanding the Turkish advance had constituted Austria's most glorious part in modern history. With the elimination of the Turkish danger, the necessity of political union among the peoples occupying the valley of the Danube was removed. The chief reason for the maintenance of an Austrian state thereby ceases to exist. Events of our own times reveal the natural working out of these international problems. As long as Mohammedanism threatened to absorb Christianity in southeastern Europe, the various peoples of the Austrian Empire stood shoulder to shoulder against a common foe. The sense of security now induces them to turn their thoughts on themselves and effectively hasten the growth of national consciousness based on ideals and aspirations which can be expressed in a common language.

The passing of Austria's usefulness as a nation has been marked by the country's growing vassalage to the leading Teutonic power. At Berlin, the center of Imperial Germany, the aim of every leader is to further the easterly expansion of the Empire. Austria, commanding the natural route to the southeast, figures as a precious asset in these imperial estimates. But success to German ambition spells defeat to the dreams of political independence cherished in the minds of the peoples of Austria-Hungary. A conflict of vital importance to each contestant is raging. The struggle is likely to be maintained wherever more than a single language continues to be spoken.

The mastery of the Adriatic, claimed by Italy at present, has been contested in the past twenty-five centuries by every people which succeeded in gaining a foothold on its shores. Illyrians, Greeks, Romans, Byzantines, Venetians and Turks each in their day acquired maritime supremacy in the Mediterranean, and naturally aspired to control this waterway. The prize was worth fighting for. It was part of the lane of traffic between the rich valley of the Po, the lands beyond the Alps and eastern countries. In the present century eastern trade generally runs in different channels. A sufficient tonnage, however, finds its way to the great harbors of the Adriatic to excite Italian ambitions. Moreover Italian manufacturers are looking forward to the establishment of crosswise trade relations with the Balkan peninsula. These are economic considerations which impart definite aim to the policy of Italian statesmen.

The most satisfactory picture of Italian desire to annex Dalmatia appears on maps of the Adriatic, which show the contrast between the opposite coasts. On the Italian side, the coast-line runs with monotonous uniformity. It is devoid of the headlands, gulfs or islands which impart economic, strategic and scenic value to Dalmatia. Barring short stretches in Puglia the entire Italian coast is shallow and sandy. Its well-known ports hardly deserve the name. Mariners are well aware of the obstacles to navigation along the whole western Adriatic shore. At the head of this sea, especially, the situation for Italian shipping is most unfavorable, owing to the large number of rivers which discharge material collected from practically the entire eastern watershed of the Alps and that of the northern Apennines. From west to east some among the most important of these rivers are the Po, Adige, Piave and Isonzo. This piling of material, added to the process of land emergence going on at the head of the Adriatic, impairs the value of the Gulf of Venice to modern navigation.

The Dalmatian coast, however, with its numerous bays and gulfs setting far into the land and broken by many headlands, is fringed by a garland of outlying islands. These natural features of the region provide the advantages denied to Italy. Almost every mile of shore in Dalmatia contains a commodious harbor for merchantmen or a well-sheltered base for war vessels. Most of the rivers originating in the mountain chains overlooking blue water flow eastward toward the Danube. Very little silt and sediment therefore finds its way to the Dalmatian coast.

Linguistically, the eastern shore of the Adriatic is Serbian or Albanian. But the history of this coastal land is Italian in spite of the showing of census returns as to the decided numerical inferiority of Italians within its limits. Rome had reached Dalmatia and the Near East by way of the Adriatic. A whole chain of imposing ruins extending to the wild Albanian shores bear the unmistakable impress of Roman splendor. In the partition of the Roman Empire in 295 A.D. Dalmatia was assigned to the western and not to the eastern half. The period of its subjection to Venetian rule is one of the most brilliant in its history. All the civilization it received came from the west.

The fact is that the Italian element has always been predominant. After 1866 its influence was viewed with disfavor by the Austrian government. Serbians and Croats were encouraged to settle in the Italian communities of the coast and officials of the Dual Monarchy were instructed to assist the Slavs in every possible manner with a view to counterbalancing Italian primacy in the province. In recent years the task of the Austrian government became doubly difficult, for its representatives could not avoid playing alternately into the hands of Serbians and Italians.

Dalmatia has always greeted Italian thought as the heritage of Rome and Venice. Its history, its most notable monuments and its whole culture are products of either Roman or Venetian influence. The maritime cities in particular still remain strongholds of Italian thought. Almost every one boasts of a native son who has distinguished himself in the cause of Italy.

Zara, which Italian authors delight in qualifying as "italianissima," is the native city of the Italian patriot Arturo Colantti. The great Dalmatian poet Niccoló Tomasseo, whose monument was erected in Sebenico in 1896, was a son

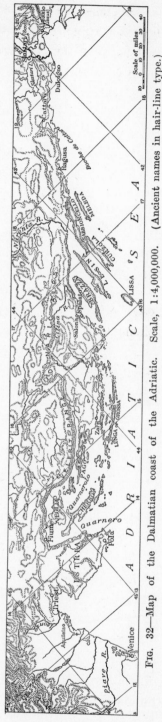

Fig. 32—Map of the Dalmatian coast of the Adriatic. Scale, 1:4,000,000. (Ancient names in hair-line type.)

of this city and, although an intensely patriotic Slav, nevertheless thus expressed himself in Italian:

> Nè più tra'l monte e il mar, povero lembo
> Di terra e poche ignude isole sparte,
> O Patria mia, sarai; ma la rinata
> Serbia guerriera mano e mite spirto,

showing thereby the extent of the hold of Italian culture over the land.   Again, Spalato is the birthplace of Antonio Bajamonti, one of the greatest exponents of Italy's claims over Dalmatia.

According to the Austrian census of 1910 the population of the province consisted of 645,666 inhabitants.   Of these it is estimated that 60,000 are Italians, who constitute the progressive and educated element of the population.   The Slav inhabitants number approximately 480,000, but only about 30,000 among them have a speaking knowledge of Italian.   The mass of this Slavic element is uneducated.

The Illyrians were early inhabitants of the eastern Adriatic coast whom the Romans had conquered in order to check piracy in the Adriatic.   After being tamed these barbarians formed the substratum of the population of Adriatic cities.   Throughout the coast their language was displaced during the Middle Ages by the Venetian of Italian traders.   In the Albanian mountains, however, the old Illyrian tongue strongly impregnated with Latin words still survives.   Roman influence could not be exerted on this rugged land as strongly as on the coast.

Rome's ancient domination of the Illyrian coast and Wallachian plains led to highly interesting consequences.   A genuine Romance language was once spoken by the mountain population of shepherds which extended across the entire Balkan peninsula from the Dalmatian coast, through the Bosnian and Serbian highlands, into the easternmost ranges of the Carpathians.   The similarity observable in Balkan and Carpathian mountain dialects thus finds its source in the original easterly expansion of Rome. The Banat territory, in which the proportion of Rumanian inhabitants is high, is the bridge land which connects the Rumanian

form of Latin used on the broad Transylvanian shelf to the
Albanian prevailing in the broken-up highlands of Albania.
Romance speech therefore found a ready soil in the Balkan uplifts.
It may even be detected in the mountainous sections of Thrace,
a province which also fell under Roman rule during the transition
period from pagan to Christian days.

The arrival of Slavs in the seventh century forced the Romans
to take refuge behind city walls, so that although the vast non-
urban part of the province became Slavic in population, the cities
remained Latin and formed themselves into a number of independent republics.   These city states passed under Venetian
protection in the ninth and tenth centuries to safeguard themselves against the piratical raids of Slavs who had succumbed to
the nefarious influence exerted by the dissected coast with its
numerous fiords and deep-water harbors.

The Venetian protectorate soon became converted into direct
sovereignty. But the yoke of the Doges lay light on the land, the
administration of cities being left entirely in the hands of the
citizens. Venetian authority was most strongly felt in Dalmatia
after the assumption of the title of Dux Histriae et Dalmatiae by
Doge Pietro Orseolo II. All the efforts of Hungarians in the
thirteenth and fourteenth centuries, and of Turks in the seventeenth, to insinuate themselves into Dalmatian affairs were futile.
The imposing barrier of the Dinaric Alps forbade intercourse
between Dalmatia and the east. Life and progress flowed into
the province from the west over Adriatic waters.

Dalmatia changed hands frequently during the Napoleonic
period. Perhaps it is on this account that the Dalmatian, when
questioned regarding his nationality, answers by stating that he
has two languages. Of these he calls one "lingua del cuore," and
the other "lingua del pane." His native province was awarded
to Austria by the treaty of Campoformio in 1797 and subsequently
annexed to Napoleon's Empire by the treaty of Presburg in 1805.
It reverted to Austrian rule in 1814. Successive masters, however, failed to root out Italian in the region. The language was
recognized as official until 1860. The formation of a united

Italian state marked the beginning of a repressive policy directed against Italians by the Austrian government. The effort of the Hapsburg administration was entirely directed towards the development of the Adriatic Slavs in order to counterbalance Italian influence. A great revival of Croatian and Serbian national feeling resulted from this policy.

The award of the entire eastern Adriatic coast to Italy would not only trespass on lands of alien speech, but would seriously hamper future economic development of Croatians and Serbians by preventing these peoples from attaining the sea. These points are admitted by most Italian irredentists. They therefore limit their claims to the Istrian peninsula and the coast region of Dalmatia comprised between the Velebiti range and the Narenta river. Italy's position in the Adriatic would be improved by the recognition of the rights of her Slav neighbors. The goodwill of a united and liberated Jugoslavia, which would be bound to Italy by ties of interest and sentiment, would thus be acquired.

The Croatian coastland, in the section which extends along the waterway of the same name from the gulf of Fiume to the mouth of the Zermagna river, is known as the Morlacca. The bay of Buccari is strategically necessary for the protection of Fiume, and Italians would probably make a strong claim for its possession in case the larger seaport came into their possession. The Serbian coastland really begins south of the Narenta river and centers around Ragusa. This is the only city of any importance on the Adriatic coast in which evidences of Serbian culture are discernible.

The old Slavic settlers were probably traders who plied between the coasts of Dalmatia and Abruzzi during the Middle Ages. In the kingdom of Naples Slav colonists are known as early as the eleventh century, during the reign of Emperor Otto I. The bulk of Slavic immigration into Italy dates, however, from the beginning of the fifteenth century when possession of the coast provinces was disputed by the Aragonians and Angevins. Both claimants induced Slavs to colonize the contested regions on condition that they would recognize the authority of those who provided them with land. At a later period the advance of Turkish hordes in the Balkans drove a large number of Slavic families westward.

The Turkish conquest of Greece also forced many Greek families to seek safety on the Italian mainland. As a result, two

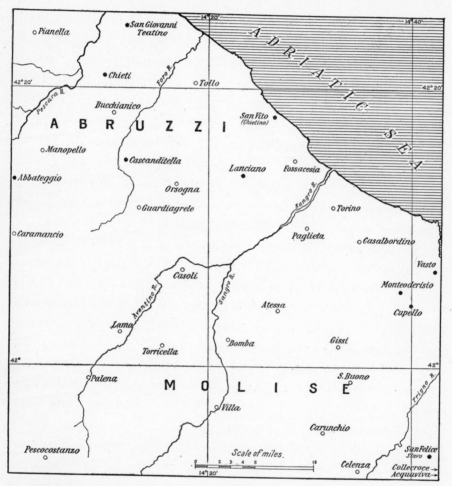

Fig. 33—The Slavic colonies of the Molise group in eastern Italy are shown by black dots.

communities of Greek speech are found on Italian territory at Lecce in the province of Puglia and at Bora in Calabria. The vernacular of both these regions contains a strong proportion of Italian words without, however, losing its affinity with the original mother tongue. The Lecce community consists of 4,973 families scattered in nine communi. The southern group is represented by 2,389 families settled in four communi of the Bora district, in Reggio di Calabria and in Palizzi. Altogether Greek is spoken as a vernacular by 30,700 inhabitants of Italy.

Still another reminder of the Turkish conquests of the fifteenth and sixteenth centuries is afforded by the presence of an Albanian element living along the eastern coast of Italy. This group consists of between 80,000 and 90,000 Albanians speaking their own language. The purity of Albanian speech and custom has been preserved by them on the alien soil skirting western Adriatic waters.[21]

This total shows a marked decrease from the figure of 96,000 reported in the census of 1901. Emigration accounts mainly for this loss. At the same time, a tendency among Albanians to forsake their vernacular for Italian is discernible as intercourse with the dominant element increases.

All these nuclei of foreign languages cannot impair the unity of Italian nationality because the racial distinctions on which they are based have been largely obliterated. The final supremacy of Italian language is already in sight. From the valleys of Piedmont to the eastern coastlands which face Albania, the alien tongues are giving way before the national vernacular, perhaps just because no pressure or effort to hasten their disappearance is being exerted by the government.

---

[21] O. Marinelli: Il numero degli Albanesi in Italia, *Riv. Geogr. It.*, Vol. 20, pp. 364-367; A. Similari: Gli Albanesi in Italia, loro costumi e poesie popolari, Naples, 1891.

TABLE I

INHABITANTS OF ITALY SPEAKING NON-ITALIAN VERNACULARS [1]

LANGUAGE	Localities	Number of Families [2] (Average of four persons to the family)
French	Saluzzo (Cuneo)	238
	Aosta (Torino)	15,692
	Pignerol	1,937
	Suse	1,779
German	Aosta (Torino)	430
	Domodossola (Novara)	250
	Varallo	412
	Asiago (Vicenza)	501
	Tregnago (Verona)	30
	Pieve di Cadore (Belluno)	299
	Tolmezzo (Udine)	280
Slovene	Cividale del Friuli (Udine)	3,769
	Gemona	120
	Tolmezzo	990
	Tarcento	1,371
Serbian	Larino (Campobasso)	1,069
Albanian	Larino (Campobasso)	2,431
	Penne (Teramo)	66
	Ariano di Puglia (Avel.)	763
	San Severo (Foggia)	832
	Taranto (Lecce)	757
	Lagonegro (Potenza)	2,319
	Catanzaro	701
	Cotrone (Catanzaro)	789
	Nicastro	434
	Castrovillari (Cosenza)	3,330
	Cosenza	1,441
	Paola (Cosenza)	408
	Rossano	1,702
	Corleone (Palermo)	385
	Palermo	2,733
Greek	Lecce	4,935
	Gerace (Reggio di Calab.)	129
	Reggio di Calabria	1,841
Catalonian	Alghero (Sassari)	2,552
	Total..........	57,715

[1] *Annuario Statistico Italiano*, 2d series, Vol. 4, 1914, Roma, 1915, p. 28.

[2] The Italian practice of computing by families is a result in this instance of the official standpoint which recognizes foreign languages as prevailing only in home life.

The proportion of inhabitants of Italian (including Ladin) speech in the Adriatic lands claimed by Italy is given as follows according to the Austrian Census of 1910:[1]

TABLE II

PROPORTION OF INHABITANTS OF ITALIAN (INCLUDING LADIN) SPEECH IN THE ADRIATIC LANDS CLAIMED BY ITALY ACCORDING TO THE AUSTRIAN CENSUS OF 1910:

COAST PROVINCES		Total number of Austrian subjects	Number of Italian (and Ladin) speaking Austrian subjects
Triest (city)		190,913	118,959
Görz "		29,291	14,812
Görz (district)		73,275	2,765
Gradisca "		31,321	26,263
Monfalcone "		47,858	45,907
Sesana "		30,078	343
Tolmein "		38,070	29
Rovigno (city)		11,308	10,859
Capodistria (district)		87,652	38,006
Lussin "		20,450	9,884
Mitterburg "		48,243	4,032
Parenzo "		60,368	41,276
Pola "		85,943	40,863
Veglia "		21,136	1,544
Volosca "		51,363	953

DALMATIA		Total number of Austrian subjects	Number of Italian (and Ladin) speaking Austrian subjects
Benkovac (district)		44,054	84
Cattaro "		36,014	538
Curzola "		29,695	444
Imotski "		42,086	46
Knin "		54,936	186
Lesina "		26,902	586
Makarska "		27,649	117
Metkovie "		15,475	32
Ragusa "		38,632	526
San Pietro " (Brazza)		22,865	265
Sebenico "		57,658	968
Sinj "		57,021	111
Spalato "		98,509	2,357
Zara "		83,359	11,768

[1] G. Lukas: Die Latinität der adriatischen Küste Österreich-Ungarns—Geographische Vorlesungen, *Pet. Mitt.*, Vol. 6, Nov. 1915, pp. 413-416.

CHAPTER V

SCANDINAVIAN AND BALTIC LANGUAGES

SCANDINAVIA's remoteness from the center of European political strife has not saved the region from the inconveniences arising from linguistic clashes. Especially is this true where political and linguistic boundaries do not coincide. The Danish-German frontier has been marked by antagonism between Danes and Germans. Denmark's hold on Schleswig-Holstein prior to 1866 had engendered bitter feeling among Germans, who considered the subjection of their kinsmen settled on the right bank of the Elbe estuary as unnatural. After Prussia had annexed the contested region, it was the Danes' turn to feel dissatisfied and to claim the districts occupied by their countrymen.

The problem of Schleswig-Holstein is a direct consequence of Germany's geography. By its position in Europe the Teutonic empire is essentially a land power. Its maritime development began in the midst of adverse natural conditions in the northern confines of the country. The southern Baltic and the North Sea are both shallow. Sandbanks and winter ice hamper navigation in the easternmost stretch of these waters. An outlet exists only in the round-about and rock-studded Danish straits. The Oder, Elbe and Ems are constantly discharging material collected from the mountainous heart of Europe. The harbors of the north-western shore are artificial and require ceaseless watching, for all of which German navigation pays a heavy annual tax.

The Danish tongue of land which divides Germany's northern sea boundary into two separate regions contains in its eastern and northern coasts the very advantages which Germany cannot find on its northern frontier. Eastern Jutland boasts a few natural harbors located at the head of the indentations which impart a fiord-like aspect to this coast and which in course of time have grown into centers of commercial activity. German shipping circles would consider the annexation of the Danish peninsula to Germany as a measure leading to high economic advantages, even though the construction of the Kiel canal has materially changed conditions which affected the Danish-German situation when the duchies of Schleswig and Holstein were annexed in 1866.

The present Danish-speaking population of Schleswig-Holstein is variously estimated at between 140,000 and 150,000. These subjects of the Kaiser occupy the territory south of the Danish boundary to a line formed by the western section of the Lecker Au, the southern border of the swampy region extending south of Rens and the northern extension of the Angeln hills. Between this line and the area in which German is spoken a zone of the old Frisian tongue of Holland survives along the western coast of the peninsula from the Lecker Au to the Treene river.[1] Frisian is also spoken in the coastal islands.

The degree to which linguistic variations adapt themselves to physical configuration is admirably illustrated in this case, by the southerly extension of Danish along the eastern section of the peninsula where persistence of the Baltic ridge appears in the hilly nature of the land. The Low German of the long Baltic plain also continued to spread unimpeded within the low-lying western portion of the narrow peninsula, until its northward extension was arrested by uninhabited heath land. The presence of Frisian along the western coast is undoubtedly connected with the adaptability of Frisians to settle in land areas reclaimed from the sea.

The province of Schleswig began to acquire historical prominence as an independent duchy in the twelfth century. Barring few interruptions its union with the Danish crown has been continuous to the time of the Prussian conquest. In 1848 both Schleswig and Holstein were disturbed by a wave of political agitation which expressed itself in demands for the joint incorpo-

---

[1] A substantial account of the tribes speaking these three languages was given as early as 731 by the Venerable Bede in his *Historia Ecclesiastica*.

ration of both states in the German Confederation. To what extent the mass of Danish inhabitants of the duchies took part in this movement is a matter of controversy. Holstein was an ancient fief of the old Germano-Roman Empire. Its population has always been largely German. But the duchy of Schleswig is peopled mainly by Danes. By the terms of the treaty of Prague of August 23, 1866, both Austria and Prussia had agreed to submit final decision on the question of nationality to popular vote.[2] The provisions of the clause dealing with the referendum, however, were not carried out, and on Jan. 12, 1867, Schleswig was definitely annexed by Prussia.[3]

Incorporation of the Danish provinces was followed by systematic attempts to Germanize the population[4] through the agency of churches and schools. In addition a number of colonization societies such as the "Ansiedelungs Verein für westliche Nordschleswig," founded at Rödding in 1891,[5] and the "Deutsche Verein für das nordliche Schleswig" were formed to introduce German ownership of land in the Danish districts. The final years of the nineteenth century in particular constituted a period of strained feeling between Danes and Germans owing to unsettled conditions brought about by duality of language and tradition.

At present the problem of Schleswig is considered settled by the German government. A treaty signed on January 11, 1907, between the cabinets of Berlin and Copenhagen defined the status of the inhabitants of the annexed duchy. The problem of the "Heimatlose" or citizens without a country[6] was solved by the

---

[2] [Translation.] "Art. V. His Majesty the Emperor of Austria transfers to His Majesty the King of Prussia all the rights which he acquired by the Vienna Treaty of Peace of 30th October, 1864, over the Duchies of Holstein and Schleswig, with the condition that the populations of the Northern Districts of Schleswig shall be ceded to Denmark if, by a free vote, they express a wish to be united to Denmark." E. Herstlet: The Map of Europe by Treaty, London, 1875, Vol. 3, p. 1722.

[3] A later treaty signed by Austria and Prussia at Vienna on Oct. 11, 1878, suppressed the referendum clause, which had never been viewed with favor by the German government.

[4] M. R. Waultrin: Le rapprochement dano-allemand et la question du Schleswig, Ann. Sci. Polit., May 15, and July 15, 1903.

[5] L. Gasselin: La question du Schleswig-Holstein, Paris, 1909.

[6] L. Gasselin: op. cit., p. 206.

recognition of the right of choice of nationality on their part.
The German government considered this measure as satisfying
the aspirations of its subjects of Danish birth. Nevertheless,
although the Danish government appeared to share these views,
the acquiescence of Danes living in Germany to any solution other

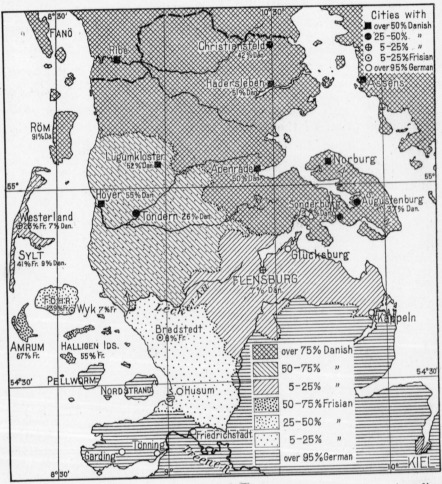

FIG. 34—Sketch map of Schleswig-Holstein showing languages spoken. According
to the German viewpoint. Scale, 1:1,200,000. (Based on maps on pp. 59, 60, Andree's
Handatlas, 6th ed.)

than the restoration to Denmark of the Danish-speaking sections
of Schleswig remains doubtful. That suspicion of the loyalty of
the Schleswig Danes is still entertained in Germany is shown
by statements like that made by Henry Goddard Leach, Secretary

of the American-Scandinavian Foundation, when he asserted [7]
that Roald Amundsen, discoverer of the South Pole, was prevented from lecturing in Norwegian, in the town of Flensborg,
because the language resembled Danish.

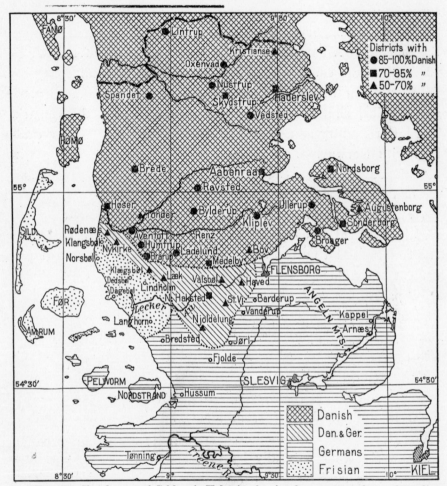

FIG. 35—Sketch map of Schleswig-Holstein showing languages spoken. According
to the Danish viewpoint. Scale, 1:1,200,000. (After Rosendal based on Clausens
and Heyers.)

In Norway the linguistic problem goes under the name of
Maalstraev. The question of language in that country was
debated with marked fervor [8] during the years prior to the separation from Sweden. "Freedom with self-government, home,

---

[7] Scandinavia and the Scandinavians, New York, 1915, p. 30.
[8] Op. cit., p. 143.

land and our own language'' was the plea of Mr. Jörgen Lövland, subsequently Premier of Norway, in an address to the Norwegian youth in 1904. ''Political freedom,'' then said Mr. Lövland, ''is not the deepest and greatest. Greater is it for a nation to preserve her intellectual inheritance in her native tongue.''

Norwegian history is not continuous, complaisant historians to the contrary. A long break occurs from the Union of Kalmar in 1397, when the country ceased to exist as a political entity, to 1814. During this period of extinction, Norway was a mere geographical shuttlecock tossed between Sweden and Denmark. The latter country as a rule obtained the upper hand in its dealings with Norway. This relation accounts for the analogies in the languages of the two nations. But although Norway had seceded from Denmark in 1814, the Danish language, representing the speech of the more energetic and better educated Danes, remained official. Four and a half centuries of union between the two countries had made Danish the medium of intellectual development throughout Norway. But this linguistic invasion was accompanied by a notable modification of Danish. Norwegian intonations and sound articulations became adapted to it and the Norwego-Danish language, which is spoken today, gradually came into use.

This hybrid language, however, does not prevail exclusively. About 95 per cent of the Norwegians speak, according to districts, different dialects derived from the Old Norse. The Norwego-Danish, or Riksmaal, is the language of polite society and the one which a foreigner naturally learns when in Norway. The language of the land, or Norsk as it is called by the Norwegians, has the merit of being more homogeneous than either Danish or Swedish.

Nationality and language have grown apace in Norway. Prior to the nineteenth century the use of words taken from the Norwegian dialects was considered bad form. The granting of a constitution to the Norwegians, in 1814, created a strong feeling of nationality throughout the land. This spirit was reflected in active research for every form of Old Norse culture. Hitherto despised patois words were forced into prose or poetry by the foremost Norwegian writers, a movement to Norsefy the Riksmaal thus being originated.

As a result of these endeavors a new language, the "Landsmaal," or fatherland speech, came into being about the middle of the nineteenth century. The name of Ivar Aasen will always be linked with it. This highly gifted peasant devoted his life to the idea of a renaissance of the Old Norse language through the unification of the current peasant dialects. Scientific societies, urged by patriotism no less than by genuine scholarly interest, granted him subsidies which enabled him to carry on his studies. Two of his works—"The Grammar of the Norwegian Popular Language," published in 1848, and a "Dictionary of the Norwegian Popular Language," in 1850—virtually established a new medium of speech in Norway.

Landsmaal was happily introduced just about the time when a sense of national consciousness began to dawn on Norwegian minds. By a number of enactments of the Storting the study of the new national tongue was made compulsory. This body first acted in May 1885 by requesting the Government "to adopt the necessary measures so that the people's language, as school and official language, be placed side by side with our ordinary written speech.⁹ Then, in 1892, the following law for elementary schools was framed: "The school board (in each district) shall decide whether the school readers and text-books shall be composed in Landsmaal or the ordinary book-'maal' and in which of these languages the pupil's written exercises shall in general be composed. But the pupil must learn to read both languages." Finally, in 1896, the study of Landsmaal was made obligatory in the high schools.

After Norway secured complete national independence, in 1905, the Landsmaal advanced rapidly. Its use was permitted in university examinations. By 1909 one hundred and twenty-five out of six hundred and fifty school districts had adopted "New Norse" as the medium of instruction.¹⁰ In the bishopric of

---

⁹ Op. cit., p. 147.   ¹⁰ Op. cit., p. 148.

Bergen the new language came to stay in 56 out of 101 country parishes. The issue between Landsmaal and Riksmaal being closely linked with nationalism in Norway, many Norwegians have now come to look upon the Danish tongue as a sign of former vassalage. New Norse, on the other hand, embodies the newly acquired national independence. In the eyes of patriots it is the language which is most closely allied to the saga tongue of their Viking ancestors. And yet it is stated that less than a thousand persons in Norway actually use New Norse in their conversation.[11] The supplanting of Norwego-Danish by the made-to-order Landsmaal bids fair to take time. But the process of welding Norwegian dialects into a single national language is going on. In this must be sought the significance of Norway's language agitation. A Norwegian tongue which will be spoken within Norwegian boundaries is being formed. In recent years it has been customary to publish all acts of Parliament both in Norwego-Danish and in Landsmaal.

The Swedish language differs from Norwegian by a typical accentuation. The growth of the language to its present form may be traced back to the Runic period of the thirteenth century. At that time Swedish was free from foreign admixture. The influence of Latin and of Middle and Low German was felt later. The language passed successively through the period of Old Swedish (1200-1500) and Early Modern Swedish (1500-1730). Its present form belongs to the Later Modern School, although it is spoken now without much change from the language of the middle eighteenth century.

The eastern half of the European continent contains a zone of excessive linguistic intermingling along the line where Teutonic and Slavic peoples meet. From the shores of the White Sea to the Baltic and thence to the coast of the Black Sea an elongated belt of lowland was ill fitted to become the seat of a single state because nature has not provided it with strongly marked geographical boundaries which might have favored the development of nationality. Hence it is that before the eighteenth century we

---

[11] Op. cit., p. 150.

do not find a single nation in possession of this region. On the other hand, it is the site on which three religions met in bloody fray in modern times. At the beginning of the modern era its northern sections became the theater of wars between Protestants and Catholics, while to the south, Christians arrayed against eastern infidels were obliged to war for centuries before the danger of the invasion of central Europe by Mohammedan hordes was totally removed.

The Finns, occupying the northernmost section of this elongated belt, are linguistically allied to the Turki. Physically they constitute the proto-Teutonic substratum of the northern Russians with whom they have been merged. Their land was transferred from Sweden to Russia in 1808. Autonomy conceded by the Czar's government provided the inhabitants with a tolerable political status, until it was rescinded by the imperial decree of February 15, 1899. The opening years of the present century marked the beginning of a policy of Slavicization prosecuted with extreme vigor on the part of the provincial administrators.

The Finnish peoples of Russia must be regarded as autochthons who have been subjected to the inroads of both Slavic and Tatar invasions. In the ninth century A.D. they formed compact populations on the European mainland directly south of Finland, where their descendants now group themselves in scattered colonies. Except in Finland they are being Slavicized at a rapid rate and the Slav population is now imposing itself on the Tatar which had once swamped the indigenous element.

Early mention of these Finns shows them divided into several tribes. The Livs and Chuds, who dwelt mainly around the gulfs of Livonia and of Finland, were the forefathers of the present inhabitants of northern Livonia as well as of Esthonia.[12] The Ingrians and the Vods inhabited the basin of the Neva. The Suomi tribes, of which the Kvens, Karels, Yams and Tavasts were the most important, occupied the Finnish territory held at present by their descendants. Every river valley of northwestern Russia was in fact a tribal homeland. The term Finnish as applied to

---

[12] A. Rambaud: Histoire de la Russie, Paris, 1914, p. 21.

these tribes refers to their culture, which was Asiatic throughout. Racially, however, they consist of Nordics with a strong addition of Tatar blood.

The area of Finnish speech forms a compact mass extending south of the 69th parallel to the Baltic shores. Its complete access to the sea is barred in part by two coastal strips in the gulfs of Bothnia and Finland in both of which Swedish predominates in varying percentages.[13] The group of the Aland Islands, although included in the Czar's dominions, is also peopled by Swedes all the way to the southwestern point of Finland.[14] This broken fringe of Swedish is conceded to be a relic of the early occupation of Finland by Swedes.[15] One of its strips, the Bothnian, is remarkably pure in composition. The band extending on the northern shore of the Gulf of Finland, however, contains enclaves of the Finnish element. This is ascribed to an artificial process of "fennification" resulting from the introduction of cheap labor in the industrial regions of southern Finland. Slower economic development of the provinces of the western coast, on the other hand, tends to maintain undisturbed segregation of the population.

The ties uniting Finland with Sweden are moral and cultural. Swedish missionaries of the twelfth and thirteenth centuries were the agents through whom Christianity was introduced into Finland. Together with religion many Swedish customs and laws superseded the primitive social organization of the Finns. The relation established was virtually that of an intellectual minority gaining the upper hand over an ignorant majority. A change in the situation came about in the middle of the fourteenth century when Finland became an integral part of the Swedish kingdom and all civil and political distinctions between the two elements of its populations were abolished.

Finland's union with the west failed, however, to bring about Swedish predominance in the land. The Finns preserved their

---

[13] Atlas de Finlande, Carte 46, Helsingfors, 1911.
[14] K. B. Wiklund: Språken i Finland, 1880-1900, *Ymer*, 1905, No. 2, pp. 132-149.
[15] R. Saxen: Répartition des langues, *Fennia*, Vol. 30, No. 2, 1910-1911, Helsingfors, 1911.

FIG. 36.

FIG. 37.

FIG. 36—View of the Lake country near Kuopi, showing the Kallavesi Sea with low islands and level shores. This is a characteristic Finnish landscape.

FIG. 37—Above the Koivukoski Falls at Kajana. Finnish waterways are the usual lanes of traffic between the inland seas of that country.

language and tended in fact to assimilate their conquerors. The physical isolation of their country from Sweden contributed largely to foster this incipient stage of Finnish nationality. The Gulf of Bothnia and the frozen solitudes of Lapland proved an effective barrier to the complete fusion of Swedes and Finns. Eastward, however, no natural obstacles intervened between Finland and Russia. The prolonged struggle between the latter country and Sweden hence inevitably led to the Russian conquest of Finland.

The peace of Nystad in 1721 enabled Russia to occupy Finnish territory for the first time. All of the southeastern portion of the duchy then became part of the Muscovite empire. A further cession in 1743 at the treaty of Åbo brought Swedish frontiers as far west as the Kymmens line. The final conquest was ratified by the treaty of peace signed by Swedish and Russian plenipotentiaries on September 17, 1809. Sweden formally renounced its rights over Finland and the duchy became part of Russia.

Today Finland is a country with three languages. Russian is the channel of official activity. Finnish, through a literary revival, has won its right to be the language of the land and this is a symbol of the Finns' desire for independent national existence. Swedish remains as the age-old medium through which Christianity and western culture were conveyed. It is also to a large extent the business language of the province, especially for communication with western Europe. Competition between the three languages is carried on with unabating energy. The struggle is an outward manifestation of the fight for independence waged by the natives of Finland in the presence of Swedish and Russian efforts to dominate the country. The common danger from Russia has lately drawn the Swedish and Finnish groups together, although the Finns were previously strongly anti-Swedish. The old antagonism still lingers in society life. The Swedish-speaking element rarely mixes with the Finnish-speaking. This is particularly noticeable at Helsingfors, where each language represents a distinct stratum of social life.

In Russia's Baltic provinces two of the world's oldest yet

absolutely distinct languages are spoken. South of the Gulf of
Finland the Esthonians or Chuds still retain a primitive form of
Mongolian. In the neighboring Letto-Lithuanian group, on the
other hand, a speech which is closely akin to the old Aryan is
employed. Almost any Lithuanian peasant can understand simple
phrases in Sanskrit. The survival of archaic languages in this
section of Europe is the result of isolation provided by a forested
and marshy country in which folk-characteristics maintained their
ancient forms. From the racial standpoint Esthonians, Letts and
Lithuanians are fair, generally tall, narrow-faced and long-
headed. In the Fellin district, in southern Estland, a very pure
Nordic type is found among peoples of Esthonian speech.

Early Russian chronicles describe the Letts and Lithuanians
as divided into several tribes.[16] The Yatvags were scattered along
the banks of the Narev. The Lithuanians proper together with
the Shmuds peopled the Niemen valley. Very little dialectical
differences exist between the two. The Shmuds cluster now in
northwestern Kovno without, however, attaining the Baltic shore.
The left bank of the Drina was occupied by the Semigals, while
on the right dwelt the Letgols who were the ancestors in direct
line of the Letts of southern Livonia. The Kors, who lived on
the western shores of the Gulf of Riga, were later to impose their
name on the province of Kurland.[17]

Two of these tribes, the Shmuds and the Lithuanians, escaped
the Teutonic conquest through the inaccessibility of their forested
and marshy retreat. Around them the Kors and the Letts, as
well as the primitive Slav occupants of Prussia, had been subjugated by the Knights of the Teutonic Order. The only salvation
for these tribes from Teutonic oppression consisted in their seeking the natural shelter occupied by the two more fortunate groups
of their kinsmen. Behind this natural barrier Lithuanian nationality was born in the middle of the thirteenth century under the
leadership of Mindvog, an energetic chieftain who insured his

---

[16] A. Rambaud: Histoire de la Russie depuis les origines jusqu'à nos jours,
Paris, 1914, p. 21.
[17] Rambaud: op. cit.

own supremacy by causing the leaders of rival clans to be put to death. With the help of the Poles the Lithuanians eventually checked the easterly expansion of the Teutons.

The region occupied by Lithuanians in former times can be traced today by the distribution of the type of dwelling peculiar to this people. The ancient area exceeds the borders of the present linguistic zone. The earliest examples of Lithuanian houses consist of a single room. The indoor life of a single family was spent within this one apartment. This primitive habitation grew into the modern style by the successive addition of rooms. In course of time a kitchen or a stable was added to the main building. Sometimes the old type of house stands to this day adjoining more modern buildings. In such cases it is used as a barn.

The old Aryan of the Lithuanians is in vogue principally along the Duna and Niemen rivers as well as around Vilna, where this people are settled in compact masses. In spite of the antiquity of their language, no texts prior to the sixteenth century are known. Emigration in the past decade to large Russian cities, and to America, has decreased their ranks appreciably. Their number is now estimated at 3,500,000.[18] In his native land, the Lithuanian is not on the best of terms with neighboring peoples. He looks upon the Russian as his political oppressor and upon the Pole as his hereditary foe. The Lett is regarded with somewhat less animosity as a rival. The Letts spread inland from the shores of the Gulf of Riga and number about 1,300,000. Owing to Polish influences, many Lithuanians are Catholics, but, in the main, both Letts and Lithuanians are stanch Lutherans.[19] Their land is the home of religious free thought within orthodox Russia. German influence prevails among them on this account, although it is doubtful whether it extends to the point of their preferring German to Russian rule. Evil memories of the attempts of the Teutonic Knights to conquer the immemorial seat of the Lettish and Lithuanian populations survive throughout their forests and marshes. Neither people has forgotten that its ancestors were

---

[18] The Russian census of 1897 showed 3,094,469.
[19] About 50,000 Letts belong to the Greek Church.

refugees who sought the shelter of their boglands as a last recourse from Teutonic aggression.

Prior to 1876, the Baltic provinces were ruled by a semi-autonomous administration headed by a governor-general whose rôle was more properly that of a viceroy. German was as much an official language as Russian and no restrictions prevented its use in courts. German schools and a German university were widely attended. Since that date, however, the Letto-Lithuanian populations have been deprived of the liberal régime they formerly enjoyed and an official "Russification" has been directed against them. Most of the Lutheran schools were closed by order of the government and the teaching of German in schools restricted or prohibited. But to this day the three Baltic provinces of Kurland, Livland and Estland are considered by German writers as a domain of German culture and Protestant faith controlled by Russian political and ecclesiastical power.

In the province of Kurland the Germans boast 51,000 resident kinsmen. As a rule this section of the population is confined to the cities. Riga, Reval, Libau, Dorpat and Mitau contain notable percentages of Germans among their citizens. The first-named city counts 65,332 of these westerners in its population, or over 25 per cent of the total.[20]

The Letts have settled mainly in the Kurland peninsula and southern Livonia. They are also found in the governments of Kovno, Petrograd and Mohilev. Lithuanians occupy the governments of Kovno, Vilna, Suvalki and Grodno. No definite boundaries between the two peoples can be determined because their intercourse is constant. The only difference between the two languages is found in the greater departure of Lettic from the old Vedic forms.

North of the Letto-Lithuanian group the Esthonians, who are Finns and speak a Finnish language, occupy a lake-covered area similar to Finland. In both a granite tableland is the scene of human activity. In spite of the drawbacks of their natural

---

[20] H. Rosen: Die ethnographische Verhältnisse in den baltischen Provinzen und in Litauen, *Pet. Mitt.*, Sept. 1915, pp. 329-333.

environment the Esthonians depend chiefly on agriculture for sustenance. This industry has attained a high stage of perfection in their hands and few peoples know how to make their soil yield a higher return than do these virile northerners.

The number of Esthonians is estimated at about one million,[21] distributed as follows: Esthonia, 365,959; Livonia, 518,594; Government of St. Petersburg, 64,116; Government of Pskov, 25,458; other parts of Russia 12,855. Large colonies of Russians, Germans and Swedes are settled in the Esthonian province. The census of 1897 showed Russians, 18,000; Germans, 16,000; Swedes, 5,800.

The number of Jews settled in the province is not high. The German and Russian elements compose the nobility. The former owned and farmed 52 per cent of the land in 1878. Since that time, however, facilities have been accorded to the peasants of the province, mostly Esthonians, to purchase farms and the proportion of native land holdings is gradually increasing.

Confusion of racial minglings complicates the problem of assigning fixed ethnic place to the Esthonians. That they belong to the Finnish family is unquestionable. Linguistically they belong to the Turkish-speaking peoples. Long-headedness prevails among them.[22] These are also the characteristics of the Livs or Livonians, a Finnish tribe formerly living in Esthonia and north Livonia, now nearly extinct, but still holding a narrow strip of forest land along the Baltic at the northern extremity of Kurland. These Livs are now classed with the Baltic Finns and probably number less than 2,000 individuals. Their language has been almost entirely replaced by a Lettish dialect.

The beginning of their history finds the Esthonians pirates of the Baltic. Danish kings found it hard to subdue them and after two centuries of struggle sold the Danish crown's rights to the Knights of the Sword in 1346. From this time on German influence was to become paramount in the province. The condition of Esthonians in relation to their Teutonic masters was that of

---

[21] Russian census of 1897.
[22] W. Z. Ripley: The Races of Europe, New York, 1899.

serfs. By the terms of the treaty of Nystad in 1721 Esthonia was ceded to Peter the Great by the Swedes, who then exercised control of the land. Since then it has remained a Russian province. Lutheranism, the religion of its people, however, has been the foundation of much sympathy for German institutions throughout the province. To combat this feeling, as well as to eradicate national aspirations, Russian authorities have resorted to those harsh and repressive measures which both church and government have often enforced throughout the Czar's country.

The Esthonians are noted for their practical turn of mind. A favorite pastime among them consists of conversing in verse. They cling tenaciously to their language, the study of which is actively maintained throughout the land. Two main dialects are in use. A northern form, known as the Reval Esthonian, is recognized as the literary language. Writers have succeeded in maintaining its perfection and beauty. Through their efforts literature that instills vigor into the national consciousness has sprung into being around the legends and folk-tales of the region.

With the exception of the Finns all the peoples of northwestern Russia are being gradually absorbed by the Slavic mass. The Slav's ability to fuse with alien peoples is a conspicuous historical fact. In the Baltic provinces he seldom holds aloof as does his German rival. A growing spirit of liberalism in Russia, and the gradual loss of influence of the German nobility, ever ready to stir the opposition of Baltic peoples against Russian institutions, are two factors which have promoted the consolidation of Russian power in its northwesternmost territory. The Slav's achievement in Baltic regions, during the past three centuries, has consisted in steadily replacing the Teutonic stratum by a layer of his own kinsmen. Swedes and Germans have either fallen back or become lost in the midst of Slavic populations. The movement can hardly be called a migration, but it is a westerly expansion of most persistent and irresistible character although never aggressively manifested. As a consequence Russia's northwestern boundary with a reconstituted Poland may be foreseen.

TABLE I

POPULATION BY GOVERNMENTS IN FINLAND ACCORDING TO LANGUAGE, 1910 [1]

	Finnish	Per cent	Swedish	Per cent	Others	Per cent
Nylands	212,315	585.1	149,173	411.1	1,391	3.8
Abo o. Björneborgs ...	413,360	866.4	63,503	133.1	240	0.5
Tavastehus	330,190	986.6	4,356	13.0	119	0.4
Viborgs	479,120	969.7	7,872	15.9	7,116	14.4
St. Michels	191,137	996.0	670	3.5	93	0:5
Kuopio	324,553	997.4	664	2.0	191	0.6
Vasa	327,828	746.4	111,094	253.0	262	0.6
Uleaborgs	292,642	988.8	1,629	5.5	1,679	5.7

TABLE II

FINLAND: POPULATION ACCORDING TO LANGUAGE, 1865–1910

	1865	Per cent	1880	Per cent	1890	Per cent	1900	Per cent	1910	Per cent
Finnish	1,580,000	857.2	1,756,381	852.9	2,048,545	860.7	2,352,990	867.5	2,571,145	880.2
Swedish	256,000	138.9	294,876	143.2	322,604	135.6	349,733	128.9	338,961	116.0
Russian	4,000	2.2	4,195	2.0	5,795	2.4	5,939	2.2	7,339	2.5
German	1,200	0.6	1,720	0.8	1,674	0.7	1,925	0.7	1,794	0.6
Others	2,045	1.1	2,263	1.1	1,522	0.6	1,975	0.7	1,958	0.7

TABLE III

FINLAND: DISTRIBUTION OF POPULATION BY LANGUAGE AND BY RELIGION, DECEMBER 31, 1910 [2]

Linguistic group	Lutheran	Methodist	Baptist	Greek Catholic	Roman Catholic	Tota
Finnish ..	2,531,014	198	1,086	38,749	98	2,571,145
Swedish ..	335,496	362	2,780	251	72	338,961
Russian ..	67	2	—	7,156	114	7,339
German ..	1,758	1	—	10	25	1,794
Lapps ...	1,660	—	—	—	—	1,660
Others ...	184	1	—	—	113	298
Total ..	2,870,179	564	3,866	46,166	422	2,921,197

[1] Statisko Årsbok för Finland 1914, Helsingfors, 1915, pp. 45-46.

[2] Bidrag till Finlands Officiella Statistik, VI, Befolkningsstatistik, 45, Finlands Folkmängd den 31 December, 1910 (enligt Församlingarnas Kyrkoböcker), Helsingfors, 1915, p. 127.

TABLE IV

FINLAND: RELATIVE DISTRIBUTION BY LANGUAGES OF THE URBAN AND RURAL POPULATION OF THE GOVERNMENTS OF NYLAND, ÅBO AND BJÖRNEBORG, AND OF VASA, IN PERCENTAGES[1]

	URBAN			RURAL		
	Finnish	Swedish	Others	Finnish	Swedish	Others
Nylands						
1880	315.7	608.2	76.1	532.8	466.6	0.6
1890	436.2	536.2	27.1	545.1	454.0	0.9
1900	489.7	488.2	22.1	570.9	428.7	0.4
1910	579.7	411.8	8.5	589.1	410.6	0.3
Åbo and Björneborg						
1880	670.4	303.0	26.6	847.6	152.3	0.1
1890	700.0	292.8	7.2	855.7	144.2	0.1
1900	757.8	239.5	2.7	864.4	135.5	0.1
1910	792.8	204.4	2.8	880.2	119.7	0.1
				695.3	304.7	[0.02]
Vasa						
1880	195.7	800.5	3.8			
1890	269.6	725.4	5.0	720.3	279.6	0.1
1900	359.6	637.9	2.5	738.8	261.1	0.1
1910	482.4	512.5	5.1	770.9	228.9	0.2

[1] Bidrag till Finlands Officiella Statistik, VI, Befolkningsstatistik, 45, Finlands Folkmängd den 31 December, 1910 (enligt Församlingarnas Krykoböcker), Helsingfors, 1915, pp. 124-125.

CHAPTER VI

THE AREA OF POLISH SPEECH

SOUTH of the Baltic shores the unbroken expanse now peopled by Germans merges insensibly into the western part of the great Russian plain. This extensive lowland is featureless and provides no natural barriers between the two empires it connects. The area of Polish speech alone intervenes as a buffer product of the basin of the middle Vistula. The region is a silt-covered lowland, the bed of a former glacial lake. It has been peopled by Slavs for over a thousand years. Upon its open stretches there was no lack of food and no reason therefore for migration. The development of Poland rests primarily on this physical foundation. Added advantages of good land and water communication with the rest of the continent contributed powerfully to the spread of Polish power, which at one time extended from Baltic shores to the Black sea.

In the ninth century the Slavic tribes of the Polish and western Russian regions differed but slightly in language and customs. Dialects spoken in the upper Vistula basin and in the upper Dnieper valley presented a degree of affinity which has disappeared from the Russian and Polish languages as spoken in our time. Differences between the two groups increased as they came respectively under eastern and western influences. Intercourse between the western group and the Slavs settled in the upper Elbe region produced a Polish contingent, while contact of the eastern body with Tatars created the main Russian group. Religious differences helped to widen the breach between these two branches of the Slavic family. The western body was naturally inclined to follow the counsels emanating from the Vatican. The eastern looked to Byzantium for spiritual guidance. These were strictly geographical relations. Eventual divergence into

111

separate nationalities originated in the conflicts of religious views and material interests among the leading members in each group.

FIG. 38—Sketch map of eastern Europe showing the areal classification of Russians into Little Russians (dotted area), Great Russians (diagonally ruled) and White Russians (cross-ruled area). The black dots indicate Masurian localities. The dotted circles show Hungarian cities peopled by Ruthenians.

The Polish language is spoken at present within a quadrilateral the angles of which are found at the Jablunka pass in the Carpathians,[1] Wissek north of the Netze near the Posen boundary,

---

[1] L. Niederle: La race slave, Paris, 1911, pp. 71-74. A digest in English of his conclusions will be found in *Ann. Rept. Smiths. Inst.*, 1910, Washington, 1911, pp. 599-612.

Suwalki in the eastern Masurian region and Sanok on the San. A northern extension is appended to this linguistic region in the form of a narrow band which detaches itself from the main mass above Bromberg and reaches the Baltic coast west of Danzig. In sum, the valley of the Vistula, from the Carpathians to the Baltic, constitutes the field of Polish humanity and institutions. In spite of the remoteness of the period when they first occupied the land, these children of the plains never attempted to scale mountainous slopes. The solid wall of the western Carpathians, between Jablunka and Sanok, with its abrupt slopes facing the north, forms the southern boundary of the country.

This region, in the midst of the diversity of surface of the European continent, has produced a distinct language in the varied stock of European vernaculars. Nevertheless there is no similarity of physical type among individuals speaking Polish. Marked anthropological differences are found between the Poles of Russian Poland and of Galicia.[2] They correspond to the classification of northern Slavs into two main groups, the northernmost of which comprises the Poles of Russian Poland, together with White and Great Russians. Traces of Finnish intermixture can still be detected among them, in spite of the process of Slavicization which they have undergone. The Poles of Galicia, on the other hand, like the Ruthenians and Little Russians, reveal mingling of the autochthonous populations with Asiatic and Mongoloid invaders of Europe.[3]

Delimitation of the area of the Polish speech is more easily

---

[2] J. Talko-Hryncevicz: Les Polonais du royaume de Pologne d'après les données anthropologiques recueillies jusqu'à présent, Bull. Int. Acad. Sc. Cracovie, Classe des Sc. Math. et Nat. Bull. Sc. Nat., June 1912, pp. 574-582.

[3] Southern Poland was overrun by Mongolians during their third invasion of Europe. The Asiatics were attacked near Szydlow on March 18, 1241, by an army of Polish noblemen recruited from Sandomir and Cracow. The defeat of the Christians enabled the invaders to plunder the latter city, besides opening the way for incursions farther north in the course of which they penetrated into Silesia by way of Ratibor and marched toward Breslau. Near Liegnitz an army of 30,000 Europeans was defeated on April 9th of the same year. These disasters were invariably followed by a westerly spread of the Tatar scourge. Traces of its passage can still be detected among the Poles.

made in theory than on the field. The transition to alien languages is rarely well defined. Such detailed work as has been undertaken in western Europe, where the predominant language in small villages and hamlets is often determined, does not exist for eastern sections of the continent. The zeal of German and Russian agents of nationalist propaganda aggravates the problem. Within Galicia the boundary line passes west of Sanok and Radymno.[4] Its southern extension skirts the foothills through Rymanow, Dukla, Zmigrod and Grybow. Thence to Jablunka pass it merges with the political boundary.

In its western section the physical boundary coincides for all practical purposes with the ethnographic line of division. The Gorales mountaineers have never aspired to cross the divide of the Beskid mountains. The result is that the gentler slopes of the southern side are peopled altogether by Slovaks, while habit and custom have prevented the Podhalians, or Polish shepherds inhabiting the high valley of the Tatra, from leading their flocks to the southern grazing slopes which form part of the Hungarian domain.[5]

Changes in the aspect of the land resulting from human activity provide an easily observable boundary between the territory inhabited by Poles and that occupied by Ruthenians. The former, proceeding from the Vistulian lowland, are now scattered over a territory in which deforestation and large areas of tilled soil bespeak prolonged occupancy. The latter, coming from the Pontic steppes, reached the Carpathian slopes much later than their western neighbors. Consequently only 20 per cent of the surface of the western Carpathians is now available as prairie and pasture land, whereas the percentage of grazing land in the

---

[4] The Poles constitute the majority of the population in many cities of eastern or Russian Galicia. In Niederle's list Bobrka, Muszyna, Sanok, Lisko, Sambor, Peremysl, Rawaruska, Belz, Zolkiew, Grodek, Ceshanow, Stryj, Kalusz, Stanislawoff, Kolomya, Tarnopol, Husiatyn, Buczacz, Sokal and Trembowla are credited with over 50 per cent Poles in their population. The predominance of German in the cities of Biala, Sczerzec, Dolina, Bolechow, Nadworna, Kossow, Kuty, Zablotow and Brody is attributed by the same authority to the Jewish element present.

[5] E. Reclus: Géogr. Univ., Vol. 3, Europe Centrale, Paris, 1878, p. 396.

Fig. 39—This view is representative of the open steppe-land of Ukraine in southwestern Russia.

eastern section of the mountain chain is twice as much.[6] The area of plowed land in the western region covers between 40 and 50 per cent of the surface. In the east it barely varies between 5 and 10 per cent. Again the Polish section is practically clear of the forests, which cover, in contrast, from 50 to 60 per cent of the eastern Carpathians. Similar differences can be noted in the valleys up to an altitude of about 2,300 feet. Within them the proportion of plowed land constitutes 88 per cent of the surface in the Polish section while in the Ruthenian valleys the proportion of plowed land does not exceed 15 per cent.

On the southwestern border a number of localities in the Teschen country are claimed alike by Czechs and Poles. The increasing use of Polish and German, however, tends to invalidate the claims of Bohemians.[7] A transition zone between Czech and Polish exists here and is characterized by a local dialect of mixed language. In the western Beskid mountains Polish and Moravian are divided at the Jablunka pass. The ancient duchies of Teschen, Auschwitz and Zator were situated in this region and at the southern end of the long Slavo-Germanic borderland. The two last-named duchies were incorporated with Poland in the fifteenth century. German language and customs disappeared from their territory soon after this fusion.

This important district is in every aspect a zone of transition. Its climate becomes alternately continental or oceanic according to the prevalence of winds from east or west. The change occurs sometimes in a few weeks. Occasionally it is sudden and atmospheric conditions have been known to have changed completely from one stage to the other in the course of a single day.[8] During periods of oceanic climate, the temperature often rises above 0° C. Snows melt and spring temperature prevails during

---

[6] E. Romer: Esquisse climatique de l'ancienne Pologne, *Bul. de la Soc. Vaud. des Sc. Nat.*, 5e Sér., Vol. 46, June, 1910, p. 231.

[7] J. Zemrich: Deutsche und Slaven in den österreichischen Südetenländern, *Deutsche Erde*, Vol. 2, 1903, pp. 1-4.

[8] Limite des civilisations dans les Beskides occidentaux, *Ann. de Géogr.*, Vol. 17, 1908, Feb. 15, pp. 130-132. Cf. also E. Hanslik: Kulturgrenze und Kulturzyklus in den polnischen Westbeskiden, *Pet. Mitt.*, Ergänzungsheft No. 158, 1907.

January and February. Again sometimes the east wind brings all the signs of winter in April. In summer western breezes bring rain and dryness prevails when eastern winds blow. As a result of this semi-continental climate wheat crops on the Polish side are from three to six weeks later than on the Moravian side.

German immigrants invaded this region in the eighth century. Their language held its own until the fourteenth, after which it is represented only by linguistic islands dotting here and there the sea of Slavs. It is, however, still possible to distinguish settlements of German origin from the old Polish villages. The latter are situated on high ground or well-protected sites. They are generally characterized by the existence of a central open space and the random distribution of houses and lanes. The German villages, on the other hand, are found at the heads of valleys and usually occupy a rectangular site spreading over the two banks of a river. Each habitation has its own land appurtenance extending rearwards towards the valley slopes. The roads follow natural depressions. Taken as a whole, these German villages are admirably molded on the relief of the surface.

The western linguistic boundary of Poland extends through the German provinces of Silesia and Posen. Here a gradual replacement of the language by German since the sixteenth century is noticeable. At that time the Oder constituted the dividing line, south of the point of the confluence of the Nissa between Brieg and Oppeln. As late as 1790 the population of Breslau was largely Polish. Today over 75 per cent of the inhabitants of the city and the neighboring towns and villages are Germans. The district north and south constitutes in fact an area of linguistic reclamation.

The westernmost extension of Polish occurs in Posen, at the base of the provincial projection into Brandenburg. Around Bomst the percentage of Polish inhabitants is as high as 75 per cent. The line extends northwards to Birnbaum, after which it assumes a northeasterly direction. In spite of this occidental reach, however, the area of Polish speech within German boundaries is broken in numerous places by German enclaves of vary-ing size.[9]

In western Prussia, the Poles form compact inclusions in the German mass and attain the Baltic shores, where they occupy the entire western coast of the Gulf of Danzig. From Oliva and Danzig the line extends to Dirschau (Tezew) and crosses the Vistula about six miles below the city. It then strikes east and turns southwards towards Marienwerder (Kwidzyn) and Grau-denz. Proceeding due east from here, the boundary passes south of Eylau, the southern territory of the Masurian lakes, and on into Russian territory, until Suwalki is reached. The eastern frontier begins at this point and is prolonged southwards, accord-ing to Slav authorities, through Augustow, Bielostok,[10] Surash, Bielsk, Sarnaki, Krsanostaw and Tomaschow.

The advance of the area of Polish speech, in the form of a tongue of land, to the Baltic coast, is a proof of intimate depend-ence between Polish nationality and the basin of the Vistula. This northernmost section of the territory in which Polish is spoken, lies entirely within Prussian territory. Centuries of Teutonic influence failed, however, to eradicate completely Slavic language or customs in the valley of the great river. Between Thorn and Danzig, on the left bank of the Vistula, it is estimated that 650,000 Poles are scattered. On the right, the Prussian districts of Lobau, Strassburg and Briesen are centers of intense Polish life and culture. The city of Danzig itself, with a Polish element of only 10 per cent, still gives strong evidence of its Polish institutions. Its monuments are memorials of Poland's history, and many of its families bear Polish names even though their members use German as a vernacular.

Originally a free town, Danzig owes its predominant German population to the inflow of traders of this nationality who have swarmed within its walls since the sixteenth century. The city,

---

[9] P. Langhans: Nationalitätenkarte der Provinz Schlesien, 1:500,000. Sonder-karte No. 1 in *Deutsche Erde*, 1906; id.: Nationalitätenkarte der Provinz Ostpreussen, 1:500,000. Sonderkarte No. 1 in *Deutsche Erde*, 1907.

[10] L. Niederle: op. cit., p. 73; but cf. H. Praesent: Russisch Polen, etc., *Pet. Mitt.*, Vol. 60, Dec. 1914, p. 257.

standing like a sentinel at the mouth of the Vistula, is in every sense a creation of the river. Traffic from Poland's innermost districts flows towards the country's great waterway to be finally landed on the wharves of Danzig. Prior to the partition of Poland, the city was nominally a dependency of that country, but its inhabitants had been granted special trading privileges as well as the right of governing themselves. The city's commercial relations were highly favored by such a régime and business men from the surrounding country were not slow to realize the exceptional advantages which settlement in the city afforded. By the end of the seventeenth century its population consisted largely of German merchants and their dependents. Frederick II with characteristic far-sightedness realized the extent to which this seaport, together with the river city of Thorn, controlled the traffic between Brandenburg and old Prussia. He did not succeed however in annexing the two cities to his dominions, for it is only since 1815 that they have formed part of Prussian territory.

The struggle for predominance between Poles and Germans along Poland's western boundary is fully nine centuries old. In the sixteenth century, Slavonic tribes had become widely distributed between the Oder and Elbe, in the course of westerly expansions which correspond to south and west migrations of Teutonic peoples.[11] Place names bestowed by the early Germans in the district between these two rivers have practically disappeared under the layer of Slavic appellations conferred between the second and fourth centuries.[12] The period between 800 and 1300 witnessed the inception of a slow and powerful Germanic drive directed towards the east. Convents and lay feudal establishments participated in this historical movement. Repeated German aggressions brought about the earliest union of all Polish tribes into one nation at the beginning of the eleventh century. It proved, however, of little avail before the fighting prowess of the Knights of the Teutonic Order, who, by the first half of the

---

[11] A. C. Haddon: The Wanderings of Peoples, Cambridge, 1912, p. 48.
[12] F. Curschmann: Die deutsche Ortsnamen in nordostdeutschen Kolonialgebiet, Forsch. z. deut. Landes- u. Volksk., Vol. 19, No. 2, 1910, pp. 91-183.

thirteenth century, had succeeded in adding all Wend territory to Teutonic dominions. This early and northerly phase of the "Drang nach Osten" brought the Germans to the coast of the Gulf of Finland. Their advance was rendered possible in part by the presence of Tatar hordes menacing southern Poland. Teutonic progress was also facilitated by the defenseless condition which marks an open plain. Between the Oder and the Vistula the slightly undulating lowland is continuous and devoid of barriers to communication which the interposition of uplifted or uninhabitable stretches of territory might have provided.

Polish history has been affected both favorably and adversely by this lack of natural bulwarks. The former extension of Polish sovereignty to the shores of the Baltic and Black seas, and to within 50 miles of Berlin and the central plateau of Russia, was a result of easy travel on a plain. This advantage was more than offset by the evident facility with which alien races were able to swarm into the vast featureless expanse forming Polish territory. The dismemberment of the country is in part the result of the inability of the Poles to resort to the protection of a natural fortress, where a prolonged stand against the aggression of foes might have been made.

At the end of the tenth century the entire Polish plain acknowledged the rule of Boleslas the Great, a prince of the Piast dynasty. Kiev then paid a yearly tribute to the Polish crown. A period of internal division follows Boleslas's rule, but in the beginning of the fourteenth century Poland was once more united under the scepter of King Ladislas. From 1386 to 1772, a period of almost four centuries, Polish frontiers remained remarkably stable. Their fluctuations were slight when compared to the changes which occurred in other European countries during the same period.

At one period of its history Poland was barred from its Baltic sea frontier in the north. In the fourteenth century the invasion of the Teutonic Knights temporarily cut off the country from the sea; but apart from this interruption Poland has always had access to the sea to which the drainage of the land naturally led.

Under the first members of the Piast dynasty the Poles had control of the Baltic coast.[13] When, in the thirteenth century, the Poles called upon the Knights of the Teutonic Order for assistance in subjugating Prussia, the two parties agreed to equal division of the conquered territory. The successes of the Teutonic Knights, however, emboldened their leaders to claim more land for their share. A state of war ensued between the two former allies until by the treaty of Thorn, in 1466, the Teutonic Knights acknowledged Polish sovereignty. This brought Pomerelia, or Prussian Pomerania, within Polish territory. In 1525 the Prussian districts east of the Vistula became part of the duchy of Albert of Brandenburg and were thus surrounded entirely by Polish territory; but that part of Prussia which extends west of the Vistula remained an integral portion of Poland until 1772.

In the fighting which marked the relations between Poland and Turkey in the fourteenth and fifteenth centuries the Poles succeeded in extending their southern frontiers to within a hundred miles of the Black Sea and in carrying their sphere of influence to the sea itself. The occupation of Kaminiec by the Turks was short-lived. In general Poland's frontier on the side of the ancient Rumanian principalities remained unchanged during the last four centuries of the country's sovereign existence.

In the fifteenth century, Poland was the dominating Slavic state. In 1386 it had been united to Lithuania by Wladislas Jagellon, the first prince of the famous dynasty bearing his name. The country at that time was protected from Turkish attacks by Wallachia, Moldavia and Transylvania. Russia was its rival for the possession of Lithuania; Austria for that of Hungary and Bohemia. Prussia and Livonia were also claimed by Poland from the Order of the Teutonic Knights. The weakness of the country lay in the jealousy of the two peoples of diverse speech from which its ruling body was drawn. The Jagellons were Lithuanian princes. They favored the claims of their countrymen, who pre-

---

[13] Marquis de Noailles: Les frontières de la Pologne, Paris, 1915, p. 21.

ferred the laws of their native land to the Polish legislation which was being forced on them. The Poles likewise had their grievances against the Lithuanians. During the rule of Casimir IV he was frequently taken to task by his countrymen for spending "summer, fall and winter in Lithuania."

Poland's easterly expansion with its prolonged and finally disastrous conflicts with Russia began after the battle of Grunwald in 1410. Although the Poles then inflicted a decisive defeat on the Teutonic Knights, the western provinces they had lost could not be regained. In the eastern field the basin of the Dnieper merged without abrupt transition into that of the Vistula, just as the basin of the Oder on the west formed the western continuation of the Baltic plain. Four centuries of struggle with Russia ensued until the Muscovite Empire absorbed the greater portion of Poland.

The German element is slowly spreading eastward throughout the eastern provinces of Prussia which once formed part of the kingdom of Poland. Emigration of Poles to central and western Germany partly accounts for the German gain. From the larger cities of eastern Germany and more especially from Posen, Bromberg and Danzig, a steady stream of emigrants make their way towards the industrial centers of the west, where they find higher wages and generally improved economic conditions. The German government favors this expatriation of its Slav subjects. None of the vexations to which the Poles are subjected by government officials on their native plains are tolerated in the occidental provinces of the Empire. The result is that notable colonies of Poles have sprung up in the vicinity of industrial centers like Düsseldorf or Arnsberg, in the Munster district and the Rhine provinces. From a racial standpoint, these Poles are practically indistinguishable from Teutonic types. Their presence in Rhenish Prussia and Westphalia is no menace to German unity. They are easily assimilated; the second generation, speaking only German, forgets its antecedents and becomes submerged in the mass of the native population. Slav settlements are particularly numerous and dense along the Rhine-Herne canal between Duisburg and Dortmund.[14]   They abound in the coal-producing Emscher valley, where their inhabitants form one-fifth of the population. The Polish settlers favor the flatlands and occupy them in preference to hilly regions. They do not confine their work to mining, but provide labor for the industrial plants clustered around the coal-fields. In the beginning of 1911 the number of Polish miners in the 19 mining districts of the "circle" of Dortmund exceeded that of any other nationality.

The heavy preponderance of Poles in certain administrative divisions of eastern Germany has, nevertheless, been unimpaired by the Polish emigration. In the province of Posen the German-speaking inhabitants still constitute the minority. As a rule Germans emigrate more readily than Poles or Masurians in East Prussia.[15] In the city of Posen, Polish nationality was asserting itself with increasing vigor year by year, before the European war. The percentage of Poles grew from about 51 in 1890 to 56 in 1900. Ten years later it exceeded 57. Correspondingly the German percentage fell from 50 in 1890 to under 42 in 1910.

Posen, of all German provinces, contains the largest number of Poles. 62 per cent of its 2,100,000 inhabitants belong to this nationality. Within provincial boundaries the process of Germanizing the people has been carried on most actively in the district of Bromberg. The reason is obvious. The region is the connecting link between Germany proper and the province of Old Prussia, which forms an enclave of German speech within the territory of the Polish language. The effort to connect the ancient cradle of Prussia with the motherland is apparent in the figures which reveal the percentage of Poles in the intermediary land. The district of Bromberg numbers 53 per cent of Poles in a population of 750,000. In the provincial district of Posen, however, the percentage of Poles attains 68 for a population of 1,350,000.

---

[14] K. Closterhalfen: Die Polen in niederrheinisch-westfälisch Industriebezirk 1905, 1:200,000. Pl. 16 in *Deutsche Erde*, Vol. 10, 1911.

[15] A. Raahe: Die Abwanderungsbewegung in den östlichen Provinzen Preussens. Einleitung und Teil I. Die Provinz Ost-Preussen. Berlin, 1910.

The German element of the province is confined mainly to the cities, the country being peopled largely by Poles. Often the proportion of this native population attains as high a figure as 91 per cent and it is rare to find it below 75 per cent. Apart from the German administration of the province, Posen thus remains Polish to the core. Its nobility and landed gentry consist mostly of Poles who have strenuously opposed German encroachments by abstaining from commercial or financial intercourse with their rulers. They founded their own banks, in order to be independent of German institutions; and by means of native agricultural associations they came to the aid of Polish farmers, who were thus saved from having recourse to German colonization banks chartered for the purpose of buying out Polish landowners. The influence of the Polish element is best shown by the fact that eleven Polish representatives are delegated by its population to the Reichstag, out of a body of fifteen sent by the province.

We thus see that the Poles scattered in the eastern section of Germany constitute the largest foreign-speaking element in the Empire's population. Their number is estimated by Niederle at 3,450,000. German census returns for 1900 give 3,086,489. The percentage of Jews in German Poland is high, particularly in the urban areas. The practice of census takers is to classify them with the German or Polish population according to their vernacular. In Russia the last (1897) available census figures report the existence of 1,267,194 Jews [16] scattered throughout the Polish provinces. This represents 13.48 per cent of the population of Russian Poland. Here, as elsewhere, they are rarely engaged in agricultural pursuits but show a tendency to invade prosperous towns and cities.[17]

---

[16] N. Troïnitsky: Premier recensement général de la population de l'empire de la Russie, 1897. Vols. 1 and 2, Petrograd, 1905.

[17] The Jews cluster especially in the eastern governments of Warsaw, Lomsha and Siedlez, where their percentage varies between 15.6 and 16.4. This ratio is lower in the southern and western administrative divisions. In Kalish it reaches only 7.2 per cent and is reduced to 6.3 per cent in Petrokow. In the cities the Jews constitute on an average slightly over a third of the population, although here again they are more numerous in the east. Cf. D. Aïtoff: Peuples et langues de la Russie, *Ann. de Géogr.*, Vol. 15, May 1909, pp. 9-25.

The Polish Jews, speaking a vernacular of their own, and conscious of the advantage derived from their number, live apart from the Poles, with whom they are generally at odds on economic questions. The presence of this racially alien element has often assisted Russian administrators in their policy of holding Polish urban populations well in hand by pitting one people against the other. Jewish parties wield considerable influence in the local politics of Polish cities. They are openly anti-Slavic and side with the German inhabitants, from whom they receive guidance regarding policy and conduct. The strength of the Polish vote was felt in the 1912 elections for the Duma when Lodz sent a Jewish representative to the national council, while in Warsaw where they form 38 per cent of the population they succeeded in forcing the election of a Polish socialist who in that same year had failed to obtain a majority of the city's Polish votes.

The confinement of Jews within the pale of Poland dates from the time of the first partition, when an edict signed by Catherine II was proclaimed, forbidding them to emigrate from the annexed territory into Russia proper. Since then every succeeding Russian monarch maintained this policy of segregation until, at the time of Poland's last partition, the ten governments into which the unfortunate nation was divided became the only territory in which the Jews were tolerated.

This arrangement was made largely because of the Jew's well-known aptitude for commerce and through fear that the unsophisticated and large-hearted Russian mujik was no match for him. The state of Poland prior to its dismemberment made such measures imperative for the Russian government. The Poles were either landowners, tillers of the soil or soldiers. Few engaged in trade. The country's commerce was in the hands of Germans or Jews. Poland's weakness in the presence of foreign aggression was due to this state of economic inferiority, no less than to her lack of natural frontiers on the east and west.

The large proportion of the Jewish element in Poland may be traced ultimately to the very circumstances which impart distinctiveness to the Polish region. It was inevitable that the Jew should find cordial welcome in the broad drainage valley of the Vistula and its tributaries, tenanted by a landed nobility at the one end of the social scale and a retinue of serfs at the other. Between these two classes the Jew supplied a needed trading element and thrived. Polish kings accordingly adopted the policy of inviting and protecting Jews within their domains as early as in the fourteenth century, a time when the Jews were being expelled in hundreds from other nations. Emigration of the Jews from Germany during the period of Catholic persecution was particularly heavy. This movement helped to increase the number of Jews in Poland.

The position of the Jews in Poland varies, therefore, according to the circumstances which determined their immigration. They may be classed into two groups. The descendants of early settlers feel the welding influence of time and are united with the Poles by the bond of historical association and of common interests. The newcomers, mostly refugees from Russian cities, form an unassimilated nucleus whose tendencies and temper differ materially from the aims that actuate the native population, whether Polish or Jewish. Racial animosity in Poland is chiefly directed against these newcomers. It has reached an acute stage in recent years, owing to the strenuous efforts of Poles to control their country's industry and commerce in face of the menace of German economic absorption.

In Galicia the Jews are competitors of the Poles. Full advantage has been taken by Austrian statesmen of the existence of a powerful clique of Jewish financiers in Vienna in order to obtain Jewish support against Slavic aspirations. Jewish capitalists were allowed to take part in the development of natural resources as well as to purchase large estates. At present fully 20 per cent of the larger private domains in Galicia are owned by Jews.[18] In the cities also the Jewish element has acquired considerable influence. This is especially observable in Lemberg and Cracow. The bulk of Galician Jews, however, are poor and uneducated.

---

[18] G. Bienaimé: La Pologne économique, *Bull. Soc. de Géogr. Comm. de Paris*, Vol. 37, Nos. 4-6, April-June, 1915, pp. 128-164.

They have little sympathy with the ideals of the Christian element, from whom they hold aloof. In the social relations of the three main elements of the Galician population, Poles and Jews generally unite to exploit Ruthenians. The Jews apparently are unable to thrive on the Poles. In the Polish sections of Galicia they constitute only 7 per cent of the population, whereas in Ruthenian Galicia this proportion rises to 13 per cent.

German Poland, from Upper Silesia to the Gulf of Danzig, contains about 4,000,000 Poles. In Upper Silesia, they constitute 61 per cent of the population and number about 1,300,000. This majority has been maintained, in the face of aggressive Germanization, since the first half of the fourteenth century. The city of Posen contains 170,000 inhabitants, of whom 58 per cent are Poles. The farming districts of the province contain only about 10 per cent of Germans. Over 900,000 Poles live in East and West Prussia. In this section of Germany, they form a sufficiently compact body to be able to send representatives chosen from their own people to the Landstag and Reichstag. The western coast of the Gulf of Danzig and the banks of the lower Vistula are almost exclusively Polish. A solid wedge of Polish humanity is here interposed between the Germans of Pomerania and of East Prussia. This thorough isolation of an important body of Germans may became a thorny problem in any eventual settlement of Polish boundaries.

Upper Silesia is the best endowed section of Polish territory. The grayish soil which forms the surface of the Oder valley is eminently fitted for cereal and beet cultivation and the farmers of this soil are generally Poles. They often represent 90 per cent of the rural population.[19] In the cities and generally speaking in the industrial field they are laborers. Capital and the management of factories and of mines are in German hands.

The most interesting feature of the clash between Germans and Poles in Upper Silesia is found in the failure of the Germans in their efforts to force their language upon an alien people. Forty years ago, Polish noblemen were apt to blush at the

---

[19] G. Bienaimé: op. cit., p. 139.

thought of their Slavic origin in the presence of the German
rulers of their land. But the vexations inflicted on them by
Prussian administration, since the formation of the German
Empire, have bred a spirit of defiance and revolt. As a result
Silesian Poles were never so conscious of nationality as they are
today. They band together in order to resist Germanization
more effectively. Small tradesmen, petty farmers and profes-
sional men organize themselves into bodies to which individual
interests are intrusted whenever German methods become intolerable. But the greatest asset of Polish nationality in this fight
against annihilation is its high birth rate. This has also led to
the emigration of Poles to the industrial districts of Westphalia,
the coal districts of the Lens basin in France and to America.
This flow of Poles comes mainly from the provinces of Posen and
West Prussia, where sandy inert soils cannot accommodate rapidly
increasing numbers.

In addition to drastic educational measures, [compelling study
of their language,] the Germans have resorted to wholesale buying
of Polish estates in the section of the kingdom of Poland which
fell to the lot of Prussia when the country was partitioned. A
colonization law (Ansiedelunggesetz), decreed on April 26, 1886,
placed large funds at the disposal of the German government for
the purchase of land owned by Poles and the establishment of
colonies of German settlers.[20] The measure was artificial and
proved valueless against economic conditions prevailing in the
regions affected. A decrease in the percentage of the Polish
population of the estates acquired by purchase was rarely
brought about. The new settlers could rarely compete with
natives. The most tangible result consisted in mere substitution
of German for Polish ownership. On most of the large estates
the mass of laborers and dependents remained Poles as they had
been before. The breach between Poles and Germans was

---

[20] A law passed in 1908 authorizes the State to acquire land in the administrative
circles in which German interests require development of colonization. B. Auerbach:
La germanisation de la Pologne Prussienne. La loi d'expropriation, *Rev. Polit. et
Parlem.*, Vol. 57, July 1908, pp. 109-125.

widened by the change of masters. Nevertheless, although results corresponding to the efforts and money expended were not obtained, the measure has contributed to the advance of Teutonism in northeastern Europe.[21]

The purpose of this colonization is to redeem Prussian soil from Polish ownership. The "Mittelstandskasse" of Breslau, and the Peasant's Bank of Danzig, are financial institutions directly interested in this work of Germanization. These banks work hand in hand with the state. Results of this activity can be observed in East Prussia where the German element has acquired preponderance in 32 communes, through the intervention of German capital. A common practice of the German loan societies is to assume the liabilities of German farmers. In many cases the peasants have been provided with funds to carry on their agricultural operations. In Western Prussia 39 estates with about 14,000 inhabitants have passed into German hands.[22] Often it has been impossible to induce peasants from other parts of Germany to settle in the Polish provinces, and the state has resorted to the importation of German peasants from the old German settlements in Russia, Galicia and Bosnia.

German colonization in Polish provinces has been accompanied by increase and expansion of urban centers. The province of Posen, which now claims 151 cities,[23] is a typical instance. The colonists' cities founded by Germans are readily recognized by their peculiar configuration. Almost all have been built on the same plan. A four-sided market-place generally constitutes the nucleus of the urban tract. Main avenues diverge from the angles of the central quadrilateral. Lateral streets extend

---

[21] P. Langhans: Nationalitätenkarte der Provinz Schlesien, 1:500,000. Sonderkarte No. 1 in *Deutsche Erde*, 1906. P. Langhans: Nationalitätenkarte der Provinz Ostpreussen, 1:500,000. Sonderkarte No. 2 in *Deutsche Erde*, 1907. Die Provinzen Posen und Westpreussen unter besonderer Berücksichtigung der Ansiedlungsgüter und Ansiedlung, Staatsdomänen und Staatsforsten nach dem Stande von 1 Januar 1911, *Deutsche Erde*, Vol. 10, Taf. 1, 1911.

[22] M. Loesener: Besitzfestigung in der Preussischen Ostmark. *Deutsche Erde*, Vol. 10, 1911, pp. 3-8.

[23] Dalchow: Die Städte des Warthelandes, I. Teil, Ein Beitrag zur Siedlungskunde und zur Landeskunde der Provinz Posen. Leipzig, 1910.

parallel to the market sides and at right angles to the main arteries.

Against the tightening hold of the Germans on their land, the Poles can offer only limited resistance. But their counteracting efforts are not devoid of value. They have taken advantage of the high prices, consequent upon the sales of the land which the government has forced on them, to buy new estates. Thanks to the high rate of birth among Poles, the proportion of Poles living in German Poland to the rest of the population remains stationary, in spite of German immigration or Polish emigration. Coöperative associations of farmers, of traders or industrial operators, present a united front in all dealings of their members with Germans. In the field of education, children are taught Polish in spite of German opposition.[24] The patriotism and courage of the Polish press are maintained in face of German persecution. The return of Polish emigrants with a little capital, accumulated by toil in foreign lands, is likewise one of the factors which contribute to the preservation of the people in their homeland. Both from the western industrial districts of Germany and from overseas, many patriotic Poles return to the land of their fathers and settle upon small farms purchased with their savings.

From the east pressure corresponding to Teutonic battering, although exerted with less intensity, is applied by Russian endeavor to create national homogeneity. Of all the different members of the wide-spread Slavic race Poles and Russians are the most closely related by speech. But the affinity ends here, for the formidable barrier of religious differences hampers fusion of the two nationalities. Caught between the hammer of Teutonic reformation and the Slavic anvil of Russian orthodoxy, the Poles have remained stanch Catholics. Creed, in this case, has played a considerable part in the preservation of national spirit.

---

[24] After having been entirely banished from secondary schools, Polish was excluded from elementary schools by a ministerial decree, dated Sept. 7, 1887. Religious instruction alone could be imparted in this language and even this privilege was removed in 1905.

In Austria alone have the Poles been relatively free from persecution. Even there, in recent times, the Austrian policy of setting her subject peoples against each other had led to a display of favoritism towards the Ruthenian neighbors of the Poles. Both of these Slavic peoples inhabit Galicia principally. The province is the relic of the old duchy of Halitch, which had Lemberg for its capital. The name Galicia originated in Austria, at the time of the partition of Poland in 1772, and was applied to that part of the dismembered country which Austria annexed. The province is peopled at present by over three million Ruthenes.

Western Galicia, including the important cities of Cracow and Tarnow, as well as the Tatra massif, is peopled almost exclusively by about 2,750,000 Poles of whom 7 per cent are Polish-speaking Jews.[25] Eastern Galicia on the other hand is the home of only 1,400,000 Poles, but here the Ruthenians make up a solid mass of 3,200,000. In the cities, however, the Poles form overwhelming majorities, although their number dwindles to insignificance as the Russian frontier is approached. Lemberg, notably, contains a high proportion of Polish inhabitants.

But the fact of paramount importance in the condition of Austrian Poles is that in spite of their minority in the largest part of Galicia, they represent the dominating element in the Galician population. Vast estates and great industries are almost exclusively in their hands. They are also intellectual leaders and the liberal professions are practically entirely held by them. The Ruthenian's lot throughout Galicia is that of the toiler, either in the field or in the factory. Descendants of Ruthenian noblemen have been absorbed by the Polish nobility, which has become the ruling class. This economic superiority, coupled to political advantages secured from the Austrian government by the Galician statutes of 1868, makes the lot of the Austrian Poles truly enviable in comparison with that of their German or even their Russian kinsmen. The province is ruled by a Diet composed of Poles and Ruthenians, each speaking his own tongue. The authority of this

---

[25] G. Bienaimé: loc. cit.

body, however, is strictly restricted to provincial affairs. Extra-provincial matters are under the direct control of Vienna.

The Ruthenian is therefore the Pole's great rival in Galicia. Although the outward manifestation of this rivalry assumes the form of nationalistic outbursts, the conflict is, in the main, social and economic. The Ruthenian proletariat is at odds with its Polish rulers. It has begun to dream of redemption from the vassalage borne for centuries. Fortunately its endeavors are a source of improvement in the lot of both Ruthenian and Polish peasants. A glimpse of the power vested in the Ruthenian mass is thus afforded. As a people these Ruthenes constitute the westernmost group of the Little Russian division of the Slavic people. They inhabit the territory of the ancient kingdom of Ukraine and number some 30,000,000 souls. Southwestern Russia is peopled by them almost exclusively. They form from 76 to 99 per cent of the population of the following districts: [26]

1. The Ukraine of the right bank of the Dnieper, Podolia, Volhynia, Kiev and Kholm.
2. The Ukraine of the left bank of the Dnieper, Tchernihov, Poltava, Kharkov, southwestern Khursk and Voronezh, and the region of the Don Cosacks to the Sea of Azov.
3. The steppe of Ukraine lying on both sides of the Dnieper and comprising Katerynoslav, Kherson and the eastern parts of Bessarabia and Tauris.
4. North Caucasus, adjacent to the region of the Don Cosacks, comprising Kuban and the eastern parts of the Stavropolskoi and Terskaja governments.

In addition about 50,000 Ruthenians reside in Bukovina, while 700,000 occupy the sub-Carpathian districts of Hungary. About 2,000,000 are scattered in Siberian settlements. In Austria the Carpathian mountains split the main body of the Ruthenians into two sections, which occupy respectively Galicia and Hungary. In

---

[26] B. Sands: The Ukraine, London, 1914, p. 8.

the latter kingdom they are distributed mainly in the northern and northeastern counties of Abanj, Bereg, Maramaros, Saros, Ung and Zemplin.

The Ruthenians claim to be the original Russians. The purity of the Slav type is better preserved among them than among any other group in Russia and they show less of the Asiatic strain. They represent the truly European Russians. Racial characteristics set them apart from the main body of Russians on the north and east of their land. Round-headedness is very pronounced among them and they tend to be tall and dark-complexioned. Dialectical differences between them and the Muscovites of the north and east also exist.

The Masurians of northeastern Germany are essentially an agricultural people who have succeeded in supporting themselves on exceedingly poor soil. They occupy the marshy belt of land which has become famous through the battles fought within and around its borders during the Great European War. It comprises the nine districts of Allenstein, Johannisburg, Loetzen, Lyck, Neidenburg, Oletzko, Ortelsburg, Osterode and Sensburg. A Masurian element constitutes the majority of the inhabitants of Augustov and Seiny, the two southernmost circles of the governments of Suwalki. The German element is strongly represented in the entire region. It forms a contingent of some 70,000 individuals in the governments of Kovno and Suwalki.[27] As far as can be ascertained, the earliest inhabitants of the land consisted of fishermen occupying lacustrine habitations resting on piles. Their villages are disposed around the hillocks to which they resorted for shelter from man and the elements in the early period of the settlement of the land. Locality names throughout the region are Polish, even in the settlements founded by the Knights of the Teutonic Order or the Hohenzollerns. Often a thin streak of Germanization has been imparted to names of villages by the addition of the prefix Neu or Klein.[28]

---

[27] H. Rosen: *Pet. Mitt.*, Vol. 61, Sept. 1915, pp. 329-333.

[28] A. Weinrich: Bevölkerungsstatistische und Siedlungsgeographie, Beiträge zur Kunde Ost-Masuriens, vornehmlich der Kreise Oletzko und Lycke. Königsberg, 1911.

FIG. 40—A Wendish loghouse in the Spreewald where ancient Slavic colonies retain their language and customs although surrounded by Germans.

Within this marshy country, a Polish folk has maintained its own institutions ever since the consolidation of Poles into a distinct people within the drainage area of the Vistula. The only feature of Germanism which took hold in the land was the Protestant religion. The 300,000 Masurians, therefore, present the queer anomaly of a Protestant Polish group. Apart from this peculiarity they are as truly Poles as their land is part of the Vistula basin. With the revival of Polish ideals in recent years the growth of Protestantism in the region has been checked. It is interesting to note that the revulsion of religious feeling had its source in the province of Posen, in the full midst of Teutonic proselytism, and not, as might have been expected, in Russian Poland.

The Wends of Germany represent the only intact remnant of the Slav populations which once filled the country. The whole plain country of northern Germany extending from the Elbe to the Vistula had been inhabited by the Wends since early Christian times. The country between the Sale, upper Havel and Spree valleys was probably their original settling ground.[29] They now occupy Lusatia and are sometimes known as Lusatian Serbians. In the Middle Ages the name of Sorabes was given to them. The Germans first began to invade the region in the eleventh century. In the fourteenth, they attained numerical preponderance. The decline of the Slav communities which was accelerated by the Thirty Years' War, begins about this time. The union of Lusatia with Bohemia helped the Slav cause for a while, but the treaty of Prague, in 1635, by which the country was awarded to Saxony crushed Slavic hopes. At present, the Slavic language has practically disappeared from the region, although the appearance and customs of the inhabitants are more Slav than German.

As late as the Middle Ages the Wends occupied an area considerably to the north of their present seat. The eastern valley of the Elbe, as well as Mecklenburg territory, was settled by them before 1160. Charters of this period such as that of the Schwerin bishopric of 1178, or of the cloister of Dargun of 1174, show

---

[29] L. Niederle: La race slave, Paris, 1916, p. 94.

Slavic place names exclusively. Among signs pointing to a pre-German spread of the Wendish element are the relics of Slavic family names and evidences of the old "Hakenhufen" division of the land in lots of 15 acres.   This last proof appears irrefutable and points, upon application, to the former extension of the

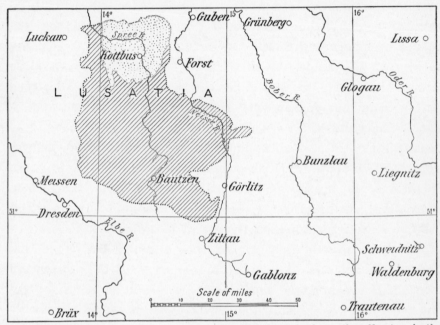

Fig. 41—The area of Wend speech. The dotted patch shows that Kottbus is the center of the district in which the majority of the inhabitants (over 50 per cent.) speak the Slav language. In the ruled area the percentage of Wends is less than 50.

Wendish element to the very shores of the Baltic.[30] Germanization seems to have been thoroughly accomplished by the second half of the thirteenth century. But even today a great part of the area east of the Elbe must be regarded as a land of German-speaking Slavs.

Surrounded by Germans, the Wendish colony is doomed to disappear in spite of a literary renascence which helps to perpetuate national consciousness in its midst. According to statistics, the number of Wends is steadily declining. The progress of Germanization is particularly apparent in Lower Lusatia, which is part of the Prussian domain. It was estimated

[30] H. Witte: Wendische Bevölkerungsreste in Mecklenburg, *Forsch. z. deut. Landes-u. Volksk.*, Vol. 16, No. 2, 1907.

in 1885 that this people comprised about 176,000 souls. Later computations place this figure at about 156,000. The absence of an intellectual class among them, compulsory military service in German regiments and the use of the German language in church favor the progress of Teutonism.[31]

The want of linguistic unity among the Wends also tends to weaken their position. Idiomatic differences between the languages of Upper and Lower Lusatia are such as to prevent the natives of the respective districts from rendering themselves intelligible to one another. The literary language of Kottbus differs from that of Bautzen. Diversity of customs and institutions is also noticeable between the two groups. German ideas increase this cultural split, the divergence from Slavic institutions and thought thus becoming accentuated. Unlike the Masurians, and because of their isolation, the Wends cannot look to eventual incorporation with the Polish body. Their political destiny is therefore distinct from that of the Poles.

We have seen in this chapter that although conquered and divided Poland still lives. A compact mass of over 20,000,000 individuals speaking the same language is a force which cannot but make itself felt. This main body of Poles resides within its own linguistic boundaries. Smaller colonies are found outside these limits. The Polish inhabitants of Lithuania and Ukraine muster about 2,000,000. Vilna alone, the capital of Lithuania, has a population of 70,000 Poles out of a total of 170,000 inhabitants.[32] The Polish colonies of Ukraine, of the coal-fields of the Donetz, and of the Caucasus comprise wealthly landholders, manufacturers, bankers and merchants. These men though living outside the ethnographic boundaries of their people nevertheless exercise the weight of their influence on its behalf. Thus the three groups into which conquest has divided the Poles remain today in intimate contact in spite of the political boundaries which separate them. It is mainly in the economic field that binding ties have been established between the three, for the Poles of the three continental empires have made it a point to promote

---

[31] Op. cit., pp. 96-97.   [32] Including 40 per cent of Jews.

trade relations with one another. This was forging a new link to their pre-existing natural ties of kinship.

The problem of delimiting Polish national boundaries is complicated on the east and west, as has been stated, by the absence of prominent surface features. On both sides the lines of linguistic parting provide the only practicable demarcation. On the north and south, however, the Baltic and the Carpathians may be utilized advantageously as national frontiers. But the fate of the Polish region is strongly outlined by nature, for the entire basin of the Vistula is a regional unit. Any partitioning of this basin would probably be followed by political conflicts.

NOTE ON THE SLAVS

In the ninth century the Slavs occupied the eastern plains of Europe between the valleys of the Elbe and the Dnieper. Southward they spread to the northern foothills of the mountains of central Europe. Although subdivided into tribes bearing different names, there existed no essential differences among them as to language or custom. The pagan divinities worshiped in the drainage area of the Vistula were the gods of the inhabitants of the Dnieper valley. Tribal authority was exercised by a chief designated as Kniaz or Voivod throughout these lowlands. Intercourse between the various groups was constant. A vague political union is even discerned by some historians. The Poles and Ruthenians and, to a lesser extent, the Bohemians, are the best modern representatives of these original Slavs. All the eastern Slavs, however, have mixed more or less with Asiatic peoples.

Some light is thrown on the European origin of the peoples of Aryan speech by the growth of the Slavs. The Slavs of Europe now form by far the most important ethnic group of that continent. They comprise about 160,000,000 individuals out of a total of 400,000,000 inhabitants of Europe. Two-thirds of this Slavic element consists of Russians (66,000,000 Great Russians, 32,000,000 Little Russians, and about 8,000,000 White Russians).[33] Next to the Russians in numerical importance are the Poles (23,000,000). The Serbo-Croatian group can only muster half the Polish array. The Bohemians follow, 8,000,000 strong, while the Bulgarian group does not quite attain 6,000,000. Smaller groups are the 2,000,000 Slovenes, the 2,000,000 Slovaks and the less important enclave communities of German lands like the Wend in Lusatia.

The homeland of the primitive nucleus of this branch of the Indo-European family is restricted in the main to the plains extending from the northwestern

---

[33] The Slavs are divided by religion into a main body of about 110,000,000 individuals belonging to the Russian Orthodox Church, about 37,000,000 Roman Catholics, 5,000,000 Raskolniks or Sectarians, between 1,000,000 and 2,000,000 Protestants and over 1,000,000 Mohammedans.

corner of the Black Sea to the sandy delta of the Oder. The valleys of the great rivers in this lowland exerted the earliest separative influence which is known to have occurred in the primitive Slav group. Niederle distinguishes three main sub-groups which fit into the frame of eastern European hydrography.[34] A northwesterly branch attained the valleys of the Elbe, Sale and Sumava, and gave birth to the Bohemian and Polish factions. A central group, originally occupying the region of the upper Vistula, the Dniester and middle Danube, rounded the southern slopes of the Carpathians and, traveling up-stream on the Danube, eventually attained the valleys of the Save and Drave. The Slavs of southeastern Europe are descendants of this group. Originally pure Slavs, they are permeated with Asiatic blood owing to repeated invasions from the east. The third group was destined to form the substratum of Slavic Russia. It radiated from the basin of the Dnieper as far north as the Gulf of Finland and eastward to the valleys of the Oka, the Don and the Volga.

TABLE I

FORMER POLISH PROVINCES UNDER GERMAN RULE AT THE BEGINNING OF THE EUROPEAN WAR [1]

PROVINCE	Area in sq. mi.	Population 1910	Period of loss to Poland
POMERANIA, regencies of Strzalow (Stralsund), Szezecin (Stettin), and Koszalin (Köslin)	11,751	1,716,921	XIIIth century [2]
WEST PRUSSIA, regencies of Gdansk (Dantzik) and Kwidzyn (Marien-werder)	9,966	1,703,474	1772 [3]
EAST PRUSSIA, regencies of Krolewiec (Königsberg), Glombin (Gumbinnen) and Olsztyn (Allenstein)	14,431	2,064,175	1656 [4]

[1] L. Strzembosz: Tableau des divisions administratives actuelles de la Pologne, Paris, 1915.

[2] Not including the circles of Lembork (Lauenburg), (479 sq. mi., 52,851 inhab.), Bytow (Bütow) (238 sq. mi., 28,151 inhab.), and Drahim land (Draheim) (197 sq. mi., 18,500 inhab.), which were lost in the first partition in 1772.

[3] Not including the circle of Susz (Rosenberg) (407 sq. mi., 54,550 inhab.), and half of that of Kwidzyn (187 sq. mi., 34,213 inhab.), which together made part of ducal Prussia and were lost in 1656.

[4] Given in fief by the Polish kings to the Dukes of Brandenburg and exonerated in 1656 from the oath of vassalage, except the four circles of Braniewo (Braunsberg) (383 sq. mi., 54,613 inhab.), Licbark (Heilsberg) (427 sq. mi., 51,912 inhab.), Olsztyn (Allenstein) (529 sq. mi., 90,996 inhab.) and Reszel (Rössel) (333 sq. mi., 50,472 inhab.), which together under the name of Duchy of Warmie made part of Royal Prussia and were lost at the first partition.

[34] La race slave, Paris, 1911, pp. 3-4.

TABLE I—*Continued*

Province	Area in sq. mi.	Population 1910	Period of loss to Poland
POSNANIA, regencies of Poznan (Posen) and Bydgoszcz (Bromberg)	11,307	2,099,831	1815 [5]
REGENCY OF FRANKFURT (Francfort-sur-l'Oder)	7,487	1,233,189	XIIIth century
PROVINCE OF SILESIA, regencies of Lignica (Liegnitz), Wroclaw (Breslau),[6] and Opole (Oppeln)	15,731	5,225,962	1335
SAXON DISTRICT OF BUDZISZYN (Bautzen)[7]	963	443,549	XIIIth century

[5] Conferred on the king of Prussia under the name of Grand Duchy of Posen at the time of the partition of the Duchy of Warsaw by the Congress of Vienna in 1815.

[6] Former appendages of a branch, extinguished in 1675, of the royal Polish house of Piast.

[7] Part of the former marquisate of Lusace.

TABLE II

POLISH ADMINISTRATIVE DIVISIONS UNDER AUSTRO-HUNGARIAN RULE AT THE BEGINNING OF THE EUROPEAN WAR

Territory	Area in sq. mi.	Population	Period of loss to Poland
MARQUISATE OF MORAVIA	866	2,622,271	XIth century
DUCHY OF SILESIA [1]	2,007	756,949	—
KINGDOM OF GALICIA with the Grand Duchy of Cracow [2]	30,615	8,025,675	1772-1795

[1] Part of the former Polish Silesia, kept by Germany.

[2] The territory of Cracow, made into a republic in 1815 by the Congress of Vienna, was annexed by Austria in 1846.

TABLE III

POLISH ADMINISTRATIVE DIVISIONS UNDER RUSSIAN RULE AT THE BEGINNING OF THE EUROPEAN WAR

Territory	Area in sq. mi.	Population in 1910[1]	Period of loss to Poland
BALTIC PROVINCES:			
Gov't of Esthonia	7,897	471,400	1660
" " Livonia	18,342	1,466,900	1660
" " Courland	10,642	749,100	1795
LITHUANIA:			
Gov't of Grodno	15,081	1,974,400 ⎫	
" " Kovno	15,853	1,796,700 ⎬	1793-1795 [2]
" " Vilna	16,587	1,957,000 ⎭	

[1] Consisting of Poles and natives.

[2] The circle of Bialystok, occupied by the king of Prussia in 1795, was ceded to Russia by the treaty of Tilsit in 1807.

TABLE III—*Continued*

Territory	Area in sq. mi.	Population in 1910[1]	Period of loss to Poland
WHITE RUTHENIA:			
Gov't of Smolensk	21,757	1,988,700	1667
" " Minsk	35,649	2,868,300 ⎫	
" " Mohilev	18,738	2,261,500 ⎬	1772-1793
" " Witebsk	17,615	1,850,700 ⎭	
KINGDOM OF POLAND:			
Gov't of Kalisz	4,436	1,183,800 ⎫	
" " Kielce	3,936	973,300 ⎪	
" " Lublin	6,567	1,556,000 ⎪	
" " Lomza	4,119	688,500 ⎪	
" " Piotrkow	4,777	1,981,300 ⎬	1815 by Congress
" " Plock	3,684	739,900 ⎪	of Vienna
" " Radom	4,817	1,112,200 ⎪	
" " Siedlce	5,591	1,003,400 ⎪	
" " Suwalki	4,895	681,300 ⎪	
" " Warsaw	6,833	2,547,700 ⎭	
RUTHENIA:			
Gov't of Kiovie	19,890	4,604,200 ⎫	
." " Podolia	16,587	3,812,000 ⎬	1793-1795 [3]
" " Volhynia	28,023	3,920,400 ⎭	

[3] The city of Kijow (Kiev) with its district (773 sq. mi., 560,000 inhab.) was lost in 1686.

TABLE IV

DISTRIBUTION OF POLES AND GERMANS IN UPPER SILESIA, ACCORDING TO 1910 GERMAN CENSUS FIGURES [1]

Locality	Population	Germans	Poles
Kreuzburg	51,906	24,363	24,487
Rosenberg	52,341	8,586	42,234
Oppeln (city)	33,907	27,128	5,371
Oppeln (district)	117,906	23,740	89,323
Gross-Strehlitz	73,383	12,616	58,102
Lublinitz	50,388	7,384	39,969
Gleiwitz (city)	66,981	49,543	9,843
Tost-Gleiwitz	80,515	16,408	61,509
Tarnowitz	77,583	20,969	51,859
Beuthen (city)	67,718	41,071	22,401
Königshütte (city)	72,641	39,276	24,687
Beuthen-Land	195,844	59,308	123,016
Hindenburg	139,810	63,875	81,567
Kattowitz (city)	43,173	36,891	5,766
Kattowitz (district)	216,807	65,763	140,592

[1] R. Baumgarten: Deutsche und Polen in Oberschlesien, *Deutsche Erde*, Vol. 13, No. 7, 1914-1915, pp. 175-179.

TABLE IV—*Continued*

LOCALITY	Population	Germans	Poles
Pless	122,897	16,464	105,744
Rybnik	131,630	24,872	102,430
Ratibor (city)	38,424	22,914	11,525
Ratibor (district)	118,923	13,316	56,765
Kosel	75,673	16,433	56,794
Leobschütz	82,635	69,901	5,178
Neustadt	97,537	51,489	43,787
Falkenberg	37,526	33,286	3,815
Neisse (city)	25,938	24,735	955
Neisse (district)	75,285	74,125	797
Grottkau	40,610	39,589	825

CHAPTER VII

BOHEMIAN, MORAVIAN AND SLOVAKIAN

The Bohemians, who with the Moravians form the vanguard of the Slavs in Europe, occupy the mountain-girt plateau of Bohemia in the very heart of the continent. Here, a steady easterly spread of Teutons has prevented expansion of these Slavs along the eastern valleys which provide them with communication with the rest of the continent. Bohemians and Moravians thus found themselves shut within the mountainous rim of their land by the Germans of Silesia and Austria proper.

The German ring surrounding Bohemia is composed of groups belonging to various types of the Teutonic family. A southwestern element consists of descendants of Bavarian settlers. Farmers and woodsmen were introduced into the Böhmerwald, as an inevitable phase of the exploitation of the mountainous area, by religious communities of the thirteenth century. The end of the Thirty Years' War was marked by a new influx of Germans needed to repopulate the sorely devastated Bohemian districts. The Bavarians, however, never reached the foot of the eastern slopes. Modern Bohemian resistance to their spread toward the plain persists unflinchingly. Northward, the Erzgebirge uplift is also a German ethnographic conquest. For centuries its mineral wealth has attracted artisans from Franconia, Thuringia and Saxony. The mountain slopes re-echo today to the sound of the dialects of these ancient countries. The Saxon element prevails particularly among the inhabitants of the Elbe valley.

Farther east, descendants of Lusatian and Silesian peasants still use the vernacular of their ancestors in the upland formed by the Iser Gebirge and the Riesen Gebirge. In modern times the valleys of these mountains yield a steady stream of German-speaking inhabitants to the industrial towns of the southern plain. The German workingman's competition with his Bohemian fellow laborer is keen in this district, but it has not been marked by a notable advance of the Teutonic idiom.

Linguistically the Bohemians and Moravians form a unit hemmed in by Germans on all sides except the east, where they abut against their Slovak kinsmen. Community of national aspirations, under the leadership of the Bohemian element, is generally ascribed to these three Slavic groups. The union has been fostered by the lack of a literary language among Moravians, who have adopted the Bohemian alphabet and style. With the Slovaks [1] inferiority of numbers helped the spread of the Bohemian language and literature.

The Czech linguistic area presents homogeneity of composition which is seldom encountered in other parts of Austria-Hungary. Intermingling of Slavic and Teutonic elements has been slight in this advanced strip of Slavdom. Overlapping of German is met in belts generally parallel to the political divide. It is particularly noticeable in the angle formed by the junction of the Böhmerwald and Erzgebirge near the western linguistic divide, where it almost attains the town of Pilsen.[2] Beyond, in a northerly direction, the volcanic area characterized by thermal springs lies within the German line. Reichenberg, a strenuous center of Teutonism, maintains easterly and westerly prongs of German in the Iser-Riesen uplifts and the Elbe valley, respectively. The German of Silesia spreads into Moravia along the Zwittau-Olmütz-Neu Titschen line.

A short stretch of the linguistic boundary coincides with the political frontier in the neighborhood of Taus, but the rest of the southern Böhmerwald overlooking Bohemian levels is German in speech from the crests to the zone in which widening of the valleys becomes established. The disappearance of this moun-

---

[1] Official Austrian figures estimate the number of Slovaks at slightly over 2,000,000. Slavic authorities generally give higher figures.

[2] J. Zemmich: Deutschen und Slawen in den österreichischen Südetenländern, *Deutsche Erde*, Vol. 2, 1903, pp. 1-4.

tainous chain, in southern Moravia, coincides with a southerly
extension of Czech in the valley of the March. Contact with
Slovak dialects begins in the Beskid area.

Celts, Teutons and Slavs have occupied the Bohemian lozenge
in turn. The appellation Czechs first appears in the sixth century. National consolidation began with the country's conversion
to Christianity, three hundred years later, and was maintained
with varying fortunes until 1620. Bohemian political freedom
was annihilated in that year on the battlefield of the White
Mountain. After this defeat the land and its inhabitants lapsed
into a state of lethargy. The high cultural attainment of a few
modern Bohemians was sufficient to rouse the country to a sense
of national feeling.[3] Fortunately native poets, historians and
scientists were successful in infusing their patriotic ideals in the
minds of their countrymen. In particular, the fire of Bohemian
patriotism has been kept alive by literary activity.

Successful attempts on the part of Hungarians to assimilate
the Slovaks has caused these mountaineers to turn to their
Bohemian kinsmen for assistance in the preservation of race and
tradition. Merging of national aspirations in this case, was
facilitated by close linguistic affinity. A Czecho-Slovak body
consisting of 8,410,998 individuals [4] thus came into being within
the Dual Monarchy in order to maintain resistance against German and Hungarian encroachments.

The struggle between Teuton and Slav in Bohemia goes back
to the obscure period of the country's early history. As late as
the middle of the ninth century Bohemia was mainly a pagan
state. German missionaries at that time were endeavoring to
convert the natives to Christianity. But the mere nationality of
the apostles of the new faith prevented them from gaining
adherents. From the heart of Europe the Bohemians looked
eastward to the Christians of the Slavic race for religious salvation. We read of envoys being sent to the court of the Byzantine emperor to beseech this ruler to send Christian teachers of

---

[3] L. Bourlier: Les Tchéques et la Bohême contemporaine, Paris, 1897, pp. 143-220.

[4] Census returns for 1910. New Inter. Encyc., New York, 1914.

the Slavic faith to Bohemia, as the German missionaries could
not make themselves intelligible to the natives.   These steps
were viewed with considerable apprehension by German bishops,
especially after the success which attended the proselytizing
efforts of Methodus and his colleagues.   The Byzantine priests
had brought with them a translation of the Bible in the Slavic
language of Macedonia.   The replacement of Bohemian by German was thus effectively prevented.   Bohemia and Moravia
definitely became bilingual countries in the thirteenth century as
a result of the inflow of German colonists who responded to
urgent appeals for settlers made by Bohemian rulers in that
period.   The belt of German towns which completely encircles
Bohemia is a consequence of this policy.   The deforested zones
of the west and northwest received the largest number of
settlers.

In western and northern Bohemia a struggle for supremacy
between German and Czech has been carried on for years with
unabated vehemence.   The scene of contest between the two
peoples is often laid in individual communes.   Clerical, industrial
and educational influences are constantly at work for the extension of the linguistic area with which they side.   On the whole
the Bohemians, being in command of superior pecuniary
resources, appear to be gaining ground, although from special
causes the German element shows an advance in certain districts.
In those parts where mixture has taken place no definite
boundary between pure German and Bohemian (i.e., in over 90
per cent of the respective peoples) can be drawn.   As a rule, it
is the Bohemians who have of late advanced their outposts into
the German sphere, the Germanization of which dates back some
two hundred years.   Although they have fallen back somewhat
in the tongue of land which projected into German ground, north
of Mies, they have gained much ground in Pilsen and in the
industrial region around Nürschan, west of that town.   Fifty
years ago only some three or four thousand out of a total population of fourteen thousand in Pilsen were Bohemians, but the
influx of population which has since taken place has been almost

entirely Bohemian. In 1890 the proportion of Germans in the city only amounted to 16.2 per cent. Nürschan, the chief center of the coal-fields of western Bohemia, boasts a Bohemian majority and if the process now going on is continued the Bohemian population will probably in time join hands with that in Mies.[5]

Further to the northeast similar conditions prevail, though the linguistic frontier is in parts more sharply defined. In the coal-fields of Brüx and Dux the Bohemian element has largely increased on the German side of the normal frontier owing to the influx of Czech miners. In Trebnitz again the Czech language has gained a firm footing, although the town at the end of the nineteenth century was entirely German. In the neighboring town of Lobositz, however, which occupies an important position at the junction of six lines of railway, the prospects from the German point of view are brighter. The accession of Charles IV to the throne of Bohemia in 1346 was an event of the utmost importance in the linguistic history of the country.[6] This sovereign, the successor of German princes who had never allowed Bohemia fair play, showed marked affection for the land he was called upon to rule and set himself to master its language thoroughly. For two hundred years prior to his reign, Bohemian stood in danger of being replaced by German. Other Slav dialects were fast disappearing before the vigorous advance of Teutonic

---

[5] Quoted from the *Geogr. Journ.*, Vol. 16, 1900, p. 553.

[6] According to data gathered by Niederle " the Bohemian boundary in the fourteenth century started at Kynwart and passed through Zdar, Kralipy and Komotan, the latter being German. Thence it attained Most and spread to Duchcov and Dieczin. Bilin and Teplitz were still Bohemian. The frontier then reached the German settlement of Benesov and extended to Jablonna and beyond the Iestred mountains until it struck the sources of the Iser river. Reichenberg was a German city in the fourteenth century. The Germans also occupied the mountainous land beyond Hohenelbe. This town was then peopled by Bohemians mainly, but Pilnikov, Trutnov, Zaclev and Stare Buky were already German. Starkov was Bohemian, but the Brunov region and the Kladsko country was Germanized. Olesnica and Rokytince were Bohemian. Beyond Policzka and Litomysl the situation was similar to that of our day. Nemecky Brod contained a German enclave. Jindrichuv Hradec as well as Budweiss, Krumlov and Prachatice were inhabited by both peoples. The Kasperk mountains were mainly German. The boundary in the Domazlice country was on Bohemian soil. Klatovy was a mixed zone, while Tachov was German."

speech. Through its literature alone the Bohemian language was preserved. This literary development was an advantage which was not possessed by the Slav languages, which gave way before German.

As a result of Charles's benevolent policy Bohemian became the language of the court. Furthermore it was used exclusively in many courts of law, which were re-established through the same influence. It was even decreed that speakers at the assemblies of town magistrates should use the language of their choice and that no one speaking only German could be appointed a judge. In this way equality for the Bohemian language was obtained in the districts in which Germans had settled.[7]

The creation of the Archbishopric of Prague and the foundation of the "new town" of Prague dated also from the reign of King Charles. Bohemian clergymen were encouraged to preach in the vernacular. Their sermons reached the people and stirred them to thought. The national movement against the Roman Church was thus facilitated. But another cause favored the spread of Protestantism in Bohemia. Antagonism to Catholicism was merely a special form of Bohemian objection to German influence in the land. The Hussite movement is therefore an episode in the prolonged struggle between Teuton and Slav.

The enlargement of Prague infused vitality into the Bohemian language. The new town was Bohemian in speech as well as in sentiment. Slavic prevailed exclusively in municipal offices and tribunals. Venceslas, who followed Charles, faithfully maintained his predecessor's attitude towards Bohemian. A notable advance in favor of the language of the land was made in his reign by a decision according to which all decrees of the court and the government, which hitherto had been rendered in either German or Latin, were to be henceforth published in Bohemian.

The University of Prague, which has always been a center of Bohemian intellectual life, was also affected by these changes. In the middle of the fifteenth century the German element in Bohemia had complete control of the affairs of this institution.

---

[7] Lützow: Bohemia, New York, 1910, pp. 71, 92.

Its chairs were filled by Teutons and its dignities awarded to their kinsmen. In 1385, swayed by national aspirations and relying on the predilection shown them in high quarters, Bohemians began to protest against the presence of foreigners in their national seat of learning. Their appeal found a response with the Archbishop of Prague, who ruled that Bohemians were entitled to priority in appointments to university offices, and that only in case of their unfitness was a German to be selected. Complaint of this decision was made by the Germans to the Pope and a compromise reached in virtue of which predominance of Bohemian rights was obtained. The appearance of John Huss on the scene of this struggle was the next step in the task of completely emancipating Bohemia from German rule.

The national movement fostered in this manner was to end disastrously at the battle of the White Mountain in 1620. The treaty of Westphalia removed all probability of the establishment of an autonomous Bohemian nation. But Bohemian patriots have a saying that "as long as the language lives the nation is not dead," and through all the dark days of the country's history, in the very heart of continental Europe, cut off from the surrounding lands by a wall of forested slopes, the Bohemian language has held its own, not merely as a vernacular but as a literary language worthy of the nation's pride.

A period of marked decline intervened, however, between the seventeenth and nineteenth centuries. The crushing blow inflicted on Bohemian nationalism in 1620 was speedily followed by a rigid German oversight of the country. Seven years later, Ferdinand inaugurated a series of measures aimed at destroying the cause for which Bohemians had sacrificed their lives. The German language began to supplant the Bohemian. The "renewed ordinance of the land," issued in 1627, contained provisions for the recognition of German in tribunals and government offices on the same terms as Bohemian. The appointment of Germans to important offices was a policy which marked this period. Its effects became perceptible in the growing use of the conquerors' language. The seventeenth century is marked by a rapid growth of the Teutonic belt encircling Bohemia. Luditz and Saaz were lost to the Bohemian language in that period. So were the districts of Rokytince and Vichlaby[8] in the eastern section of the country. But since the beginning of the eighteenth century little change has taken place in the German-Bohemian linguistic boundary.

Among the causes which contributed to the decline of the Bohemian language about this time were the land confiscations which were carried out on an extensive scale by the Imperialists.[9] Most of the noblemen of Bohemia were deprived of their estates. As a result about half the landed property of the country was taken away from its Slav owners. This spoliation was carried on by the Catholics, the despoiled and exiled Hussites being replaced by Germans, Spaniards, Walloons and even Irish. This foreign element naturally adopted the German language and Bohemian was abandoned to serfs and peasants.

The humble tillers of Bohemian soil proved faithful custodians of their native speech. They stored the language during two centuries as though they had been gifted with the foreknowledge of the splendid literary revival which was to mark its renaissance at the magic touch of Kolár, Sofarik and Palacký. Coincident with this movement national consciousness was reborn among Bohemians. Writers and poets naturally took the past greatness of their native land as the theme of their compositions. They told their countrymen of the glorious days of Bohemian history. The movement fortunately took place when the wave of liberalism set in motion by the French Revolution was still advancing into the recesses of central Europe. By the year 1840 all Bohemia had awakened to the idea of national independence. Attempts to secure partial autonomy proved abortive, however. Revolutionary outbreaks in 1848 were quickly repressed by Austrian troops, but the struggle between the two elements increased in bitterness as years went by.

At present two-thirds of the inhabitants of Bohemia are

---

[8] L. Niederle: La race slave, Paris, 1916, p. 109.
[9] Lützow: op. cit., p. 294.

Bohemians, and this Slavic element is gradually forcing its way into districts which were formerly occupied exclusively by Germans. The causes of this shifting are economic. The German element, controlling industry and vested with authority, has attained a state of relative prosperity. Even its poorest members are not attracted by the prospect of work held out by Bohemia's growing industry. The less advanced Bohemians, however, not so content with their lot, are attracted by certain kinds of labor which the German element spurns. Having fewer local ties than their Teutonic countrymen, they easily move from place to place. It thus happens that out of the thirty-six German districts of Bohemia, twenty-two are now fully 5 per cent Bohemian.[10]

The inhabitants of the Margravate of Moravia are also true Bohemians. This state is a crown-land of Bohemia, to the east of which it lies. Its population consists of 1,870,000 Bohemians and 720,000 Germans. Close affiliation with the kingdom of Bohemia is revealed in Moravia's past history. The two states formed the nucleus of the Bohemian nation. At present Moravia is even more truly Bohemian than her larger sister state, since three-fourths of the landowners of Moravia are Bohemians, while in Bohemia that element holds only about three-fifths of the soil. In spite of the mountainous character of the country, and the isolation produced by it, very slight traces of early tribal differences can be detected among these Bohemians. In Moravia alone three distinct types can be distinguished by their dialects and their physical or ethnographic features. Dress in the last case plays an important part.[11]

The northeastern section of Moravia is known as the Lassko country and is peopled by Lassi Moravians. This group occupies districts mainly around the towns of Moravska-Ostrava and Frydland. South of them a number of Slovak villages are found within the Moravian border. Their inhabitants, sometimes known as Moravian Slovaks, are emigrants from the Hungarian moun-

---

[10] V. Gayda: Modern Austria, New York, 1915.
[11] L. Niederle: La race slave, Paris, 1911, p. 127.

tains who reached the western Carpathians in the eleventh and twelfth centuries. Although they speak Bohemian, their customs differ considerably from Bohemian usages. The balance of Moravia is peopled by Hanaks, who are easily distinguished by temperamental differences from the previous two groups. The Hanaks as a rule are calm and inclined to ponderous ways of thought and action, whereas both the Lassi and Slovaks are quick-minded and lively.

German expansion into Moravia is facilitated by the valley of the March, which penetrates into the heart of the Margravate. The Elbe and Moldau in Bohemia play a similar part as agents of Germanization. As in Bohemia, the Germans are confined to the border heights or the towns. In the thirteenth century many German fortified towns existed in Moravia. The rise of a powerful German middle class dates from this period. Intellectually as well as industrially the Teuton element is the more advanced. Racial and linguistic differences are accentuated by religious antagonism, the German element being Roman in creed. The clergy in fact have acted as a powerful agent of Germanization in Moravia.

The Slovaks are dwellers of the northern highland border of Hungary who reached Europe in the sixth century B.C. They are closely related by racial and linguistic affinity to the Bohemians and Moravians. The course of centuries has failed to change their customs or the mode of life they led in the western Carpathians. The Hungarian plain spread out below their rocky habitation without tempting them to forsake the huddled conditions of their native valleys. Their language holds its own as far east as the Laborec valley. Junction with Polish is effected in the Tatra.

Once only in their history did the Slovaks succeed in creating a great nation. In 870 A.D., under the leadership of Svatopuk, they established the short-lived Great Moravian Empire. Unfortunately his successors were unable to maintain the independence of the nation he founded and the empire crumbled to pieces before the repeated attacks of the Hungarians. By the tenth century the political ties between Bohemians and Slovaks were completely severed.

In the fifteenth century the two peoples were drawn to each other by ties of religion. An enthusiastic reception had been given to the teachings of John Huss by the Slovaks. They adopted the Bohemian translation of the Bible. Religious reformation was followed by a literary revival and Bohemian became the language of culture among them. It was mainly among Protestant Slovaks, however, that the influence of Bohemian prevailed. The Catholic clergy opposed the movement by encouraging literary development of Slovakian. This linguistic struggle is maintained to the present day. In spite of opposition, however, Bohemian remains the literary language of the Slovak people. John Kollar, one of the greatest writers of Bohemian poetry, was a Slovak.

The Slovaks number approximately two million souls spread over ten of the "comitats" of northern Hungary. Their occupation of this region antedates the coming of the Magyars. Survivals of ancient Slovak populations are still met in the villages of central and southern Hungary. Bohemian refugees of kindred speech and religion reinforced this autochthonous element after the battle of the White Mountain in 1620. These circumstances perhaps have prevented their assimilation by the conquering race. The aristocracy alone has intermarried with the Hungarians. The masses have no more intercourse with the rulers than they can help. Linguistic and religious differences intensify the breach.

While the Slovaks form compact populations in the mountains of northern Hungary, their colonies are found scattered throughout the southern parts of this country except in the Transylvanian districts. The campaign waged by Hungarians to suppress Slovak national aims renders the lot of these Slavs particularly trying. The ancient names of their villages and towns are being officially replaced by Magyar names, even where most of the inhabitants use Slovakian as their vernacular.

Although Slovak-land is an integral part of the Hungarian

kingdom, it has proved an attractive field for German colonization since the ninth century. The comitat of Zips was settled
by a large colony of Germans in the middle of the twelfth century. Fifty years later the Teutons began to invade the comitats
of Pressburg and Neutra [12] by advancing from the west. In Bars
and Hont, to both of which they proceeded from the south, they
were not known before the thirteenth century. The Germanization of Slovak districts was particularly intense during the
Tatar invasion of this period. Hungary had been grievously
affected by this eastern scourge, and its kings offered special
inducements to repopulate their devastated provinces. Their call
was heeded by numerous families of German peasants. In the
first half of the sixteenth century almost every town within
Slovak boundaries contained one or two German families at least.
The heart of this German colonization was situated in the mining
districts of the country. Kremnitz and Nemecke Prava, as well
as adjoining districts, attracted heavy contingents of Teuton
workers. This movement ended in the seventeenth century when
the inflow of German colonists was checked by special legislation
and the foreign element was absorbed by either the Slovaks or
the Hungarians.

The modern boundary of Slovakian language in Hungary
starts according to Niederle at Devinska Novaves near the
confluence of the Morva [13] and Danube. From this point it
extends southeastward to Novezansky and Leva. Thence it is
continued south of Abanj as far as Huta, which is the easternmost Slovak village. The line now turns westward and skirts the
Galician frontier as far as the German border.

The area included within these confines is not altogether
homogeneous. The comitats of Neutra, Turocz, Bars and Gömö
contain enclaves of Germans. Polish and Hungarian settlements
are also known between Vrable and Neutra as well as at Abanj,
west of Kashau. Many Slovak communities exist, however,
beyond the region outlined above. These extra-territorial nuclei

---

[12] L. Niederle: La race slave, Paris, 1916, p. 106.
[13] The March acquires this name in its last stretch.

more than counterbalance numerically the alien total in Slovak-land.

The most important localities inhabited by Slovaks outside of their native land are Gran, in the comitat of Esztergom, and Budapest. The Hungarian capital probably contains between 25,000 and 40,000 Slovaks. Their number in Vienna is estimated at 50,000. In other parts of Hungary, as for instance at Kerepes and Pilis, highly ancient Slovak communities are believed to represent survivals of the people who lived in Hungary prior to the appearance of the Hungarians.

Bohemia's national enfranchisement, if carried out on a linguistic basis, will rescue the old lands of the Bohemian crown, namely Bohemia, Moravia and the Slovak districts of north-western Hungary, from Teutonic rule. The historical validity of Bohemia's claims to independence and the failure of centuries of Germanization to deprive the Bohemian of his individuality establish the country's right to a distinct place in a Europe of free and harmonious nations. The Bohemian has his own objects in self-development and the achievement of his independence should be no disparagement of the aims and pursuits of other nations.

CHAPTER VIII

THE LANDS OF HUNGARIAN AND RUMANIAN LANGUAGES

THE presence in Europe of Hungarians, a race bearing strong linguistic and physical affinity to Turki tribesmen, is perhaps best explained by the prolific harvests yielded by the broad valleys of the Danube and Theiss. Huns, Avars and Magyars, one and all Asiatics wandering into Europe, were induced to abandon nomadism by the fertility of the boundless Alföld. Western influences took solid root among these descendants of eastern ancestors after their conversion to Christianity and the adoption of the Latin alphabet. So strongly did they become permeated by the spirit of occidental civilization, that the menace of absorption by the Turks was rendered abortive whenever the Sultan's hordes made successful advances towards Vienna. At the same time, fusion with the Germans was prevented by the oriental origin of the race. The foundation of a separate European nation was thus laid in the Hungarian plains.

Language to the Magyar has always represented nationality. When in 1527 St. Stephen's crown was offered to Ferdinand of Austria in order to strengthen Hungary's resistance against the Turk, the new ruler pledged himself not to destroy this sacred token of Hungarian political independence. "Nationem et linguam vestram servare non perdere intendimus" was his solemn promise. The germ of a dual form of government was thus created in the presence of the Sultan's barbarous hordes, but Hungary always preserved its individuality, for at no time did the kingdom form part of the Holy Roman Empire. Closer union with Austria towards the end of the seventeenth century when the right of succession to the Hungarian throne became hereditary in the Hapsburg family, failed to Germanize the land during all the eighteenth century. Later, up to 1867, the persistent struggle of the Magyar against the Austrian was kept up. Attempts to replace German by Hungarian in the governing bodies of counties and muncipalities were merely the outward expression of the contest.

When, in 1825, the Hungarian Academy of Science was founded by a group of patriotic leaders, the movement was little more than an attempt to revive the Magyar tongue. Count Stephen Széchenyi's words on this occasion betray the consciousness of the intimate relation between language and nationality which is felt in every country during periods of actual danger. "I am not here," he said, "as a great dignitary of the kingdom; but I am an opulent landowner, and if an institution be established that will develop the Magyar language and, by so doing, advance the national education of our countrymen, I will sacrifice the revenues of my estates for one year." The impetus given by this statesman, and a few equally earnest compatriots, to the cultivation of national literature in Hungary became a potent factor in the shaping of the country's modern political destiny. It liberated the Magyar from the Germanizing influences of Austrian rule and ultimately paved the way to the establishment of a dual government in the Empire.

The linguistic boundary between Hungarian and German is found in the eastern extremity of the Austrian Alps. The southern side of the valley of the Danube between Pressburg and Raab is German. Magyar spreads however to the north to meet the Slovak area. South of Pressburg the shores of Lake Neusiedler are included in the German area. The line then crosses the upper valley of the Raab and attains the Drave, which forms the linguistic boundary between Croatian and Hungarian. East of the Theiss, contact with the Rumanian of Transylvania begins in the vicinity of Arad, on the Maros river, and extends northward in an irregular line, hugging the western outliers of the Transylvanian Alps and attaining the sources of the Theiss. In the northeastern valley of this river, Hungarian and Ruthenian languages replace each other. The area of Magyar speech thus defined lacks homogeneity in its western section lying west of the Danube. Important enclaves of Germans are solidly intrenched in this portion of the Hungarian domain. The central portion of the monotonous expanse unfolding itself between the Danube and the Theiss is, on the other hand, characterized by uniformity of the Hungarian population it supports. Enclaves however exist all along the border of this eastern area.

Hungarian nationality asserted itself definitely in the nineteenth century in the face of strenuous effort on the part of Germans to assimilate the Magyars. The latter took advantage of the defeat of the Austrians at Sadowa in 1867 to reach a compromise with their masters. The Hapsburg Empire was then converted into a Dual Monarchy. For a time the economic advantages of this union lay entirely with Austria. The Hungarian plain, vast and fecund, bestowed the wealth of its fertility on Austria. A land of farmers it also became an important market for the industrial output of its German partner-state. This economic relation was maintained until the beginning of the twentieth century, when Hungary made rapid progress in industry and forced Austria to seek Balkan markets for the disposal of its manufactured goods.

Austria's unsuccessful attempt to dominate Hungary's economic life accelerated the growth of the germ of dissension between the two countries. The tie that links Budapest to Vienna, at present, is strengthened by Hungarian dread of the Slav. It might have given way long ago otherwise, for in truth Hungary has to face the menace of Pan-Germanism as well. The percentage of native Hungarians in their own country is under 55 per cent and gives them a bare majority over the combined alien peoples.[1] The number of Germans scattered in Hungarian districts is 2,000,000. The only advantage which the natives of the soil possess lies in their occupation of the richest lands in their country.

---

[1] An increase in the percentage of the Hungarian element in Hungary at the expense of the other nationalities and particularly of the Germans is shown by official figures. The following table is instructive:

A minor group of Hungarians have settled on the eastern edge of the Transylvania mountains. Here they live surrounded by Rumanians on all sides except on the west where a lone out-post of Saxons brings Teutonic customs and speech to the east. The name of Szekler, meaning frontier guardsmen, applied to this body of Magyars is indicative of their origin. Their pres-ence on the heights overlooking the Rumanian plain bespeaks the desire of Hungarian sovereigns to control the site of a natural rampart dominating their plains. At the end of the thirteenth century this Hungarian colony was in full development. Its soldiers distinguished themselves during the period of war with the Turks. Prestige acquired on battlefields strengthened the separate and semi-independent existence of the community. The region occupied by these Hungarians is situated along the east-ernmost border of the Austrian-Hungarian Empire. It extends west of the uninhabited mountain-frontier district between Tölgyes Pass and Crasna. The towns of Schässburg and Maros Vasarhely lie on its western border. But the area of Rumanian speech situated between the land of the Szekler and the main Hungarian district is studded with numerous colonies of Magyars, thereby rendering delimitation of a linguistic boundary in the region almost impossible.

The Saxon colony adjoining the Szekler area on the west is also a relic of medieval strategic necessities. In spite of the name by which this German settlement is designated, its original members appear to have been recruited from different sections of western European regions occupied by Teutons.[2] Colonization

---

Percentages of the Population of Hungary, without Croatia (after Wallis).

	1880	1910
Magyars	46.7	54.5
Germans	13.6	10.4
Slovaks	13.5	10.7
Rumanians	17.5	16.1
Ruthenians	2.6	2.5
Serbs and Croats	4.6	3.6
Others	1.5	2.2

But cf. in this connection B. C. Wallis: Distribution of Nationalities in Hungary, *Geogr. Journ.*, Vol. 47, 1916, No. 3, pp. 183-186.

[2] F. Teutsch: Die Art der Ansiedelung der Siebenbürger Sachsen, *Forsch. z. deut.*

had already been started when King Gesa II of Hungary gave it a fresh impulse, in the middle of the twelfth century, by inducing peasants of the middle Rhine and Moselle valleys to exchange servitude in their native villages for land ownership in the Transylvania area.[3]

To promote the efficiency of these colonists as frontier guardsmen an unusual degree of political latitude was accorded them. In time their deputies sat in the Hungarian diet on terms of equality with representatives of the nobility. Prolonged warfare with the Tatar populations who attempted to force entrance into the Hungarian plains, led to the selection of strategical sites as nuclei of original settlements. These facts account for the survival of the Teutonic groups in the midst of Rumanians and Hungarians. Today the so-called Saxon area does not constitute a single group, but consists of separate agglomerations clustered in the vicinity of the passes and defiles which the ancestors of the Teutons were called upon to defend. The upper valley of the Oltu and its mountain affluents, in the rectangle inclosed between the town of Hermannstadt, Fogaras, Mediasch and Schässburg, contain at present the bulk of this Austrian colony of German ancestry.

The Rumanian problem in Hungary is mainly economic. The chief aim of Hungarians is to maintain political supremacy in the provinces containing a majority of the Romance-speaking element. The Rumanian communities are scattered over an area of about 76,000 square miles (122,278 sq. kms.) which comprises Transylvania and its old "exterior" counties as well as the Banat. This region is peopled by 6,305,666 inhabitants according to recent census figures. Of these 87.8 per cent consist of peasants. The number of Rumanians is officially estimated at

---

Landes- u. Volksk., Vol. 9, 1896, pp. 1-22. Cf. also O. Wittstock: Volkstümliches der Siebenbürger Sachsen, in the same volume. The name "Saxon" appears to have been applied indiscriminately in the Middle Ages to settlers of German speech in the Balkan peninsula. "Saxon" miners and "Saxon" bodyguards were also known in Serbian countries in that period.

[3] Luxemburg and the regions comprised between Trèves, Düsseldorf and Aix-la-Chapelle furnished German colonists during the middle of the twelfth century.

FIG. 42—View of the Transylvanian plateau near the western edge of the Carpathians. Hosszufalu (Langendorf) in the distance.

2,932,214. Rumanian students, however, point to official Austrian returns for the year 1840 which placed the number of their countrymen at 2,202,000 [4] and lay stress on the coefficient of increase for the period 1870 to 1910, which is 15.5 per thousand in Rumania and 10.8 per thousand in Hungary. Applying the Rumanian rate to the Rumanian subjects of the Hapsburgs they find that their kinsmen in Hungary ought to number approximately 3,536,000. Otherwise it is necessary to admit that between 1840 and 1890 Magyars increased 54 per cent, and Rumanians only 17 per cent, in spite of the recognized fact that Rumanian peasants have larger families than their Hungarian masters.[5]

Social grouping in Transylvania shows that the dominating Hungarian class consists largely of city dwellers and government employees. These are the characteristics of an immigrant population which is not solidly rooted to the land. The Szekler alone among Magyars are tillers of the soil and in intimate contact with the land on which they live. Few of the Rumanians are landowners. The estates held by an insignificant number of their kinsmen generally form part of ecclesiastical domains and are of restricted size. They own however a relatively large proportion of Transylvania's forested areas, which the Hungarian ruling class is endeavoring to acquire by imitating Prussian methods of absorption of Polish lands.

The Germans and Hungarians who founded settlements on the Transylvanian plateau were unable to impose their language on the inhabitants of the mountainous region. Rumanian, representing the easternmost expansion of Latin speech, is in use today on the greatest portion of this highland [6] as well as in the fertile valleys and plains surrounding it between the Dniester and the Danube. A portion of Hungary and the Russian province of Bessarabia is therefore included in this linguistic unit outside

---

[4] Hungarian statistics show 2,470,000 in 1870; 2,403,000 in 1880 and 2,589,000 in 1890.

[5] Cf. V. Merutiŭ: Romînii între Tisa şi Carpaţĭ, raporturĭ etnografice, *Rev. Stiintifică Vasile Adamachi*, Vol. 6, No. 2, 1915.

[6] N. Mazere: Harta etnografica a Transilvanei, 1:340,000, Inst. Geogr. al Armatei, Iasi, 1909.

of the kingdom of Rumania.[7]   Beyond the limits of this continuous area, the only important colony of Rumanians is found around Metsovo in Greece where, in the recesses of the Pindus mountains and surrounded by the Greeks, Albanians and Bulgarians of the plains, almost half a million Rumanians [8] have managed to maintain the predominant Latin character of their language.[9]

Rumanian is derived directly from the low Latin spoken in the Imperial era. In syntax and grammar it reproduces Latin forms of striking purity. Words dealing with agricultural pursuits, however, are generally of Slavic origin. The closeness of Rumanian to Latin can be gathered from the following two specimens of Wallachian verse and their Latin rendering:

1.

Rumanian	*Latin*
Bela in large valle amblà	Puella in larga valle ambulabat,
Erba verde lin calcà;	Herbam viridem leniter calcabat,
Cantà, qui cantand plangeà,	Cantabat et cantando plangebat,
Quod tódi munti resunà;	Ut omnes montes resonarent:
Ea in genunchi se puneà,	Illa in genua se ponebat,
Ochi in sus indireptà;	Oculos sursum dirigebat;
Ecce, asi vorbe faceà;	Ecce, sic verba faciebat:
" Domne, domne, bune domne."	" Domine, domine, bone domine."

2.

Rumanian	*Latin*
Nucu, fagu, frassinu	Nux, fagus, fraxinus,
Mult se certà intra séne.	Multum certant inter se.
" Nuce," dice frassinu,	" Nux," dicit fraxinus
" Quine vine, nuci college,	" Quisquis venit, nuces legit,
" Cullegend si ramuri frange	" Colligendo ramos frangit:
" Vaide dar de pelle a tua;	" Vae itaque pelli tuae!
" Dar tu fage, mi vecine,	" At tu fage, mi vicine,
" Que voi spune in mente tene:	" Quae exponam mente tene?
" Multe fere saturasi;	" Multas feras saturasti,
" Qui prébéne nu amblasi;	" At haud bene ambulasti;
" Quum se au geru apropiat	" Quum gelu appropinquat
" La pament te au si culcat,	" Ad pavimentum de deculcant
" Si in focu te au si aruncat, . . .	" Ad focum averruncant, . . .

---

[7] G. Weigand: Linguistischer Atlas des dacorumänischen Sprachgebietes, Leipzig, 1909.

[8] Their number is given at 750,000 by G. Murgocè and P. Papahagi in " Turcia cu privire speciala auspra Macedoniei," Bucarest, 1911.

[9] The total number of Rumanians in the Balkan peninsula is estimated at about 10,300,000, distributed as follows: Rumania, 5,489,296 or 92.5 per cent of the population; Russia, 1,121,669, of whom 920,919 are in Bessarabia; Austria-Hungary, 3,224,147, of whom 2,949,032 are in Transylvania; Greece, 373,520; Serbia, 90,000.

The prevalence of Latin in an eastern land, and in a form which is stated to present closer analogies with the language of the Roman period than with any of its western derivatives, had its origin in the Roman conquest of southeastern Europe in the early part of the first Christian millennium. Occupation of the land by important bodies of legionaries and a host of civil administrators, their intermarriage with the natives, the advantages conferred by Roman citizenship, all combined to force Latin into current use. And when in 275 Aurelian recalled Roman troops from the eastern provinces of the empire, the vernacular of Rome had taken too solid a footing on Dacian soil to be extirpated.

Abandonment of the region by the Romans is cited for political reasons by the Magyar rulers of Transylvania to refute Rumanian claims to this Hungarian province. Rumanian historians, however, have been able to demonstrate the untenability of this assumption.[10] They have shown that many of the customs of their country are distinctly reminiscent of Latin Italy. It is still customary in many Rumanian villages to attach a small coin to the finger of the dead after an ancient Roman custom of providing the soul with its fare across the Styx. Bands of traveling musicians in Balkan or Hungarian cities are known to be composed of Rumanians whenever their members carry an instrument which is a faithful imitation of the pipes of Pan as sculptured upon Roman and Gallo-Roman monuments. Rumania's national dance, the Calusaré, commemorates the rape of the Sabines to this day. Neither does the list of these analogies end with the examples given here. Furthermore the evidence afforded by geography tends also to validate Rumanian claims.

From the valley of the Dniester to the basin of the Theiss the steppes of southern Russia spread in unvarying uniformity save where the tableland of the Transylvanian Alps breaks their continuity. The entire region was the Dacia colonized by the Romans.[11] Unity of life, in this home of Rumanian nationality,

---

[10] A. D. Xénopol: Les Roumains au Moyen-Âge, Paris, 1885.

[11] W. R. Shepherd: Historical Atlas, New York, 1911, pp. 34, 35, 39.

has been unaffected by the sharp physical diversity afforded by the inclosure of mountain and plain within the same linguistic boundary. The thoroughness with which Rumanians have adapted themselves to the peculiarities of their land is evinced by the combination of the twin occupations of herder and husbandman characteristic of Moldavians and Wallachians. Cattle and flocks are led every summer to the rich grazing lands of the Transylvania valleys. In winter man and beast seek the pastures of the Danubian steppes and prairies. Rumanians thus maintain mountain and plain residences, which they occupy alternately.[12] This mode of life is the transformation which the nomadism of the Asiatic steppe received on Rumanian soil. It is a true relic of past habitat. These seasonal migrations also account for the intimacy between highlanders and lowlanders in Rumania, besides affording adequate explanation of the peopling of the region by a single nationality.[13]

There was a time, however, when Rumanian nationality was entirely confined to the mountain zone. Invasions which followed the retirement of the Romans had driven Rumanians to the shelter of the Transylvanian ranges. Perched on this natural fortress, they beheld the irruption of Slavs and Tatars in the broad valleys which they once held in undisputed sway. Only after the flow of southeastern migrations had abated did they venture to reoccupy the plains and resume their agricultural life and seasonal wanderings.

The outstanding fact in these historical vicissitudes is that the mountain saved the Latin character of Rumanian speech. Had the Romanized Dacians been unable to find refuge in the Transylvanian Alps their language would probably have been submerged by the Slavic or Tatar flood. As it is, the life of Rumanians is strongly impregnated with eastern influences.

---

[12] Typical examples of seasonal migration are found in Switzerland, where conditions prevailing in the higher and the lower valleys of the Alps have induced the inhabitants to shift their residence with the seasons.

[13] A similar nomadism is observable among the Rumanians of the Pindus mountains. Cf. A. J. B. Wade and M. S. Thompson: The Nomads of the Balkans: An Account of Life and Customs among the Vlachs of Northern Pindus, London, 1914.

Oddly enough its Christianity was derived from Byzantium instead of from Rome and, were it not for a veritable renaissance of Latinism about 1860, its affinity with the Slavic world would be manifest with greater intensity than is apparent in the present century.

The preservation of Roman speech was not confined to the Transylvanian mountain area. In spite of Rome's waning power in the Balkans, her language had taken such solid root in the peninsula that it has maintained itself to this day in the Pindus mountain region intervening between Epirus and Macedonia. Here the Kutzo-Vlachs of the region speak a language identical with that spoken in the last stretches of the valley of the Danube. In Albania also the same cultural heritage has been treasured to this day in the mountainous tangle of the land. Albanian however is further removed from Latin than Rumanian, probably on account of less intercourse with the Roman world.[14]

The name of Kutzo-Wallachians or Aromunes is given to the mountaineers of Rumanian speech peopling parts of Macedonia, Albania and Thessaly. This detached band of Rumanians occupies mainly the region between the mountains of the Pindus range and the Serbian boundary. In Albania they are found scattered along the upper reaches of the Semeni and Devoli rivers. In Greece, the channels of the Voyussa, the Arta, the Aspropotamos, the Bistritza and the lower Vardar likewise constitute their favorite tramping grounds. A shepherd people, roaming with their flocks, their life is spent either in the valleys of their summer mountain resorts or in the plains which they favor in winter. Tribes or clans among which dialectical differences can be found occur according to locality, but they nevertheless compose when taken together a compact mass of Rumanians settled far from the main body of their kinsmen by speech.

A group 5,000 to 6,000 strong live near the sources of the Aspropotamos around Siracu, and between Kalarites and Malakasi. Northwards this clan extends to Metsovo.[15] In the Olympus

---

[14] About one-third of the words in Albanian are of Romanic origin.
[15] *Bull. pour l'étude de l'Europe Sud-Orientale*, June, 1915, p. 112.

mountains Rumanians are known at Vlakho-Livadi and adjoining districts. Eastwards, the Veria Rumanians are found in the villages of Selia, Doliani and Kirolivadi. West of the latter locality, the settlements of Vlakho-Klissura, Blatza and Sisani are likewise composed entirely of Rumanian inhabitants. The same is true of the villages of Nevesca, Belcamen and Pisuderi as well as of Gramosta, in the recesses of the Grammos mountains and of Koritza and Sipiska. Other colonies exist at Okrida, Gopes, Krushevo, Molovista, Tirnova, Magarevo and Monastir. The Struga and Geala settlements are also part of the preceding groups.

Within Albanian territory the village of Frasheri is the most important Rumanian settlement. Its name has passed to the Frasherist group of western Rumanians. Around Berat, a strong contingent occupies about 40 villages and can muster ten thousand men. In the Vardar valley various settlements aggregating 14,000 individuals, all farmers, are distributed near Guevgueli as well as in localities north and south of this town. Many of these peasants are Mohammedans and speak a dialect of their own. A Rumanian settlement is also found in the Jumaya Pass south of Sofia and along the old Turco-Bulgarian frontier.

The nomadic character of these isolated adherents of a Latin language is shown in many of their villages, which are occupied during part of the year only. As an example the villages in the vicinity of Frasheri, the ancient "Little Wallachia," are inhabited during winter alone. Many Frasherists can be met along the Albanian coast between Kimara and the bay of Valona, as well as along the eastern coast of Corfu and in villages of the Moskopolis and Koritza districts. As a rule they are peddlers and confine their commercial nomadism to profitable routes just as pastoral nomads, who are their kinsmen, seesaw back and forth between the mountain districts nearest their plains.

The three areas of Romance language in the Balkans attest, by implication, the powerful influence attained by Rome in the peninsula prior to the rise of the Slavic flood. The presence of the Slavs began to be felt about the seventh century and two hundred years later the Balkan peninsula had become heavily Slavicized. Before that period, however, every nook and corner of the land area between the Adriatic and the Black and Ægean seas must have been under effective Roman jurisdiction. Lanes of travel from the coasts of Albania to the famous Thracian rendezvous were frequented by Roman traders and colonists with increasing regularity in the early centuries of the Christian era. The growing estrangement of Byzantium from the west, Slavic inroads and later Turkish advances all but destroyed the social unity which must have characterized the Balkan region in Roman times. Of this unity, the Rumanian and Albanian languages alone have survived along different coasts. Both languages are knit together structurally as well as by outward harmony.

Through the survival of Romanic languages in the Balkan peninsula an excellent glimpse is obtained of the conditions preceding the Slavic migrations which, beginning at the end of the third century, burst into full strength at the opening of the sixth. The Slavic flood was both heavy and prolonged. Its strength can be surmised from the survival of Slavic place names in the sections of Balkan territory under Greek, Rumanian or Albanian control. But the Slavs mastered only the drainage area of the Danube and its tributaries. The twin basins of the Save and Drave afforded them westerly routes of penetration without, however, providing channels of southerly advance. The watershed coinciding roughly with easterly longitude 21° in Albania and attaining the Pindus mountains therefore remained closed land to the Slavs. As a result Albania and Macedonia are to be considered as areas in which Romance speech once prevailed. The signs of this linguistic relation are numerous in Albania because the country is less open to invasion than the Macedonian basin.

A territory of Romance languages extending continuously from the Atlantic to the Black Sea probably existed prior to the immigration of Slavs into southeastern Europe. The areas of Romansh, Friulian, Ladin, Albanian and Rumanian are remnants of this ancient language zone. Even the Slavic language of the

Macedonian peasant is a layer superimposed on the linguistic stratum prevailing before the period of Slavic invasion. It is therefore about thirteen centuries old. The changes undergone by the earlier form of Macedonian in this span of centuries have been so sweeping as to obliterate altogether the character of the pre-Slavic tongue. Rumanian vernaculars of the Pindus extended therefore to the east and not improbably into Thrace. A claim

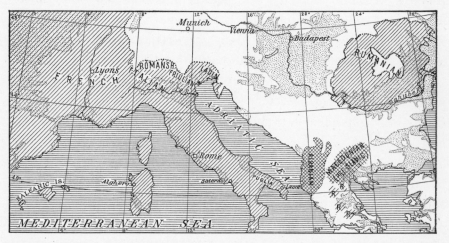

FIG. 43—The easterly sweep of Romance languages. The dotted areas are low-lands. Romance languages are spoken in the diagonally ruled areas. Cross-ruling represents the connecting areas between eastern and western Romance languages. Pindus localities in which Rumanian is spoken are indicated by R. Scale, 1:12,500,000.

upon Macedonia based on this assumption has even been put forward by Rumanians.[16]

No fair conception of the character of the Rumanian population can be attained without thorough realization of the extent to which the land has been open to the invasions of Asiatic nomads of the steppes. The intensity of this movement can be ascertained for the historical period. Back of that time, however, the interminable stretch of centuries must have been character-ized by the same inflow from the east, else the Rumanian population would not betray today such distinctly Tatar ear-marks. The eastern sections of the country, those nearest to,

---

[16] A. A. C. Stourdza: L'Héroïsme des Roumains au Moyen-Âge et le caractère de leurs anciennes institutions, Paris, 1911.

and forming practically a continuation of Russia, teem with settlements of pure Tatars.

The earliest inhabitants of Rumania are tall, dark brachycephs —the Cevenoles of Deniker's classification. This original element has been repeatedly diluted by Slavic and Tatar percolation. The Roman conquest, which together with the "pax Romana" brought civilization to the land, was not an ethnical victory. The Romans, a mere minority of leaders, ruled in the land much after the fashion in which the British govern India at present. But this occupation of the land by men representing a superior civilization sufficed to stamp the speech of Rome upon Rumania.

Rumania's past differed from that of the other Balkan nations. During the centuries in which the destiny of the ancient world was controlled largely by Byzantine statesmen, Moldavia and Wallachia seldom took part in the quarrels that pitted Slavs against Greeks. Balkan conflicts seemed then to be restricted to the populations living south of the Danube. Excellent relations were maintained between the rulers of Rumanian principalities and the Byzantine court. It was always felt at Constantinople, throughout the centuries of bitter struggle against Islam's waxing might, that the voivodes' aid against the Turks was assured.

After the terrible blow inflicted on Christendom by the fall of Constantinople, the two principalities of the northern Danubian bank managed to preserve autonomy. This is a highly significant fact in Rumanian history, for it meant that the country was spared the effects of racial blendings or upheavals consequent to the Ottoman occupation of southeastern Europe. Religious and national antagonism between the various elements of the Christian populations under the Sultan's rule were incessantly fostered by the Turks as a means of consolidating their own sovereignty.

The rôle played by Rumania during the long period of Christian servitude entitles the country to the gratitude of the other Balkan states. The land beyond the Danube became a haven to which victims of Mohammedan persecution repaired whenever possible. Noblemen despoiled of their estates, traders menaced with execution for having claimed payment of debts incurred towards them by the followers of the Prophet, students whose only crime consisted of having interpreted Christian doctrines to their co-religionists, all found refuge under the banner of the cross flying on the north bank of the Danube. Hungary itself has incurred a heavy debt of obligation to Rumania, for both Moldavia and Wallachia served as a buffer against which Turkish blows directed at Magyar power spent themselves in vain.

The province of Bukovina, once the borderland between Rumanians and Ruthenians, has become in modern times the meeting place of both peoples. According to recent Austrian statistics its population is as follows:

	1900	1910
Germans	159,486	168,851
Bohemians and Slovakians	596	1,005
Poles	26,857	26,210
Ruthenians	297,798	305,101
Slovenes	108	80
Serbo-Croatians	6	1
Italians	119	36
Rumanians	229,018	273,254
Hungarians	9,516	10,391
Total	723,504	784,929 [17]

The Rumanians and Ruthenians are the oldest and most numerous inhabitants of Bukovina. The former are generally confined to the southeastern districts of the province while the majority of the Ruthenians inhabit the northwest. The mountainous sections are peopled by the Huzuli, a folk whose speech and customs contain traces of Slavic influence. The remainder

---

[17] Divided according to religion, the census of 1910 shows the following figures:

Roman Catholics	98,565
Greek Catholics	26,182
Armenian Catholics	657
Orthodox Greeks	547,603
Gregorian Armenians	341
Lipps	3,232
Protestant sects	20,518
Jews	102,919
Unaccounted	86
Total	800,103

of the inhabitants of Bukovina consists of descendants of immigrants who settled in the province about five or six centuries ago.

Germans, mostly traders and artisans from Transylvania and Galicia, made their first appearance in Bukovina in the fourteenth century. Occasionally German priests and warriors

FIG. 44—Sketch map of the Rumanian area (diagonally ruled) in Bukovina and Hungary. The blank area is overwhelmingly Slavic (Little Russians or Ruthenians). The dotted patches in Hungary represent areas of Hungarian speech.

would also find their way into the province and decide to settle permanently within its borders. A fresh impetus to German colonization was given by the fall of Bukovina into Austrian hands in 1774. Under the rule of Maria Theresa and Emperor Joseph II Germans of all classes and conditions were induced to seek the province and Germanize the land. They came as officials, teachers, soldiers and merchants and took up their abode generally in special cities.[18]

This German element was derived chiefly from Swabia, Bohemia and German Austria. The Swabians were the earliest colonists and are found scattered in the best farming districts of the province.[19] The Zips of northern Hungary are generally found in the mountains of southwestern Bukovina which they had occupied originally as miners.[20]

The Hungarians of Bukovina are not descendants of immigrants from Hungary but from Rumania. Their ancestors were the Magyars and Szeklers who had been dispatched by Hungarian kings to defend the passes of Transylvania. After Bukovina's annexation to Austria, efforts were made to induce the descendants of the old frontier guardsmen to live within Austrian boundaries. The call was heeded by many who as a result selected Bukovina as residence. One of the earliest colonies was founded at Istensegitz, while Hadikfalva and Andreasfalva became sites of their settlements during the reign of Emperor Joseph.

The Poles emigrated to the province mainly from Galicia between the years 1786 and 1849. They are found scattered in the larger cities, notably at Czernowitz. The Slovaks came later. Prior to the nineteenth century they had no colonies of any importance in Bukovina. In 1803 they appear around the glass factories near Crasna, where they were employed as woodcutters. Between 1830 and 1840 they founded the settlements of Neusolonetz and Pojana-Mikuli.

Many Bukovinan localities are inhabited by Lippowans, who are Great Russians and who on the basis of language are considered as Ruthenians by Austrian census-takers. The Lippowans

---

[18] Czernowitz, Storozynetz, Sereth, Suczava, Radautz, Gurahumora, Kimpolung were among the cities most often selected.

[19] Their colonies are found at Rosh, Molodia, Tereblestie, Hliboka, St. Onufri, Altfratanz, Milleschoutz, Arbora, Itzkani, Ilischestie, Unterstanestie, Storozynetz, Neuzadowa.

[20] Their settlements are found at Jakobeny, Kirlibaba, Luisenthal, Pozoritta, Eisenau, Freudenthal, Bukschoja and Stulpikani.

belong to the sect of Old Believers which seceded from the
Russian Orthodox Church in the middle of the seventeenth century. Persecution forced them to flee to neighboring countries
and they flocked in large numbers into Bukovina. Their descendants now inhabit principally the towns of Mitoka-Dragomirna
and Klimutz as well as neighboring villages.

By the acquisition of Bukovina in 1777 the Hapsburgs
increased their territory by about 6,200 sq. m. (10,000 sq. km.)
and a population of 75,000 inhabitants, consisting largely of
Rumanians.[21] Nistor estimates the population at the time of this
annexation at 56,700 Rumanians, about 15,000 Ruthenians at the
most and 5,000 Huzulis, who, from the border bandits that they
were, settled finally in western Bukovina.[22] According to
Rumanian historians the Slavic element of Bukovina was
negligible in the fourteenth century. It was a common occurrence
for Ruthenian peasants to escape from Polish serfdom and settle
in Moldavia, the land of free farmers. The fugitives, dribbling
on Rumanian soil in small numbers, became merged in the mass
of the native population. The consolidation of large estates in
the seventeenth century and the resulting agricultural boom
obliged landowners to induce peasants of neighboring countries
to settle in Bukovina. The emigration of many Ruthenians can
be accounted for by this economic change.

After the Turkish conquest of Kamieniec-Podolski the new
provinces of the Dniester valley were populated by Slavs drawn
from among Little Russians. The district of Hotin in eastern
Bukovina was colonized at that time. Again Sobieski's victories
over the Turks were followed by a temporary Polish occupation
of northern and western Moldavia and a renewed inflow of Slavs.

Ruthenian invasion of the soil of Bukovina persisted steadily
from the eighteenth century on. Galician serfs were driven by
oppression to this hitherto unexploited territory. In 1779 the

---

[21] Today the predominance of Ruthenians in Bukovina is contested by Rumanians
who claim that Austrian statistics are deliberately padded.

[22] I. Nistor: Romănŭ si Ruteniĭ in Bucovina, studiu istoric si statistu, Bucarest,
1915, p. 72.

number of Ruthenians in Bukovina was estimated at 21,114. Tombstones of that date found between the Dniester and the Pruth are almost entirely in Rumanian. In 1848 the Ruthenian element in the province numbered 108,907 against 208,293 Rumanians. The census of 1910 places the number of Russian-speaking inhabitants at 305,101, while the users of Rumanian are placed at 273,254. Rumanian authorities, however, call attention to the fact that these figures are determined on the basis of the language most commonly used and not on that of the inherited mother tongue.

Rumanian also holds easy predominance in the strange medley of languages which can be heard in the Russian province of Bessarabia. The region forms a natural extension of Moldavia, east of the Pruth furrow, and has always been intimately connected with Rumanian life. It became part of the Czar's dominion in 1812, after the treaty of Bucarest of May 28 of that year, but the southern part was reincorporated with the principality of Moldavia after the Crimean war. This section was restored, however, to Russia by a decision of the Congress which met in Berlin in June 1878. It has since remained Russian territory. These changes, no less than its position as the narrow corridor between the Asiatic steppeland and southern Europe, have made it the meeting land of Europe's most untutored elements.

The broad hilly spurs bounded by the Dniester and the Pruth contain the bulk of these Bessarabian Rumanians, who make up half the population of the province or nearly one million souls. Interspersed with this native element, German colonists and Bulgarian immigrants,—the latter brought wholesale in the course of Turkey's European recessional,—and Serbian or Greek cultivators are to be found in many of the villages that nestle in the broad and smiling valleys of the low plateau. The flat marshy tracts along the Pruth and at the mouth of the Danube are occupied by Cosacks and Tatars, while a numerous gipsy element manages to subsist on the rest of the inhabitants by juggling or fortune telling, or frequently by pilfering.

The national consolidation of the Rumanians of Bukovina, the Banat and Bessarabia with the main body would supply a non-Slavic linguistic wedge between Russians and Balkan Slavs. But apart from this linguistic difference, Rumanian life and institutions present close analogies with their Russian counterparts. From the standpoint of the anthropologist both countries contain a Slavic substratum strongly diluted by Tatar infiltration. Religious views nursed and cherished in the Kremlin hold spiritual sway throughout the length and breadth of Rumania. And yet, in spite of such strong bonds, and that of immediate neighborhood, language with nationality remains sharply distinct in the two kingdoms.

CHAPTER IX

THE BALKAN PENINSULA AND ITS SERBIAN INHABITANTS

THE Balkan peninsula presents in its physical features a clue to our understanding of the development of separate languages and nationalities within its area. Its mountainous center has always exerted a centrifugal action on Balkan peoples. This influence has been strengthened by the existence of important routes to the mainland of Europe and of Asia. Throughout historical times the region formed, with Asia Minor, a natural bridge joining the east with the west. Before mankind had begun to record its past, it had afforded a natural passage for the westerly migrations of Asiatic peoples. Today the region bids fair to maintain the same connecting rôle. But in future the human stream appears destined to be directed towards the east.

Physical environment forced Asiatic tribes to rove because the barren steppes of their birthplace failed to provide more than could be harvested at a single halt. These ancestors of the modern Khirgiz poured into Europe from protohistoric times. They were herded along by nature toward that most favored parallel of latitude, the fortieth, near which civilization has flourished preëminently. In their quest for sustenance they wandered along a path that led far into Europe as well as toward the smiling regions bordering the Mediterranean basin. Here fertility of soil and propitious climate rendered settlement possible.

How readily the peninsula affords easy access between Europe and Asia can be gathered from the map. The narrow watercourse which begins at the Ægean mouth of the Dardanelles and extends to the Black Sea entrance of the Bosporus provides, at both its extremities, the shortest fording places between the two continents. At Chanak, on the Dardanelles, about one mile and

Fig. 45—The Bosporus seen mid-channel at its narrowest point.

FIG. 46—A bit of Sarajevo with ample evidence of former Turkish rule over the Serbians of Bosnia.

a half of channel separates the peninsula of Gallipoli from the Anatolian coast. The very outline of the European shore is symbolical, for in the Thracian and Gallipoli promontories the Balkan peninsula seems to stretch out two welcoming arms to Asia and thus invite intercourse. South of the straits, the deeply indented coast lines of Greece and of Asia Minor teemed with matchless harbors. Their shores became the birthplace of adventurous sailors. The Ægean itself, with its numerous islands, provided so many stepping-stones jutting out of its choppy waters to aid daring pioneers in their expeditions.

Every race of Europe and of western Asia has marched at some time or other through the valleys that extend in varying width between the uplifts rising south of the Danube and the Save. The attempt to determine the original element is almost futile in the face of the constant stream of invaders. To go back only to the period following the one in which the Thracians dotted the southeastern area with their quaint tumuli we find the peninsula already settled by Illyrians on its western border. The Albanians are supposed to be direct descendants of this ancient people. Secluded in their mountain fastnesses from contact with subsequent invaders of the peninsula, they best represent today the type of the peninsular inhabitant of about 2000 B.C. To the east the basin of the Danube was peopled subsequently by Dacians and Gaetes, who presumably were the ancestors of the peasants now occupying the Dobrudja.

North of the boundary-defining rivers dwelt the Scythians and the Sarmatians. The story of their migrations is the same for different epochs. It tells either of the appearance of sturdy barbarians before whose dash the settlers, somewhat effete on account of acquired comfort, give way. Or else it is the tale of the settler who has had time to organize his forces into orderly fighters and whose disciplined bands go forth to conquer new territory at the behest of his civilization. Thus did Roman legions sweep away the barriers to the acquisition of new colonies.

Following the Roman occupation of the peninsula a steady flow of uncouth northerners began to appear. Under the names of Sarmatians, Goths of various sorts, Huns, Bulgarians to whom the Byzantines gave their appellation because they came from the banks of the Volga, and Avars, they spread havoc far beyond the western limits of the Adriatic. These barbarians were followed by Slavs. The eastbound journeys of the Crusaders next intervene; then a final mighty onslaught of Turkish hordes whose savage fury seemed for a moment to obliterate the laboriously-reared western civilization.

To this bewildering succession of human types the extraordinary complexity of stock characterizing the present population of the peninsula is directly ascribable, each race or people having left some trace of its passage. The compilation of an ethnographical map of the region results in the representation of the most mosaic-like surface imaginable. Nor are the actual evidences of these ancient invasions lacking to the observant eye. Take, for instance, the fair-haired, blue-eyed Greeks, totally devoid of traces of nigrescence, who are by no means uncommon in Macedonia.[1] In them the Nordic type, due in part to the Achæan conquerors, has survived. To this day the tourist, wandering in any town formerly occupied by the Turks, may suddenly behold in the streets as pure a Mongolian type as is to be found on the highlands of western central China. In the Bosnian town of Sarajevo, as in the Macedonian villages north of the Ægean, the ugly features of these Asiatics often reveal but too plainly their origin.

Traces of these wanderings have lingered in the relics of former habitat observable in Balkan countries. Any one whom fate has made the guest of Turkish hosts will remember how toward bedtime rolled bundles leaning vertically against the corners of the rooms are brought out and laid open on the floor. These are the beds which the members of the household use. They consist of a mattress, sheets and blankets which had been removed during the day from the mat over which it is customary to spread them at night. Although it is centuries since the Turk

---

[1] I have also seen this type among Anatolian Greeks. It is observable among Greeks living in New York.

has ceased living in tents, he still adheres to this custom of his nomad forefathers. The fact is observable in the two-storied dwellings of the Mohammedan sections of Adrianople or Constantinople. But the practical conversion of bedrooms into sitting rooms is only one of the many phases of Turkish indoor life which recall tent life. Rooms altogether destitute of furniture are quite usual. I am now referring to the average Turkish home —not to the relatively few in which European customs are observed. In the majority of cases the only furniture consists of rugs spread on the walls and floors. Articles of household use are kept in closets. No chairs or tables help to relieve the bareness. At meals the family will squat in groups around circular trays supported on low stools. A bowl of "yoghurt," or curdled milk, is the invariable accompaniment of each repast. Indulgence in this preparation is observable with similar frequency in a broad belt which begins in the Balkan peninsula and extends eastward between parallels 45° and 35° of latitude to Mongolia. Signs pointing to Asiatic origins can likewise be witnessed outside the houses in Turkish cities. The national coat of arms, conspicuously displayed over the gates of government buildings, bears two horsetails surmounting the Prophet's coat. In this emblem we see Tatar chieftains' insignia of rank which have been coupled to Mohammedan symbolism.

In this same line of thought we find that traditions furnish evidence of a remarkably significant character. A tradition flourishes to this day among the Turks that their occupation of European territory could not be permanent. Often have I heard this voiced by Turks who simultaneously added by way of explanation that it could not be otherwise, since they were Asiatics. It is this feeling which lies at the root of the Turk's unwillingness to be buried on the European side of the Bosporus or the Dardanelles. The same sentiment accounts for their relatively larger burying grounds along the Asiatic shores bordering the peninsula, as compared with those on the European coast.

In the present era of world-wide industrial expansion, the Balkan region retains its place as one of the most notable of international highways. So centrally is the peninsula situated with reference to Europe, Asia and Africa that its valleys afford the most convenient overland passage for the products of European ingenuity and science on their way to market in the populous centers of Asia and Africa. Even the air line connecting central Europe and India passes over the Balkans. The superiority of the Mediterranean–Red Sea route over the other avenues of traffic leading from west to east led to the construction of the Suez Canal. The advantages of this line still exist. With the march of events, however, the main commercial thoroughfare from Europe to the Orient is shifting gradually from the waters between the Eurasian and African continents to a more easterly and at the same time far speedier overland route. The tracks of the Oriental, Anatolian and Bagdad railroad companies form at present the northern section of the trunk of this system. Incidentally, it should be noted that nature's provision for this world route is so well marked in the Balkan peninsula that the luxurious cars of the Orient Express roll over a steel-clad path which coincides remarkably with the trail followed by the first crusade— the one which Godfrey de Bouillon led along a path marked by nature. The prolongation of these railroads to Delhi and the shores of the Indian Ocean by junction with the railroads of British India advancing toward the northwest is now economically desirable.

Through connection with the Cape of Good Hope by way of Ma'an and the Egyptian frontier, over the Sinai peninsula and the Cape-to-Cairo line, will probably be exacted by the requirements of trade. In that case railroad ferries over the Bosporus will enable the same car to be hauled directly from the coast of the Baltic Sea to the shores of the Indian Ocean or to cities at the southernmost points of Africa. There is reason to believe, however, the Bosporus will be crossed by a bridge over the half mile of sea that separates the European and Asiatic fortresses facing each other at Rumeli Hissar.

Within the Balkan peninsula every economic need which has determined the foreign policy of the several states is related to

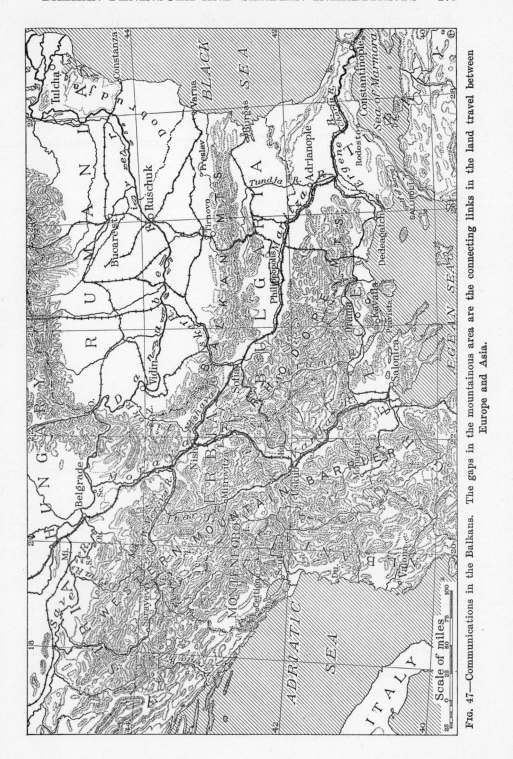

Fig. 47—Communications in the Balkans. The gaps in the mountainous area are the connecting links in the land travel between Europe and Asia.

a given feature of the land. The seaward thrust of Serbia towards the Adriatic is naturally directed along the narrow Drin valley, cutting across the long chain of the Dinaric Alps. But the country's efforts to obtain mastery of this important gap were blocked by the creation of an independent Albania. Bulgaria's trade and industrial development is likewise hampered by the lack of a favorable issue towards southern seas. At present the connection between the east-west mountainous country formed by the Balkan ranges and the lowland extending to the Ægean involves the climbing of steep slopes. Bulgarians therefore naturally coveted the Struma valley which runs in Greek territory to the west of the Chalcidic peninsula. The Montenegrins living in a rocky land which cannot support its inhabitants look covetously on the narrow defiles which lead towards the Adriatic and their longing for Scutari is merely for the possession of agricultural lands. War with the Turks once forced them to retreat into their mountains. Now that that danger is over they are coming out of their fastnesses and endeavoring to resume intercourse with the outside world.

Geography is therefore stamping its impress on the political status of the modern inhabitants of the Balkan peninsula. We have just seen how this region forms a section of a great international commercial route. Coupling this fact with industrial requirements which find expression in the demand for unhampered right of way for products of toil and thought in transit to market, it can be understood how great European powers keenly desire to secure control, or at least maintenance of equal rights of passage, over an avenue so happily situated. The matter is vital because it is based on economic grounds. Continued operation of many Old World factories, or their shut-down, often depends on conditions prevailing on the site of that battle royal of diplomacy known as the Eastern Question. The matter of Serbia's access to the Adriatic or the withholding of Austria's acquiescence to Montenegrin occupation of Scutari must, therefore, be ultimately explained by the geographical causes which have converted the peninsula into a highway of such importance that the paramount influence of a single nation over its extension cannot be tolerated by the others. A clear view of this fundamental principle leads us to realize that the presentation of an ultimatum to Serbia by Austria on July 23, 1914, was the preliminary step toward opening a pathway for Germany and Austria to Salonica and Constantinople. Then, as soon as Austro-German power should be solidly established athwart the Bosporus, the intention was to secure control of the land routes to Egypt, the Persian Gulf and India.

As matters stand at present the balance of power oscillates between two groups represented by Teutonic and Slavonic elements respectively. Their clashing zone is the Balkan peninsula. The "Drang nach Osten" of Pan-Germanism found concrete geographical expression on the map, in 1908, by Austria's final absorption of Bosnia and Herzegovina. A further step in the same direction was marked by the creation of a new Balkan nation, Albania. All this was a result of efforts to obtain control of the remarkable highway we have been considering. This easterly spread was hampered, however, by the steady southerly progress made by the Balkan countries. Their victories in 1912 and 1913 lengthened perceptibly Russia's southwesterly strides toward ice-free coasts. The process taken as a whole is one of recurrence. Time has converted the stream of early Asiatic invaders into these two opposing currents. The Teutons are now repeating the exploits of the Greeks, the Macedonians, the Byzantines and the Crusaders. The Slavs, whose differentiation from Altaic ancestors has not been as thorough as that of their western neighbors, are likewise playing anew the part of their forefathers seeking milder regions by way of the Balkan peninsula.

South of the Hungarian and Slovene linguistic zones the Austro-Hungarian domain comprises a large portion of the area of Serbian speech. The language predominates everywhere from the Adriatic coast to the Drave and Morava rivers as well as up to the section of the Danube comprised between its points of confluence with these two rivers. Serbian in fact extends slightly east of the Morava valley towards the Balkan slopes lying north of the Timok river, where Rumanian prevails as the language of the upland.[2] To the south contact with Albanian is obtained. The area of Serbian speech thus delimited includes the independent kingdoms of Montenegro [3] and Serbia. Within the territory of the Dual Monarchy it is spoken in the provinces of Croatia, Slavonia, Bosnia, Herzegovina and Dalmatia. The language is therefore essentially that of the region of uplift which connects the Alps and the Balkans or which intervenes between the Hungarian plain and the Adriatic.

Union between the inhabitants of this linguistic area is somewhat hampered by the scission of Serbians into three religious groups. The westernmost Serbs, who are also known as Croats, adhere to the Roman Catholic faith in common with all their kinsmen the western Slavs. Followers of this group are rarely met east of the 19th meridian. A Mohammedan body consisting of descendants of Serbs who had embraced Islam after the Turkish conquest clusters round Sarajevo as a center. The bulk of Serbians belong, however, to the Greek Orthodox Church. Cultural analogies between the Mohammedan and orthodox groups are numerous. Both use the Russian alphabet, whereas the Croats have adopted Latin letters.

Much has been made in interested quarters of the difference between Catholic Croat and Orthodox Serb. Intrigues directed from Vienna and Budapest have sought to accentuate these differences and to foment hatred where Christian charity would speedily have produced concord and understanding. Even in Russia, there have been fears lest close political contact between Serb and Croat dilute the purity of Serb orthodoxy. In other quarters political ambition has made use of divergence of creed as a pretext for seeking to perpetuate political division between

---

[2] Serbian authorities usually extend the zone of their vernacular to points farther east. Cf. J. Cvijić: Die ethnographische Abspreuzung der Völker auf der Balkanhalbinsel, *Pet. Mitt.*, Vol. 59, 1913, No. 1, pp. 113-118.

[3] Montenegro is peopled by descendants of Serbians who took refuge in its mountains after the crushing defeat of Serbia by Turkey on the battlefield of Kossovo in 1389.

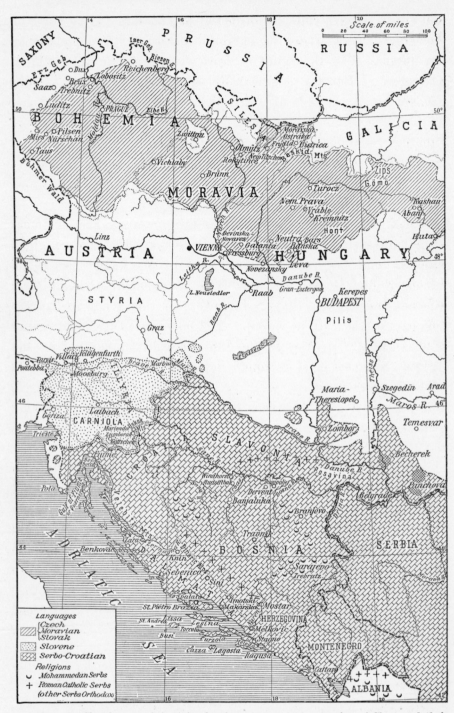

FIG. 48—Sketch map of Austria showing westernmost extension of Slavs and their
languages in Europe. The German-Hungarian wedge between northern and southern
Slavs is shown. The small cross-ruled patches are areas of Rumanian language.

the two main branches of the southern Slav race.   But a Serbian saying, which can be heard in Bosnia, Croatia or Montenegro, is the best refutation of the existence of any political differences between Serbs of different creeds.   "Brat yay mio Koye vieray bio," "A brother is always dear whatever his religion."   A simple phrase, but one with national significance.

The Serbo-Croatian group made its appearance in the Balkan peninsula at the time of the general westerly advance of Slavs in the fifth and sixth centuries.   A northwestern body of this people, wandering along the river valleys leading to the eastern Alpine foreland, settled in the regions now known as Croatia and Slavonia.   Here the sea and inland watercourses provided natural communication with western Europe.   Evolution of this northwestern body of Serbians into the Croatians of our day was facilitated by the infiltration of western ideas.   But the great body of Serbians, occupying the mountainous area immediately to the south, had their foreign intercourse necessarily confined to eastern avenues of communication.   They therefore became permeated with an eastern civilization in which Byzantine strains can be easily detected.

In spite of these cultural divergences, the linguistic differentiation of the Croat from the Serbian element has been slight. The Serbian sound of "ay" is generally pronounced "yay" by Bosnians and "a" by Dalmatians.   The Croatian "tcha" corresponds to the "chto" of the Serbian.   As a rule variations are slight, and natives of the different districts not only understand each other, but can also detect respective home districts quite readily on hearing each other.

Today the political aspirations of this compact mass of Serbians are centered around the independent kingdom of Serbia, which is regarded as the nucleus around which a greater Serbia comprising all the Serbian-speaking inhabitants of the Balkan peninsula will group.   This Serbo-Croatian element is estimated to comprise at least 10,300,000 individuals.[4]   The southern Slav

---

[4] J. Erdeljanović: Broj Srba i Khrvata, Belgrade, 1911.

question centers chiefly around the fate of those unredeemed populations. The Near Eastern Question cannot be settled without cutting away from Austria-Hungary, and uniting with Serbia and Montenegro, all the southern Slav provinces of the Hapsburg crown. It is stated of Metternich that he had openly proclaimed his belief in the necessity of annexing Serbia to either Turkey or Austria. That was in the day, however, when popular claims counted for little.

Southern Slav unity and independence are both necessary to Europe. Serbia, or rather Serbo-Croatia or "Jugoslavia," is reared on a land-gap that provides Europe with a gateway to the east. The freedom of Balkan peoples and to a great extent the freedom of Europe depend upon the power of the southern Slavs to hold the gate. It is therefore to the advantage of European countries to strengthen the southern Slavs by every means in their power. A partial unity that would leave any considerable portion of Jugoslavia unredeemed would but divert southern Slav energy into irredentist channels and deflect it from its chief mission.

The ties which unite Serbians and Croatians have led writers to consider the two peoples as one under the name of Serbo-Croatians.[5] In the eleventh century Skilitzer, a Byzantine writer, alludes to the "Croatians, who are called Serbians." Little distinction was made between their tribes when they first made their appearance in Balkan lands. Both peoples are Slavs and it is not unlikely that they are derived from a common stock. The location of the territory they occupied affords a clue to the origin of differences between them. Their homelands lie on the confines of the two Roman empires which ruled respectively over eastern and western Europe. It was natural that some groups of the Serbo-Croatian element should follow the religious leadership of Rome while others rallied to the Orthodox teachings of Byzantium. The main distinction between Serbians and Croatians is found in this diversity of religious views.

[5] E. Haumant: La nationalité serbo-croate, *Ann. de Géogr.*, No. 127, Vol. 23, Jan. 15, 1914, pp. 45-59.

From a geographical standpoint the area of Serbian speech presents excessive diversity of features. National unity within its bounds is therefore apt to be sorely hampered. Dalmatia, teeming with islands and fiords, enjoys the advantage of easy access to all its districts by way of the sea. The Dinaric Alps separate it, however, from the land of the ancient kingdom of Serbia which arose on the basins of the Save and Morava. The two areas form in reality isolated compartments. A capital suitable to both cannot be located. Belgrade or Nish is appropriate enough for the valley of the Danube, Spalato or Ragusa for the coastland. Uskub is perhaps more centrally situated on the road connecting the Danube to the Adriatic. But this city also belongs to the eastern watershed of the isolating mountains. Whatever be the political destiny of this linguistic area, it is bound to be divided into two parts with outlets respectively on the Adriatic and the Danube.

Between the sixth and thirteenth centuries, the Serbian invaders of the Balkan peninsula grouped themselves into a number of independent tribes. The Serbian state to which the smaller units adhered politically came into being in the thirteenth century. That it was inhabited by a prosperous people is proven by numerous works of art which are still preserved in the churches of the land. A hundred years later the kingdom of Serbia attains its widest extension. Under Stephen Dushan, the country spreads from the Black Sea to the Adriatic and from the Danube and Save valleys to the Ægean. In 1346 Dushan is crowned emperor at Uskub. He is about to march on Constantinople, but death puts an end to this project. Henceforth Serbian power is to be on the wane. The appearance of the Turks in the Balkans in the last decade of the fourteenth century marks the end of Serbian independence. In the ensuing four hundred years, Serbian lands and their inhabitants are the prey of merciless Asiatics. The devastating grip of Turkish oppression begins to be relaxed in 1815 when, under the leadership of Miloch Obrenovitch, the Serbians laid the foundation of their modern independence by forcing the Turks to grant them a partial self-government. Thence to the year 1867 political emancipation from Turkey progressed steadily.

The Adriatic Sea alone provides the Serbo-Croatian peoples with a definite boundary. The line of the Drave on the north once formed a frontier for the twin group. In modern times a number of Croatian settlements have pushed forward along the Raab valley toward Slovak territory. Here they stand in danger of becoming lost in the midst of the Hungarian population, as were the Serbian settlements which in the seventeenth century were scattered as far as Budapest. On the southwest, the boundary of the Serbian linguistic area presents many obstacles to accurate delimitation. There was a time when all northern Albania was part of the Serbian empire. In the eleventh century the Serbian kingdom, established in the Lake Scutari district, comprised Albanian populations within its boundaries. Immediately before the Turkish conquest Serbian language and customs had advanced as far south as Epirus. The coming of the Asiatics caused profound changes in the distribution of Balkan populations through the conversions to Mohammedanism by which it was attended. Many Serbians who had penetrated to the south and a large number of Albanians became followers of the Prophet. Their descendants became ''Turks'' and as such endured the vicissitudes which marked the decline of Ottoman power. The Serbian element lost its individuality in the midst of Albanians. A record of its former advance in northern Albania subsists in the Serbian villages which are scattered in the region.

Small areas of Serbian are found at Zumberak and Mariondol on the southern slope of the Uskok mountains in Croatia near the Carniola boundary. These Serbian groups occur on the border line separating Croats from Slovenes. They were founded by refugees from the south and east who had settled in the military confines of the Empire previous to 1871. In 1900 the population of Mariondol consisted of a few hundred inhabitants, many of whom have since emigrated to the United States. In Zumberak for the same year the number of inhabitants was estimated at

11,842, of whom 7,151 were "uniats" and 4,691 Catholics.[6]   The conversion of these Serbians from Greek orthodoxy was accomplished in the eighteenth century.

Scattered Serbian settlements are found between the Danube and Theiss valleys as far north as Maria-Theresiopel and farther south at Zombor and Neusatz.   The rich corn-growing districts southeast of Fünfkirchen (Pechui) contain some of the most important Serbian centers in Hungary.   Serbian is the language of the entire district of confluence of the Theiss and Danube as well as of many colonies in the Banat of Temesvar.   Religious diversity alone has prevented fusion of these Serbians with the Hungarian majority of the land.   Whenever they come into contact with Rumanians of the same religion the Serbians lose ground and become merged in the bosom of the Latin population. "A Rumanian woman in the house," says the Serbian proverb, "means a Rumanian home."   Such Rumanian households are now solidly established north and south of the Danube valley in the northeastern angle of Serbia where a century ago they were practically non-existent.[7]

Among these Serbian settlements of southern Hungary those in the Banat of Temesvar are the most important. Temesvar itself although an ancient seat of Serbian voivodes [8] contains fewer Serbians than Germans and Hungarians.   The Slavs however occupy the western part of the Banat and form majorities between Zombor and Temesvar, Becherek and Panchova.   Around Maria-Theresiopel (also known as Subotica or Szabadka) the Serbian element contains many Roman Catholics —the so-called Bunjevci, who were emigrants from former Turkish provinces, mainly Herzegovina.

The old sanjak of Novibazar, which became part of Serbia after the last Balkan war, is largely Serbian in people and

[6] N. Zupanić: Zumbercani i Marindolci, prilog antropologii i etnografiji Srba u Kranjskoj Prosvetni Glasnik, Belgrade, 1912.

[7] E. Haumant: La nationalité serbo-croate, *Ann. de Géogr.*, No. 127, Vol. 23, Jan. 15, 1914, p. 48.

[8] A. Evans: The Adriatic Slavs and the Overland Route to Constantinople, *Geogr. Journ.*, Vol. 47, No. 4, April 1916, p. 251.

Fig. 49.

Fig. 50.

Fig. 49—The broken aspect of the Dalmatian coastland is strongly represented in this view of Lussinpiccolo and surrounding islets.

Fig. 50—Usual landscape in mountainous Montenegro.

speech.   In the long centuries of Mohammedan rule the Turks
had become possessors of the majority of cultivated lands.' But
the task of farming was left entirely in the hands of the Serbian
peasants—whether of Mohammedan creed and known as Bosh-
naks, or Christians.   The Moslem element as a rule resided in
the towns which grew around a castle or fortress.

From the twelfth to the fourteenth century the great commercial route which led from the Adriatic at Ragusa to Nish and
Byzantium passed through Sienitza and Novibazar.   Prosperity
never since equaled flowed with the commerce from Venetian
cities and the Dalmatian coast to the Orient.   The districts of
the sanjak then boasted of denser and wealthier populations.
The Turkish conquest, however, diverted this trade route into
the Morava valley with the result that the erstwhile frequented
sanjak became almost completely isolated and neglected.   West
of the Lim the sanjak has always been predominantly Serbian.
East of this river the pure Serbian type is preserved in the districts of Stari Vlah, Novi Varosh and Berane.   The region's
earliest inhabitants are found in the secluded gorges of the Tara
and the Ograyevitza tableland.   Albanian settlements are met
in Peshtera and Roshai.

Like Albania, Bosnia was originally peopled by Illyrians, a
people of Alpine race whose living representatives are found
among the Skipetars or rockmen of Albania.   Although the land
was conquered by the Romans, its inhabitants were never thoroughly Romanized.   The mountainous character of Bosnia accounts
for this failure of Latinism.   Many traces of the Roman invasion
are being continually discovered on the sites of ancient military
camps and in inscriptional remains which are frequently unearthed
in the territory comprised between the Adriatic and the Danube.
Dalmatia and Pannonia were the two provinces into which the
Romans had subdivided the region for administrative purposes.
The Slavs who began to appear in the middle of the sixth century left a deep impress on the inhabitants.   The influence of
these latest comers is the only one that has prevailed to our day.

The coming of Hungarians in Europe may be likened to a

wedge driven into the mass of Slavic populations. The success
of these Asiatics brought about the separation of the southern
Slavs from their northern kinsmen. In the course of these
adjustments Bosnia and its inhabitants became part of the
kingdom of Croatia which originated in the valleys of the Drave
and Save. The province was administered by a Ban, who,
though a vassal of the Croatian crown, always managed to retain
a certain measure of independence.[9]

After the Hungarian conquest of Croatia, the Bans were
allowed to maintain their rule. Their policy consisted in culti-
vating friendly relations with the ruling element and at the same
time in drawing closer to the Serbian populations in the east.
The intimate connection between Serbia and Bosnia dates from
the end of the twelfth century. Two hundred years later Stephen
Turtko, the son of Serbia's greatest monarch, was crowned king
of Serbia, Bosnia and the Littoral provinces at the shrine of
Saint Sava. But the independence of Greater Serbia was short-
lived. Hungarian arms were soon in the ascendant and Bosnia
became a prey of feudal lords—a land divided against itself.

The Turks found it in this condition in the fifteenth century
and easily subdued its petty princes. They used their rights of
conquest to force Mohammedanism on the Bosnians. The mass
of the landed gentry accepted the Arabic faith in order to retain
possession of their property. Many of the Bosnian Mohammedans are descended from adherents of Bogomil heresies
who welcomed this method of finding relief from persecution.
The fanaticism of these converts and that of their descendants
became noteworthy even in the midst of Turkish religious
intolerance. It has delayed the expulsion of the Turks from this
region, prevented the consolidation of Bosnia with Serbia in the
early years of the nineteenth century and finally paved the way
for the Teutonic advance towards eastern lands.

The Austrian occupation of Bosnia in 1879 was followed by
a current of German immigration. The new settlers came from
Germany and the German-speaking provinces of Austria. To

---

[9] G. Blondel: La Bosnie, *Bull. Soc. Norm. de Géogr.*, Jan.-March 1912, p. 18.

weaken Serbian influence in the land the flow of this human tide was favored by the government. Engaging terms were offered to the colonists. The land they took up was turned into home-steads which became the property of the settler on easy terms, and after ten years' occupation Bohemians, Poles and Ruthenians were also lured to Bosnia. The Posavina district teems with these Slav immigrants. German peasants however were con-sidered the most desirable element in the eyes of Austrian officials. Through this migration Windhorst is now peopled mainly by Germans from the Rhine provinces and Rudolfthal by Tyrolese. Swabians from Hungary founded a large colony at Franz-Josefsfeld, while Germans from the same country created settlements at Branjevo and Dugopolje. Although these German emigrants constitute a numerically unimportant fraction of the Bosnian population, their presence has sufficed to warrant them the solicitude of Pan-Germanist writers in whose works they are referred to as "Our German brothers of Bosnia." [10]

By its geography, no less than racially, Bosnia is an integral portion of Serbia. For over a thousand years Bosnians and Serbians have had a mutually common civilization. The same historical and political vicissitudes have been shared by the two peoples. Common economic aims and the identity of inhabited territory have furthermore acted as unifying factors. Whatever be the name applied to Croats, Dalmatians, Slavonians, Bosnians or Serbs, all speak the Serbian language. All have striven for centuries to promote their individuality as a nation. To help them realize themselves as a political unit merely implies fur-thering the process begun by nature.

---

[10] C. Diehl: En Méditerranée, Paris, 1912.

CHAPTER X

LANGUAGE PROBLEMS OF THE BALKAN PENINSULA

The Serbian linguistic area, noticed in the preceding chapter, is both the political and physical link connecting central Europe with the Balkan peninsula. Beyond Serbia, to the south or southeast, the true Balkan domain is reached. This region is occupied chiefly by Greeks and Bulgarians. The Albanian and Rumanian populations of its western section, although distinct in speech, nevertheless lack the cultural and historical background required in the formation of nationality.

The Albanians inhabit the rugged lands which were known as Illyricum and Epirus in classical times. Secluded within the narrow, trough-shaped relics of ancient mountain folding, the natives had no immediate contact with their Greek neighbors on the south, or with Serbians on the north. Hence Albanian has survived in the most inaccessible portions of the Dinaric rocky country. In its grammar Skip or Modern Albanian is exclusively Aryan in form. Nevertheless only four hundred entries out of a total of 5,140 listed in G. Meyers' Etymological Dictionary of Albanian can be classified as unalloyed old Indo-European. The intrusion of Tatar modified into Turkish words is considerable and amounts to no less than 1,180 words. Romanic enters into the total to the extent of 1,420 forms, thus predominating. Some 840 words are Greek, while 540 are of Slavic origin.

In the belief of some etymologists the name Albania is related to the old Celtic form Alb or Alp, which means mountain. Comparison with the Celtic form "Albanach," used in Scotch vernacular to name the mountainous section of Scotland, is of utmost interest and significance. The Albanians, however, do not call themselves by this name. They designate themselves as Skipetars or rockmen, and apply this appellation indiscriminately to all the inhabitants of Upper and Lower Albania who do not use Greek, Serbian or Rumanian as a vernacular. Many resemblances in the language spoken by Albanians and Rumanians point to a probable early association of the two peoples.

Albania is still a land of mystery. Few European travelers have ventured within its inhospitable confines. It is a country without a master, a country where the head of every family is sole ruler of his inherited plot of land. It is scantily populated. Its inhabitants are divided into hostile groups by religion and tribal rivalry. No common aim on which to found nationality exists among them. The only bond that holds them together is perhaps their intolerance of alien authority.

Latitude divides the Skipetars into two main groups. A northern branch is known by the name of Gheks, while the dwellers of southern Albania go by the name of Tosks. The Skumbi river valley, running at right angles to the Adriatic, separates the country into the two sections inhabited by each of these peoples. Each of these branches is further divided by religion into Mohammedans and Christians. The Christian Gheks inhabit principally the valleys of the Drin and the Mati. The powerful Mirdite clan draws its adherents from this group. They are Roman Catholics and strongly under Italian influence, which dates back to the beginnings of Venetian trading on the eastern shores of the Mediterranean. The Christian Tosks have been affected by the views of the Eastern Church. Almost all recognize the religious authority of the Phanariot clergy. The Mirdites form a compact community to the south of the Drin. The group consists of some 300,000 individuals scattered over a territory about 375 sq. m. in extent. An hereditary chief is acknowledged head of the clan, his authority being even recognized by many non-Mirdite tribes. With their allies the Mirdites number approximately half a million souls while the clan's sphere of influence extends over a territory about 1,000 sq. m. in area.

Both of the Christian groups of the Albanian people have been mercilessly persecuted by the Mohammedan element, which represents the landed gentry and nobility of the country. The name of Arnaut applies generally to the Mohammedan Albanians. All are descendants of converts who embraced Islam at the time of the Turkish invasion. By adopting the faith of their conquerors, they were allowed to retain possession of their farms and property. The Christians became serfs, and were set to work on the lands under a system of feudal servitude which was exceedingly onerous.

The inhabitants of Albania are totally devoid of national feeling.[1] Various causes militate against national unity. Primeval patriotism, expressed by love of tribe rather than of country, is one of them. Furthermore the peculiar shape of their country transforms it into a number of compartment-like areas beyond which tribal activity rarely extends. The setting up of an independent state in 1913 was a purely political move undertaken by Austrian statesmen to prevent Serbian expansion to the Adriatic. Within the boundaries determined by the ambassadorial conference held in London in that year strife and dissensions prevail now as intensely as during the Turkish régime. Natives of the northern sections of the country speak Serbian dialects and favor union with Serbia or Montenegro rather than independence. Malisori tribesmen fought side by side with Montenegrin troops in the fall of 1912 as their ancestors had done in the campaign of 1711 against the Turks. The Albanians of Ipek, however, gave assistance to Turkish regulars. The inhabitants of the valley of the upper Morava sent supplies to Serbian troops against which the chieftains of central Albania led their men. The purest type

---

[1] Reliable estimates of the population of Albania are given by Petrovich in " Servia: Her People, History and Aspirations," London, 1915, p. 175. According to this author the country is inhabited by:

Arnauts (Mohammedans)	350,000
Tosks (Orthodox)	350,000
Mirdites (Roman Catholics)	300,000
Serbs (Orthodox)	250,000
Greeks (Orthodox)	150,000
Bulgarians (Orthodox)	50,000
Turks (Mohammedans)	50,000
Total	1,500,000

FIG. 51.

FIG. 52.

FIGS. 51 and 52—Albanians in native costume. The men shown in the upper photograph are "Arnauds" or Mohammedans. The lower illustration shows two Albanians of the shepherd class.

of Albanian found in the vicinity of Elbassan, Koritza and Valona[2] is practically submerged in a sea of Greeks. Under these circumstances, partition of the country between Greece and Serbia might not be incompatible with native aspirations. Political stability could be obtained in this case without paying attention to linguistic unity. Nevertheless Albania is not without national boundaries. The valley of the Drin and the range of the Pindus have left their mark in the development of the Albanian people, while the sea on the west provides the country with a most desirable confine.

On the east and south, the limits of Albanian language and nationality become indefinite owing to the intermingling of foreign populations. In the Ipek district, along the northeast corner of the country, two centuries of Albanian invasions have failed to insure preponderance of the Albanian over the Serbian element. Nevertheless at the London ambassadorial conference in 1913 Albania was awarded the only available road between Montenegro and Serbia. The route, cut in the mountainous tangle which characterizes this region, follows the Clementi gap, a district settled by shepherds of the tribe of the same name. The Prokleita mountains allotted to Albania form here a natural boundary. The inclusion of this uplift within Serbian territory would have enabled the Serbians to maintain communication with their Montenegrin kinsmen. Albanians would have lost little in the transaction, as can well be inferred from the name of the mountain, which is Serbian for "accursed."

A small strip of Montenegrin territory which extends from Podgoritza to the sea at Antivari and Dulcigno is peopled almost exclusively by about 10,000 Albanians. This district was annexed to Montenegro by the treaty of Berlin in exchange for the districts of Plava and Gusinje which were then awarded to Turkey in view of the predominantly Mohammedan religion of their inhabitants.

Montenegrin covetings of the Lake Scutari area are based on economic grounds. The eastern shore of this inland body of water

---

[2] G. Gravier: L'Albanie et ses limites, *Rev. de Paris*, Jan. 1, 1913, pp. 200-224.

contains broad agricultural tracts which can supply the small state with food products unobtainable from its rocky surface. The award of a small strip of the old sanjak and a portion of the Ipek district, at the end of the Balkan wars of 1912 and 1913, failed to meet Montenegrin requirements. The new districts are separated from the country proper by a tangle of well-nigh impenetrable mountains. At Podgoritza, the commercial center of Montenegro, it is still possible to buy cereals from Albania more advantageously than from the Ipek region. Furthermore the acquired territory is relatively densely populated and hence unfit for settlement or colonization. Under the circumstances the economic advantages secured by Montenegro by the increase of its territory in 1913 were slight.

The area claimed by the highland country comprises the shore district of Scutari Lake and the Boyana valley. To satisfy Montenegrin aspirations the Albanian boundary should follow the Drin valley to the point of confluence of the Black and White Drin and extend along the Drinassa river. Thence, passing through the coast ranges, it should attain the Kiri river by way of a canal connecting this waterway with the Boyana. Beyond, the line might appropriately be carried to Bredizza and the Adriatic between San Juan de Medua and the mouth of the Boyana.

Such a revision of Montenegro's frontier would provide the soil which the country needs for tilling. The valley of the Boyana and the drained lake district would soon be taken up by Montenegrin colonists who, now that the Turkish danger is over, are eager to descend into the lowland from their mountain fastness. The connection between the coast and inland districts would likewise be favored by the changed course of the boundary line.

In southern Albania Greek claims to Epirus are not without foundation. Hellenic language and customs prevail throughout the province. The hopes entertained at Athens originally aimed at the establishment of a northern boundary which would have included Valona. In order to satisfy Italian demands, however, a less comprehensive line was advocated, beginning at Gramala bay and extending to the Serbian frontier in the center of the western shore of Lake Okrida.   It comprises the districts of Kimara, Argyrocastro, Premeti, Koritza and Moskopolis.   According to official Turkish statistics, published in 1908, the region was peopled by 340,000 Greeks and some 149,000 Mohammedans.

The Greek proposals laid before the London ambassadorial conference suggested the following delimitation of the line between Greece and Albania.   Starting from Gramala bay on the Adriatic sea, the frontier was to extend to Tepeleni and thence to Klisura.   From this point the line was to coincide with the crest of the Dangli mountains and, crossing the basin of the middle Devoli river, attain Lake Okrida, thus connecting with the eastern boundary of Albania.

The thwarting of these Greek aspirations was followed by an insurrection of the Epirote inhabitants of Albania in 1914. The movement aimed at annexation with Greece.   Rebel troops lost no time in occupying the region of Greek speech between Kimara and Tepeleni, comprising the coast and the northern extension of the wide valley of Argyrocastro.   On February 25, 1914, the autonomy of Epirus was solemnly proclaimed by the inhabitants of Kimara assembled in their cathedral.   In the fall of 1914 the Hellenic government, taking advantage of the European war, despatched regular troops into the territory claimed by its citizens.   As a result of this invasion the Albanian area of Greek speech was brought under the direct authority of the Greek government.[3]

The determination of the boundary between the Albanian and Greek languages presents little difficulty.   The upper course of the Voyussa and the road from Delvino to Ostanitza passing by Doliano mark the divide approximately.   North of this line the prevailing language is Albanian.   To the south it is Greek.   On the Albanian side the village schoolhouse maintained by Greeks is no longer found.   Delvino itself is a town in which the two

---

[3] L. Büchner: Die neue griechisch-albanische Grenze in Nordepirus, *Pet. Mitt.*, Vol 61, Feb. 1915, p. 68.

peoples are equally represented. The language of commerce however is Greek and as a rule the Albanian townsmen speak the rival tongue with high fluency, while the knowledge of Albanian possessed by the Greek inhabitants is restricted to the few phrases needed in daily contact.

History, legend and myth, as well as language, testify to the Hellenic character of the Epirote land. These ties are too strong to allow the Greeks to relinquish complacently any portion of Epirus to Albania. Greece's dawning consciousness of nationality was nursed in the mountains of Epirus long before the Christian era. Every step in the rugged country raises the dust of Hellenic antiquity. Among the fateful oaks of Dodona the land is aglow with tradition. At a short distance from Filiates, at the junction of the Kalamas and the Cremnitza, shepherds feed their flocks about the thick walls of Passaron. Near Delvino may be seen the remains of the once prosperous city of Phoenike. Every mountain and stream in the Epirote districts of Albania is part of the foundation on which Hellenism was built. The annals of modern Greece also are replete with the heroism of Greeks who claim Epirus as their native country. The land which produced so daring a leader of men as Pyrrhus in ancient times, later counted Miaoulis, Canaris and Botzaris among its sons.

The Greek occupation of Janina and the district surrounding the city raised difficulties of a practical nature. As is generally the case in conquered countries land was found to be held by the dominating element, that is by Mohammedans, whether Albanian, Turkish or Greek. The Christian Greeks forming the majority of the population constituted the working, peasant class. The end of Turkish rule in Europe placed Mohammedan landholders in the unenviable situation of suppliants before a people whom they had mercilessly maltreated. Many were ruined and their land taken over by Greeks without compensation. A general disturbance of the economic life of the region ensued as agriculture had been its most important industry.

Geographically—as well as economically—the nation holding

Janina is entitled to Santi-Quaranta. This harbor is likewise the outlet for the products of the district surrounding Argyro-castro. In fact access to the sea for the entire Greek-speaking inland districts of southern Albania is obtained through Preveza or Santi-Quaranta. The latter harbor alone however is safe for large vessels.

The importance of Albania in European politics is largely due to the commanding position of the country's seaports at the mouth of the Adriatic. Austrians, Italians, Serbians and Monte-negrins covet them equally. South of the Montenegro frontier the first of these harbors is San Juan de Medua, situated on the northeast corner of the Gulf of Drino about 11 miles southwest of the mouth of the Boyana river.

This port, which is in reality a bay of restricted dimensions, is considered by the natives as the most favored on the Albanian coast. A bank extending to the south of the bay affords shelter from high seas. The region is the resort of local fishermen and is especially favored during winter months. In summer the swampy nature of the environing country converts it into a malarial district. Small vessels of the coastwise trade find shelter at the extreme inland extension of the bay. Ocean-going steamers anchor in the middle of the bay between the mouth of the Drin and San Juan Point.

San Juan de Medua is the harbor of the Montenegrin town of Scutari. It is also the proposed sea terminal of a railway to be built between the Danube and the Adriatic. As such it might in time become Serbia's economic outlet to the Adriatic. But the construction of a railroad connecting the valley of the Danube with the Adriatic presents well-nigh insurmountable difficulties on account of the mountainous character of the intervening country. The bay of Rodoni, in the southern part of the Gulf of Drino, is one of the safe anchorages. A commodious harbor could be provided here by modern engineering devices. The southern shore of the bay could be converted into a long wharf at no great cost. A jetty thrown out on the northern side would afford protection from the "bora" or northern wind.

Between the bay of Rodoni and Durazzo the two roadsteads of Lales and Pata intervene. Both are resorts of fishermen and petty freighters seeking refuge from the vehemence of the bora. The shallowness of the waters in both preclude their utilization as western terminals for central Balkan traffic. Beyond however, to the south, the spacious bay of Durazzo offers ample harbor facilities to Adriatic shipping.

Durazzo has undoubtedly the most commodious harbor of northern Albania. From Cape Durazzo to Cape Laghi the bay is about 11 miles long. Shoals and banks protect its northern entrance. Engineers would find little difficulty in deepening the bay in conformity with the requirements of modern navigation. This accomplished, Durazzo might again become the naval station and port of commerce which gave fame to its name in ancient times.

Its site is hallowed to history. To the Corcyreans by whom the first town was founded it was known as Epidamnus, the "far away." The Romans changed its name to Dyrrachium. In classical times the port was the point of transshipment for merchandise en route from Italy to Macedonia or northern Greece. At the height of Venetian commercial supremacy, the seaport fully retained its ancient prosperity. The wharves to which Venetian galleys were moored are still intact. Although the city is the modern commercial center of Albania it has lost much of its ancient activity.

None of these Albanian harbors are comparable in strategic importance to Valona, which is situated opposite Brindisi and on that portion of the Albanian coast nearest Italy. The holders of this seaport will control the strait of Otranto and thereby have mastery of the Adriatic. From a military standpoint, the bay facing the town is eminently suited to become a strongly fortified naval station. It is provided with a number of safe anchorages. The island of Sasseno facing the entrance affords shelter from the roughness of the open sea and forms at the same time a natural outpost. Italian and Austrian statesmen, the former especially, are fully aware of the importance of this Albanian harbor in the Adriatic question. The aim of each is to plant their country's flag on the crenelated remnants of the ancient forts which overlook the bay. Greece also aspires to the possession of the seaport. In her case the claim is made that the majority of the inhabitants are of Greek descent. An attempt to obtain mastery of the position was made by Greece in the spring of 1913 when she landed in Sasseno. An energetic protest from the Italian government forced Greece to recall her troops. The island was occupied by Italian troops in the fall of 1914.

Valona is the outlet of a region whose population consists mainly of Mohammedan Albanians. Its commercial insignificance is largely due to the character of its inhabitants. Had it been peopled by a majority of Greeks, or even Christian Albanians, its influence might have been felt in the midst of international rivalries. Whatever destiny is in store for Albania, it seems as if, in view of the non-Greek character of the Valonian population, Italian or Austrian claims would stand greater chance of being heeded.

Of the 8,000 or 10,000 inhabitants of Valona over one-half are Albanian Mohammedans who adhere to the use of their vernacular. Greek is spoken extensively by Orthodox Albanians and Greeks, who together form the next largest religious community. Among Catholics the cultural influence of Italian prevails. In fact most of the Albanian Catholics residing in the town have forsaken their native language for Italian. Through the medium of these Catholics the only sphere of Italian influence in Albania deserving mention is found in Valona and the environing district. This western influence is hardly felt, however, beyond a distance of about 35 miles inland from the harbor or by more than 20,000 souls. Albanian anarchy holds sway to the north. Southward Greek influence is strongly exerted through the agency of the Orthodox church.

Elsewhere in the Balkan peninsula linguistic groupings now conform largely to the political divisions which ended the wars of 1912-1913. The future will undoubtedly afford an increasingly satisfactory perspective of the results which followed this attempt to eliminate totally the Turk from this portion of the European continent. Racial siftings followed close on territorial readjustments. Turks from all parts of the former Turkish provinces transferred their lands to Christian residents and emigrated to Asia Minor. Special arrangements for this exodus were provided by the Turkish government. Greeks who were settled in the newly acquired Bulgarian and Serbian domain similarly sought new homes within the boundaries of the Hellenic kingdom. A heavy flow of Bulgarian emigrants was also directed to Bulgaria from Bulgarian-speaking territory allotted to Serbia.[4]

But pressing need of further boundary revision on the basis of language is felt in the peninsula. Resumption of hostilities in this part of Europe in 1915 was due principally to the moot case of the nationality of the Slavs of Macedonia. Serbs and Bulgars both claim them as their own. In reality the Macedonians are a transition people between the two. They occupy a distinctive area formed by the twin valleys of the Vardar and Struma and surrounded by a mountainous bulwark assuming crescentic shape as it spreads along the Balkan ranges and the mountains of Albania and the Pindus. For centuries this Macedonian plain has constituted the cockpit of a struggle waged for linguistic supremacy on the part of Bulgarians and Serbs. The land had formed part of the domain of each of the two countries in the heyday of their national life. To this fact in part the present duality of claim must be ascribed.

The entire northwestern Macedonian highland was under Serbian rule until the fall of 1915. East and south of the mountains Bulgarian speech predominates in districts peopled exclusively by Macedonians. The Greek element is practically entirely absent here; Serbians begin to appear in small numbers; south of Monastir and Okrida offshoots of the Pindus Rumanians are found; but the Macedonian element is present everywhere in overwhelming majority.

---

[4] Such migrations generally follow boundary revisions. The crossing of Alsatians into French territory since 1870 has been already mentioned. A large number of Danes abandoned their home in Schleswig-Holstein in 1865, and wandered into Denmark.

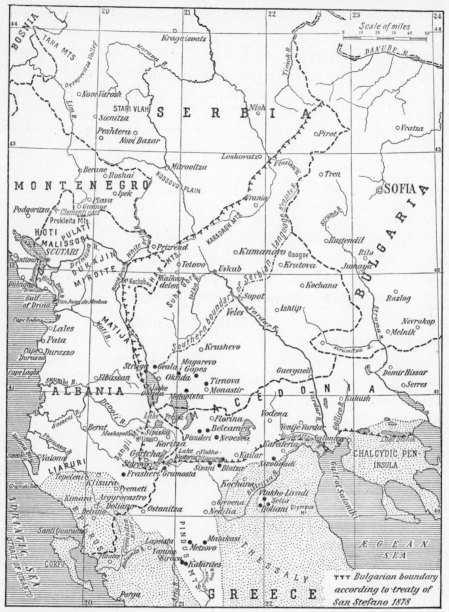

FIG. 53—Sketch map of the western Balkans. The dotted area represents the northern area of Greek language. Black dots show Rumanian settlements of the Pindus mountains and adjoining regions.

Physically Macedonia is the region of the basins of the Vardar and Struma. Under Turkish rule it was divided into the vilayets of Monastir, Uskub and Salonica. The area is isolated from the rest of the peninsula by a practically continuous line of mountains, which, starting with the Pindus, Grammos and Albanian ranges on the west, extend through the Shar, Suhagora, Osogov and Rilo uplifts on the north and connect on the east with the Rhodope massif. Macedonia is thus well defined on the surface. Within these natural boundaries, it may be divided into an elevated region extending over its northwestern portion and a lowland spreading thence to Ægean waters. The Bistritza valley forms a convenient feature to mark the beginning of the modern Hellenic area.

In a restricted sense physical Macedonia may be defined as the southerly extension of the Serbian mountain belt whose drainage leads to the Ægean. Thus it consists first of a mountain belt extending between the upper valleys of the Black Drin and Struma. To this zone must also be added a hill country which forms its continuation to the Ægean Sea. The Vardar valley is entirely within this area and divides it into equal east and west sections. The northern boundary of the area is found at the central watershed north of Uskub. Four important basins lie within these boundaries. The Tetovo basin, west of Uskub, lies close to the watershed. Southward the Monastir and Strumitza basins occupy approximately homologous positions with respect to the Vardar cut. The twin basin of Serres and Drama extends over the southeastern portion of the country. These basins have been the only important centers of Macedonian populations.

The Macedonian highland is peopled by shepherds and woodcutters. The lowlanders are husbandmen. All are generally bilingual, speaking either Greek and Bulgarian or Bulgarian and Serbian. A knowledge of Turkish usually prevails among all classes. Occupation generally affords a reliable national clue. As a rule the Macedonians, and by this term we shall hereafter denote the Bulgarian-speaking element of Macedonia, are tillers of the soil. The Greeks are traders and control a large share of the commerce of the entire region. Land is held by the Macedonians or the former ruling Turkish gentry. It is worked however by the Macedonians.

The inhabitants of Macedonia may be divided into four groups according to their vernaculars. The number of individuals in each group is estimated as follows:[5]

Bulgarians	1,172,136 or 81.5%	of the total Christian population.
Greeks	190,047 " 13.22	" " " " "
Rumanians	63,895 " 4.44	" " " " "
Albanians[6]	12,006 " 0.84	" " , " " "

The Bulgarians form a compact mass containing slight admixture of alien elements in northern and central Macedonia. Many of the occasional Greek communities encountered within this area are former Slav or Albanian centers having passed under the sphere of the Greek religious propaganda which has been actively carried on as a means of increasing the Hellenic domain. The instrument of Hellenization was the Patriarchate at Constantinople. The Patriarchs, bearing the title of Œcumenical, considered themselves as apostles of the Greater Greece idea. After the fall of Byzantium, and notably after the closing of the Bulgarian Patriarchate of Okrida, the Œcumenical Patriarchate of Constantinople was the only official church established in Turkey for Christians. Its influence, directed through schools and churches, aimed above all to Hellenize Christians. The clergy was directed to convert to Orthodoxy the greatest possible number of Christians of alien denomination and, at the same time, attempt to enforce the use of Greek speech among non-Mohammedans.

The Greeks of Macedonia are as mixed a people as can be found on the surface of the earth. Inhabitants of cities are strongly mixed with Albanian and Slav populations. Strains of Tatar blood can even be detected among them. The Mediterranean type becomes more pronounced as Thessaly is approached. In unfrequented villages, however, the tourist will not uncommonly find living impersonations of the sculptor's classical conception of the human form. This Greek element predominates in the

---

[5] D. M. Brancoff: La Macédoine et sa population chrétienne, Paris, 1905.

[6] The number of Serbians scattered in the highland region of northern Macedonia has been omitted, probably owing to its relative inferiority.

valley of the Bistritza, which, regionally, should be considered as the northeastern boundary of the area of the Greek speech.

The Slavs of Macedonia are, in many respects, distinct in character from the other Slavs of the Balkan peninsula. National feeling among them is less strongly developed than with the rest of the southern Slavs. They are industrious and frugal—even grasping. Yet there are marked exceptions which seem to prove that these qualities are not natural to them but have been acquired under the stress of circumstances. Macedonia is a land of poverty. It may rank with southern Greece as the poorest land in the Balkan peninsula. Of little fertility, extensively deforested and without particularly good pasture land, the country cannot support its relatively numerous population, and therefore an important occupation with the Macedonians is the taking of service in menial capacity in foreign countries—"Petchalba," as it is called.

The language of the Macedonians is intermediate between Serbian and Bulgarian. Its affinity with the latter, however, is sufficiently pronounced to have led generally to merging. Travelers in the land of the Macedonian Slavs soon learn that a knowledge of Bulgarian will obviate difficulties due to ignorance of the country's vernaculars. Serbian, however, is not as readily intelligible to the natives. This relation has favored the Bulgarian side whenever controversy arose and compilers of linguistic or ethnographic maps have generally abstained from differentiating the Macedonian from the Bulgarian area.[7] The impossibility for Bulgarians to regard the terms of the treaty of Bucarest as final is, therefore, obvious. Extension of the Rumanian boundary to the Turtukai-Black Sea line was also an encroachment on soil where Bulgarian was the predominant language.[8]

---

[7] D. M. Brancoff: La Macédoine et sa population chrétienne, Paris, 1905. The Serbian viewpoint is resumed by J. Cvijić in " Ethnographie de la Macédoine," *Ann. de Géogr.*, Vol. 15, 1906, pp. 115-132 and 249-266.

[8] R. A. Tsanoff in the *Journ. of Race Develop.* (Jan. 1915, p. 251) estimates that 1,198,000 Bulgarians have passed under foreign rule as a result of the treaty of Bucarest. Of these 286,000 have become subjects of Rumania, 315,000 of Greece and 597,000 of Serbia.

The area of Bulgarian speech awarded to Greece by the treaty of Bucarest in 1913 attains the Albanian boundary near Lakes Prespa and Kastoria. The upper valley of the Bistritza river crosses a region peopled by Macedonians. The former Turkish caza of Kastoria contained a majority of Bulgarian-speaking inhabitants. The domain of Greek speech begins south of Lapsista and extends eastward halfway between Kailar and Kochana. Greek predominance is maintained around Karaferia. The environs of Salonica contain a slight excess of Greek inhabitants over Bulgarians, but the Greek element is not as closely attached to the land as the Bulgarian. The line of lakes on the north of the Chalcydic peninsula forms the boundary between Greeks and Bulgarians, the latter element extending north of these inland waters to the present Bulgarian frontier.

The loss of Macedonia was bitterly resented by Bulgarians, not only on account of the racial ties which bind them to Macedonians, but also because their country's economic development is hampered by the want of the harbors which constitute the natural sea outlets for the rearlands under Bulgarian rule. The industrial and commercial development of southwestern Bulgaria is handicapped at present by the necessity of shipping the products of the region over a devious stretch of railroad through Sofia-Philippopoli-Dedeagatch. The alternative via Serbia or Greece is equally costly. The population of a considerable portion of the country is, therefore, unable to compete with rival producers of the two neighboring countries.

In the first half of 1913 negotiations between the Greek and Bulgarian governments were in progress for the division of lands conquered from the Turks. At that time the Greek government was willing to recognize Bulgarian sovereignty over the cazas of Kavalla, Drama, Pravista, Serres, Demir-Hissar and Kukush. This was done on Mr. Venizelos' understanding that these districts were sparsely inhabited by Greeks,[9] and that Kavalla

---

[9] A. Schopoff: The Balkan States and the Federal Principle, *Asiat. Rev.*, July 1, 1915, p. 21.

was the natural seaport of the districts of Strumnitza, Melnik, Jumaya, Nevrokop and Razlog.

Many of the districts thus offered to Bulgaria were peopled mainly by Turks. According to Turkish statistics the caza of Kara-Shaban does not contain a single Christian village. Its population consists almost entirely of Turks numbering about 15,000. The caza of Kavalla, having a population of 30,000, is likewise largely Turkish. The Greek element is reckoned at about 4,000, while some 3,500 Pomaks or Bulgarian Mohammedans are scattered in many villages.

Of the 50,000 inhabitants of the caza of Drama fully one-half were Turks, the number of Greeks hardly attained 4,000, while the Bulgarian element consisted of 20,000 inhabitants divided into equal numbers of Exarchists and Pomaks. In the caza of Serres, the Bulgarians number approximately 40,000, while the Greek population comprises 27,000.[10] The caza of Demir-Hissar contains 33,000 Bulgarians out of a population of 50,250. The Greeks number about 250. In Kukush there are no Greeks at all. The population of this caza consists mainly of 20,000 Turks out of a total of 23,000 inhabitants. It should be remembered that the Turks emigrated en masse from this district after the treaty of Bucarest and that, barring forcible expulsion by the Greeks, the population of all this section of southeastern Macedonia is now overwhelmingly Bulgarian.

Prior to Philip's time, Macedonia was a little-known mountainous province constantly overrun by Thracians and Illyrians. Soon after the overthrow of the Macedonian Empire by the Romans in 168 B.C. the region took its place among Roman provinces and eventually formed part of the Byzantine Empire. Rapacious Goths under Alaric brought havoc to the land after its fortunes were bound to that of the dominant eastern state. The Slavs made their appearance during the reign of Justinian. Their colonies had attained importance while Heraclius was on the throne. In the tenth century, Macedonia became part of the

---

[10] Brancoff: op. cit., p. 23.

great Bulgarian kingdom, but gravitated later towards Byzantium, though not without having been the scene of disastrous struggles between Byzantine hosts and their barbarian foes. Turks and Tatars first overran the country in this period and even founded colonies. The two invasions from the east, of the Slavs and of the Turks, must have wrought profound changes in the Macedonian populations. A short period of Serbian rule was undergone in the fourteenth century. In the fifteenth, Macedonia became an integral portion of the Ottoman dominions and preserved this political status until its rescue during the Balkan wars of 1912-1913.

Ethnically Macedonians and Bulgarians consist of mixed European and Asiatic elements. The oldest layer in the population is Thracian. This local stock peopled the land at the time of the Roman conquest and was strongly Romanized during the subsequent centuries. Slavs overran the country in the sixth century. The Bulgarians made their appearance in the seventh. Turks, or rather Mongol and Tatar hordes, began their invasions in the eighth. These Asiatics were nomads. They made excellent soldiers but poor settlers. Their settlements, which were made at strategic points, can be recognized today by their commanding sites.

It is hard to determine how much of the Slav or of the Tatar exists in the average Bulgarian of our day. The history of the land during the second half of the first Christian millennium is a record of constant invasions from the east. The invaders appear at first to have been Slavs from the southern steppes of western Russia. As time goes on, however, Bulgaria is seen to absorb wanderers proceeding from more and more distant districts in the southern belts of the steppeland which forms the continuation of Europe into Asia. Slavic culture and speech preserved by the Bulgarians seem but the veil that hides their strong Asiatic affinity.

The fundamental difference between the temper of the Serbian and the Bulgarian is apparent to travelers in Balkan lands. The former are true Slavs. They are lighthearted and always ready to make merry. Their mountains re-echo with folk songs of the genuine Slavic type. The Bulgarian on the other hand is inclined to silence. Both peoples are equally industrious, but in the Serbian the mobile and restless spirit of the west is discernible, while the Bulgarian is as slow and ponderous a thinker as ever was bred on the vast and open stretches of Eurasia's central lowlands.

Proof of the Altaic origin of some of the Bulgarians is derived from philology. To be sure, the Bulgarian and Turkish languages, as now spoken, prevent mutual understanding, even though a number of Turkish words have crept into Bulgarian in the course of the centuries of Turkish rule. These are mostly modern words, however, which did not exist at the time of the Asiatic migrations. On the other hand, a deeper etymological bond is found in the words for both wild and domestic animals, which are very similar in the two languages. In the same way the old stock of words relating to agricultural or pastoral pursuits are very closely akin in Turkish and Hungarian. An interesting feature of the peopling of Bulgaria is the modern tendency of the Bulgarian to abandon his ancient home in the Balkan mountains and seek the fertile lowlands of the country's main valleys. A steady emigration from mountain to plain has been going on since the Turks withdrew their garrisons from Bulgaria. This movement reflects a sense of security which followed the expulsion of the Turks. It is not yet ended. The fertile basins of southeastern Bulgaria are still sparsely populated. The reason is clear. They were peopled largely by Turks who preferred to retire on Turkish soil after the Balkan wars of 1912-1913. The Bulgarians have not yet had time to occupy the territory abandoned by the Turks.

After the Turkish conquest Turkish historians, particularly Evlia Tchelebi and Sa'aeddin, constantly refer to the Macedonians as Bulgarians. This belief was held by the Turks until the end of their rule of the province. The first Bulgarian bishop authorized by the Turkish government was appointed for the diocese of Uskub and southern districts. This appointment followed census-taking in the district which indicated Bulgarian predominance.

In southwestern Macedonia the inhabitants of the districts of Kastoria, Florina and Kailar are generally Bulgarians. Even in the Mohammedan villages, as, for example, Grevena and Nedilia, nothing but Bulgarian is heard. The fundamental Bulgarian character of the entire region is furthermore established by place names which are Bulgarian in spite of secular infiltrations of Greeks, Albanians and Turks.

This portion of Macedonia along with the Vodena, Yenije-Vardar and Salonica districts which were lately allotted to Greece, constitute an interesting linguistic zone. Here alone, of all Bulgarian-speaking regions, have been preserved forms peculiar to the old Bulgarian language. The speech of the inhabitants of Kastoria in particular reveals antiquated styles which are found only in the first manuscripts prepared for the use of Christian Slavs.

At the ambassadorial conference of Constantinople in 1876 the cazas of Kastoria and Florina were included within the boundaries of the proposed autonomous province which was to have Sofia as its capital. The treaty of San Stefano likewise comprised the districts under the newly created Bulgaria. These considerations suffice in themselves to demonstrate the Bulgarian nationality of the inhabitants of the present northern confines of Greece.

The Serbian claim on portions of Macedonia acquired after the Balkan war of 1913 rests largely on a relatively short term of military occupation at the height of the Serbian might in the fourteenth century. This is made the basis of an historical plea. The crowning of Dushan, their most renowned ruler, in the city of Uskub however did not change the national character of the inhabitants of the city or the districts surrounding it. Furthermore, Serbian rule in Macedonia was preceded by Bulgarian sovereignty and was followed by Byzantine supremacy over the land. Greeks and Bulgarians may therefore buttress their claims on equally valid historical contentions. Samuel, one of the Bulgarian Czars, had extended his domain as far west as the Adriatic. His success in adding the seaport of Durazzo to his land, however, failed to change the Serbian nationality of the western districts he managed to conquer.

Only in recent years have Serbian claims on Macedonia been set forth by Serbian scholars. Historians like Raitch, Solaritch and Vouk Karadjitch formerly concurred in setting southern Serbian frontiers at the Shar mountains. In 1860 Serbian scientific societies had joined in the publication of Macedonian songs collected by Verkovitch under the title of "Bulgarian Songs." Serbian writers of the period around 1870 describe inland inhabitants of Thrace, Rumelia and Macedonia as Bulgarians, while they recognized the coast dwellers as Greeks.[11]

A transition dialect between Bulgarian and Serbian is spoken by the inhabitants of the Krajste and Vlasina valleys in eastern Serbia. The Krajste, an ill-known region, skirts the Serbo-Bulgarian boundary and spreads eastward to the basins of Tren and Kustendil. The Vlasina upper valley is known to Serbians as containing the most important peat bog in their country. The two districts are characterized by seasonal migrations of their inhabitants which acquire decided intensity in the Vlasina valley.[12]

In its westernmost area the delimitation of a Bulgarian linguistic boundary is greatly hampered by the relatively large Serbian-speaking element on the north and a corresponding mass of Greeks on the south. Reliable statistics are still unavailable. Figures supplied by rival nationalist propaganda institutions are for obvious reasons open to suspicion. The region where the determination of this linguistic boundary is most difficult is found in the neighborhood of Pirot and Vrania. Here the language of the Slavic natives departs equally from the Bulgarian and Serbian. This region, however, lies north of Macedonia proper. At the same time there appears to be little room to

---

[11] *L'Écho de la Bulgarie*, Dec. 20, 1914.
[12] R. T. Nikolić: Krajste i Vlasina, *Nasetia Srpskikh zrmalia*, Vol. 8, 1912, pp. 1-380.

doubt that the area of Bulgarian speech attains the zone of the eastern Albanian dialects and that it attains the Gulf of Salonica. But the seafaring population of the Ægean coast is largely Greek.

Salonica itself is by no means a Bulgarian city, but an excellent type of the polylingual cities of the Near East. Out of a population of 160,000 inhabitants, it contains 20,000 Greeks and an equal number of Europeans and Turks respectively. Its Bulgarian population is negligible. The most numerous element is made up of Jews who, it is estimated, constitute about one-half of the population. Next to Constantinople, Salonica is the best harbor in the Balkans. It is coveted by the Bulgarians on the plea that the population of the country environing Salonica is mostly Bulgar.

The city occupies a dominating position on the Ægean coast halfway between Piraeus and Smyrna and has always been a meeting-point of Europe and Asia. In a sense it is the eastern terminal of continental lines with which it is connected by the railroad which passes through Nish and Uskub. In this light the city may be likened to one of the piles of a gigantic bridge thrown across the Ægean to connect Europe and Asia. It is the natural outlet of the greatest part of Macedonia. Inland towns all the way from Ipek, Prizrend and Mitrovitza to Monastir, Ishtip and Serres obtain the goods which they need through Salonica. The products of the fertile valleys of the Vardar and the Bistritza are almost exclusively directed toward this harbor. The exchange of commodities between Salonica and its rearlands reaches a yearly value of about $100,000,000.

Whatever be the prevailing language spoken in this city, its greatness depends entirely on the degree of freedom with which its inhabitants can maintain trade with the districts extending north and northwest. To maintain its size, or grow, the city must continue to be the receiving point of manufactured goods shipped into Macedonia as well as parts of Serbia and Albania. It must also remain the shipping point for the natural products from those same districts. To separate Macedonia from Salonica, its natural harbor, is to create an unnatural condition. The city draws its life from the resources of Macedonia. Its prosperity is therefore directly related to the political fate of that country.

Bulgaria was independent during three different periods of its history. The first kingdom was founded in 679 when Bulgarian bands led by Asparush crossed the Danube and conquered the Slavs who had previously occupied Bulgaria. Conquest carried his successors to the very gates of Constantinople. At the end of the ninth century under the reign of Simon, the second Christian ruler of the country, the kingdom comprised all of Hungary, Rumania, Macedonia, Thessaly, Epirus and Serbia in addition to its present territory. Preslav was its capital. Bulgaria had then an area of 233,300 sq. m.

The Byzantines conquered Bulgaria in 1018 and maintained their supremacy until 1186. The second kingdom was reëstablished in that year with Assen I as its sovereign. In the reign of Assen II (1218-1241), Bulgarian territory reached the Adriatic, Ægean and Black seas and the Danube formed its northern frontier. Tirnovo was the capital of the second kingdom. Bulgaria was at that time one of the great European powers. Its area was then 113,100 sq. m. The third kingdom dates from the year 1877.

Several attempts have been made in the past to create a Bulgaria which would extend as far as the country's language was spoken. Towards the end of 1876 an international conference was held in Constantinople to put an end to the intolerable condition of the Christians inhabiting this portion of the Balkan peninsula. The delegates decided to form two new Turkish provinces, the boundaries of which would coincide with the ethnographic limit of the Bulgarian people. Sofia and Tirnovo were selected as the chief towns of the new provinces. The Sultan's government succeeded in blocking the execution of this project. War with Russia followed and Russian victories forced Turkey to sign the memorable treaty of San Stefano on February 19, 1878.

The boundary then decided upon was practically identical with that provided by the ambassadorial conference of Constantinople. Bulgaria however obtained in addition a band of territory in Thrace and access to the Ægean through the seaport of Kavalla and the mouth of the Vardar. In exchange, the principality lost the Dobrudja to Rumania and a portion of the sanjak of Nish with the towns of Nish and Leskovatz to Serbia. Russia at San Stefano had, therefore, merely enforced execution of the agreement reached jointly by the representatives of European powers. The treaty she imposed on the Porte was from the linguistic standpoint an improvement on the ambassadorial plan elaborated at Constantinople.

Unfortunately for Bulgaria, the unity of the nation failed to receive the sanction of Europe at the treaty of Berlin in spite of the sound scientific basis on which it was founded. Political and strategical considerations, on the plea of which many international blunders have been committed, prevailed. After this act of injustice Bulgarians organized themselves to reclaim the land of which they had been despoiled. Thirty-five years were spent in preparation. On February 19, 1913, Bulgar guns and bayonets, backed by Bulgar determination, had almost reëstablished the national unity for which they had striven. This new effort was not to be crowned with success. Only in the winter of 1914-1915 were the Bulgarians able to occupy with their arms the territories of Bulgarian speech which had been allotted to Serbia by the treaty of Bucarest. The permanency of this occupation is, needless to state, subject to international approval.

The extreme southeastern angle of the Balkan peninsula, east of the Maritza river, is probably the most polyglot region in Europe. The valley of the Maritza is mainly Bulgarian. Numerous colonies of Greeks settled along the coast between the Dardanelles and the Black Sea entrance of the Bosporus ply their trade as fishermen or sailors. The petty coastwise traffic is almost entirely in their hands. The Bulgarians are mainly farmers. Their properties are scattered east to the very walls of the world-metropolis which brings fame to the region. Within Constantinople itself truck gardens are generally owned and exploited by Bulgarians. Bulgarian and Greek languages are therefore common in this peninsula extremity of Europe. The latter however is in constant use by most of the inhabitants, whereas Bulgarian is restricted to the Slavic element.

The Turkish masters of the land were never able to impose their language on the Christian population. Many of the Greek and Bulgarian inhabitants of the region cannot speak a word of Turkish. The fact is particularly observable among Greeks. The language of the conqueror hovers over the land as the medium of administration. Its function ceases then, as far as the Christian element of the region is concerned. The Turkish population in this bit of the Balkan peninsula is numerous, owing to the attraction exerted by the capital. Reliable census figures are unavailable. Thanks to the presence of a strong garrison and a host of civil-service officials the Turkish population of Constantinople, added to the Turks remaining in the strip of European Turkey still owned by the Sultan after the treaty of Bucarest of 1913, probably musters as many individuals as those to whom Greek is vernacular. An important Armenian colony is centered at Constantinople and radiates in settlements without the capital. These Christians also have held fast to their native speech, although most of them can claim proficiency in Turkish. This familiarity with the language of their conquerors betrays their Asiatic origin, in contrast with the ignorance of Turkish found among the Greeks, who never forget their European affinities.

In Europe the Turk, child of the ungrateful Asiatic steppe-land, has always been the heartily despised intruder. He has shown himself incompetent to follow up the task of conquest by assimilating the peoples he subdued. Perhaps his lack of national ideals lies at the root of his failure. The language he imposed on his Christian subjects never replaced their vernacular. It was spoken only by the males of the subdued populations. Only in rare instances did it penetrate within their households. Hence, Turks never felt at home in Europe. They knew that their nomad's tent was pitched only for a while on the continent in which they sojourned as conquerors and as strangers. They were emigrants who had lost all memory of their land of origin and who nevertheless could not adapt themselves to the land which their bravery had won. The state they founded had a weak head and no heart whatever. Under these conditions the expulsion of Turks from Europe could always be foreseen in spite of the weary years it took to accomplish it.

Every boundary revision that marks the successive shrinking of Turkish territory in Europe has been attended by wholesale emigration of Mohammedans from lands reclaimed by Christians. Immediately after the Balkan wars of 1913 about 50,000 Turks voluntarily departed for Asia Minor from territory allotted to Greece. An equal number left sections of Macedonia taken over by Serbia, while about 25,000 abandoned land annexed by Bulgaria.

The historical fact is that Turks have never consented to live in a land governed by Christians. In 1882 Thessaly was annexed to Greece by a decision of European powers. No armed conflict between Greece and Turkey took place on that occasion and racial hatred had not been increased by the horrors of war. The Greek government at that time offered special inducements to the Turkish inhabitants of the ceded territory to remain on their land and continue their agricultural pursuits. The Turks, however, preferred to emigrate to the Sultan's domain.

When Crete was awarded to Greece over 50,000 of the 80,000 Turkish inhabitants of the island abandoned their homes and decided to settle in Asiatic Turkey. This exodus took place in spite of the perfect security of life and property that had prevailed in the island since its administration was taken over by a committee of Europeans in 1877. This tendency of Turks to forsake Christian countries is observable even in Bosnia and Herzegovina, where the Austrian government has shown decided favor toward Mohammedan inhabitants, considering them more loyal than other elements of its southeastern population.

The Turk's last stand in Europe marks the final stage of his colossal struggle to retain mastery over the Dardanelles and Bosporus to which the highways of Europe and Asia lead. The

Bosporus is the junction of two important world routes. One of these connects the peoples of central Europe with the crowded settlements of British India. The other is the line of communication between the commercial ports of the Mediterranean and the caravan terminals on the Black Sea coast. Each of these highways has constituted a channel through which the trade between eastern and western lands has been directed from the very beginnings of commerce. The narrowness of this Eurasian waterway permitted continuous travel between two continents, while the straits allowed uninterrupted maritime travel from Black Sea harbors to distant seaports of the western world. Modern railway communications have benefited by the former circumstance. The sea commerce of medieval days thrived on the latter.

The entire European coast of the elongated waterways which connect the Ægean and Black seas is inhabited by peoples speaking languages each of which symbolizes conflicting aims and aspirations without being strong enough to silence its rivals. From the political standpoint the linguistic factor appears to be of slight value in this case. Economic needs, to the exclusion of other considerations, will probably determine the destiny of this region.

The relation of a region to the world depends in general upon its economic value. The importance of this southeasterly strip of the Balkan peninsula is therefore affected by its central location with reference to the continents of Europe, Asia and Africa. Between Paris and Bagdad, or the Cape of Good Hope, the overland route is continuous save for a short mile of water at the Bosporus and an equally insignificant crossing at the Isthmus of Suez, in the case of African travel. Herein lies the economic relation of this portion of the Balkan peninsula to the rest of the world. But the European coastland of the intercontinental strait separating Europe from Asia does not constitute a complete region. The Asiatic coast of the waterways must be taken with the European and a single district formed out of the Dardanelles, the Sea of Marmora and the Bosporus with their coasts and shores. This region is the threshold of Asia and conversely the entrance to Europe from the east.

A Balkan zone of depression extending west and south of the Balkan uplift affords natural access between the valley of the Danube proceeding from the heart of Europe and the Dardanelles-Bosporus passage. This convenient gap is provided by the wide valley of the Morava and the narrower Nishava course which lead to the Sofia basin, whence penetration into the Thracian plains is obtained by the Maritza valley. The corresponding function for the Asiatic shore is performed by the valley of the Sakaria and in a less degree by the Pursak river depression— both trending westward from the high plateau of western Asia.

The main roads from the Bosporus and the Dardanelles to the Sakaria river valley skirt the shores of the straits of the Marmora, as they follow a coastal lowland which fringes the Dardanian and Bithynian heights. At Panderma however the old highway strikes inland slightly south of east to Brusa in order to avoid the elevated plateau intervening between the Marmora and Lake Abullonia. Thence, still following a line of least elevation, it winds towards the small harbor of Ghemlik (the Cius of Graeco-Roman times) until beyond Isnik (ancient Nicaea of ecclesiastical fame) it debouches into the waters of the Sakaria.

These natural features connect the heart of Europe with the high plateaus of western and central Asia as well as with the fertile Mesopotamian lowland and the Indian peninsulas. The silk sent to Europe from eastern Asia in medieval days followed this road. The route has declined since the construction of the Suez waterway. Railway lines planned to connect Channel ports with the Gulf of Persia will restore the commercial value of the region. The value of the Bosporus as an avenue of trade remains unimpaired in modern days. It is the only maritime outlet for the export of the cereals and farm products of southern Russia and the oil of the Caucasus.

Hence the commercial importance of Constantinople. The city is a huge caravanserai—the meeting place of traders from the world's remotest corners. Control of its commanding position is coveted by every nation whose citizens depend on industry and trade for their welfare. The commerce of three continents lies within its grasp. The political status of the extreme southeastern corner of the Balkan peninsula, together with that of the extreme northwestern corner of Asia Minor, therefore affects the interests of the entire community of European nations.

We have in this a factor which may exert greater weight than language in the eventual formation of an independent political unit comprising the elongated zone of coastland inclosing the Dardanelles, the Sea of Marmora and the Bosporus. A convenient boundary for this territory in the Balkans might start at the Gulf of Saros and, coinciding thence with the heights overlooking Rodosto, might reach the course of the Chorlu. From here to the Black Sea coast the administrative boundary of the vilayet of Constantinople might be converted into an international frontier. This delimitation would leave the valley of the Maritza in Bulgarian hands. This award is justifiable not because the beauty of the river banks is proclaimed in the Bulgarian national hymn, but rather on the grounds of Bulgarian linguistic preponderance in this valley. Substantial coincidence between Bulgarian political and linguistic boundaries on the southeast would then have been obtained.[13]

---

[13] On the Asiatic side the valley of the Sakaria and a long fault revealed by the line of lakes east of the Marmora provide ready-made frontiers which could be conveniently extended to the Gulf of Adramyt on the Ægean. This line constituted the Asiatic boundary of the Latin Empire of Constantinople in the period intervening between the years 1204 and 1261.

CHAPTER XI

THE GEOGRAPHICAL CASE OF TURKEY

TURKEY, by virtue of position, has always stood closely related to every section of the European mainland. The country's fate has affected the destiny of every European nation. The modern importance of Turkish affairs in European international problems is a measure of the extensive influence of the Near East over Europe. A study of European nationalities cannot therefore be complete without reference to the empire of Turkish Sultans.

A strong contrast constantly engages attention in the history of Ottoman lands. Of old, the world's highest civilizations, its purest religions, arose within their confines. In modern days decadence on the heels of a steady recessional marks their lot. The explanation usually advanced is that Mohammedanism has impeded Turkish progress. But this religion was no obstacle to cultural growth in the countries surrounding Turkey. In Egypt, as in Arabia, Persia and northern India, the thought of the natives grew to splendid maturity. The intellectual life of these Mohammedan countries is altogether beyond the grasp of the Turkish mind.

The foundation of Turkey's weakness as a nation and the failure of the cause of civilization within its boundaries lie in the country's situation. The land staggers under the load of misfortune which its central position in the eastern hemisphere has heaped upon it. Its native populations have never been able to develop freely. The country is an open road alongside or at the ends of which nationalities have blossomed. It has been the prey of invaders by which it has been overrun. The Turks find themselves on this land today because they are descendants of wanderers. They have occupied the road because they ignored the ways of stepping off its path. Having come in numbers sufficiently strong, they managed to subdue the original inhabitants, who in their groping for the higher life had given the world a number of great conceptions in learning, art and religion. But hardly had the easterners occupied the road before the process of clearing it began.

Turkey has been a highway of commerce and civilization between Europe on the one hand and Asia and Africa on the other. The history of this country and of its inhabitants cannot be understood unless one is thoroughly impressed by this fundamental fact. On the east the Persian Gulf followed by the Mesopotamian valley, its natural prolongation, formed a convenient channel for the northwesterly spread of human intercourse. To the west, land travel between Europe and Africa drained into the Syrian furrow. Both of these natural grooves led to the passes which carried the traveler into Asia Minor. The peninsula therefore was both an important center of human dispersal and a meeting place for men of all nations.

The through roads converging into Turkish territory are probably the oldest commercial routes of the world. At any rate they connected the sites on which the most ancient civilizations rose. The remotest past to which the history of humanity carries us centers around the large river valleys of the tropical and subtropical zone in the eastern hemisphere. The banks of the Nile, of the Euphrates, of the Indian rivers, or of the broad watercourses in Chinese lowlands were nurseries of human culture. Abundance of water, together with a profuse flora and fauna, gave early man ease of life. Hunters, fishermen and shepherds were naturally converted into farmers. A short wait and the seeds they planted would grow to maturity without exacting other attention than the preliminary act of sowing. The life men led afforded time for thought. Curiosity was awakened regarding lands beyond. Ample provision of natural products furnished them with stocks available for barter. These conditions favored the development of commerce and stimulated the creation of trade routes, which were coveted by many as they became more and more trodden.

Between Europe and Asia the great movements of peoples have followed two parallel directions north or south of the central belt of high Eurasian mountains extending from east to west. Men have traveled back and forth in these two lines from the earliest known period. But exchange of ideas has been practically confined to the southern avenue. In the cold of the Siberian or northern European lowlands men had little opportunity to acquire refinement. They were active and energetic, while the followers of the southern pathways were thinkers.

From the dawn of history to our day only two departures of importance have taken place from this east-west traffic. Both were modern events. One occurred in the middle of the fifteenth century as soon as the Turks acquired mastery of western Asia and the Balkan peninsula. The Christian sailor-trader of that time was then obliged to circumnavigate Africa in order to reach eastern seaports. The other change took place when the Suez Canal was completed. This waterway diverted to its channel much of the overland Asiatic traffic routed between the Black Sea and the Persian Gulf or the Indian Ocean. But even these two diversions failed to eliminate entirely the picturesque caravans which plied over Turkish roads. Thus it may be assumed that these routes have been used uninterruptedly for about 10,000 years at least, that is to say, before the time in which their known history begins.

The southeastern portal of these celebrated highways is situated at the head of the Persian Gulf. The broad Tigris and Euphrates thence mark the northerly extension of the routes. On the western river, the natural road leaves the valley above Mosul and penetrates into the Armenian highland through the gorges in the neighborhood of Diarbekir. The very name Mosul, a contraction of the Greek "Mesopylae" or Central Gates, suggests its origin. The city grew at the meeting point of routes from the Caspian, Black and Mediterranean seas and from the Persian Gulf. The through highway links once more with the

Euphrates in its upper reaches around Keban Maden in order to reach the Anatolian plateau. The passes are precipitous and the waters flow southward closely hemmed in by steep and rocky barriers. Access to the billowy surface of Armenian mountain lands is obtained by means of either the Murad Su or the Kara Su. The union of these two rivers into the single watercourse known as the Euphrates at a short distance above Keban Maden has at all times attracted much of the traffic and travel between Armenia and Mesopotamia. The eastern affluents of the Tigris south of Lake Van, on the other hand, reach the uplifted core of Armenia where they are lost in the tangle of steep valleys and deeply broken surfaces.

Because it is a region of water dispersal, Armenia is also the gathering-site of the heads of outflowing watercourses. If the distance at the divide between the uppermost reaches of two divergent watercourses be short, it is hardly a barrier to human intercourse. This condition prevails in the uppermost reaches of the Euphrates and of the Aras. The important town of Erzerum is the symbol of this union. Within its walled area the traffic of the central plateaus of Asia joined with Mesopotamian or Black Sea and Mediterranean freight, after having followed the easterly approach to Turkey through Tabriz and the southern affluents of the Aras, north of Urmiah Lake. Through this eastern avenue of penetration Asiatic peoples and products have been dumped century after century into Turkish territory.

The valley of the Euphrates, rather than that of the Tigris, is therefore the main artery of communication between north and south in eastern Turkey. It is the avenue through which the ideas of Iran came into contact with Semitic thought. But the uniting influence of the great river was far from being exerted on Oriental peoples alone. In its broad southern course, the river provided ancient merchants with a short-cut which greatly facilitated land travel between the Ægean or Mediterranean and the Persian Gulf. Another city, Aleppo, is the geographical monument which grew with the increase of travel in this stretch of the Euphrates or declined as the channel became less and less frequented. It is the western counterpart of Mosul in the sense that it also is a point of convergence for routes proceeding from every quarter of the compass.

The chief Turkish route leaves the Euphrates at the angular bend near Meskeneh. A two-days' journey across the desert brought the traveler to Aleppo. Beyond, the ancient road hugged the shores of the northeastern corner of the Mediterranean and, passing over the dull gray of the broad Cilician plain, headed for the huge cleft in the limestones of the Taurus, known as the Cilician Gates. Past this breach it is the plateau of Anatolia— a region whose physical isolation has always influenced the life of its inhabitants. Today, south of the Cilician Gates, the land is Arabian in speech and Semitic in thought, while in the country to the north the prevailing language is Turkish, which differs from the refinement of Arabian as markedly as the crudity of the Turkish mind differs from the intellectuality of the Arabian.

Thus through mountain tract and mountain trough the east found its way into the Anatolian plateau. Conversely the west made several successful scalings of its slopes. The valleys leading westward into the Ægean or northward into the Black Sea acted as breaches which facilitated human travel. Among these the Meander, Gediz and Sakaria are noteworthy. The "Royal Road" of the Persian period connected Ephesus with Susa by way of the Cilician Gates. It is described by Herodotus. Official despatch-bearers traveled over it in the fulfilment of their missions. Ramsay places this road north of the desert center of Asia Minor[1] and considers the southern route as the highway of the Graeco-Roman period. This last road is the shortest and easiest between Ægean ports and the Cilician Gates.

The history of inland Asia Minor is the record of travel over the network of the region's roads. Its chief events consist of military marches and trade travels. Urban life on this section of the peninsula had its origin in caravan halts. The cities of inner Anatolia represent successive stages of east-west travel.

---

[1] The Historical Geography of Asia Minor, *Roy. Geogr. Soc. Suppl. Papers*, Vol. 4, 1900, p. 27.

Their alignment serves to trace the course of the road. To our own day this part of Turkey has not been a land of settlement.

In the southeastern half of Turkey human life has also been confined to highway regions. This part of the world is known to us as Syria or Mesopotamia. Both are depressed regions—channels of human flow—bordering the western and eastern sides of the Great Syrian desert which, wedge-like, interposes its shifting solitude of sand between the two as far as the foothills of the mountains on the north. West of Syria lies the Mediterranean; east of Mesopotamia the mountains of Persia. With such a pattern of land carving, it was natural that life and activity should have gathered in the precise regions where the historian finds them.

A dominant fact recurs in every stage of the region's history. Turkey is so placed that its possession is the goal of every nation which has risen to eminence in or around Turkish lands. Its control ushers in a period of great prosperity in every instance. Trade flows freely in the highways, carrying prosperity in its wake. The energy of the fortunate nation is spent to maintain the economic advantages secured. The loss of the highway zone is accompanied by national decline. A new nation rises and obtains the mastery of the road, and the cycle is repeated. The western Asiatic highway may aptly be named a highway of wealth or of misfortune.

At the beginning of the first pre-Christian millennium the struggle for the possession of this highway was as keen and sanguinary as it is at present. The empires of the Nile and Mesopotamian basins, of the Syrian strip and of the Hittite mountain lands mustered the flower of their manhood in yearly arrays for the purpose of seizing or guarding the great arteries of west Asiatic traffic. The short-lived prosperity of the Jewish empire, at the time of Solomon, was attained immediately after the country's boundaries extended from the Red Sea and the Mediterranean to the Persian Gulf. Judea grew to splendor by becoming sole mistress of the international routes which traversed Syria and Mesopotamia. Her greatness was transmitted to Assyria with the loss of the land routes to that same empire in the eighth century B.C. A hundred years later the Chaldeans obtained possession of the highways. It is now their turn to impose their will on neighboring nations. Another century slips by and with it the greatness of Semitic states. In the east, men of Aryan speech, mostly Persians, have begun to value the present Turkish land routes. In 560 B.C. Cyrus is at the head of cohorts which soon after give him mastery of Turkish Asia from the Ægean to the Persian Gulf. To this conquest Darius adds Egypt and India.

All these events center around one of the greatest struggles ever fought between men. It is the conflict between Europeans and Asiatics immortalized in Hellenic literature,—the clash between two continents, each battling for the exclusive control of the highway connecting them. The contestants met on this Turkish highway, they fought over its plains and defiles, and battled for its possession in the realization that the economic prosperity upon which national wealth and greatness rest could be secured only by its conquest.

A significant fact of the celebrated struggle is revealed by the inability of the Greeks to conquer the Persians. They defeated them and checked their westerly advance. The Ægean and Eurasian waterways of Turkey proved an impassable moat to the Persian invaders. As long as the Persians retained control of the highways the menace of their brutal despotism faced the liberal spirit of the Greeks. The danger was dispelled by Alexander's conquest of the highway. No better instance of the power vested in the effective hold of these lines of communication between the east and west can be found.

All the history of Turkish lands is conditioned by their location on the map. The region has occupied a conspicuous position on the stage of world events since the earliest known times. Faint rays of prehistoric light reveal it as the bridge over which the race of round-headed men crossed into Europe from Asia. During antiquity we find it to be the original seat of civilizations which radiate outward in every direction. In medieval times it is the great half-way station of the main artery of world trade. We know of it in modern days as the center of a mighty international struggle familiarly known as the Eastern Question.

A world relation of such an enduring character must obviously rest on exceedingly firm foundations. A search for its causes leads us straight into the field of geography. Three elements, namely, those of position, form and natural resources are primarily accountable for the extraordinary interest which Turkey has always awakened. The region is the Asiatic extension of Mediterranean lands nestling against the great central mountain mass of Asia. It is sharply separated from the rest of the continent by a mountain wall which extends continuously from the Black Sea to the Persian Gulf and is made up of the Armenian and Zagros ranges. It is a peninsula, itself formed by two distinct peninsulas, and one of the unit divisions of the Asiatic continent in the sense that it is the only part of the entire Asiatic continent subject to Mediterranean climatic influences.

By position first, at the junction of three continents and therefore on the main field of history; secondly, as the site of convergence of the main avenues of continental travel and, thirdly, by its situation in one of the two regions in which climatic conditions proved most favorable for the early development of humanity, Turkey, at first glance, appears to have been eminently favored by nature. These advantages made it the meeting place of races which are generally associated with the three continents which the country unites. Aryan, Tatar and Semitic peoples therefore are strongly represented in the land.

In considering Turkey as the meeting place of three continents it is necessary that we should confine our conception of this fact to the strictly literal sense of the term. The country is a meeting place and nothing more. It has never been a transition zone physically and, as a consequence, there has been very little mingling of the different elements in its population. The very shape of the land prevents fusion of the inhabitants into a single people. The interior upland rises abruptly above a narrow fringe of coastal lowland. Its surface features, consisting partly of deserts and saline lakes, recall the typical aspect of central Asia. On the other hand, the rich vegetation of the maritime fringe reflects European characteristics. No better relic of Asia Minor's former land connection with Europe exists than this strip of the west soldered to the eastern continent. But the physical union is clean-cut and, as a result, the change from the low-lying garniture of green scenery to the bare tracts of the uplands is sharp. These features make of Turkey a land of strange contrasts. Its coasts are washed by the waters of half a dozen seas and yet in places a journey of barely twenty-five miles from the shore lands the traveler squarely in the midst of a continental district.

So diversified a country could not be the land of patriotism, and as we pick up the thread of its troubled history we find a woeful absence of this spirit. In Byzantine times as in Ottoman a selfish bias towards local interests, a parochial attachment of the sordid type, pervades its population. A medley of peoples, each filling its particular geographical frame and animated by widely divergent ideals, are constantly engaged in looking abroad rather than toward the land for the attainment of their hopes. Nature fostered this condition. Communications between the different regions have always been difficult. From the narrow fringe of coastland to the interior plateau the ascent is steep. More than that the maritime dweller of the lowland dreaded the total lack of comfort which he knew awaited him on the arid highland. Conversely the indolent inhabitant of this elevated district realized that were he to settle near the coast he could not compete successfully with the more active seafarers. As time went on the coastal peoples—mainly Greeks—accustomed themselves to look beyond the sea for intercourse with the outside world while the Turkish tenants of the interior land still kept in their mind's eye the vast Asiatic background out of which they had emerged.

In the same way the imposing barrier of the Taurus prevented contact between the occupants of the districts lying north and south of the mountain. The significance of this range to Europeans cannot be overestimated. The mountain has proved to be the chief obstacle to the northward spread of Semitic peoples and their civilizations. Successive waves of southern invaders, invariably of Semitic descent whether highly civilized or drawn from tribes of savages, spent themselves in vain dashes against the rocky slopes. The fact is verified historically whether we consider the failure of Assyrians in antiquity, of the Saracens during Middle Ages, or of the Egyptians and Arabs led by Mehemet Ali in modern days. At present the linguistic boundary between Turkish and Arabic occurs in this mountain chain and Hogarth has expressed the fact in a realistic phrase by stating that, at an elevation of about 2,000 ft., the Arabic speech is chilled to silence.

To come back to the factor of Turkey's geographical position, we find that while this feature has generated an attracting force the shape of the land, on the other hand, promoted a constantly repellent action. We have in this situation a remarkable conflict which has exerted itself to the detriment of the inhabitants. The centripetal action of position was always reduced to a minimum by the centrifugal effects of form. The mountainous core made up by the Anatolian table-land and the western highland of Armenia was a center of dispersal of waters, and hence to a large degree of peoples. Furthermore, however much the land was a single unit with reference to the broad divisions of Asia, the fact remains that it was greatly subdivided within itself. The six main compartments into which it may be laid off have fostered totally divergent civilizations. All of these conditions were fundamentally fatal to the formation of nationality. They only favored intercontinental travel and trade. In this respect the country has been of the highest importance in the history of the eastern hemisphere, and at present commands world-wide attention.

In only one respect did position and form operate harmoniously. Both agencies combined to create Turkey's relation with the world beyond its borders. This relation was facilitated by the admirable set of natural routes which led in and out of the country. Beginning with the broad band of the Mediterranean Sea, land and water routes succeed each other in close sequence. The inland sea itself is prolonged through the Ægean and the Turkish straits into the Black Sea, the shores of which are closely dotted with the terminals of great avenues from northeastern Europe, as well as all of northern and central Asia. On the European mainland, the far-reaching Danube has an outlet into Turkey through the Morava-Maritza valleys in addition to its own natural termination. The Dnieper valley plays an exceedingly important share in connecting Turkey to northern lands. To the east the trough-like recesses in the folds of the mountains of Armenia and Kurdistan lead to the great Tabriz gate beyond which the Persian Gulf affords sea travel to centers of civilization of the monsoon lands or westward to the African coast. Land connection with this continent also exists in the rift valley of Syria where the beginning of the African rift system is found. Through the occurrence of all these channels of penetration the history of Turkey finds place as a special chapter in the history of the world's great nations. A greater share of responsibility falls on the land for this relation than on the Turks themselves.

The world relation of Turkish lands antedates, however, the coming of the Turks by many a century. Problems summarized in the familiar term Eastern Question have their origin in the existence of the narrow waterways consisting of the Dardanelles, Marmora and Bosporus. This water gap has exerted profound influence in shaping the relation of Turkish territory to the outside world. The Eastern Question is as old as the history of civilization on this particular spot of the inhabited world. It could not be otherwise because, fundamentally, this momentous international problem is merely that of determining which people or nation shall control the strait. Who shall gather toll from the enormous transit trade of the region? This is the economic problem which has always deeply agitated the leading commercial nations of the world. Its continuity is a proof of its geographical character. As long as these straits exist at the point of nearest convergence of the Balkan and Anatolian peninsulas, identical problems are bound to recur on their site. Beneath the shifting scenes of human events the abiding stage persists in directing them into its own channels.

Accordingly as early as in late Minoan times and surely in full Mycenean period, some fifteen hundred or two thousand years before our era, we find the Eastern Question already vexing the world. It centers first around Troy, because the city commanded the southwestern outlet of the straits and played the same leading part in the history of its day as Constantinople has played since then. The shifting of the site to the northeastern end of the waterway represents the gradual spread of Hellenic influence in northeastern maritime territory.

We can only come to an adequate conception of the rôle of Troy in history by a clear understanding of the value of its site. The city was a toll-station. Its citizens accumulated wealth in the manner in which the burghers of Byzantium laid the foundations of their vast fortunes. Schliemann's excavations brought to light amazing treasures of precious metals and jewelry. These riches may well be regarded as the price paid for the right of the passage of vessels and their freight through the straits. Nor is it strange to find that coincident with the decline of the Homeric city, the earliest mention of Byzantium, its successor, appears. Consistently with this method of viewing Trojan history it becomes possible to reach a rational understanding of Homer's classic epic as the account of a secular struggle for the possession of an eminently profitable site.[2] The testimony of history on the number of sieges which Constantinople has undergone is at least precise, although no literary masterpiece sheds lustre on the events. It is impossible to escape from the parallelism in the histories of Byzantium and Troy simply because the geographical background of both sites is similar in every respect. In the case of Troy, it meant convenient access to the Pontine rearland, probably the first El Dorado recorded

---

[2] W. Leaf: Troy, A Study in Homeric Geography, London, 1912.

by history—the land of fabulous treasures, in search of which the Argonautic expeditions were equipped. With Byzantium, it meant access to the luxuries which Asia could supply as far as the Pacific.

So much for the antiquity of the Eastern Question. Passing to another phase of Turkey's world relation we find that the land's influence has even affected the discovery of America. We now stand on the threshold of modern history and deal with a broad economic problem which affected late medieval commerce and which is an ever recurrent theme in that splendid period of active human enterprise known as the Age of Discovery. The dominant idea of the day was to find means of facilitating east-west trade in the eastern hemisphere.

From earliest times commercial relations between the land of Cathay and Europe had been one-sided. The east sold and the west purchased. There was very little exchange. The products which came from the east could all be classed as luxuries. They constituted freight of small volume such as precious stones, fine woods, essence and spices, the value of which generally ran high. These commodities had been shipped to Europe for about two millenniums prior to the fourteenth century of our era. Overland the caravans plowed their way across the southern expanse of Russia's interminable steppeland and penetrated finally into the plateaus of Iran and Anatolia. Their home stretch lay in Turkey. By sea the traders were accustomed to end their journeys at the head of the Persian Gulf, whence the valuable wares would be shipped farther west via Mesopotamia. In this case again the home stretch is found on Turkish soil. It was not until about the end of the fourth century B.C. when the Egyptian hamlet of Rhaecotis changed its name into that of Alexandria, that this sea route was extended into the Red Sea and Mediterranean. At this time the vision of acquiring wealth through the eastern trade began to dawn on the minds of the inhabitants of the Mediterranean seaboard. Many centuries were to elapse, however, before westerners realized that fortunes could be made by venturing into eastern fields. The profits and the splendor of the eastern trade were popularized by Christendom when the accounts of Marco Polo and the friar travelers of his time became available. Then the ambition of every adventurous merchant was to act as middleman in the trade with Cathay.

The bulk of the east-west trade in medieval time flowed through the same two main arteries. The northern land route from China through central Asia passed through the Tabriz and Erzerum gates and ended at Trebizond, the rest of the journey being made by sea through the Bosporus-Dardanelles passage. The southerly course was an all-water route from the sea of China to the Mediterranean.

The incentive to reduce cost of transportation was as strong in those days as it is at present. The northern route being mainly overland was a source of incessant worry to the trader. The unrest which followed the appearance of Mohammedanism, the reluctance of the adherents of Islam to deal with infidels, rendered commerce more and more risky. Transportation by land was slower and less profitable than by sea, as it is now. Caravans could not avoid brigands as easily as ships could escape pirates. It was not only a case of argosies reaching port but also of camels escaping highwaymen. In addition, duties had to be paid at four or five different points of transshipment. If we examine the pepper and ginger trade alone—the supply of both of which came from the east—we find that from Calicut, the great emporium of trade on the Malabar coast, these spices were carried by the Arabs to Jiddah and thence to Tor, on the Sinaitic peninsula. Overland journeys began at the last point and extended to Cairo. From the city a river journey on the Nile to Rosetta followed, after which the freight was packed on camels and sent to Alexandria. All these conditions made for the increase of cost of the eastern wares which were supplied to Europe.

With the cost of eastern commodities rising higher and higher, as land transportation became more and more hazardous, the minds of navigators naturally turned to the possibility of discovering a sea-way to India and Cathay. The discovery of

America in the course of these endeavors to lower prevailing freight rates was an inevitable consequence of economic conditions. The chief point of interest resides in the fact that the discovery which immortalized Columbus' name was accelerated by fully half a century through the falling of Constantinople into the hands of the Turks in 1453.

The capture of the Byzantine capital came as the death-blow to an already declining commercial intercourse. Henceforth the Moslem was to stand guard at the western gate through which east-to-west intercontinental trade had passed; and there seemed to be no doubt that he was firmly resolved to prevent the Christian from traveling back and forth through his dominions. It meant the definite closing of the western gate to eastern commerce. The first evil effects of the Turkish conquest were felt by the Venetians and Genoese. The Venetians especially incurred the wrath of Mohammed the Conqueror on account of the aid they had rendered to the beleaguered capital. Greater leniency was shown by the Turks to the Genoese, who had refrained from open manifestations of sympathy with the Byzantines.

The Sultans themselves as well as their ministers were willing to foster the trade which traversed their lands. It left a share of its proceeds in the Turkish treasury. As a matter of fact, commerce between Turkish lands under Mohammedan rule and the west existed only because of the income it brought to the Turkish government. But the Turk could not compete successfully with the Christian in the markets of the world and this proved a barrier to commerce. The significance of the Turkish conquest of the Byzantine Empire is to be found therefore in the fact that it practically cut off land communications between western Europe and eastern Asia. Incentive to western exploration was intensified. Before the fall of Constantinople the discovery of a western sea route to the east was regarded as highly desirable. It now became a necessity.

The possibility of reaching the Far East by a voyage through the pillars of Hercules had suggested itself to the active intellect of the Greeks and Romans, yet the incentive to undertake exploration did not acquire intensity until the latter half of the fifteenth century. The Turkish advance into western Asia came, therefore, as a shock whose impact forced trade out of the Mediterranean through the straits of Gibraltar into the wide Atlantic.

But there was another important result of the Turk's conquests in the Balkan and Anatolian peninsulas. The diversion of the eastern trade from European land routes into sea lanes impoverished the German-speaking inhabitants dependent on the Danube artery of continental life. The land on either side of this main highway was blessed with natural wealth, but its treasures had been drained by the Vatican. The reformation, which combined religious and political aspirations, was an excellent opportunity for the chiefs of the small states scattered in the long valley of the great river to pounce upon the landed property owned by the Roman church and establish economic conditions favorable to themselves.

The present world relations of Turkey may be summarized by the statement that the country lies squarely in the path of both Teutonic and Slavic advance. A natural course of expansion is leading Germany to the southeast across the Balkan peninsula into Turkey. The extension of frontiers required by Russia likewise impels Slavic conquest of Turkey. Overpopulation in the one case and the need of access to ice-free waters in the other make the contest inevitable. The Teuton is answering the call of the land, the Slav that of climate. In both the problem is mainly economic. At bottom it is the modern phase of the Homeric struggle idealized in the Iliad.

The dismemberment of Turkey into European colonies is the goal steadily held in view since the loss of the Holy Land to Christendom. It will be the last chapter in the long history of Europe's commercial conquest of western Asia. Three causes militate in favor of an eventual partition. The country is rich in natural resources. It is held by a people whose incompetence to convert nature's gifts into use or profit is historically patent. It also happens to occupy a commanding situation with reference to the trade of Europe with Asia and Africa. These three points are fundamental in the solution of the Turkish problem.

The European nations most vitally concerned in the dismemberment of the Sultan's dominions are four in number. Great Britain's interest is born of the Empire's relation to Egypt and India. The cause of Russian progress depends on the country's access to warm seaports. Germany is the newcomer on the scene and, as a land power, is engaged in extending her land area. To her sons Turkey offers an attractive colonization area and at the same time the land route which will render them independent of the sea-way passing through Suez to the east. As a colonial power of the first magnitude, no less than on account of her millions of Mohammedan subjects, France cannot be disinterested in the fate of the corelands of Islam.

Turkey is the Asiatic pendant of the intercontinental highway represented in Europe by the Balkan peninsula. Through Asia Minor the land provides a convenient causeway between Asia and Europe. Through Arabia it connects Asia to Africa. Again, through the combined position of Asia Minor and Syria it becomes possible to maintain continuous land travel from Europe to Africa. Turkey is thus the ideal center of the eastern hemisphere. Mastery of its territory is bound to turn the flow of intercontinental trade into the lap of its holders. The entire history of European conflict over Turkish lands is wrapped up in this geographical fact.

Italians were the pioneers of European trade with Turkey after the consolidation of Ottoman power. In this Genoese and Venetian traders merely followed in the footsteps of their fathers, whose dealings with the Byzantines had been considerable. French merchants were not slow to compete with Italians. In the fifteenth century British drapers and commissioners begin to appear in the Levant. Germans show signs of activity a hundred years later, but confine their operation mainly to the European dominions of the Sultans. From these beginnings to the twentieth-century territorial claims of the great powers is but a natural economic unfolding.

Turkey's remarkably central position in the eastern hemisphere makes the country the threshold of Great Britain's Asiatic dominions as well as the natural land connection between British Africa and British Asia. From India westward and from the British zone in southern Persia as defined by the Anglo-Russian convention of 1907, to the Sultanate of Egypt, southern Turkey, represented by Lower Mesopotamia and Arabia, is the only stretch of territory in which the British government does not exercise direct control; and the task of consolidating British influence in these two regions of the Turkish Empire is well advanced.

In the economic life of modern Mesopotamia British influence is paramount. About 90 per cent of the trade of Basra and Bagdad is in British hands. Steam navigation on the Euphrates and Tigris with its attendant privileges of transportation is a monopoly exercised by the British. This means that all the Persian trade which enters or leaves the country through its southern Turkish border must pay toll to British capital. Most important of all, the stupendous task of reclaiming the great twin-river valley has been undertaken by British enterprise.

The area of agricultural lands in Lower Mesopotamia is generally calculated at ten times the total surface of farming land in Egypt. The territory suited for cultivation extends northward from the Persian Gulf roughly to a line drawn from the bend of the Euphrates at Anah to Tekrit on the Tigris. Its eastern boundary is defined by the Zagros and Pusht-i-Koh mountains. On the west it reaches the Great Syrian desert as far as its junction with the plateau of Arabia. Thus defined the region is the great alluvial plain of Mesopotamia. A stretch of land remarkably rich in humus, it only needs a just rule and competent engineers in order to become highly productive.

In olden days the entire district was one vast field. Its fertility had earned it the name of granary of the world. Herodotus extols its productivity: ". . . In grain it is so fruitful as to yield commonly two-hundred fold. The blade of the wheat

plant and barley plant is often four fingers in breadth.''[3]   In
their present state the once productive lands present the appearance of a desert.   The old irrigation ditches are in ruins.   Mile
upon mile of parched, cloggy soil or dreary marsh take the place
of ancient fields.

The reclamation of this arid country was undertaken in 1908
by British engineers headed by Sir William Willcocks.   In the
Delta region of Mesopotamia, comprising the entire drainage
valley extending south of Hit on the Euphrates and of Samarra
on the Tigris, between 12 and 13 million acres of first-class
irrigation land were to be converted into productive areas.   In
spite of Turkish opposition the work advanced with sufficient
rapidity for the Hindiyeh Barrage to be inaugurated in 1914.
At a distance of twenty centuries a handful of plucky northerners had, notwithstanding well-nigh insurmountable obstacles,
put the last touches to a drainage project begun on the same
spot by Alexander the Great, the construction of a new head for
the Hindiyeh branch or Pallocopas having been that monarch's
first public work in Babylonia.[4]

In the Persian Gulf British influence advanced by great
strides during the present century.   Within the last ten years
the policing of the gulf waters and harbors has been undertaken
by Britain's men-of-war.   An appreciable curtailment of the
trade in firearms followed the tracking of gun-runners by British
captains.   The important towns of the Persian and Arabian
coast are virtually British possessions.   Bushire[5] on the eastern
shore, Koweit on the west are protectorates.   The trend of it all
is to advance India's western frontier to the line of the
Euphrates.

For Great Britain's attitude toward Turkish politics is
dictated by Delhi rather than London.   As ruler of the most

---

[3] Bk. 1, Chap. 193.   Babylonia's fertility is also noticed by other ancient writers.
Cf. footnote of Rawlinson's Herodotus, New York, 1859, Vol. 1, p. 258.

[4] W. Willcocks: The Irrigation of Mesopotamia, New York, 1911, pp. 13-14.

[5] Bushire with a population of about 20,000 inhabitants owes its importance to its
being the southern sea terminal of the caravan route which starts at Teheran and
passes through Isfahan and Shiraz.

numerous political group of Mohammedans in the world, the king of England's residence in his European capital cannot affect India's geographical needs, among which the maintenance of a clear road from its shores to the mother island is of prime import. Thus the establishment of a British zone in southern Persia and the attempt to substitute British law in Mesopotamia where, after all, the Sultan's authority is most precarious in character, merely reveal England's necessity of consolidating her power over the approaches to her great Asiatic colony.

In dealing with Indian geography and the vast body of Mohammedan Hindus, attention is necessarily riveted on the question of Arabia. British stewardship of the peninsular table-land seems inevitable. Not that those huge wastes of burning sand contain resources convertible into profit; but Arabia represents a wedge of barbarism driven in between the civilizing influences exerted by Great Britain in Egypt and India. The danger of its becoming a generating center of revolutionary currents involving British colonial policies in destruction is not mythical. Millions of Indian Moslems turn daily in prayer toward the direction of the Kaaba. A glance at India's history suffices to reveal the extent to which the Sea of Oman has linked the two peninsulas.

To detach Arabia from a shadowy allegiance to the Sultan of Turkey and bring it within the uplifting sphere of British activity was part of the political program elaborated at Downing Street after the bombardment of Alexandria in 1882. In pursuance of this policy British influence is now markedly felt along Arabia's three coasts. It is firmly planted on the southeast, where Arabia is nearest to India. From Koweit to Muscat every petty potentate exercising an antiquated patriarchial authority has learned to rely on British protection against Turkish encroachments. Aden, on the southwest coast, is a lone outpost of civilization from which western ideas radiate and occasionally reach the plateau land of Yemen or the niggardly wastes of Hadramut. This British seaport is the natural outlet of Yemen. Products of the favored districts around Kataba, as well as between this town and Sana'a, can be transported with greater facility to Aden than by the arduous routes which lead to Red Sea harbors.

The question of Arabia involves other considerations. Mecca and Medina, its holy cities, are essentially the religious center of the Islamic world. From their sites Mohammedanism has spread about 4,000 miles both east and west. Among Arabs as well as the majority of Mohammedans outside of Turkey desire for the restoration of the Caliphate at Mecca is strong. Arabs especially consider the Sultans as usurpers of the title. Selim I had been the first to adopt it after the conquest of Egypt and Arabia in 1517. Arabs however refuse to recognize the right of any but descendants of the Prophet's family to this supreme post of the Mohammedan ecclesiastical hierarchy. According to Islamic traditions the Caliph must be a member of the Koreishit tribe. This explains why any ambitious leader who succeeds in circulating the report of his relationship with Mohammed's progeny has always secured a following among his co-religionists in Asia or Africa.

The Arabs have aired this chief grievance of theirs in English ears. They found ready sympathy among British officials no less than among the leaders of their faith in Egypt or India. The complete severance of the Mohammedan Caliphate from the Turkish Sultanate will, therefore, be a probable result of Franco-British success in the present war. The reëstablishment of the Prophet's family in its hereditary right and capital will have the advantage of providing Islam with a geographical center at the very point of its birth.

Modern German ascendancy in Turkey has constituted the gravest menace to the British project of uniting Egypt to India by a broad band of British territory. German diplomacy has exerted its best efforts during the past generation in the attempt to defeat this design. In overcrowded Germany the need of land for colonization is felt as keenly as the necessity of providing new markets for the country's busy industries. Germany does not contain within its borders an agricultural area of sufficient extent for the requirements of its fast-growing populations. Against this it has been estimated that with adequate irrigation Asia Minor can turn out a million tons of wheat annually, as well as at least 200,000 tons of cotton. The basis of Teutonic southeasterly expansion lies in these facts. The immediate aim of German imperialism is to spread through Austria and the Balkan peninsula into Turkey down to the Gulf of Alexandretta and the shallow waters of the Persian Gulf. But its realization implies the shattering of British projects.

This rivalry in the west Asian field became inevitable from the moment that men of German speech became conscious of the power they had acquired in 1870 by banding together in a single state. The task of national consolidation once accomplished, the thought of German leaders naturally turned eastward in the direction in which land extended. Eight years later the prestige acquired by the newborn empire gave it a decisive voice in the treaty of Berlin. The first peg in the line of the Teutons' southeasterly march was driven then by the revision of Bulgarian frontiers delimited by the treaty of San Stefano. The Slavic obstacle seemed removed from the Teutons' path and its place filled by the more easily negotiable Turkish obstruction.

From the date of that treaty to the events of these years of war Germany's conduct in Turkey has been determined entirely by the call of the land. In 1882 a German military commission undertakes to reorganize the Turkish army. In 1889 the Deutsche Bank—whose directors are leaders of Germany's oversea affairs —is granted a concession for a through line from Constantinople to Konia. This concession has since been modified so as to comprise the trans-Anatolian trunk railway which connects the capital with Bagdad. In 1898 the Kaiser visits Damascus in person, there solemnly to proclaim assurances of his unalterable good-will to the millions of Mohammedans scattered over the surface of the earth. In 1902 the Bagdad line is definitely awarded to a group of capitalists, among whom Germans represent the majority of investors. From that date on, railroad, mining and irrigation concessions in Turkey seemed to have been reserved exclusively for Germans. The transfer of Turkey's unexploited riches to German ownership became almost an accomplished fact.

It was the "Drang nach Osten," a movement directed primarily by the valleys of the Danube and the Morava, and forking out subsequently along the Vardar and Maritza gaps. To clear this road to Turkey, Serbia was wiped off the map of Europe in the fall of 1915 by Teutonic armies. For this too had Serbian nationality been split into three separate bodies at the behest of Teutonic diplomatists. Bosnia and Herzegovina, lands Serbian in heart and logic, were administered by Austria, an empire in name like Turkey but virtually ruled by Prussia since the day of Sadowa. Montenegro, of old the refuge of martyred Serbia, had always been prevented by Austria from uniting with its sister state. In truth Serbia lay under the bane of a geographical curse. It was always in the way.

The misfortune of position is shared fully by Turkey. Coming at right angles to Germany's southeasterly drive, Russia's steady southwesterly advances in the nineteenth century foreshadowed the conversion of all the Black Sea and its Bosporus entrance into Russian waters. With the most inaccessible parts of the Armenian mountains in Russian hands since 1878, further expansion through western Armenia into Anatolia cannot be delayed much longer.

The Russian viewpoint deserves every consideration. Russia lies benumbed by the cold of her frozen land. She has had one long winter since the dawn of her nationality. The chief reason why her sons have been laggards in the liberal progress of the past hundred years must be sought in this simple fact of geography. Russia does not need more land or fresh resources. She only seeks the warmth of the sun's rays. Geographically it is Russia rather than Germany who is entitled to "her place under the sun." Today more than ever, and because of her newly-won liberty and democratic institutions, Russia needs a window on the sunny side of her national dwelling.

Russian access to the open sea in the southwest can be

secured either at Constantinople or Alexandretta. The Bosporus route is the more advantageous, as the markets for products of the plains of southern Russia are strewn along Mediterranean coasts. But mastery of the Bosporus is of little value to Russia without possession of the Dardanelles strait. The Marmora is but the lobby of the Black Sea. The entire Bosporus-Dardanelles waterway must, therefore, be Russian in order to allow the country to reap the full advantages of attaining ice-free seas. If fifty years ago the question was merely one of political foresight, today it has assumed vital importance, for southwestern Russia's economic development, in the present century, has made the country absolutely dependent on Balkan and Mediterranean markets.

As an alternative, the harbor of Alexandretta finds favor among Russians. It lies at a distance of only 450 miles from the southern Caucasus frontiers. Moreover, it is part of the ancient land of Armenia, which sooner or later is destined to become a Russian province in its entirety. Such an extension of Russian territory to blue water on the Mediterranean has significance in two ways. It would redeem a land that has remained Christian in spite of centuries of Mohammedan yoke and it might effectively bar German access to the Persian Gulf.

Russian influence in Turkey differs signally from the control exerted by its three western competitors. British, German and French encroachments on Turkish sovereignty have increased in proportion to the amount of capital expended by each of these countries for the development of Turkish resources. In this respect Russia, which is not a country of financiers, stood at a disadvantage. To overcome this handicap Russians resorted to borrowing from France and England, mainly the former, and invested the funds thus obtained in Turkey. Such transactions have in reality been the means of strengthening French and British ascendancy in the Ottoman land. The northeastern region of Anatolia, which, owing to its contiguity to Russia, was regarded as a sphere of Russian influence, has lately been looked upon often as a zone of French interests, owing to the participation of French capital in its development. But from a geo-

FIG. 54.

FIG. 55.

FIG. 54—View of the harbor of Odessa.
FIG. 55—Export wheat ready to be loaded at Odessa.

graphical standpoint this French zone is artificial. Its depend-
ence on Russia cannot be altered as long as its position on the
map remains unchanged.

France's natural sphere of interest in Turkey will be found
in the Syrian vilayets. This is not due to the financing of Syrian
public utilities and indus-
tries by French capitalists
as is often alleged. It is
the offspring of the Mediterranean which, since the
dawn of history, has con-
nected the southern French
coast to Syrian harbors.
Phœnician oversea trade
in the first millennium before the Christian era
had reached the coasts of
Provence and Languedoc.
Marseilles, a city born of
this intercourse, has maintained commercial rela-
tions with Syria uninter-
ruptedly down to the present time.

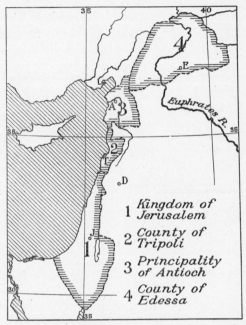

FIG. 56—French states in Syria at the
time of the Crusades. Scale, 1:11,500,000.
Based on Pl. 68, Historical Atlas, by W. R.
Shepherd, Holt, New York, 1911.

Franco-Syrian ties were strengthened considerably during the
Crusades. The conquest of Syria and Palestine by the Arabs
diverted the thoughts of Christendom from the economic importance of these lands to their religious appeal. France, "the
eldest daughter of the Church," took the lead in the attempt to
wrest the Holy Land from its Mohammedan conquerors,—
"Gesta Dei per Francos." Many of the petty states founded by
noblemen who took part in the Crusades were ruled by Frenchmen. Antioch and Tripoli had French princes, Jerusalem a
French king. The title of Protector of Oriental Christians conferred by the Papacy on French kings had its origin in the active
part played by France in the Crusades.

France has exercised a dominant intellectual influence in the Levant for at least seven centuries. Turks bestow the appellation "Frank" on Europeans without discrimination of nationality. Western ideas which have trickled down to Turkish soil are French in character. French schools in Turkey are more numerous than any other. The civilizing power of French culture showed its strength by the readiness with which it asserted itself in the midst of uncongenial Turkish thought. France's hold on Turkey is thus of a high moral order. It differs in this respect from the material claims of the other European powers.

At the same time through the investments of French capitalists a well-defined zone of French interests has been created in Syria. Excepting the Hejaz line every railroad in the province has been financed in France. The silk factories of the Lebanon, around which the whole industrial life of Syria clusters, were started by French citizens. Their annual product, usually estimated at half a million kilograms of silk, is exported to France. Syrian silk farmers in need of funds for the annual purchase of cocoons raise their loans exclusively among the banking houses of Lyons. French interests are not confined to Syria alone; fully one-half of the amount of one billion dollars representing Turkey's official debt to Europe has been advanced by French financial institutions.

It is difficult to assign a place to Italy in the array of European claimants for Turkish territory. The trade between Italian and Turkish seaports has lost the relative importance it had acquired in medieval times. Italian pretensions to Adalia Bay and its rearland are of quite recent date and the result of conquests in Libya. But beyond vaguely formulated promises for railway concessions from the Turkish government no ties bind the region to Italy. Italy however created its own sphere of interest somewhat unintentionally by the occupation of the islands of the Dodecanesia. By this act it distanced every other European country in the race for a share of Turkey.

The group of islands lying off the southwestern coast of

Anatolia is now held by Italy in virtue of stipulations covenanted with Turkey at the treaty of Lausanne. According to the terms agreed upon, Italy was to occupy the islands in guarantee of Turkish good faith pledged to prevent anti-Italian agitation in Libya. Upon complete pacification of the latest territorial addition to Italy's African domain, the political fate of the islands was to be determined jointly by the six Great European Powers.

The islands, between twelve and fifteen in number, are peopled exclusively by Greeks. Hellenic customs, language and religion have survived upon each in spite of centuries of Turkish rule. Italian sovereignty, however benevolent or likely to promote the welfare of the islanders, is disliked equally at Patmos, Leros, Cos and Rhodes. The remaining islands are relatively unimportant, some consisting of mere uninhabited rocks emerging two or three hundred feet above the sea. But to the smallest inhabited islet, annexation to Greece is keenly desired. The Italians were hailed as liberators from the Turkish oppression by the hardy fishermen who labored under the impression that their island homes had been rescued in order to be annexed to Greece. Their disappointment was expressed in mass meetings at Patmos and Cos in 1913.

Racial and historical considerations add their weight to the linguistic claims advanced by Greeks in Greece and the Dodecanesia. As sailors the islanders have maintained to this day classical traditions of Hellenic maritime activity in the region. The islands in fact constitute lands of unredeemed nationality whose natives are without a single exception akin to the continental Greeks.

This fact combined with a distribution of a numerically preponderant Greek element along the western coast of Anatolia makes the Ægean a truly Greek sea. Structurally the coast lands encircling this body of water are identical. In the east as in the west they constitute the warped margin of a subsided area. Identity of land and peoples has given rise to Greek claims on western Turkey. Greece, therefore, keeps in line with other European nations in expecting a share in the inheritance of the moribund Turkish state.

The claim is historical no less than economic. The association of the Ægean religion with centuries of Hellenism and fully one millennium of Byzantinism is by no means severed in modern days. For the second time in its glorious history the ancient city of Athens has become the social, political and intellectual center of the Greek world. In one and the same prospect the Greek capital can point with pride to the Hellenic splendor exhaled from Anatolian ruins and to her modern sons achieving daily economic victories over the Turk in his own land.

In this spectacle of nations lying athwart each other's path the clue to the adequate settlement of the Turkish problem may be found. Turkey is before anything else a roadway—a bridgeland. As soon as this point of practical geography is recognized it will be easy to provide international legislation in which the claims of interested powers will be harmonized. But no solution of the political problem involved can ever be attained without full consideration of its geographical aspects. Failure to recognize this would leave the Eastern Question in the hopeless tangle in which it has lain for over a century.

As the seat of through routes Turkey and its railroad play a great part in international transportation. Hence it is that the Turkish lines, with exception of the Hejaz railroad, are controlled by financiers grouped according to nationality. At present the majority of shareholders in each of the concessions belong to one or the other of the great European powers.

The broad Eurasian landmass contains three densely populated areas. Of these central Europe is the westernmost. The Indian peninsula follows, situated approximately midway between the European area and the coastlands and islands of eastern Asia, which form the easternmost of the three. In these three regions only does the average density of population exceed 64 inhabitants to the square mile. The speediest and most convenient routes between the westernmost and the two Asiatic regions must inevitably cross Turkey. This feature, together with the fact that Asiatic Turkey is a land richly endowed with natural resources and that, although lying at Europe's very door, it is still undeveloped, confer upon Turkish railroads an importance which has always been keenly realized by enterprising business men the world over.

All travel between Europe and Asia is deflected into northern and southern channels by a central mass of mountains which separate a vast lowland of plains and steppes on the north from the tablelands of southern Asia. Age-old avenues of human migration and of trade in the northern area have the disadvantage. of traversing sparsely inhabited regions. To build transcontinental railroads along this route implies scaling some of the highest mountain ranges in the world in order to tap the populous centers of India. Although this is not beyond the engineer's ability, capitalists decline to consider it. Southern routes, on the other hand, link with the seas that set far inland on Asiatic coasts. The function of the Turkish trunk lines is to provide the shortest connection between European railways and the steel tracks of southern Asia or to connect with the sea routes that link harbor to harbor from the Persian Gulf to the China Sea.

Although lying at Europe's very door and in spite of its extreme antiquity as the abode of civilized man, Asia Minor presents the strange anomaly of being one of the world's least developed regions. It was only after the Crimean War that railroad construction was undertaken within the peninsula. The granting of railway concessions enabled the Sultan to pay his debt of gratitude to the western nations which had assisted him in checking the natural efforts of the Russians to add a strip of ice-free coast to their country's southwestern boundary. With the exception of a single line every kilometer of track in the peninsula has been built by Europeans. As is always the case in undeveloped areas, the districts tapped by the various lines became economically dependent on the roads that hauled their products and supplies. This circumstance induced tacit recognition of spheres of foreign influence in which commercial, and attendant political, preponderance leaned strongly towards the country which supplied the capital with which the railroads were built. Wherever, as in Syria, vaguely defined spheres of European influence had previously existed, the advent of engines and cars contributed to strengthen them considerably. The routes determined by the steel-clad tracks may therefore be considered as approximate center-lines of these spheres of foreign influence. It is on this basis that six distinct spheres may be marked out as follows:

(1) A British sphere extending over the entire drainage basin of the Meander and traversed by the British-owned Aidin railway.

(2) A French sphere which was originally confined to the drainage of the Gediz river, the ancient Hermos, but which, through privileges acquired as a result of the successful operation of the French-owned Cassaba railway, now extends northwards to the Sea of Marmora. This additional sphere is divided into two equal east and west areas by the French-owned Soma-Panderma railroad.

(3) A German sphere—the most important of these spheres of foreign influence—which, beginning at the Bosporus, traverses the entire peninsula diagonally by way of the inviting routes provided by surface features and extends southeasterly through Mesopotamia to the Persian Gulf.

(4) A Franco-Russian sphere which was originally allotted to Russia and which comprises all of the area north of the German zone described above. Russia's inability to finance railway enterprise in this area, no less than political ties which bind this country to France, led to French participation. As a result of this dual arrangement construction on the French-owned Samsoun-to-Sivas line was begun in 1913.

(5) A second French sphere comprising all of Syria. It is considered by Frenchmen as their most important sphere of influence in Turkey. The French-owned Beirut-Aleppo, Tripoli-Homs and Jaffa-Jerusalem lines are operated in this area.

(6) An Italian sphere extending inland from the extreme southwestern coast of Asia Minor so as to include the hinterland of the Gulf of Adalia. Italy is a recent invader of this field. Its ambitions were revealed in the fall of 1913, after it became known that negotiations had been carried on between the representative of the Italian bondholders of the Ottoman Public Debt and the Turkish government for the concession of a railway line to connect the seaport of Adalia and the town of Burdur, the southeasterly terminus of the Aidin railway.

(7) With these six spheres a contested seventh should be mentioned, which is constituted by the exceedingly rich mineral district situated at the northern convergence of the valleys of the Tigris and Euphrates. Russian, French and German interests claim respective rights of priority to its exploitation.

None of these divisions would be recognized officially as such in Turkey. But then ethnographic boundaries are likewise strictly ignored by the rulers of that country. Definite official recognition of these spheres is nevertheless implied in the terms of a number of commercial covenants signed by Turkey and various European powers according to which the right to operate railroads, and even mines sometimes, is granted by the Turkish government exclusively to a single company which in almost every instance is owned by capitalists of the same nationality. The Russo-Turkish convention of 1900, which reserved to Russians rights of preëmption on railroad building in the area called the Franco-Russian sphere, may be mentioned as an example. Similarly the Bagdad Railway Convention of 1902, formally signed by the German ambassador and the Turkish Minister of Public Works, recognized the exclusive rights of the Bagdad Railway Company—a German enterprise—to build the important trans-peninsular route which will link Europe to Asia and Africa.

One might infer that the existence of these six spheres should be attributed to Turco-European agreements. Closer scrutiny brings to light, however, the working of purely natural forces, explanation of which is to be found in the geography of Asia

Minor. These international railroad conventions, and the areas determined by their text, represent in reality the outcome of the geographical conditions which are grouped here under the two major heads of world relation and regional features.

World relation is an attribute of geographical location. Situated as a junction area, a bridge as it were, between two continents, Asia Minor stands out as an excellent type of an intermediate region which has participated in the life of both. This two-fold influence has been particularly marked whenever general progress in either continent culminated in an overflow beyond continental boundaries. The feats of Greeks and Persians, and of Byzantines and Turks, may be considered as successive cycles in which the spirit of Europe or of Asia predominated in turn. At the end of each cycle life on the peninsula would revert to conditions determined largely by regional influences. The past sixty years have witnessed the beginning of a process of slow liberation from the effects of the last cycle of Asiatic invasion. The spirit of the west is ushered in once more for the simple reason that it has become necessary to maintain a clear road over which the products of overworked European factories will be transported to populous markets in southern Asia. The primary cause of European influence must therefore be traced back to Asia Minor's location, by virtue of which the peninsula has always been the site of an important world route. Aryans of the present century are merely preparing themselves to travel by rail the highway over which their far-removed ancestors tramped on foot.

Besides offering the shortest overland route between the Baltic Sea and the Indian Ocean, Asia Minor's favored location affords the same convenience with regard to land communication between Europe and Africa. Any line diverging southwards at a suitable point on the main trunk which traverses the peninsula diagonally may be prolonged through Syria to the Turco-Egyptian frontier and extended in Africa so as to connect with the Cape-to-Cairo railroad. While no definite steps have yet been taken to secure this desirable connection, the project has

been under consideration for over a decade and it may be surmised that its execution will not be deferred much longer.

But world relation is also determined by a region's natural
resources. Notwithstanding its undeveloped state, Asia Minor is
known to have been abundantly endowed with all the primary
products required by modern man's complex life. The valleys
connecting its coast line with the inland ranges are exceedingly
fertile. This is particularly true of its western and northern
area. The high plateau of the interior needs only to be irrigated
in order to become a vast granary. Its mineral wealth is so
abundant and varied that it may be asserted that no other area
of the same dimensions can be compared to it. Its flora is
extremely diversified. Its forest belts are still considerable,
despite a lack of legislation for insuring their conservation and
rational exploitation. The slopes facing its three seas from the
upper coniferous belts to the lower olive tree zone, support a
great variety of economic species. We have here all the elements
which satisfy man's natural desire for space after he has reached
a given stage of development. This desire is imposed by
economic requirements which impel activity in fields that must
be kept expanding. The zones must be hence regarded as spheres
of economical rather than political influence. They indicate
natural foresight on the part of powerful political agglomerations
preparing the way for future industrial and commercial advantages. At bottom it is an expression of man's growing ability
to shape his destinies according to his requirements and free
himself from the limitations imposed by frontiers. The economic
phase of Asia Minor's geography thus contributes its full share
in the determination of these spheres of foreign interests.

Asia Minor may be considered as the eastern emergence of
the continental shelf supporting the European peninsula. Its
salient physical features are a central plateau surrounded by a
rim-like succession of ranges which are fringed in turn by a
coastal strip of land. A gradual ascent from west to east can be
observed. The western ranges have a mean altitude of about
2,000 feet above sea level. The plateau has an average height of

3,000 feet. The Armenian upland generally exceeds 4,000 feet. Access from the sea to the interior is impeded by the mountainous barrier reared as a natural bulwark. The gaps made by watercourses alone permit communication. As most of the rivers are not navigable, an important method of exploration is thus closed to adventurous roamers, whether native or foreign. This lack of fluvial communication has greatly hindered intercourse. Rivers have constituted the ancient ethnic boundaries between the inhabitants of the peninsula.[6] Communication between districts has been carried on mainly from harbor to harbor. Although the peninsula is in direct contact with three seas its mountainous rim prevents benign maritime influences from extending to its interior. Its climate may therefore be classed as extreme Mediterranean in type. All these combined factors annul to a large extent the effects of peninsular conditions.

The region is not as salubrious as its elevation might imply. It is an area which has been occupied by communities of men actively engaged in human pursuits at various periods of history, and which has been subsequently abandoned to itself or rather to the working of causes in which man had no part. Gradual desiccation of the plateau is evinced by the presence of desert wastes coated with alkaline precipitates, by receding lakes and all the manifestations accompanying the decline of a hydrographic system. The salt lake occupying the central part of the plateau is in reality nothing but a vast marsh. Hydrographic changes are not confined merely to the interior of Asia Minor but exert their action on the coast itself. The bays of Tarsus and Ephesus are now much shallower than they were two thousand years ago.[7] The general result is to impair settlement. Reoccupation of the soil must often be preceded by sanitation and it is only within recent times that this important tool has been perfected by man so as to enable him to wield it effectively in the conquest of fresh sites of occupancy.

Viewed therefore from its broadest aspect the problem of

---

[6] Vivien de St. Martin: Asie Mineure, Vol. 11, p. 386.
[7] Reclus: Asie Antérieure, pp. 509 and 522.

European control of Asia Minor resolves itself into one of renewed settlement. It is therefore pertinent to inquire how this condition coupled with regional influences has affected each of the six spheres.

Englishmen were the first to engage in Turkish railway building. The Aidin railway, which links the thriving port of Smyrna to the Anatolian plateau at Dineir, represents an investment of about $50,000,000, or about a third of all the money invested in Turkey by the British public. This road taps the fertile Meander valley and has proved a remunerative undertaking to its owners, although it has not been subsidized by the Turkish government. The line is credited with the best management in Turkey. Its well-ballasted track and the splendid condition of its rolling stock impress the traveler most favorably. English capital is also represented in other lines built in Turkey, though only as minority holdings.

This British zone of influence is at present the best developed region in Asia Minor. Its northern boundary is determined by the divide separating the watersheds of the Gediz and the Meander rivers. The Aidin railway follows the course of the last-named river to its very sources at about 1,000 feet below the general western level of the plateau.[8] The eastern boundary of the sphere is defined by the end of the natural road at one of the abrupt slopes leading to the plateau in the vicinity of lakes Burdur and Ajituz. Its southern frontier reaches the districts which supply the railroad with traffic drawn from the border line of the Carian ranges and the foot of the northern slopes of the Lycian Taurus.

The sound establishment of Great Britain's commercial influence in this locality dates from the year 1856, when construction on the Aidin railway was inaugurated. Its real beginning can be traced back to the dawn of the nineteenth century, when English naval supremacy replaced France's hitherto paramount maritime influence in the Levant. In recent years an interesting expansion of British trade ascendancy in

---

[8] Hogarth: The Nearer East, New York, 1902, p. 33.

this zone can be detected since the products of the area tapped by the Aidin railway, whether they consist of cereals, fruit, ores or local manufactured goods such as rugs, are mainly exported nowadays to Great Britain, the United States and Australia.

Throughout history the valley of the Meander has constituted a region in which natural features of the surface have been eminently favorable to man's development. In addition to the wealth of its natural resources it is provided with a deeply indented coast line, in which commodious natural harbors occur. Here is found the maximum density of population for the entire peninsula—70 inhabitants to the square mile.[9] Within this restricted area Greek influence first took root about 2,600 years ago before spreading throughout Asia Minor. The origin of this movement must be ascribed to the local advantages which invited human activity by the display of favorable regional features. It is safe to surmise that the same geographical agencies have been again responsible for the striking parallel afforded by the first establishment within contemporary times of a sphere of western influence in the region.

Italy's connection with Turkish railroads has consisted in providing labor and in laying claim to franchises in southern Asia Minor. These claims are of recent date, and have been put forth since the occupation of the islands of the Dodecanesia by Italian troops. Specifically the claim is made for the right to build a railroad from Adalia northwards to Burdur. The region to be tapped by this line is a strip of broken lowland intervening between the Lycian and Cilician Taurus. The valleys of the Aksu and Keuprusu, bordering the east and west slopes of the Ovajik massif, join in forming a deltaic area in which sub-tropical cultures, rice, cotton and tobacco thrive. Plains and wide valleys, which are probably ancient lakebeds, occur between the smaller ranges of the zone. They contain arable lands which might be turned to account were the region more thickly settled. A number of smaller rivers discharge their contents into the gulf

---

[9] Hogarth: op. cit., p. 155.

of Adalia. The gulf itself is shallow, devoid of harbors, and open to southerly winds. Lack of natural harbors and remoteness from the main highways of the peninsula have contributed to the sphere's isolation. It is still imperfectly known through a few route surveys and occasional descriptions.

The most important road in Turkey is the partially completed trunk line running diagonally across Asia Minor and beyond into Mesopotamia. The line is German-owned, although French and English capital is represented. The concession for the first stretch, extending from Constantinople to Konia, had been granted to German and Austrian railroad builders in 1888. The celebrated Bagdad railroad is the prolongation of this line. Its construction was turned over to German promoters by a firman (decree) dated January 21, 1902. The financial burden of the enterprise was estimated at about $200,000,000.

The Bagdad railroad is the final link of the shortest overland route between Europe and Asia. In the minds of Germans it is destined to compete with the sea-way controlled by England. The road was conceived in order to connect Teutonic centers of industry and Asiatic markets. The speediest sea route between Europe and Asia passes through straits guarded by British sentinels. As long as Gibraltar, Suez and Aden form part of Great Britain's colonial domain, they can be closed at will to competitors of British manufacturers.

The great trade routes which link Europe to Asia have always crossed Turkish territory. One of the most widely traveled of these highways formerly connected the classic shores of Ionia to the fever-laden coast of the Persian Gulf. It was the road to India. The spices, gems and silk of the East reached European buyers by way of this trunk land route. For countless centuries caravans have plied back and forth over the barren plateau of Asia Minor and the sweeping plains of the Mesopotamian depression. This traffic is still maintained although it is now much on the wane. Long files of camels proceeding leisurely at a swinging gait are met occasionally by the traveler in Anatolia. A patient ass leads the way as of old. The turbaned driver plods along unmindful of the historical associations accumulated over his path. He knows however that the steam engine, devised by western ingenuity, is about to deprive him of the scanty pittance which his journeys yield.

Germany is essentially a land power. It was natural that the country should seek to establish land routes over which its control would prove as effective as England's oversea highways. With this aim in view, the German government lent unreserved support to German captains of industry striving to obtain sole mastery of the great Turkish trunk line. Asia, teeming with thickly populated districts, lay at hand. Britain's unrivaled sea power afforded its people adequate transportation to these centers of consumption. The Germans realized that a land power could not compete successfully with rulers of the waves. They resolved to acquire commercial supremacy in Asia by the creation of a land route. The Bagdad railroad is the outcome of this realization.

The road starts at Konia at the southeastern terminal of the Anatolian railroad, also a German line, whose tracks reach the Asiatic suburbs of Constantinople. Konia lies in the very heart of the Anatolian plateau, a stern and melancholy land, destitute of trees and sparsely peopled. Here at an average elevation of 2,500 feet above sea-level, the tracks are laid over the ancient highway which leads to Syria. In spite of its mournful scenery, the region is a veritable paradise to the archeologist. It is studded with prehistoric ruins and contains secrets of Hittite history which await the scholar's investigation. Here and there along the line the dilapidated remnant of a Seljuk building reminds the traveler of the peculiar charm of Mohammedan art.

Beyond the plateau the road plunges into a tangled mountainous district known as the Taurus. The famous Cilician Gates are the only practicable gap provided by nature among bold and abrupt peaks in this region. The armies of Pagan, Christian and Mohammedan monarchs have marched through this gorge in the long struggle between the East and the West which enlivens the history of the ancient East. Cyrus with his retinue of

Persian lords and his bands of Greek soldiers found it a convenient opening. Alexander the Great stepped between its narrow walls on his way to conquer the world. Detachments of Crusaders under Tancred and Baldwin bore the banners of the cross through the rugged pass. Later Mongolian hordes sang of loot as they swarmed through the mountain cut.

Unfortunately the ride through this mountain section of the Bagdad line will not be made uninterruptedly in broad daylight. The engineering problems involved are of considerable magnitude. The mountain can be conquered only by means of tunnels and the cost of this method of advance is naturally enormous. It has been estimated at a minimum of $140,000 per mile. In addition to tunnels considerable stretches of very heavy earthwork are required. If the undertaking delights the engineer's heart, it is on the other hand apt to dismay the capitalist.

The drive through the Taurus does not end the difficulties of construction. This mountain is succeeded immediately by the equally lofty and precipitous Amanus range. Another arduous tunneling section is encountered. Of the two the last is the most difficult and costly. An idea of the heavy expense incurred in this construction work is conveyed by the cost of the wagon road built to reach the mouth of the first tunnel. It has been estimated that over one million dollars have been spent in this preliminary work.

The descent towards the Cilician plain is steep. To the west Tarsus, the birthplace of the Apostle Paul, looms a blot of white over the grayish green of the surrounding land. The change from the dreary scenery of the plateau is a delight to the eye. The valleys leading to the Mediterranean coast are wooded. Vegetation soon assumes a southern aspect of luxuriance. The sensation of finding oneself in an altogether different country is especially felt on hearing the sonorous accents of Arabic now spoken in place of Turkish.

From the site of the Amanus tunnels to Aleppo the line was completely built in 1915. Thence it strikes eastward only to turn south after reaching the Euphrates river. From here on to

Bagdad trains will run through the great alluvial flood plains of Mesopotamia. This is a rainless district. The present large cities, Mosul, Bagdad and Basra, have no important share in world affairs in comparison with the political and cultural influences which radiated far outward from the precincts of ancient Nineveh and Babylon.

Between Konia and Bagdad the railroad is 1,029 miles long. For convenience of operation it is divided into sections of approximately 130 miles in length or more correctly of 200 kilometers. Construction on the first section was begun shortly after the award of the concession. This portion of the road was opened to traffic in 1904. Building was abandoned until 1910 owing to lack of funds. In May of that year operations were resumed at different points of the line. By the middle of 1913 about 400 miles had been completed.

Since the beginning of the European war, construction has been pushed with increasing speed. In northern Mesopotamia the construction of a bridge over the Euphrates at Jerabluz allows the laying of tracks with a fair degree of rapidity in the northern stretches of the Syrian desert. Work was also undertaken at Bagdad in a northerly direction. In the last days of 1914 trains were running regularly in the valley of the Tigris between this city and Samarra. Since then, according to reports, the tracks have advanced farther north.

Work on the sections in northern Mesopotamia does not present great difficulties. There is reason to believe that construction here proceeded with feverish haste during the European war. The main obstacles to rapid track-laying are found in the mountainous district which intervenes between the Anatolian plateau and the plains of Syria and Mesopotamia. According to reports the tunnels in the Amanus mountains were driven from end to end by the summer of 1915. It will probably take longer to complete construction through the mountainous wall which connects the Chakra valley to the Tarsus river in the Cilician Taurus. This section of the road is only 22 miles long. It crosses however an extremely rugged district and requires four separate tunnels which together measure some 10½ miles. In May, 1914, three tunnels had been started and the ground cleared at the approach of the fourth.

A number of branch lines are included in the concession of the Bagdad railroad. The products of some of Turkey's most promising districts will pass over their tracks toward the trunk line, thence to be finally transported overland through the Balkan peninsula and Austria to German manufacturing centers. A side line projected to extend northeast of Aleppo will tap eventually an exceedingly rich mineral belt situated at the northern convergence of the Tigris and Euphrates. In this district the celebrated copper mines of Argana are found. They are worked in desultory fashion by the Turkish government. In spite of crude methods of extraction and long camel-back hauls the ore is of sufficiently high grade character to yield ample returns. Silver, lead, coal and iron also exist in the same zone of mineralization.

An important branch connecting the trunk line with the Mediterranean at Alexandretta has been in operation since 1913. The line is only about fifty miles in length and traverses the heart of a rich orange-growing district. The northern track of this branch crosses the plain of Issus where Alexander battled against Darius. At about six miles from its southern terminal the line hugs Mediterranean waters and crosses the spot where, according to statements of the natives, the whale relieved itself of the indigestible burden of the prophet Jonah.

In central Mesopotamia, branch lines extending in easterly directions will tap rich oil-fields and may eventually provide connection with future trans-Persian railroads. The history of this Mesopotamian region abounds in stirring chapters. The most favored section is found in the narrow neck of land extending for a short distance at the convergence of the courses of the Tigris and Euphrates. This site was marked by nature for the heart of great empires. After the fall of Babylon, the neighboring cities of Seleucia and Ctesiphon became in turn the capitals of Greek emperors and of Parthian and Sassanid sovereigns. Here Bagdad, rich in human history, grew to world fame. The farms and palm groves surrounding the city spread on the east and west until they almost reached the banks of the rivers which carried life and fertility in their waters. At the time of Arab prosperity Bagdad was one of the most magnificent cities of the Mohammedan world. As a center of Mussulman art the city had no peer. The Turkish conquest, which swept light a blight over the land, put an end to the city's prosperity.

In modern times, Persians and Turks have vied with each other to retain possession of the land. Bagdad then became the center of the struggles waged between Caliphs and Imams. The conflict which splits Islam into the two rival camps of Sunnis and Shiites revolved around the city. The mausoleums and mosques which annually attract thousands of pilgrims are the sanctuaries in which upholders of the divergent beliefs elbow each other oftener than in any other Mohammedan city.

Should the Bagdad railroad be destined to remain German property the line is bound to become the backbone of German supremacy in western Asia. Germania, helmeted and carrying sword and shield, will ride over its rails to conquer Palestine and to wrest the wealth of the Nile and Ganges from British grip. But the foreign interests of every European nation are affected by the construction of this celebrated railway. It is the most direct route to Asia for all of Europe. The question of its internationalization is therefore one of the problems of European diplomacy.

The extensive zone traversed by this railway comprises the fertile and well settled valleys of the Sakaria and the Pursak, practically the whole of the interior plateau to the foot of its surrounding mountains and the eastern section of the Mesopotamian valley. Within this belt the most populous inland towns of the peninsula succeed each other at regular intervals. This circumstance indicates their former importance as stages on the long journey between the Bosporus and the Persian Gulf. Casual inspection of their crowded bazars would dispel doubt on

FIG. 57—One of the many shops in a Turkish bazaar. All commerce in Oriental cities was formerly centered under a single roof. This feature of Oriental commerce is gradually disappearing.

this score. Attention must be called here to the geographical significance of these bazars in the Orient. Every urban center is provided with one. It is usually a roofed inclosure within which the city's business is carried on. Caravans proceeding from remote sections of the continent have their rendezvous outside their gates. The size of these bazars and the activity displayed in each is the measure of an eastern city's intercourse with the rest of the world. In the geographer's mind their significance is the same as that of railroad stations.

By acquiring this trunk line the Germans succeeded in taking a first mortgage on Turkey. It was the first signal success of the policy of directing Teutonic ambitions into eastern channels which Bismarck had adopted immediately after the consolidation of the German Empire. He had a vision of an all-German line of traffic starting at Hamburg and crossing the Bosporus towards the Far East. In one direction German calculations miscarried. Germany was unable to finance the undertaking without the support of British and French capitalists. The international character of the line became more and more pronounced between the years 1908 and 1911. During this period a number of agreements were signed between Great Britain, France, Germany and Turkey in which a notable percentage of German interests passed over to the two rival countries, the Germans emerging out of the transaction with a bare control.

The project of an all-German route received another setback when England was awarded the final section of the Bagdad line. This successful stroke of British diplomacy consolidated British influence in the Persian Gulf. Koweit and the environing districts ruled by petty Arabian chiefs became British protectorates and the long-planned German through line merely butted against a solid wall raised by British ability.

The French have invested twice as much capital as the English in Turkish railroads. The lines they manage and own directly are the Syrian railroads and the Smyrna-Kassaba line. They are also interested in the construction of roads in the northeastern districts of the country where concessions have been awarded to Russians. Muscovite inability to provide capital is responsible for the transfer of the building and operating grants to Frenchmen.

The sphere of French influence comprising the Gediz valley and its adjacent territory to the Sea of Marmora lies entirely out of the beaten track of intercontinental travel. Its economic prosperity is therefore governed by purely regional influences. The valley of the Gediz river itself compares in fertility with that of its southern consort, the Meander. Tracts of arable land in its northern area and the occurrence of extensive mineral deposits, a few of which are among the most heavily exploited in Asia Minor, combined with genial climate and the accident of position which places the zone directly opposite the European mainland, all tend to impart elements of economic significance which have allured French enterprise.

As has been shown already, the zone of paramount French influence in Asiatic Turkey lies, south of Asia Minor, in Syria. "La France du Levant" is a term which is not uncommonly applied by Frenchmen to this Turkish province. The origin of this intercourse may be traced to the trade relations between Gaul and Syria in the fourth century B.C. During antiquity a widely traveled road, albeit of lesser importance than the peninsular highway of Anatolia, connected the Mediterranean and the Persian Gulf. This route started from Egypt and Syrian harbors and skirted the western and northern edges of the Arabian desert before assuming a southerly strike which led it through the Mesopotamian basin. The populous cities of Damascus, Homs, Hama and Aleppo lie on this ancient avenue of trade. Here, as in the case of the Anatolian cities mentioned, their present population is altogether out of proportion to their resources or activity. It can only be regarded as a sign of the importance they once had as stages in this southern east-west route. The Syrian littoral, described by Hogarth as the garden of Arabia,[10] must be regarded therefore as an intermediate region connecting Asia and the country lying west of its Mediter-

---

[10] Op. cit., p. 194.

ranean border. This influence of location prevailed throughout history.

The conquest of Syria by Frankish Crusaders gave renewed impetus to commercial relations between Syria and France. A regular trade route between Marseilles and Syrian ports was established. The treaty of alliance between the Sultan of Turkey and the King of France the first half of the sixteenth century contributed to bind this province more firmly to France. At the end of the seventeenth century French trading-centers had been established in all the important cities of Syria. Napoleon's invasion of this province as a result of the Egyptian campaign and French intervention in the Lebanon in 1859 likewise increased French prestige in the region. The confinement of this western hold to Syria can be ascribed to the influence exerted by the boundaries of the province. It forms with Palestine an excellent type of regional unit consisting of an elongated mountainous strip barely 50 miles wide. With the Mediterranean on the west, and deserts on the south and east, its only outlet to the world lay on the north.

French builders first undertook to connect the province of Lebanon with the sea by constructing the Beirut-Damascus line. The tracks were subsequently extended to Aleppo, a city whose greatness was founded on its situation along the natural road which connects the Mediterranean with the Persian Gulf. As a railroad center Aleppo's future looms bright, for the city lies also in the path of the tracks which will connect the Black Sea with the Mediterranean.

In southern Syria, the outlook for French enterprise was dimmed for a few years by the construction of a Turkish line from Damascus southwards. Branch lines were carried to the sea. Harbor concessions, however, were granted to French firms. French interests thus retained a notable share of the control over the traffic in and out of Syria. Furthermore, a concession for a line from Rayak to connect with the Jaffa-Jerusalem road which they obtained in 1914 will enable them to compete with the Hejaz line.

The last railroad agreement between the French and Turkish governments was signed on April 9, 1914. Concessions on the part of the Turkish government are bestowed in return for French financial support. The lines granted will tap northern Anatolia and Armenia. Connection with the German lines will be made at Boli and at Argana. The area tributary to this line contains fertile plains and plateaus. It is known to be rich in mines, notably in copper. The advent of the railroad will undoubtedly brighten the outlook of the Turkish mining industry.

In southern Arabia a railroad concession was awarded to French promoters in 1908. The line was to connect the seaport of Hodeida with Sana'a. It was intended to divert into Turkish territory the large trade with the interior which now passes through Aden. Strategic reasons also weighed heavily in the decision to build this road. At no time have the Arabs of the Yemen shown sympathy for their Turkish rulers. Every commander sent to quell their incessant rebellions ascribed his failure to lack of transportation facilities. It was mainly in view of this condition that steps were taken to connect this section of the Arabian table-land with the sea.

The Franco-Russian sphere is the outcome of privileges originally conceded to Russia by Turkey. The terms of the agreement under discussion call for the construction of railroad lines as follows: The trunk line is to start at Samsoun and to end at Sivas.[11] A westerly branch line will diverge from Tokat towards Yozgat without reaching this city, however, or extending beyond the divide between the Yechil and Kizil rivers. A second branch will start at Tokat and reach Erzindjian, whence it will be turned northwards to Trebizond. Beyond Sivas the line will be extended to Kharpout and the vicinity of the important Argana copper mine. Connection with the Bagdad railway will be made beyond this point. Finally an important branch will leave the trunk line at Kazva to extend to Kastamuni and Boli.

The zone defined by these projected lines covers the greater

---

[11] *Asie Française*, Oct. 1913, p. 402.

part of northern Asia Minor. It forms a region in which relief and the rigor of the climate have retarded the development of the population.[12] These geographical disadvantages are compensated by ample natural resources. The eastern section is known to contain a rich copper belt which bids fair to become the site of a thriving industry. The deltaic strips and river valleys will permit extensive tobacco culture and fruit raising. The passing of this zone under the sphere of western influence is a mere result of Russia's constant endeavor to obtain a coast line which will not be closed to navigation during the winter.

The only line owned by the Turks in their country is the narrow-gauge railway known as the Hejaz line which starts from Damascus and is intended to reach the holy town of Mecca. The financing of this line has been unparalleled in the annals of railroad building. Ostensibly the purpose of the construction was to provide traveling conveniences to 250,000 pilgrims who, it is estimated, came annually from all parts of the Mohammedan world to worship at the Kaaba. In the belief of many, the line was built for strategical reasons and to enforce Turkish sovereignty among the Arabs, who have always been loath to admit the Sultan's claims to the Caliphate.

The funds for the construction and equipment of the road were obtained by appealing to the religious feelings of the 230,000,000 Mohammedans scattered in widely separated regions of the globe. Stress was laid on the pious character of the undertaking. According to reports, $14,000,000 were collected soon after the enterprise was launched. Thereafter about $12,000,000 were contributed annually for several years. The operation involved no responsibility to the promoters, headed by Abdul Hamid, the former Sultan of Turkey, all the funds being bestowed in the form of donations. The road has thus no shareholders and no bonded indebtedness, its capital being spontaneously wiped off.

The religious character of the undertaking is apparent in the mosque-wagon attached to each train. Seen from the outside,

___

[12] Hogarth: op. cit., p. 244.

the prayer carriage is distinguished only by means of a diminutive minaret six and a half feet high. The interior is fitted out according to religious custom with rugs on the floor and framed Koranic verses in letters of gold on the walls. The direction of Mecca is indicated by a map at the end of the car, so as to enable the faithful to orient themselves properly when engaged in prayer.

A hopeful view of the future of Turkey's economic position may be entertained by remembering that the land is still unexploited and that the resources of its soil and subsoil await the handling of western energy. It is expected that as fine a cereal crop as can be obtained anywhere in the world will be raised in the region between Eskishehir, Angora and Konia. Five million dollars spent by Germans on irrigation at Chumra in the vicinity of the last-named city has proved conclusively that a thriving agricultural industry can be established on the interior plateau of Asia Minor. The Cilician plain, where cotton and cereals are cultivated, contains vast tracts of swamp land which can be reclaimed. Here, too, irrigation would greatly improve cotton culture. Many of these rich soils are parts of Turkish crownlands which have been estimated by some to amount to one-tenth of the entire area of Turkey. The lands owned by the Evkaf, or Ministry of Religious Foundations, also cover vast areas. Estates held under either of these forms of tenure can be rendered highly productive under western management. The southernmost end of the Bagdad line taps rich oil fields which are situated in the area of transition between the plateau of Iran and the Mesopotamian depression. The railroad traverses the western end of this oil basin. Its eastern section in Persia has been developed since 1908 by British firms.

The international control of Turkish railroads reflects the transitional character of the land over which they are built. Ownership in Turkish lines is of practically no value to so backward a people as the Turks have proved themselves to be. It is of vital importance to the industrial communities of the countries which hold the extremities of the roads of which the Turkish system is but a link. Germany, Austria and France at the western extremity of the transcontinental line, Great Britain in India at its eastern end, have interests which affect a large proportion of their population. In the west the great through line starts in some of the busiest industrial centers of the world. In the east it taps coveted markets. The attention of European manufacturers is directed towards densely populated India or China simply because profitable trade is found where numbers exist.

A comprehensive glance at the spheres of foreign influence in Turkey shows that the most satisfactory evidence of the control of geography over the development of railway zones and spheres of foreign influence in Asia Minor is obtained by mere reference to the regions in which adverse geographical conditions prevail. The Italian and Russian spheres are both characterized by physical and climatic conditions which have stood in the way of human development. The map reveals the absence of railways in both.

In the more favored zones western influences are shown by the presence of modern surface features. Striking examples of German enterprise can be observed along their extensive sphere of action. Grain warehouses at Polatli on the Angora line receive the crops of the environing country. In the plains of Konia canals and locks of varying dimensions have been built and the former swampy area is fast becoming a heavy producer of wheat. Farther south near Adana over 200,000 acres have been reclaimed mainly for cotton growing. In this district important harbor works have been undertaken at Alexandretta which it is planned to make both the outlet of all southern Asia Minor and the terminal of the sea route from Europe to the east.

Similarly French influence in Syria is observable in the macadamized highways of the Lebanon no less than in the development of a thriving silk industry. In the British zone of the Meander valley mines have been opened up by British capital. Along with this economic progress education is also advancing. Numerous European and American schools were in existence in

Asiatic Turkey prior to the European war. The mere presence of European employees of the railroads in the Anatolian towns is enough to infuse new thoughts into the minds of the inhabitants. On the whole the locomotive is performing its civilizing work and Asia Minor is gradually becoming Europeanized.

Summing up we find that we have dealt with a connecting region which may justly be considered as the classical type in geography. A land which by its position was everyman's land, and which, because of its geography, was of greater interest to the outsider than to its own inhabitants. Being a part of three continents it became part of the life which flourished in each. A nation formed on such a site belongs more to its neighbors than to itself. In this respect its future will resemble its past.

CHAPTER XII

THE PEOPLES OF TURKEY

THE peoples and ideas emanating from within the realm which still bears the name of Turkey have left an indelible mark on the rest of the world. Crossed by some of the great highroads of history, the land is inspiring in every aspect in which it is regarded. Its heritage of memories and the prestige of a happier and grander past are undisturbed by marks of decadence. Most of the foundations of our progressive spirit were laid in that eastern region. From a purely scientific standpoint, its human grouping and surface configuration present highly interesting interdependence.

The region is divisible into six major geographical sections. Each forms a background against which distinct types of the human family are displayed. The various groups differ from one another in religion and language, often even in race. A fringe of fresh and verdant coastland which surrounds the elevated shelf of Asia Minor is largely Greek and Christian. The only foothold which western thought, art or temper ever obtained in Asiatic Turkey is found within this wave-washed strip of land. The plateau-heart of Anatolia is predominantly Turkish and Mohammedan. The Christian element scattered on its steppe-like surface is unable to assert itself and yields to Oriental ascendancy. The high and broad mountain masses which border it on the east are the home of the Armenoids, generally Christians, sometimes Mohammedans, but almost always characterized by broad-headedness accompanied by a peculiar flattening of the back of the skull. Beyond this mountain barrier Asiatic Turkey becomes entirely Semitic, being mainly Arabian in speech and overwhelmingly Mohammedan in creed. Three main regions characterize this southern area. The long and narrow corridor of Syria became the highway which in antiquity bound the flourishing empires of the Nile basin to the powerful kingdoms of the Hittite highlands and the Mesopotamian low-lands.   Its motley population, containing representatives of every race, is a relic of former to-and-fro human displacements along its trough-like extension.   In the adjoining desert Bedouin tribes find their favorite tramping ground.   The twin valley of Mesopotamia is the home of peoples in whom fusion of Semitic and Indo-European elements is observable.

The history of this land is that of its invaders.   Successive streams of humanity poured into it from four superabundant reservoirs.   Its central mountain zone was the motherland of a virile race whose sons went forth at intervals to breathe vitality into gentler populations scattered between the Ægean coast and the valleys of the Nile and Mesopotamia.   Armenians and a number of Mohammedan sects represent today this Alpine race. Mediterranean men proceeded constantly from the south and west to new homes in the pleasant valleys that connected eastern Ægean shores with the interior table-land.   Mobile Semitic hosts abandoned the plateau of inner Arabia before the time of our earliest records and drifted naturally northwards towards the fertile Tigris-Euphrates basin or the commercial routes of Syria.   Finally a Turki element, lured out of its mountain cradle in the Altai by scattered grass lands extending westwards, swarmed in successive hordes into Asia Minor and even beyond, well into the heart of Europe.

In addition to the foregoing fundamental wanderings, the inflow of an Iranian element, composed of men of Aryan speech, may be observed.   This contingent marched out of the plateau of Iran and reached the Turkish highland without having to scale its slopes.   As a result of this migration Persian words permeate Armenian [1] extensively.   The Turks also have appro-priated a certain amount of Persian words and culture from the

---

[1] Fully one-third of Armenian consists of words of Persian stock. Some Armenian philologists point to the existence of a small remnant of highly ancient words which cannot be traced to Aryan forms and which probably represent the survival of a language indigenous to the Armenian highlands.

same source. Racially, however, the eastern element was absorbed by the Armenoid population.

The present inhabitants of the diversified domains of the Sultans have been welded by the run of history into a shadowy political unity which has failed to harmonize their incompatibilities of origin and ideals. Turkey is a thoroughly theocratic state. Its sovereign-caliph and his subjects have always considered it their most important mission to bring Islam to the infidel. So great is the hold of ideals over the human mind, however, that the non-Mohammedan populations have clung passionately to their religious beliefs. We are forced to seek in creed the main distinguishing traits which, outwardly at least, divide the inhabitants of Turkey into groups of different names. We shall see, however, that in the minds of many of them, language or historical traditions have little significance. At the same time it is believed that distinctions of a more fundamental character will be brought out in the course of this chapter.

The Greeks

Our knowledge of the first appearance of Greeks in Asia Minor has undergone radical revision in recent years. Their prehistoric culture can be traced as far back as the Neolithic. The chief interest of modern discovery centers around the now accepted fact that Greek culture originally invaded the region from the south and that the Indo-European element which brought Aryan speech to the land is a later wave which flooded the original Mediterranean stock at some time during the transition from the Age of Bronze to that of Iron.[2] The southwestern coast was first colonized. A northerly extension occurred thence and proceeded mainly along the coast.[3]

The sequence of geological events preceding man's appearance upon the Ægean coast of Asia had imparted features which were destined to favor human development to an excep-

---

[2] H. R. Hall: The Ancient History of the Near East, London, 1913, pp. 31-79.
[3] R. Dussaud: Les civilisations préhélleniques dans le bassin de la Mer Egée, Paris, 1914, pp. 414-455.

tional degree. A land-bridge connecting the Balkan and Anatolian peninsulas occupied the site of the Ægean Sea at the dawn of quaternary times. The subsidence of the land during this period was accompanied by heavy fracturing trending in east-west lines. The Ægean archipelago, studded with islands and surrounded by deeply indented coasts, conveys a vivid picture, on the map, of the crustal deformity which occurred.

Climate also conferred its share of advantages. The long and narrow valleys are sheltered by mountains on all sides except to seaward. Northerly air currents cannot reach them. Frosts or snows are therefore unusual.[4] The course of moisture-laden winds blowing landward from the seas that wash the three coasts of Asia Minor is arrested by the mountainous rim of the peninsula. Precipitation is almost entirely expended upon the narrow shore lands. Copious rainfall and flowing rivers thus provide this historic Anatolian fringe with patches of luxuriant vegetation and green valleys. The interior plateau, on the other hand, remains parched and barren during the summer months.

A splendid stage for Greek history was thus built during the prehuman period. Early Mediterranean oncomers discovered sheltered havens and fertile inlets along the entire development of the fancifully dissected coast. A natural festoon of outlying islands increased their security by providing them with advanced posts for the detection of hostile raids. Erosion along the parallel lines of east-west rifts had carved fair valleys in which the winding rivers of classical literature found a channel. But above all, the sea contributed commerce and cosmopolitanism, both great elements of world power. These in turn favored the growth of tolerance,—a trait which has ever marked the western mind and which, at that particular spot, was to constitute a bastion destined to remain impregnable to the opposing spirit of the east.[5]

Intermediate site, low relief above sea level and genial climate

---

[4] D. G. Hogarth: The Nearer East, New York, 1902, p. 102.

[5] D. G. Hogarth: Ionia and the Near East, Oxford, 1909; J. L. Myres: Greek Lands and the Greek People, Oxford, 1910.

combined to give the Greeks a full share of the joy of life. These are the physical elements upon which the striking cultural superiority of Hellenism is founded and without the concourse of which it has never set permanent foot anywhere. The brilliant florescence of Greek civilization in pagan time attained its apogee wherever these three geographical factors prevailed. The Byzantine Empire succumbed before eastern onslaught because it was gradually converted into an Asiatic state and thus exceeded the boundaries marked by nature for Greek humanity.

The sixth century of the pagan era was the Golden Age of Hellenism in Asia Minor. The elongated seaward valleys became the seat of flourishing and independent nations. A strong democratic spirit prevailed among their inhabitants. City states or self-governing communities were numerous. Their merchant princes drew on the vast eastern rearland for supplies which they sold to Europe. They also collected heavy tolls from freight going eastwards. A double stream of wealth thus flowed into their treasuries. The prosperity of this period has never since been paralleled in the region.

Creative art found a home upon a site so eminently favored by nature. The heart and mind of its inhabitants throbbed responsively to the stirring events which were the result of their country's situation at the junction of the most important sea and land highways of the then known world. There the antagonism between east and west, out of which so much world history has been made, broke into violent clashes after periods of commercial interchange. Talent was spurred to high achievement under the stimulus of foreign contact, wealthy patronage and genial environment. Imposing ruins and prolific discoveries of master-pieces of art convey ample testimony of nature's concentrated prodigality on this famous coastland.

The present Greek occupants of the Anatolian shores reflect the pleasant character of their environment in the lightness of heart which is one of their distinguishing characteristics. Their craving for gaiety, society and enjoyment is unfailing. Even the gloom of Asiatic dominion does not prevent merrymaking at every opportunity. In these respects the Greeks share to an eminent degree the feelings of the nations of the western world.

With the exception perhaps of the Circassians, the Greeks are the handsomest of the inhabitants of Asiatic Turkey. Classical forms of the head and of the general cast of countenance are met in every nook of the Anatolian seaboard. Their profiles are those of the gently curving lines of ancient Greek statues and medals. Among women graceful carriage of the head and neck adds to their charm. The men are erect and firm of gait.

Fishing and sailoring are the hereditary occupations of the coastal Greek populations of Asia Minor. Inland they become traders. The "corner" grocery or the village butcher shop is generally owned by a Greek. In recent years the Greek has learned to play the part of the promoter in the growing development of Asia Minor. He is often the middleman who brings western capital to eastern opportunity. Herein his rôle differs but slightly from that of his Lydian or Carian ancestors.

The true Greek is met only as far inland as a whiff of the salt sea air can be inhaled. Eastward, on the Anatolian tableland, Greek communities of the ancient Phrygian and Cappadocian lands differ from kindred coastal populations as widely as the fascinating greenswards of the one vary from the semi-arid steppe of the other. Once beyond the range of maritime influences, Greeks often forget their own language and adopt Turkish instead. This is frequently the case in many of the inland settlements where Turkish is now the only medium of oral expression for Christian thought.[6] Racially, too, the Greeks of the inland towns and villages betray Alpine or Armenoid origin rather than Mediterranean descent. Short stature, ample chest development and broad-headedness are conspicuous among them. The rock-hewn villages south of Mt. Argaeus afford a clue to the origin and antiquity of these mountain Greeks.[7] They are descendants of the natives who were conquered by the armies

---

[6] In many of these Anatolian communities Greek is written with Turkish characters.
[7] G. de Jerphanion: La région d'Urgub (Cappadoce), *La Géogr.*, Vol. 30, No. 1, July 15, 1914, pp. 1-11.

of Greek pagan states or by Byzantine troops. The conquerors brought language and culture to the upland populations but were numerically insufficient to impose a new racial stratum. Later the wave of Turkish invasion drove out Greek and forced Asiatic speech on the same mountain populations without always replacing Christianity by Mohammedanism.

Duality of language is sometimes accompanied by a strange duality of creed among Anatolian Greeks. At Jevizlik, on the road between Trebizond and Gumushchane, dwell crypto-Christian Greeks who publicly profess Mohammedanism while maintaining in secret the Greek orthodox faith.[8] The inauguration of a constitutional form of government in 1908, with its promise of religious liberty, gave the members of the community an opportunity to renounce their outward form of faith and proclaim complete adherence to the religion they had never really forsaken.

To the philologist these ancient Greek communities are veritable treasure grounds, especially when found in mountainous districts. Archaic forms of speech are in current use among their inhabitants. In many, the purity of the ancient Greek dialects of Asia Minor has been preserved with but slight contamination from later literary influences. The very names of those who speak these vernaculars show interesting connection with the classical period of Hellenism. Socrates or Pericles will cook daily for the traveler, and Themistocles supply him with tobacco. More than that, they all make themselves intelligible in the style—and the spirit, too—of inscriptional language. But the old Hellenic dialects should not be confused with the still unknown Lycian, Lydian and Carian languages found in inscriptions. There is reason to believe that these primitive speeches of the Anatolian plateau represent exceedingly early stages in the development of Indo-European forms.

Many of the Greek communities owe their survival to the proficiency of their members in a particular industry. The settlements of Greek miners scattered in the Pontic and Tauric

---

[8] In the Levant they are called Mezzo-Mezzos.

mining districts are instances in point. The Turkish conquest of
the Byzantine Empire was accomplished by Asiatic barbarians
who knew how to fight but included no artisans in their ranks.
They were therefore obliged to rely upon the populations of the
conquered lands for the maintenance of industrial and commercial activity. This notorious incompetence of the Turk for any
pursuit other than that of soldiering is, at bottom, the prime
cause of the survival of Christian communities within Ottoman
boundaries.

The Turks

The appearance and establishment of the Turks in a land
which was not that of their origin follows their life as nomad
tribesmen of the vast steppeland of central Asia. They were
men at large upon the world's largest continent, the northerners
of the east who naturally and unconsciously went forth in quest
of the greater comforts afforded by southern regions. The
flatlands which gave birth to their race lie open to the frozen
gales of the north. Their continental climate, icy cold or burning
hot in turn, is cut off from the tempering influences prevailing
behind the folds of tertiary mountain piles to the south. As the
steppemen migrated southward their gradually swelling numbers
imparted density to the mass they formed because expansion on
the east or west was denied them. China and the Chinese,
admirably sheltered by barriers of deserts and mountains,
stopped their easterly extension. Christian Russia stopped them
on the west, though at a heavy cost to herself, for no obstacle
had been raised by nature to meet their advance. The open plain
of central Asia merges insensibly into that of north Europe.
That is why incidentally Russia is half Tatar today. The
Asiatic was forced upon her. She sacrificed herself by absorbing
him into her bosom, saving Europe thereby from this eastern
scourge, but forfeiting the advantages of progress.

Cut off from east and west in this manner, the only alternative left to the Turk was to scale the plateau region of western
Asia and to swarm into the avenues that led him to conquered

Fig. 58—A group of Turks who have none of the racial traits indicated by their name. The seated members in the foreground are typical inhabitants of the Anatolian plateau. The Greek type, closely resembling the Italian, appears in the background.

territory where he succeeded in attaining power and organizing his undisciplined hosts into the semblance of a state. The presence of the Turk upon the land to which he conferred his Mongolian name and the very foundation of the Turkish state can in this manner be attributed to outward causes rather than to local development. It was essentially a process of trans-plantation. The consolidation and rise to power of the Ottoman Empire between the thirteenth and sixteenth centuries were largely due to foreign conditions, for during that interval Europe was busily engaged in extirpating feudalism and the objection-able phases of medieval clerical influences from its soil.

The Turks and their name were first known to the western world in the sixth century of our era. But their invasion of Asia Minor should rather be considered as a gradual infiltration begun in prehistoric times. Hittite carvings represent, among others, a recognizable Mongoloid type of Tatar soldiers who fought as allies of the great mountain state.[9] Pig-tails, high cheek-bones and oblique eyes have been conspicuously modeled by the sculptor. Tatar migrations are thus discerned in the morning of the history of Asia Minor. The early invaders were steadily reinforced from the east by their kinsmen. The rise of the Seljuk Turks to dominance was the explosion of energy accumulated in the course of the centuries in which this move-ment of Altaic tribes had persisted. The consolidation of Ottoman power marked its culmination. A single tribe could never have acquired sufficient strength to establish a mighty empire had not its ranks been swollen by members of kindred groups encountered during its migration. This is what actually happened when Jenghiz Khan and Timur appeared on the stage of history. Turkish accounts describe both as fiery leaders, men who could command the adherence of the vast swarm of descend-ants of their kinsmen, in whose footsteps they marched. Sultan Osman, the founder of the present Turkish dynasty and reputed to be of the same caliber, likewise drew on a human legacy of centuries for the accomplishment of his designs.

---

[9] J. Garstang: The Land of the Hittites, London, 1910, p. 318.

Unfortunately, the Turks bear a name which is utterly void of significance. They themselves apply it to every Mohammedan inhabitant of Asia Minor without discrimination of race or origin. But for fully eight centuries they have stocked their harems with women seized from conquered populations. It is no exaggeration to say that this human tax has been levied on almost every family of the Caucasus, western Asia and the countries of the Balkan peninsula. Today the net result of this variegated intermixture is that the Tatar origin of the average Turk, so called, is entirely concealed by the mingling with Mediterranean, Armenoid-Alpine and even Nordic elements. Except in a few isolated instances the Turki type of central Asia is rarely met within Turkish boundaries. Clearly no valid claim to racial distinctiveness can be set up by the Turks.

In religion the Turk is no innovator. He has merely taken unto himself the idealism of Arabia. And yet his efficient wield of the fine edge of Mohammedan fanaticism failed to sever the ties which bind Islam to this land. Even his language is not his own. The splendor of Arabian syntax and the supple elegance of Persian style alone confer literary flavor upon it. Over 70 per cent of the words in Turkish are Arabic retained in unalloyed purity. A scant sprinkling of Tatar words merely recalls by their sound the raucous articulations which form the nomad's speech, while their paucity is a true measure of the limited range of concepts which find lodgment in his mind.

Turkish nationality is equally meaningless. The descendants of Asiatic nomads became masters of western Asia without ever conferring the boon of government or of nationality upon the land and its peoples. In Gibbon's mordant words "the camp and not the soil is the country of the genuine Tatar." And Turkey is still a vast field in which the Turk has pitched his tent and merely waits, knowing that the day is not far off when he will have to break camp and seek new pasturages for his herds and flocks. But the site on which he has settled for the past five centuries had been the seat of a highly organized government. Seeing himself master of this estate the Turk unhesitatingly adopted its institutions. Thus, under the mantle of Islamic theocracy, Byzantine government and customs have continued to flourish in Ottoman dominions. Barring special features belonging to Mohammedanism, the ceremonials of the Sultan's court may be traced, step by step, to Byzantine forms. The very absolutism of the caliphs is alien to the fundamentally democratic character of both Tatar societies and Koranic teaching. It is Byzantine and a relic of the despotism of the Roman Caesars.

In speaking of the Turks it is necessary to carry two distinct types in mind. The pure Tatar vagrant, true to his native indolence, which unfits him for sedentary occupation, is in the minority. The mass of the Turkish population consists of a mixed element in which the racial strain of given localities persists along with characteristics imparted by fusion with Turki conquerors. This mingling is indicated further by the spirit which moves this people in the performance of their daily tasks. Its members are recruited among the plodding, gentle-mannered and kind-hearted peasants of the land. Local influence accounts for these qualities. Occasionally, however, the foreign strain will crop out. Then, like their nomad ancestors, who, from peaceful shepherds roaming leisurely from patch to patch of green, are transformed into fiends incarnate by the approach of a thief or a beast of prey, or whom a passing storm will throw into fits of uncontrollable rage which vents itself in passionate outbursts of shrieking and gesticulation, the Turkish peasants can cast their natural softness of character to the winds and become either bloodthirsty murderers smiting unarmed Christians or else heroes performing gallant deeds on the battlefield.

The majority of this Turkish population finds a congenial home on the Anatolian upland. Their ancestors beheld here an environment in which the physical characteristics of the plateaus of central Asia were reproduced. They took to it naturally. The table-land is a rolling expanse mournfully devoid of vegetation, save for rare clusters of stunted trees. Scanty plots of grass, surrounding sickly pools or streams, resemble holes in a ragged garment spread over its surface. Sun-baked in summer, chilled in winter, with a climate too deficient in moisture for the favorable development of human societies, the land could only appeal to Asiatic sons of semi-arid areas. In recent years, the tendency of Turks to retire to this region is observable wherever the industry of Christian populations of the encircling coastland has rendered life too arduous for Turkish love of ease.

The penetration of this table-land by nomads from the heart of Asia goes on today as in the past, albeit with abated intensity. It is no rare occurrence in Asia Minor to meet Tatars or Turkomans who have been on a slow westerly march for periods of from five to ten years at a time. Most of them come from the Kirghiz steppes. A vague desire to change their residence from a Christian to a Mohammedan country impels their wanderings, according to their own accounts. Constantinople looms as an objective nebulously impressed in their minds. But the goal is rarely attained. In reality their migration is as unconscious as that of their forefathers and merely carries them out of sheer necessity from pasturage to pasturage in the manner it affected former generations.

Mohammedan Immigrants

Ever since the establishment of Turkish authority in western Asia the policy of the Sultan's officials has been directed towards attracting Mohammedan settlers from foreign countries to the unpopulated districts of Turkey. Particularly at the end of unsuccessful wars, special efforts are made to induce Moslem inhabitants of lost provinces to return within Turkish boundaries, where land often exempt from taxation is assigned to them. Widely distributed Circassian, Tatar and Turkoman settlements owe their origin to this Turkish method of increasing the Mohammedan element in the country. The Bithynian peninsula, where Cretaceous limestones and sandy Eocene beds provide excellent soils, is a region favored by immigrants.

Russia's southwesterly spread of empire is responsible for

the movement of some 500,000 Circassians from the Caucasus highlands to Asiatic Turkey. Lithe of figure, brilliant-eyed and nimble in mind, these immigrants are morally and physically far superior to their new countrymen. They bring with them the higher standard of living of their native land. Their dwellings are more solidly built than the customary shanties or hovels of the Anatolian table-land, and their food is of the average European quality. Wherever settled, they live in a degree of comfort unknown to the Turkish peasant. Flourishing farming communities have grown up around their villages. In cities they are distinguished by a natural aptitude for commerce, and many an able government official has been recruited from their numbers.

In race, language and religion the Circassians of Turkey present, according to tribal origin, the confusion existing in their cradle land. The Kabardian group of the Uzun Yaila are of western Caucasus extraction and speak an incorporative language. The Chechen settled in Syria are derived from Daghestani highlanders. In some cases Circassians bear Christian names, but worship in mosques. Representatives of central Asiatic, European and even Semitic races are found among them.

A colony of Noghai Tatar refugees was founded in the lower Jeihun valley after the Crimean War, at which time it consisted of some 60,000 individuals. Their numbers were speedily reduced, however, by the malaria and fevers of the unhealthful Cilician coast land. A decimated remnant is now engaged in farming the marshy lands originally bestowed on their fathers. They maintain excellent relations with the Turks, with whom they intermarry.

The Turkomans of Asia Minor are, according to their statements, refugees from Muscovite Christianity. In reality they seek escape from Russian pressure exerted to force them to abandon nomadism. This name is applied generally to immigrants coming from Turkestan who preserved their roving habits. The cruel Turki type of lineament and expression is observable on their faces. They are Sunnis, or orthodox Mohammedans, and a Turkish-speaking people, but have little intercourse with native Turks.

The Karapapaks, or Black Caps, known also by the name of Terekimans, are Shiites, or adherents of the eastern branch of Mohammedanism, from Russian Armenia, who have crossed the Turkish frontier and settled near Patnoz in the Van vilayet. The original seat of this people is between Chaldir and Daghestan. Racially they are of Turki stock. Tatar types predominate among them, although Circassian and Persian physiognomies are by no means uncommon.

The Lazis of northeasternmost Turkey, who are sometimes known by the name Tchan, form the connecting link between the Caucasian and Anatolian populations. Many of them have forsaken their Russian homes in the past thirty years for the land of their kinsmen on the Turkish side of the frontier. They occupy, in fairly dense communities, villages nestling on the forested seaward slopes of the Pontic Alps, as well as the narrow strip of coast east of Platana. Former generations looked on them as pirates or brigands. They now follow less irregular pursuits, but still bear the reputation of being daring smugglers. The Turkish navy recruits sailors from among them.

By race the Lazis are allied to the Georgian group of Caucasus peoples, and their intermixture with ancient Armenian populations is probable. Their adherence to Mohammedanism is lax. They speak a southern dialect of the Grusinian language closely allied to Mingrelian but mingled with Greek and Turkish words. In some localities Turkish entirely replaces their vernacular. The limits of their language in Turkey coincide with the western boundary of the sanjak of Lazistan. They extend thence eastward, in a belt fringing the southern base of the Caucasus, all the way between the Black and Caspian seas.[10]

---

[10] Many Moslem immigrants from eastern Europe are also found in Asia Minor. Bosnians, Albanians, Pomaks and, in general, members of every Mohammedan community in the Balkan peninsula consider Asia Minor as a favorable land in which to settle.

FIG. 59.

FIG. 60.

FIG. 59—"Turkish" crowd in an Anatolian city (Trebizond). A gathering in these Turkish cities contains representatives of almost every race in the world.

FIG. 60—A group of Maronite women. Their sturdy appearance suggests their highland origin.

Mohammedan Dissenters

A number of communities whose origin is wrapped in obscurity are found off well-beaten avenues on the Anatolian table-land. A mild, temperate lot, broad-shouldered and open-faced, they have much in common, in spite of diversity of worship and isolation. Racially they present few of the Turki features. Their speech is usually Turkish, but they keep rigidly apart from the Turks. They are Mohammedans in name only. Having secured immunity from the fanaticism of the masters of the land, they have secretly maintained ancestral beliefs to their full extent. When the light of ethnographic research shall have been fully shed on their rites, it is likely that the transition of religious thought from the paganism of Hellenic times to the Christianity of the Byzantine era will be made clear.

To this group belong the inhospitable Tahtajis (known also as Chepmi and, in their westernmost extension in the Aidin vilayet, as Allevis), who are the woodcutters of the upper recesses of the Lycian mountains. A people of almost primitive manners, they form a community of about 5,000 souls. Eastern and western culture swept by their mountain homes, leaving the faintest of traces among them. Having neither priests nor churches they are held in disrepute by the Turks. Similarity with eastern religions can nevertheless be traced in their worship. They wail over the corpses of their dead as do the Egyptians. A vague connection with Iranian ideas is discernible in the belief they hold regarding the incarnation of the devil in the form of a peacock. They cannot be induced to discuss their rites with strangers. In their simple minds faith is all in all, and well accentuates the separatist tendency determined by their rugged mountains.

A more important group, the Kizilbash, present racial characteristics peculiar to the Nordic race, although they too have mingled extensively with the Armenoid natives of the Anatolian mountains over which their settlements are scattered. The name is pure Turkish for "red head," but cannot be traced to head-gear in Turkey. In Persia however allied communities are known whose members wear scarlet caps. The bends of the Kizil Irmak [11] and of the Yechil Irmak contain their villages.[12] They also have settlements in the highlands which extend from the Taurus to Upper Mesopotamia.

A Turkish-speaking people of peaceful habits, engaged exclusively in the tillage of their lands, submissive to authority, frugal and industrious, such are the Kizilbash in the midst of their Turkish, Kurdish and Armenian neighbors. They are usually on excellent terms with the Christians. But to this day, after centuries of occupation of the valleys of the Sakaria and Halys, they have remained as foreigners among the Turks who colonized their territory long after them. Probably on account of religious divergences the newcomers have always held them in contempt.

It is not unlikely that the Kizilbash are lineal descendants of the Galatae of Asia Minor. This western people entered the peninsula through the notch cut by the valley of the Sakaria—an avenue also chosen by the Phrygians sung by Homer. Later the Cimmerians also followed the same route. All these invasions from the west brought blondness into Turkey—though not of the pure Nordic type, for the roads leading out of northern Europe had their longest stretches in the brunet territory of central and southern Europe. Nevertheless mingling incurred in the course of migration, as well as after settlement, has not obliterated entirely the fair ancestral type. The strongest argument in favor of the relationship between the Galatae and the Kizilbash lies in the identity of the territory occupied by both peoples. The racial distinction between the two lies in the greater admixture of Tatar blood in the Kizilbash of our times. Gradual change of the Galatian of European provenience into

---

[11] R. Leonhard: Paphlagonia, Berlin, 1915, pp. 359-373; J. W. Crowfoot: Survivals among the Kappadokian Kizilbash (Bektash), *Journ. Anthrop. Inst.*, Vol. 30, 1900, pp. 305-320.

[12] The distribution of Kizilbash villages in the Yechil Irmak valley is shown in G. de Jerphanion's Carte du Bassin du Yéchil Irmak, 1:200,000, Paris, 1914.

the Kizilbash type of Asiatic affinity was accompanied by the replacement of Celtic by Tatar culture.

Galates to the Greeks meant any western barbarian. The term was applied to the foreigners whose coming was always marked by destruction and who, in the third and second centuries B.C., terrorized Thrace before crossing into Asia Minor. Here they introduced Celtic forms of speech which were current in their settlements as late as the fourth century of our era. At that time the language spoken in parts of Anatolia was similar to the dialect of the Traveri, a Celtic tribe on the Moselle whose name has been perpetuated in that of the city of Treves.[13] Arrian, a native of Bithynia, describing the customs of the Celts gives accounts of usages, such as the worship of the oak, which prevailed in his country and which on investigation are found to have their counterparts in Europe.

In religious thought, the Kizilbash may be classed as the most liberal among the Mohammedans of Turkey. Their interpretation of the Koran exempts them from keeping fasts and allows them the use of wine. They permit their women to go about with a freedom which has never been tolerated among Sunnis. Christian rites, such as the custom of praying over bread and wine, are performed among them. Fragmentary survivals of pagan observances likewise form part of their worship.

The Kizilbash are closely affiliated with the Bektash confraternity, a once powerful Islamic organization which still owns a large number of convents (tekkes) and churches in Turkey. Indiscriminate use of the two names has led to much confusion in the writings of travelers. It seems preferable to restrict the name of Kizilbash to the group of Anatolian people whose mountain origin is amply proven by somatic traits and whose cultural development denotes amalgamation with invaders of the table-land. The term Bektash can then be applied to the form of religion to which this people adheres at present. The connection is probably founded on the ease with which Bektash proselytism

---

[13] J. G. Frazer: The Golden Bough, the Magic Art and the Evolution of Kings, London, 1911, Vol. 2, p. 126, footnote 2.

drew recruits from among Kizilbash populations. In the light of this distinction the so-called Bektash people of the Lycian mountains are merely a sub-group of the Kizilbash, to whom they are related in part by race, language and religion.

The Balikis, or Belekis, living on the southern fringe of Sasun,[14] are probably also a remnant of the old highland population. The Mohammedanism they profess is tainted with dim reminiscences of Christian worship and was probably adopted as a self-preservatory measure. Religious beliefs weigh lightly however on this community. Its members possess neither church nor mosque. A term of residence among them would probably enable an observer to discover survival of very ancient customs. The passing traveler can do little more than note the unusual freedom with which their women go about unveiled or note the mixture of Arabic, Kurdish and Armenian words in their language.

The Avshars, descended from Persian immigrants mingled with native hill populations, are settled mainly on the eastern slopes of the Anti-Taurus facing the northern end of the Binbogha range.[15] The two elements which are blended in this people are also represented in their religion. The newcomers brought Shiite Mohammedanism and insured the predominance of their views over the relics of the nature cults of the aboriginal groups. Traces of Christian influence are observable in their daily life. Around Cesarea these Avshars give the shape of a cross to the loaves of unleavened bread they bake. In view of the deep-rooted aversion of Mohammedans towards any trace of Christian symbolism, it is evident that we are here in the presence of an old-established usage rather than one adopted in post-Mohammedan times. But in speech, custom and occupation the community differs in no respect from neighboring Turks.

The nomad element of the Anatolian plateau is represented mainly by the Yuruks, whose wanderings range from the northern landward slopes of the Cilician Taurus to the mountainous tract

---

[14] H. F. B. Lynch: Armenia, London, 1901, Vol. 2, p. 430.
[15] Earl Percy: Highlands of Asiatic Turkey, London, 1901, pp. 89-90.

surrounding Mt. Olympus. They are divided into tribes of varying size, some not exceeding twenty tents. Their number is estimated at about 200,000. Roving over barren districts, the members of this group are half-starved human products bred in areas of defective food supply. The men know no other occupation than that of tending their sheep and horses. The women are noted carpet-weavers. Strangers passing within sight of their tent settlements can generally rely on finding the nomad's proverbial hospitality under their felt roofs.

In common with kindred plateau communities, the Yuruks hold severely aloof from the Turks. But they have adopted Turkish speech, and it is gradually replacing their ancient vernacular. They have sometimes been connected with European gipsies, although the little that is known concerning their history and traditions hardly warrants such an assumption. A promising field for ethnographic research still awaits exploitation among their settlements. They call themselves Mohammedans and circumcise, but have no priests or churches.[16]

The Aptals of the lofty valleys of northern Syria also have nomadic habits and appear to be closely related to the gipsies. Although they claim to be Sunnis they rarely intermarry with settled Mohammedans. Their roaming life carries them from village to village, generally in the capacity of musicians and entertainers. According to their traditions they were expelled from the lower Tigris regions in the ninth century.[17]

THE ARMENIANS

The table-land on which Armenian life unfolded itself was faulted into blocks and covered by flows of huge volcanoes after the Miocene. Pontic ranges fringe it on the north and thereby forbid access to the Black Sea.[18] On the south, the folds of the Anti-Taurus mountains likewise act as successive barriers. But

---

[16] C. Wilson: Handbook for Travelers in Asia Minor, Transcaucasia, Persia, etc., London, 1911, p. 68.

[17] The gipsies of Syria are known by the name of Nawar, or Zotts.

[18] Cf. inset on accompanying map entitled "Part of Asiatic Turkey showing Distribution of Peoples."

no mountain obstacles intervene to the east or west of Armenia. Close racial, linguistic and historical relations can therefore be traced between Armenians and Persians today. Furthermore, the existence of important Armenian communities scattered all the way west of Armenia to the coasts of the Ægean becomes intelligible. The very crowning of Armenians as Byzantine emperors may ultimately be explained by this east-west extension of relief in western Asia.

The heart of the Armenian plateau is found in the gently folded limestones and lacustrine deposits surrounding Lake Van. Here an elevated plain relieves the ruggedness of environing peaks. Here, too, our earliest knowledge of Armenian history is centered. But the formation of nationality upon the surrounding sites of intricate relief was a long-drawn process. A highland dissected into numerous valleys could not become the seat of a united people. The region, being broken up, favored division. Accordingly feudalism flourished undisturbed throughout its extent. Each valley or habitable stretch was governed by its own princeling. These petty chiefs relied on the security provided by their rugged environment and were naturally disinclined to acknowledge authority emanating from outside their valley homes.

The plain of Van has always loomed large in the history of Armenia. This interesting depression occupies the southeastern corner of the great central plateau and lies surrounded by volcanoes which were centers of lively eruptive activity during the Pleistocene. Together with the plain of Mush it forms a single basin which was once a lake bed. The heavily saline waters of Lake Van still cover its deepest section. The exposed lake bottom consists of volcanic matter carrying fertilizers in abundance. Rich brown loams contributed to the region's famed fertility. Between the tenth and ninth centuries B.C. the Vannic community became the nucleus of a confederacy of mountain tribes forming the kingdom of Urartu,[19] which extended to the

---

[19] The Mexican parallel is too striking to be omitted here. The southern end of the plateau of Anahuac, on which the waters of Lake Texcuco receded within historical

FIG. 61—The plain of Van. The photograph shows the three features which make the site a center of Armenian history. The plain afforded farming land and was dominated by a lone eminence to the protection of which Armenians have resorted to this very day. The broad lake in the background added to the natural strength of this position.

heads of the valleys debouching on Assyrian territory.[20] After successful resistance against Assyria the independence of the Armenian state became well established about 800 B.C.

The ancient history of the Armenians is closely related to that of the Hittites. The appearance of the former is coeval with the disappearance of the latter. The probability of a common origin is strong. Enough light has been shed on the history of the Armenian table-land prior to 700 B.C. to enable us to divide its political subdivisions into two great groups. The Vannic states of the kingdom of Urartu held sway in the northern ranges. Hittite dominance extended to the southern group of mountains. It may be assumed that the Armenians of the present day are direct descendants of these ancient populations, due allowance being made for the invasion of Iranian peoples who brought eastern culture to the land. The free inflow of this eastern element was impeded, however, by the highly dissected table-land of Armenia. It trickled westward without ever assuming the proportion of a flood. Hence the Armenian physical type is preserved with considerable purity beneath the shroud of Aryan culture.

The Armenians call themselves Hai and trace their descent to a mythical mountain chief Haik. Hai-istan is the name of their native land in Armenian. The word Armenia itself is of Persian derivation and foreign to Armenian. A remote possibility of the connection of Hai with the old name Hit or Hatti may be advanced in view of the frequency with which the elision of the letter t and the replacement of d-t sounds by y occur in Armenian.[21] The etymology of the name, however, still awaits more thorough elucidation.

Although the relation between the Hittite and Armenian

---

times, is the center of the stage of Mexican history. Surrounding this open land numerous narrow valleys were peopled by independent tribes which eventually banded together under the leadership of the community living near the central body of water. This lake confederacy became Cortez's most powerful opponent when the conquistadores undertook their memorable expedition. Cf. F. J. Payne: History of the New World Called America, Oxford, 1899, pp. 450-463.

[20] D. G. Hogarth: The Ancient East, New York, 1914, p. 74.

[21] Notably t is entirely eliminated from the third person singular.

languages yet remains to be determined, and the secrets of the old Vannic language are not fully revealed, enough is known to prove Armenian an Aryan infiltration from the west. Herodotus refers to them in a natural manner as the Φρυγῶν ἄποικοι (VII, 73), "Phrygian colonists." It is significant to note that this Greek appellation was bestowed on the Armenians at a time when western Asia was better known to the civilized countries of the world than it is at present. Modern research, however, places the inhabitants of the plateau of Anatolia and of the Armenian mountain land in the same racial type.

Planted squarely on the scene of the secular conflict between the civilization of Europe and Asia, Armenia became the prey of the victor of the moment. But the united influence of site and configuration was more than once during this long struggle strong enough to confer independence on the Armenian. As a buffer between eastern and western empires the country enjoyed three distinct periods of native rule prior to the Ottoman conquest.

Throughout these vicissitudes, Armenian life centered mainly around its mountain home. Nevertheless, altitude alone does not suffice to explain the characteristics of the people. Climate must also be taken into account. Armenians are distributed in a belt extending one degree on either side of the line of north latitude 39°. Within this zone the products of the soil as well as the customs are those of temperate regions bordering on the warm. The narrow highland valleys are wonderfully fertile. Wheat is harvested before July at an elevation of 3,600 feet in many districts. The country enjoys fame for the variety and excellence of its fruits.

Little wonder, then, that traits which distinguish populations reared in sunny lands should also prevail among the dwellers of this rugged mountain zone. Voluble in the extreme, endowed with a highly developed imaginative sense and with an innate tendency to aggrandize and glorify the facts of ordinary life, the Armenian is often an eastern counterpart of the celebrated Tarasconese created by Daudet's genial fancy.

But a rocky environment is equally reflected in the minds of the Armenians. Harshness of manner and a certain degree of uncouthness are present along with tenacity of purpose and moral fortitude. Through the latter, endurance of Turkish persecution, which has generally assumed exceedingly savage form, was made possible. Armenians are also known for their martial spirit. Dwellers of many of the less accessible recesses of the Tauric or Armenian highlands held their Turkish foes in check for centuries and managed to maintain a state of semi-independence in their conqueror's land until confronted by modern artillery.

Again, the influence of the mountain home of the Armenians is expressed in their art. Poems and songs often extol the fairness of the valleys where rest will be found after descent along interminable slopes. Sometimes the beauty of lakes, embosomed in high plateaus, fires the poet's fancy. Towering summits figure in legend as steeples from which melodious chimes send forth their tones. Armenian music, too, resounds with echoes that seem to reverberate from valleys cut deep in the sides of their mountains.

Perhaps it is these varied influences which convert the rough and mannerless mountain boors into the most polished and cultured citizens of Turkish cities. Armenians have the reputation of being energetic business men. Their honesty was proverbial among the Turks, who generally intrusted the management of estates or domains to their hands. Among them alone throughout the inland districts of Asiatic Turkey, western progress found receptive minds.

The size of the Armenian population of Asiatic Turkey has never been accurately determined. The inaccuracy of Turkish statistics is notorious. Furthermore the boundaries of Turkish administrative provinces have been drawn with the sole view of creating groups in which the Mohammedan element would predominate. The estimate of 2,100,000 Armenians for Asiatic Turkey given by so reputable a writer as Major-General Sir

Charles Wilson [22] is undoubtedly high. Cuinet's figures given by Selenoy and Seidlitz [23] probably come nearer the truth. The wholesale massacre of Armenian males which has been systematically conducted by the Turks for the past twenty years and which culminated in the massacres and deportations of the past two years, makes it improbable that over 1,000,000 Turkish Armenians still live. Prior to the European war, the only districts of any size in which they constituted a majority of the population were found west of Nimrud Dagh in the plains surrounding Mush as well as in the Kozan district north of the Cilician plains.[24]

The Kurds

An Alpine zone of transition connecting the plains of northern Mesopotamia with the surrounding mountains on the north and east became the homeland of the Kurds. In a broad sense it is the drainage area of the Tigris and Euphrates. It is also the site of important mountain gaps through which human movements from east to west or vice versa have proceeded. Before the consolidation of Turkish authority in this region, a matter of less than a century ago and still in an imperfect stage of completion, Kurdish clans, each under the sole leadership of their respective chieftains, controlled the pass through which traffic from the southern lowlands or the eastern plateau was directed

---

[22] Handbook for Travelers in Asia Minor, Transcaucasia, Persia, etc., London, 1911, p. 75.

[23] *Petermanns Mitt.*, Vol. 42, Jan. 1896, p. 8; and for details V. Cuinet: La Turquie d'Asie, Paris, 1891-94, Vols. 1-4.

[24] The Armenian population of Turkey is divided by creed into three distinct communities. The vast majority—probably about ninety per cent—belong to the Gregorian sect of Christianity. Adherents of the Roman Catholic faith are found chiefly in western Asia Minor. Protestant congregations have sprung up around the educational institutions maintained by British or American missionary societies. Let it be noted here that many Mohammedan communities in Armenia consist of Armenoid individuals whose membership in the fold of Islam is the result of forcible conversions since the rise of Ottoman power. The Dersimlis, who inhabit the region between the two main branches of the Euphrates, have the reputation of being crypto-Christians of Armenian blood. Moslems of Armenian origin are also known in the village of Karageben on the Tehalta river east of Divrik. In Russia the Armenians number a scant million souls. Half of this community is scattered in the valley of the Arax and in the Erivan province.

towards the Anatolian table-land. They exacted heavy tolls from passing caravans and derived their chief source of revenue from these levies.

Their manner of living conforms with the intermediary character of their habitat. The semi-nomads of the plains and southern hills seek cool uplands during the summer months. In winter they descend to the warm plains with their flocks and herds and mingle with their Arab neighbors. Their instinct for seasonal migrations has been developed to such an extent that they cannot refrain from maintaining their semi-annual movements in the Armenian districts to which they have been forcibly removed by the Turkish government, desirous of insuring Mohammedan predominance in the Christian valleys of Armenia.

Language and religion carry the Kurds back to eastern ancestry. However diverse their dialects, Aryan roots forming the framework of their speech have survived in spite of the admixture of Turkish and Arabian words. By creed they are generally upholders of Shiite tradition in its westernmost confines. But their religious views vary from tribe to tribe and present as composite a character as their race. Many are Sunnis. Wandering into eastern Asia Minor since hoary antiquity they have culled from Paganism, Christianity and Islamism alike. The predominance of the ideals which inspire these faiths among the individual clans probably affords a clue to the period of their arrival in the localities which they now inhabit.

Similarly, the racial relation of the Kurds with peoples found east of their land is well established.[25] They undoubtedly belong to the European family, though perhaps not in the sense suggested by von Luschan, who would connect them with inhabitants of northern Europe. From the writer's own observations the "generally blue eyes and fair hair" are by no means dominant in the regiments of Hamidyeh cavalry recruited exclusively from

[25] F. von Luschan: The Early Inhabitants of Western Asia, *Ann. Rept. Smithsonian Inst.* for 1914, pp. 561-562.

among Kurdish tribesmen.[26] The three groups studied by the eminent anthropologist near Karakush, on the Nimrud mountain, and at Sinjirli were probably remarkably pure, as might be inferred from the nature of their secluded districts. As early invaders of a transition land the Kurds have intermingled extensively with both highland and lowland populations.[27] The Kurd varies therefore according to region, the inhabitants of the elevated sections being stocky and of massive build, while the tall and sallow Semitic type appears among those on the southern plains.[28]

The Kurds, particularly in the semi-nomadic state, are noted freebooters. Travel in the districts they occupy is generally unsafe. Armenians and other Christians find them an inexorable foe. They are none too loath to prey even on Turks, although as a rule the latter obtain immunity in return for the lenient dealing of the government in cases of Kurdish depredations on non-Moslem communities. The strong arm of an organized police alone will end the lawlessness with which their name is coupled in Turkey.

Good qualities are not wanting among them. A Kurd is generally true to his word. The rude code of honor in vogue among their tribes is rarely violated, and, whenever disposed, the Kurd can become as hospitable as his Arab neighbors. The tempering influence of a settled existence among sedentary tribes is marked by harmonious intercourse with surrounding non-Kurdish communities. At bottom their vices are chiefly those of the restless life they lead in a land in which organized government has been unknown for the past eight centuries.

THE SYRIANS

Syria is the elongated land passage, barely fifty miles in width, which connects northern Africa with western Asia. It is

---

[26] "Rarely of unusual stature . . . complexion dark" is Wilson's description. Handbook for Travelers in Asia Minor, Transcaucasia, Persia, etc., London, 1911, p. 64.

[27] Mark Sykes: The Kurdish Tribes of the Ottoman Empire, *Journ. Anthrop. Inst.*, Vol. 38, 1908, pp. 451-486.

[28] B. Dickson: Journeys in Kurdistan, *Geogr. Journ.*, Vol. 35, No. 4, April 1910, p. 361.

FIG. 62—A Kurdish village in Upper Mesopotamia with characteristic stone shanties peculiar to semi-arid regions.

FIG. 63—A harvest scene in Upper Mesopotamia with Kurds at work.

one of the world's best-defined natural regions. The sea on the west, and the desert on the east, sharply mark off its fringe-like extension. On the north the Amanus ranges constitute a wall that has proved well-nigh impassable to Semites. To the south the land naturally ends in the Sinai peninsula.[29]

The province is mountainous in its northern half. Its mountains are the monuments that throw light on the utter failure of the cause of human progress in northern Syria. A single redeeming feature, the Orontes river valley, favored foreign contact. At its mouth on the Mediterranean western ideas filtered into the land while a blend of eastern influences, Persian and Arabian, flowed down with its waters. All converged at Antioch, the region's greatest center of life and a true product of the Orontes' lower course. Absence of relief in southern Syria, however, was coupled to a Mediterranean climate and fertile soils. These permitted the development of the flourishing civilizations of antiquity. Herein lies the physical basis of the historical evolution of the Syrian fringe and the explantion of the growth of nations and of world religions in its southern lands.

As a land-bridge of early humanity Syria was necessarily the scene of much coming and going at a time when the civilization of the world was largely confined to what is now known as Asiatic Turkey. Its population therefore presents a mixed character. Hittites, Arameans, Assyrians, Egyptians, Greeks, Romans, Arabs and Turks conquered the land in turn and imparted their native customs to its inhabitants. The inhabitants of its southern area are now transformed almost beyond the possibility of analysis. The settlements of the elevated and broken northern area, on the other hand, represent very ancient communities.

The mountains of Syria harbor strange denizens in their northern end. In the northern Lebanon many villages of the western slopes are inhabited by the Metauilehs, who are Shiite

---

[29] De Torcy: Notes sur la Syrie, *La Géogr.*, Vol. 27, No. 3, March 15, 1913, pp. 161-197; No. 6, June 15, 1913, pp. 429-459.

dissenters and bear unenviable reputation for ignorance and inhospitality.[30]   Their own traditions point to Persian or Arabian origins.   Religion seems to confirm the former claim.   At the same time they are known to the Syrians as a sturdy mountain people.   Scattered through the same mountain districts the Ismailyehs, another highland folk who under the name of Assassins enjoyed sinister fame during the Middle Ages, maintain their abode in inaccessible valleys.   The epithet which is coupled to their name is an altogether illogical rendering of the Arabic "hasheeshin" and does not convey any worse meaning than that of "hasheesh" fiends.   They live mainly in groups around old Saracen castles.

THE ANSARIYEHS

The Ansariyehs, or Nusariyehs, form an important group among northern Syrians.   Their settlements are generally confined to the grassy seaward slopes of the mountains stretching north of the Nahr-el-Kebir towards the Gulf of Alexandretta. They also occupy villages in the plains surrounding Antioch.   In recent years they have shown a tendency to abandon their mountain homes for the less arduous life of the plains.   Officially they are regarded as Mohammedans and bear Mohammedan names, but the religion which differentiates them from the other inhabitants of northern Syria teaches Christian and Sabean doctrines alike.   It is believed that they still maintain observances of exceedingly ancient nature cults.   The fundamental principles of their creed are transmitted by word of mouth and with injunction to secrecy.[31]   Their deification of the conception of fertility is couched in highly metaphorical language in which the productivity of the earth and of the human race is extolled.   By making proper allowance for the imagery which clothes the wording of their prayers it will probably be found that their religion resolves itself into a relic of the worship of the mother-goddess

---

[30] L. Gaston Leary: Syria, the Land of Lebanon, New York, 1913, p. 10.

[31] R. Dussaud: Les Nossairis, *Bibl. de l'École des Hautes Études, Sciences, Philosophie et Histoire*, Paris, 1900, Vol. 129.

which was deeply rooted throughout the mountain districts of Asia Minor. Hints of nocturnal orgies accompanying their worship should be taken with a grain of suspicion, as orthodox Mohammedans are prone to such imputations whenever dissension from the Koran is suspected. In this Mohammedans merely follow the lead of Byzantine Christians in whose eyes the relics of Anatolian paganism were as obnoxious as the heresies of their own times.

The ancestors of the Ansariyehs and other small sects in northern Syria were closely related to their powerful Hittite neighbors. These peoples all occupy, together with the Druzes and Maronites, the southern limit of known Hittite monuments.[32] Their land is the frontier zone between Syria, Asia Minor and the Armenian highland. It is studded with ruined strongholds which figured prominently in ancient battle.

THE DRUZES

The southern Lebanon and Anti-Lebanon ranges in the rearland of the Haifa-Beirut coast[33] are inhabited by Druzes. Tribes of this people are met as far southeast as the Hawran volcanic uplift, whither they have steadily emigrated from the Lebanon in the course of the past hundred years and where they have succeeded in dislodging the former Bedouin inhabitants. These Druzes are best known for their warlike disposition. Although numerically inferior to the Christian population of their native districts, their bellicose qualities have won them predominance in central Syria. In religion they are pure monotheists. Their standard of morality is high. They call themselves Mohammedans but do not maintain mosques and rarely practise polygamy. Orthodox Moslems generally repudiate them on account of the discrepancy between their teachings and the tenets of the Koran. As far as can be determined the doctrines

---

[32] J. Garstang: The Land of the Hittites, London, 1910, pp. 15, 16.

[33] About forty towns and villages are held by the Druzes in the southern Lebanon. In the Anti-Lebanon districts they people eighty villages and share possession of about two hundred with their Christian kinsmen, the Maronites.

of the Mosaic law, the Gospels, the Koran and Sufi allegories
are represented in their creed. Often when with Christians they
will not hesitate to assert belief in Christianity. The leaven of
Iranian influences which pervades their doctrines estranges them
from the surrounding Semitism just as their highland home
separates them from the plainsmen settled around them. The
dominance of this eastern strain in their thoughts does not, however, necessarily indicate racial migrations. Historical testimony is available to prove that the known form of Druze religion
can be traced to the teachings of Hamze, a Persian disciple of
Hakem.[34] The case is more probably that of an infiltration of
foreign ideals and its retention within a region deprived by its
relief from intercourse with the more progressive life of the
surrounding lowland.

THE MARONITES

Closely related to the Druzes are their northwestern neighbors, the Maronites, a Christian people, who seceded from the
Roman Church in the great schism that followed the council of
Chalcedon in 451 A.D.[35] They form a compact mass settled on the
western slopes of the Lebanon mountains between the valleys of
the Nahr-el-Kebir and the Nahr-el-Barid. Mountain isolation
and intermarriage among them have maintained an old type with
remarkable purity. Being better farmers than warriors they
have suffered from the oft repeated depredations of their warlike neighbors.[36] Enmity with their Mohammedan neighbors

---

[34] Hakem was a Fatimite caliph of Egypt, who ruled in the early eleventh century.
He incurred the hatred of his subjects by causing the incarnation of God in himself to
be preached in Cairo by Darasi, his chaplain. Both became so unpopular that they
were forced to escape from the capital to the Lebanon, where they succeeded in imposing
their doctrines on the mountaineers. The name Druze is believed to be derived from
Darasi.

[35] In recent years the Maronites have submitted to the authority of the Vatican.
In return certain privileges, such as that of retention of Syriac liturgy, have been
accorded to them. They constitute a veritable theocracy, all tribal and community
affairs being handled by the clergy.

[36] The French military expedition to the Lebanon, undertaken in 1860, was caused
by the massacre of over 12,000 Maronites by the Druzes in that year.

dates from the time of the Crusades when the Maronites had sided with the Christian knights.

THE JEWS

The Jews of Turkey include a small remnant of the captivity settled around Jerusalem and in Mesopotamia.[37]   After the destruction of Jerusalem, the valley of the Tigris became the most important seat of the Hebrews. Parthian tolerance granted them a partial autonomy under the authority of a chief chosen from among the descendants of the house of David.[38]   This liberal régime ended with the decline in power of the Abbasside caliphs of Bagdad. The Jews were then forced to abandon Chaldea. Many emigrated to Spain. Later, under the reign of Ferdinand and Isabella, they were compelled to flee from Spanish persecution and seek a home again in Turkey. Descendants of these emigrants, known as Sephardim, are settled in cities of Asia Minor and Syria. Small colonies of Ashkenazim Jews are also scattered in various Turkish towns. An old colony of a few hundred Samaritans survives in the vicinity of Nablus.

The Jews are an exceedingly composite people and, contrary to popular belief, do not represent as pure a type of the Semitic race as the Bedouin Arabs. Southern Syria was a prey to invaders from every quarter of the compass. It was the clashing ground of Hittite and Nilotic civilizations. From the west, Mediterranean seafaring populations swarmed in from earliest antiquity. At least three great waves of Semitic migrations overwhelmed the land prior to the coming of the Arabs. The Jew, therefore, represents the fusion of four distinct races of men. The purity he has retained is that of the fused type. His language alone is Semitic. His physical appearance recalls Hittite traits more prominently than Semitic and this probably accounts for the frequent mistaking, in western Europe and in the United States, of Armenians for Jews.

---

[37] This group comprises about 90,000 souls in Syria and 40,000 in Mesopotamia.
[38] E. Aubin: La Perse d'aujourd'hui, Paris, 1908, p. 418.

ARAMEANS

The Arameans are either direct ancestors of modern Jews or else close congeners of early Hebrews. Both peoples are closely allied. They represent one of the many waves of Semitic humanity which have rolled out of Arabia's highland steppes. A period of settlement in the fertile districts around the mouth of the Euphrates and Tigris precedes their spread throughout Mesopotamia and northeastern Syria. References to their history abound in sacred texts, as well in inscriptional remains [39] found throughout western Asia. The accounts, however, are fragmentary and so far have made possible only partial reconstitution of their history. An Aramean nation or a number of Aramean states undoubtedly existed in the tenth century B.C. This body subsequently acquired considerable power and founded colonies all over Mesopotamia and Syria. Damascus and Hamath, both in the latter province, became the greatest centers of Aramean power, owing to the natural resources of the districts around their sites as well as to their commanding position on important trade routes.

It seems established that the vast territory designated by the Assyrians by the name of "Mat Aram," or land of Aram, did not necessarily contain Aramaic populations. It was more probably conquered by Arameans, who imposed their language on the subjugated peoples. Soon after the capture of Damascus by the Assyrians in 732 B.C. the Aramean nation disappears from history. Aramaic, however, survived and was even adopted by the victors.[40] But, in common with other Semitic languages, it could not withstand the advance of Arabic. The only locality in which it is now spoken is found northeast of Damascus in the environs of the villages of Malula, Bakha and Yubb Adin, where the natives still use a dialect similar to the Palestinian Aramaic spoken thirteen centuries ago. There is reason to believe that this sub-group of Syrians represents today the old Aramean

---

[39] The Elephantine papyri discovered on the island of Elephantine in southern Egypt between 1903 and 1906 contain Aramaic texts of great historical value.

[40] O. Procksch: Die Völker Altpalästinas, Leipzig, 1914, p. 30.

stock in as pure a degree as is consistent with the secular mingling of peoples which has taken place in the region.[41]

The Yezidis

The Sinjar range of hills stretching in a westerly direction from Mosul is the only upland of importance in the Mesopotamian valley. The largest compact mass of Yezidis are domiciled in this hilly country. A minor group occupies the Samaan mountains in Syria.[42]

The appellation of devil-worshipers which generally accompanies the name of Yezidi conveys a totally erroneous impression regarding their beliefs. They recognize, in fact, a benign deity, the Khode-Qanj, who reigns supreme over creation but with whom is associated an inferior divine essence, the Malik-i-Tawus, or Peacock King, who is lord of all evil and whom they consider necessary to propitiate in order to avert misfortune. But the ceremonies and sacrifices performed in honor of the subordinate deity do not interfere with the primary worship with which the God of Good is revered.[43] This interpretation of divinity bears deep analogy to the Iranian cult which revolves around the central figures of Ormuzd and Ahriman, respectively the good and the evil principle. The language of the Yezidis, which is akin to Kurdish, brings added evidence of the eastern derivation of their culture.

According to their own traditions the Yezidis came originally from the districts of the lower Euphrates. Certain Sabean features of their religion indicate intimate contact with Semitic populations. Little is known about their curious religious celebrations, to which strangers are never admitted. Their practice of bowing before the rising sun is a clear relic of Zoroastrian influence. They also perform rites which have analogy to

---

[41] At the end of the pre-Islamic period the region west of the Euphrates to the eastern slopes of the Lebanon mountains was known to the Arabs as " Beit Aramyeh," or the land of the Arameans.

[42] H. Lammens: Le Massif du Gebal et les Yezidis de Syrie, *Mélanges Faculté Orient. Univ. Beyrouth*, 1907, pp. 366-407.

[43] W. B. Heard: Notes on Yezidis, *Journ. Anthrop. Inst.*, Vol. 41, pp. 200-219.

Christian commemorations. In a land overrun in all directions no simple feature of the views they hold can account for their origin. The religion of the moment was imposed by the dominant element over all the peoples of Asiatic Turkey. Hence a given group merely shows successive strata of religious invasions.

The sturdily-built Yezidi is active and hardy. His energy sets him apart from the lithe-limbed and easy-going Arabs. His vigor and fighting blood saved him from the frightful persecutions for which the particularly obnoxious feature of his dual deity was responsible. Byzantine bishops and Arabian mollahs in turn reserved the wildest thunder of their intolerance for the Yezidi, whom they execrated beyond all others among heretics and unbelievers. This hatred of the presumed worshiper of the devil has not yet been outlived, and a devout Mohammedan will today spit upon the ground and mutter a curse whenever the abhorred name crosses his lips.

The Yezidis enjoy fame as agriculturists who know how to exact good yield from their mountain farms. They live a retired life and rarely allow strangers to travel through the Sinjar range. The modern armament of Turkish expeditions has cowed the present generation into a submission which their fathers would have scorned. But they still remain unwilling tax payers who rely on the natural disinclination of Turkish tax collectors to mountain-climbing.

THE NESTORIANS

The Nestorians, a Christian sect, are descendants of the followers of Nestorius, who seceded from established orthodoxy in the sixth century. They inhabit scattered villages in a region which changes from mountain to plain as it extends west of the Persian frontier to the Tigris river, roughly between latitudes 34° and 38°. On the north they rarely venture beyond the Bohtan river. The mountainous tract produces a manly set, who have more than held their own against the martial Kurds. Poverty and dependence mark the lot of the plainsmen in spite of their industry as agriculturists.

To say that the inhabitants of Turkey have religious nationality is perhaps the happiest way of accounting for the presence of large numbers of independent communities owing political allegiance to the Sultan. The bond of faith in the case of the Nestorians is one of remarkable strength, because this community represents the persecuted remnant of the ancient church of central Asia. Owing to its situation on the very outskirts of early Christianity the church became engaged in propagating the Gospel on a scale exceeded only by the see of Rome in the sixth and sixteenth centuries.[44] Consciousness of this tradition has not forsaken the Nestorians of the present day. The great influence wielded by their patriarch or religious head, the Mar Shimun, as he is called, is a relic of former authority.

The speech of the Nestorians is a Syriac dialect in which Persian, Arabic and Kurdish words have found place. Religious services are conducted, however, in the uncontaminated language. The Nestorians call themselves Syrians and refuse to recognize any other appellation. Owing to this fact much confusion has arisen in the minds of travelers who have attempted to describe them.

The Chaldeans

The Chaldeans are racially akin to the Nestorians, with whom they formed a single religious community prior to the seventeenth century. The hope of obtaining relief from Mohammedan persecution induced an important section of the old community to join the church of Rome at that time. In recent years, however, many have forsaken Roman Catholicism and formed a new sect which is known by the name of New Chaldeans. Protestant communities of this people as well as of Nestorians and Jacobites exist.

The Jacobites

The rugged limestone district around Midyad is the home of another mountain people known as the Jacobites. Banded

---

[44] A. P. Stanley: Lectures on the History of the Eastern Church, New York, 1909, p. 58.

together by the ties of religion they form a community of husbandmen living aloof from their neighbors of divergent religious
views.   They are described as of warlike nature and independent
spirit.   Language also differentiates them from other Ottoman
groups, a Syriac dialect differing considerably from Nestorian
being in use among them.[45]   In Turabdin they speak an Aramaic
dialect known as Turani.   The Jacobites are noted for their aptitude for business.   The important colony of traders founded in
the eighteenth century in the vicinity of Bagdad owes its origin
to the desert traffic and the Indian trade by way of Basra.

This people traces its religious origin to the teachings of
Jacobus Baradeus,[46] who, in the middle of the sixth century,
traveled through Asia Minor and consolidated scattered groups
of Monophysite recusants into a single body.   They constituted
a large sect during the Middle Ages, but defections, notably in
favor of the Roman Church, have thinned their numbers considerably since then.   At present they muster hardly more than
15,000 individuals.

The Sabeans

We are still in the dark concerning the history of the
Sabeans, a people of Semitic origin who profess Christianity.
That they once formed a powerful nation is attested by numerous
ruins and inscriptions.   This state began to decline in the first
century of the Christian era and had completely disappeared by
500 A.D.   They call themselves Mendai and are often known by
the name of Christians of St. John.   The community is small,
numbering hardly 3,000 souls, mostly goldsmiths and boat-
builders who ply their trade in the Arab encampments of the
Amara and Muntefik sanjaks in the vilayet of Basra.   They talk
a Semitic dialect and dress like the Arabs, from whom they can
scarcely be distinguished.   Their original homeland is believed
to have been Yemen.

---

[45] H. Trotter: *Geogr. Journ.*, Vol. 35, No. 4, 1910, p. 378.
[46] F. J. Bliss: The Religions of Modern Syria and Palestine, New York, 1912.

FIG. 64.

FIG. 65.

FIG. 64—Kurd children of the Armenian borderland. The poverty of the land is reflected in their appearance no less than in the arid background of the photograph.
FIG. 65—A family of sedentary Arabs in Mesopotamia.

FIG. 66—In the desert of Syria. A tribe of Anezeh Arabs moving from an exhausted pasture to a fresh one.

THE ARABS

The Arab folk, sparsely distributed over the Syrian desert and forming the majority of the inhabitants of the featureless downs of Mesopotamia, represent the ebbing of the last tide of Semitic invasion. In the sandy waste of their western extension, their tribes, shifting perpetually from seat to seat, like the dunes around which they roam, consist of Bedouin or "tent men." The contribution of these nomads to society is as insignificant as the yield of the unproductive lands of their wandering. Towards the east, however, where two mighty rivers bring fertility and life to the soil, the genius of the race blossomed untrammeled and gave Mohammedan civilization to the world.

The purest living representatives of the Semitic race are found among these Bedouins. Civilization pursued its steady growth around their tent homes without affecting their lives. Better favored belts encircling the Syrian desert attracted the human migrations which took place in western Asia. From the last out-liers of the hill system fringing the southern Taurus to the northern confines of the Arabian peninsula, the patriarchal state of society prevailing today differs little from the condition in which a dreamer well past middle age found it fourteen centuries ago and brought it within the pale of modern thought by inspiring it with the enthusiasm of his own belief in a single God. Stripped of his religion and of his rifle, the Bedouin stands today before the historian as the living image of long remote ancestors whose invasions caused profound upheavals in the societies established east and west of his present tramping ground.

But the Arab settled in the long elongated plain watered by the Tigris and Euphrates can never lay claim to equal purity of stock. He lives in a land which by virtue of a great twin river system gave rise to the oldest civilization of the world. Its inhabitants, whether aboriginal or invaders from the table-land on the east, derived more than mere sustenance from prox-imity to these mothering watercourses. Surrounded by desert and mountain, this region naturally became a seat of population.

Its native element, already much mixed, was assimilated to a large extent by the Arabs since the period of their appearance in Mesopotamia.

The floating masses of Bedouins have successfully resisted Turkish effort to induce them to abandon nomadism. Occasionally, as in the belt of Tauric precipitation or along the borders of the zone of Mediterranean rains no less than under the benign influence of Mesopotamian rivers, they become sedentary. They are then known as *fellaheen*. But the change is incompatible with their immemorial restlessness and implies loss of caste in their own eyes.

TABLE I

NAMES AND PEOPLES OF SOME NON-TURKISH VILLAGES IN ASIA MINOR

Peoples designated as follows:

Alevi	Al.
Armenians	Ar.
Avshars	Av.
Chaldeans	Ch.
Circassians	Cir.
Greeks	Gr.
Karapapaks	Kpk.
Kizilbash	Kz.
Kurds	Kd.
Nestorians	N.
New Chaldeans	N. Ch.
Tatars	Ta.
Turkomans	Tkn.
Yezidi	Yd.

Name of Village	Peoples	Name of Village	Peoples
Aghje Kaleh	Kd.	Atess	N.
Agh-ova	Kd.	Avviran	Gr.
Aivali	Gr.	Bazarjik	Kd.
Ak-bunar	Cir.	Berar	Ar.
Akdam	Ar.	Bey	Ch.
Akhlat	Kd.	Birgami	Kd.
Akstafa	Kpk.	Chateran	Ar.
Alaklissia	Gr.	Chevirme	Kd.
Alexandropol	Ar.	Chukh	Ar.
Alkosh	N. Ch.	Deliler	Kd.
Altea	Gr.	Derendeh	Ar.
Angora	Ar.	Diz-deran	Kd.
Arabja Keupri	Gr. & Cir.	Ekrek	Ar.
Ardia	Cir.	Feshapur	Ch.
Arji	N.	Funduk	Cir.

Name of Village	Peoples	Name of Village	Peoples
Furinji	Kd.	Misli	Gr.
Garib	Kd.	Mush plain	Ar.
Garni	Ar.	Nerdivan	Kd.
Gemerek	Ar.	Nerib	Kd.
Gunderno	Ar.	Nigdeh	Gr.
Gunig-kaleh	Ar.	Niksar	Gr.
Gurgujeli	Tkn.	Norchuk	Ar.
Gurun	Ar.	Omar	Kd.
Haik	Ar.	Orbülu	Kd.
Hamsi	Gr.	Pekarieh	Ar.
Hanefi	Al.	Pingan	Ar.
Harras	Kd.	Porrot	Kd.
Helais	Kd.	Pulk	Ar.
Hornova	Ar.	Rabat	Kd.
Hoshmat	Ar.	Redvan	Yd.
Inevi	Tkn.	Samsat	Kd.
Instosh	Ar.	Sekunis	N.
Isbarta	Gr.	Semil	Yd.
Isoghlu	Kd.	Serai	N.
Jenan	Kd.	Shabin Kara-Hissar	Ar.
Jessi	Kd.	Shahr	Ar.
Kaialik	Kd.	Sha-uta	N.
Kainar	Cir.	Sheik Adi	Yd.
Karachu	Kd.	Sheikh Amir	Kd.
Kara-geben	Ar.	Sheikhan	Kd.
Keklik-oghlu	Kd.	Shen	Kd.
Kelebesh	Gr.	Shernak	Kd.
Kemer	Av.	Sultan Oghlu	Tkn.
Keupri	Tkn.	Tadvan	Ar.
Kezanlik	Cir.	Takvaran	Kd.
Khakkaravokh	Kd.	Tashan	Ar.
Khasta-Khâneh	Av.	Tashbunar	Cir.
Khusi	N.	Terzili	Ar.
Kinskh	Kd.	Thorub	Ch.
Kizil-doghan	Gr.	Tokat	Ar.
Kilisse	Ar.	Tomarze	Ar.
Kochannes	N.	Top-agach	Ar.
Koch-hissar	Ar.	Tor	Tkn.
Kojeri	Ar.	Ulash	Ar.
Koshmet	Kz.	Uzum Yaila	Cir.
Kotni	Kd.	Vurla	Gr.
Kula	Gr.	Yakshi-khân	Ta.
Kwaneh	N.	Yalak	Av.
Maden	N.	Yarzuat	Ta.
Madrak	Kd.	Yeni Keui	Kd.
Mansuriyeh	Ch.	Zara	Ar.
Melendis	Gr.	Zela	Ar.
Mervanen	N.		

TABLE II
CLASSIFICATION OF THE PEOPLES OF ASIATIC TURKEY

NAME	RACE	RELIGION	SPEECH	HOMELAND	ESTIMATED NUMBER
Allevis (see Tahtajis)					
Ansariyehs	Armenoid	Monotheistic	Arabic	Syrian mts. and Cilician plains	175,000
Aptals	Armenoid	Sunni	Arabic	Syrian mts.	uncertain
Arabs	Semitic	Mohammedan	Arabic	South of Tauric and Armenian mts.	300,000 ?
Arameans	Semitic	Hebrew	Aramean		300
Armenians	Armenoid	Christian	Armenian (Aryan)	Armenian highland, Taurus and Anti-Taurus ranges	1,000,000[1]
Asdias (see Yezidis)					
Avshars	Turki	Shia	Turkish	Anti-Taurus	uncertain
Balikis	Armenoid	Mixed Mohammedan and Christian	Mixed Arabic, Kurdish and Armenian	Near Sasun	uncertain
Bejvans	Semitic	Mixed Mohammedan and Christian	Arabic	Near Mosul	uncertain
Chaldeans	Semitic	Roman Catholic	Syriac, Kurdish and Arabic	Near Diarbekr and Jezireh; Sert and Khabur basin	50,000
Chepmis (see Tahtajis)					
Circassians	Mixed Turki and Indo-European	Mohammedan	Turkish	Anatolia, N. Syria, N. Mesopotamia	500,000
Druzes	Armenoid	Mohammedan	Arabic	Lebanon; Anti-Lebanon, Hawran mts., around Damascus	200,000
Greeks[2]	Mediterranean	Christian	Greek	Coast districts, mining districts, large cities	2,000,000
Ismailyehs	Armenoid	Mohammedan	Semitic	Northern Syria	22,000
Jacobites	Semitic	Christian (Monophysites)	Syriac	Syria, Mesopotamia	15,000
Jews	Mixed Semitic, Mediterranean and Armenoid	Hebrew	Hebrew	Jerusalem; environs of Damascus	150,000
Karapapaks	Turki	Shia	Turkish	Tutakh-Patnoz	3,000
Kizilbash	Armenoid mixed with Turki	Shia, or mixture of Shiism, Paganism, Manichaeism, and Christianity	Turkish	Angora and Sivas vilayets; Dersim	400,000
Kurds	Indo-European	Mohammedan	Aryan languages	West of the Sakaria river; Kurdistan	1,500,000
Lazis	Georgian branch of the Caucaso-Thibetan peoples	Mohammedan	Grusinian	Lazistan; north of Choruk Su, around Riza	uncertain
Maronites	Armenoid	Christian	Arabic	Mt. Lebanon, Anti-Lebanon	350,000
Metauilehs	Probably Armenoid	Shia	Arabic	Northern Lebanon	under 50,000
Nestorians	Armenoid	Christian	Syriac	Basin of the Great Zab; valleys of the Bohtan and Khabar	60,000
New Chaldeans	Semitic?	Christian	Syriac	Alkosh	uncertain
Sabeans	Semitic	Christian	Syriac	Amara and Muntefik sanjaks of the Basra vilayet	3,000
Samaritans	Semitic?	Hebrew	Hebrew	Near Nablus	300
Syrians	Semitic;	Christian and Mohammedan	Arabic	Syria and Mesopotamia	uncertain
Tahtajis	Armenoid	Mohammedan	Turkish	Lycian mts.	5,000
Tatars	Turki	Mohammedan	Turkish	Anatolia and Cilician plains	25,000
Terekimans (see Karapapaks)					
Turkomans	Turki	Mohammedan	Turkish	Angora, Adana and Aleppo vilayets	uncertain
Turks	Turki mixed with Armenoid	Mohammedan	Turkish	Anatolia mainly	8,000,000
Yezidis or Asdais	Mixed Armenoid and Indo-European	Devil-worshipers, mixture of the old Babylonian religion; Zoroastrianism, Manichaeism and Christianity	Kermanji	Kurt Dagh on the W. to Zakho E. of the Tigris; Badi near Mosul; Sinjar range	40,000
Yuruks	Armenoid	Mohammedan	Turkish	Konia vilayet	200,000
Total........	....	....	....	....	15,048,600

[1] The figures for Armenians and Greeks require revision in view of the systematic efforts of the Turks to extirpate these two peoples. The massacres of the entire Greek population of villages of the Ægean coasts and atrocities of a most inhuman character perpetrated on the Armenians of inland communities have largely depleted the ranks of these two Christian subject groups.

[2] Hellenes, or subjects of the King of Greece, number about 20,000.

TABLE III

THE CHRISTIANS OF THE TURKO-PERSIAN BORDERLAND

I. *Mosul and the Valley of the Tigris (by families)* [1]

District of Mosul.

City of Mosul	2,000 R. C. [2]	
City of Mosul	1,200 J.	
City of Mosul	400 R. C. s.	
Telkief	2,000 R. C.	
Bagdair	700 J.	
Bartila	300 R. C.	
Batnai	400 R. C.	
Tel Uskof	450 R. C.	
Alkosh	700 R. C.	
Dohuk	150 R. C.	
Bait Kupa	300 R. C.	
Mar Yakob & Sheus	100 R. C.	
Total	8,700	8,700

District of Sapna.

Mangeshie	200 R. C.	
Dihie	30 P.	
Daviria	100 R. C.	
Tinn	70 R. C.	
Aradin	200 R. C.	
Haszia & Benata	50 R. C.	
Bibaidi	30 N.	
Diri	40 N.	
Dirginie	35 N.	
Lower Barnai, Maisie, Chamankie, etc	120 R. C.	
Total	875	875

District of Zakhu.

Zakhu	100 R. C.	
Bait Daru	90 R. C.	
Peshawur	110 R. C.	
Bersiwi	70 R. C.	
Sharnish	50 R. C.	
Margu & Baiju	95 R. C.	
Wasta	80 R. C.	
Total	595	595

[1] Figures supplied by Dr. W. W. Rockwell, Editor of the American Committee for Armenian and Syrian Relief. See Rockwell: Pitiful Plight, second ed., pp. 66.

[2] Abbreviations; R. C.: Roman Catholic Uniats, "Chaldeans." R. C. s.: Roman Catholic Uniats, "Syrian Catholics." J.: Jacobites. N.: Nestorians, "Assyrian Christians." P.: Protestants.

TABLE III—*Continued*

District of Bohtan.

Tilkuba	60 R. C.	
Jazera (Jezireh)	150 R. C.	
Mansuria	60 P.	
Hassan	70 N.	
Shakh	30 P.	
Mar Akha	30 P.	
Mar Yohannan	10 P.	
A few other villages	50 N.	
Total	460	460

District of Zibar.

Esan	30 N.	
Argin	7 N.	
Shushu & Sharman	25 N.	
Shaklawa (in Akra)	500 R. C.	
Akra	300 R. C.	
Total	862	862

District of E. Berwar.

Aina d'Nuni	50 N.	
Duri	35 N.	
Ikri & Malakhta	40 N.	
Bait Baluk	20 N.	
Four villages, including Halwa, Khwara	50 N.	
Dirishki	20 N.	
Maiyi	25 N.	
Haiyiz	30 N.	
Bishmeyayi	20 N.	
Iad	20 N.	
Tashish	30 N.	
Musakka	20 N.	
Three small villages	25 N.	
Jadeda	15 N.	
Chalik	30 N.	
Kaneba Labi	20 N.	
Total	450	450
		11,942

II.   *The Highlands of Kurdistan*

Tyari	5,000
Tkhuma	2,500
Baz	800
Tal	700
Diz	600
Jilu	2,500

TABLE III—*Continued*

Berwar (Qudshanis included)	900	
Lewan (west of Julamerk)	300	
Serai (45 miles east of Van)	300	
Eleven villages around Serai	400	
Norduz (on Van-Julamerk road)	200	
Albak (near Bashkala)	300	
Gawar	400	
Six villages in Nerwan & Rekan	200	
Shemsdinan & Bar Bhishu (estimated)	200	
Total families	15,300	15,300
Grand total		27,242
Total individuals at six to a family		163,452

CHAPTER XIII

SUMMARY AND APPLICATIONS

THE science of geography attains its highest usefulness when called into the service of man. Having in mind the influence of regional environment upon human societies and particularly upon language and nationality as shown in the foregoing chapters, let us next look at the bearing of our conclusions on the determination of international frontiers. The problem consists in ascertaining the logical or natural limit of the spread of language and nationality. Growing at first in listless response to environment, natural frontiers eventually attain a stage where intelligent conformity to the same environment becomes necessary. Here the linguistic factor based on a sound geographical foundation acquires practical value though it is not necessarily the only determining element.

The spirit of nationality represents the highest development of the idea of self-preservation. Its growth can be traced from the individual to the family, thence to the tribe and city, until the formation of the political state is obtained. In the last stages of this process, nationality attains perfection through homogeneity of its component individuals. The men who compose a single nation must think together. Their ideals and aims must be one and they must be conscious of a common destiny. Language, as the currency of thought, naturally becomes the unifier. To a notable degree areas of homogeneous language in Europe have been spared the havoc of battle or siege. On the other hand, linguistic borderlands have always been scenes of armed struggle and destruction.

Community of origin is not essential among members of the same nation. The bond of language and identity of historical destiny suffice for the creation of nationality. An English-

314

speaking immigrant on United States soil, imbued with the spirit of the principles on which the country's independence is founded, finds himself in a state of response to the idea of American nationality. And yet, the idea of nationality is no mere integration of historical associations. It stands enthroned in the land. The poet touches his compatriot's heart by recalling the murmur of the forest or by a picture of the winding shore. Through the charm of living green enshrined in circling hills, at times through an appreciation of the solemn peak rising heavenward, man found love of homeland. A strong tie between humanity and the land was created by these relations.

Nationality cannot depend on language alone, for it is founded on geographical unity. The past thousand years of European history contain sufficient proof of the fact. The three southern peninsulas Spain, Italy and Greece are homelands of an equal number of nations. A single language is current in each. To the north a similar differentiation of nations adapts itself to regional divisions. Plains, mountains and seas have limited European nationalities to definite number and extension.

Thus every people acquires a peculiar genius which expresses itself in characteristic fashion and cannot be made to assume a guise alien to its own spirit. It absorbs the idealism of its captors and molds it into its own form. The poet's intuition rarely echoed deeper truth than in the oft-quoted passage which immortalized the spirit of Hellas:

> Graecia capta ferum victorem cepit, et artes
> Intulit agresti Latio.

Europe was stirred to the consciousness of nationality by the French Revolution. Nations began finding themselves when the doctrine of man's equality, proclaimed on French soil, found responsive welcome among the peoples of the continent. But the new spirit caused dismay in every court circle. The inevitable reaction that followed was reflected in the treaty of Vienna of 1815, when national aspirations were ignominiously ignored and peoples beheld themselves bartered as chattels. The delegates in attendance sat as representatives of dynastic interests. Their interest in remodeling the political map of Europe was absorbed wholly by the idea of securing compensation for the spoliation of the territorial property of their sovereigns. Their labors meant triumph for autocratic rule. Popular clamor for national grouping was unheeded. Instead of quieting Europe, the treaty of Vienna was a virtual admission on the part of less than three dozen men that Europeans were incapable of bearing the glorious burden of their own destinies. The tares of monarchical despotism were left to stain the field of popular freedom.

But the seed sown by the great act of the French Revolution was hardy. It was too late to eradicate liberal spirit from European society. A mighty struggle of ideas ushered in the revolts of 1830 and 1848. Twenty odd years more, and for the first time in its history western Europe was parceled into linguistic nations. The birth of Germany during this period was significantly heralded by an outburst of patriotic literature which for fire and enthusiasm was unprecedented. Geibel's demand for a united Germany in Heroldsrufe was but the echo of the aspirations of millions of his countrymen. France emerged out of these ordeals without loss of her linguistic territory. The area of German speech received marked attention. In truth the morning of modern German nationality may be said to have broken in 1815. A year prior to this historic date, the decision had been reached at the treaty of Paris (March 30, 1814) to unite the German states into a single confederation. The dominating thought of European diplomacy, at the time, was to prevent a recurrence of Napoleonic disturbances.

With their restricted territories, as well as by the jealousies which animated their rulers, the German states lay, an easy prey, at the mercy of any ambitious foreign leader. In their union, Europe hoped to lay the foundations of continental peace. Such a federation, it was thought, would safeguard the other European countries from a concerted German attack, as it seemed highly improbable that the entire confederacy would join in a war undertaken by any one of its members for purposes of self-aggrandizement. By this arrangement provision was made for the strengthening of a number of weak states without the creation of a new powerful unit in the group of European nations. Thirty million Germans, comprising by far the majority of the German-speaking inhabitants of the period, were thus politically welded for the first time in modern history.

The idea of nationality had received scant attention in Germany before the nineteenth century. Kant, Fichte and Hegel contributed powerfully to its awakening. Hardly had the concept become familiar to German thought before its relation with language became established. The trend of feeling on the subject is best expressed by Arndt about half a century before the fruition of Bismarck's life project at Versailles:

> Was ist das deutsche Vaterland?
> So nenne endlich mir das Land!
> So weit die deutsche Zunge klingt
> Und Gott im Himmel Lieder singt,
> Dass soll es sein, dass soll es sein,
> Das ganze Deutschland soll es sein.[1]

A literary history of a country is, in great measure, the mirror of its political growth. The development of social aptitudes, of intellectual faculties or of material wants within a given area is, in the last resort, an expansion of the living forces which make for nationality and which, ultimately, find their way to literary records. Nationality and literature are thus bound together by geography and history. Whatever be the period under observation, the spirit of the day pervades them both. A striking example of this relation is observable in medieval

---

[1] What is the German's Fatherland?
O name at length this mighty land!
As wide as sounds the German tongue,
And Germans hymns to heaven are sung,
That is the land;
That, German, is thy Fatherland.

[Translation from J. F. Chamberlain's Literary Selections as an Aid in Teaching Geography, *Journ. of Geogr.*, Sept. 1916, p. 12.]

France, where the troubadours personified the feudal conditions which prevailed in the country. And furthermore literature, as a human product, partakes of all the limitations which are subtly imposed by the land on the fancy. It varies therefore, according to region, in mental temperament, tastes and emotions or modes of thought.

So because it is part of life and a living influence, literature has always consolidated the nation-forming power of language. Poetry, especially, is often an intensified reflection of national thought and life. In the words of Irving, "Poets always breathe the feeling of a nation." The cultivation of literature serves national ends. In the very child, love of country is instilled through the medium of doggerel—sometimes through lines of exquisite simplicity. In thus strengthening the idea of nationality, literature may be compared to the statue hewn from the marble of language by patriotic and artistic thought.

Belgian writers, in this respect, occupy a place of their own in European literature. Verhaeren and Maeterlinck voice the depth of their sincerity in the language of their Walloon colleague Lemonnier. Love of country in Spaak, a Fleming, is sung in French verse:

> Oui, sois de ton pays. Connais l'idolatrie
> De la terre natale! Et porte en toi l'orgueil
> Et le tourment de ses jours de gloire et de deuil.

Antoine Clesse, the poet of Mons, likewise expresses popular feeling in French:

> Flamands, Wallons,
> Ne sont que des prénoms
> Belge est notre nom de famille.

No matter how the works of these poets are analyzed, in the inmost souls of these writers it is the land that speaks. Belgium is fathomed in their hearts. Their eyes lingered lovingly on the scenery in the midst of which they lived. Flat roads winding interminably over flat lands, chimes whose tones mellow with age ring from the crumbling tops of old towers, rustic feasts enlivened by the roaring mirth and joviality celebrated by Flemish painters, these are the visions which are evoked by the French words assembled by Belgian writers in their compositions. One would seek in vain, however, for these Belgian scenes in French literature. Like the Belgicisms which abound delightfully in every Belgian writer's works, they portray the soul of Belgian poetry as sincerely as they afford genuine glimpses of Belgian lands. The same subtle sensation of the living earth has been felt on the troubled surface of mountainous Switzerland. For of Swiss lands and life few descriptions will ever combine the charm and faithfulness which characterize the works of Gottfried Keller, foremost among the country's writers who drew on the joint inspiration of flaming patriotism and the incomparable beauty of Swiss landscape.

And how often has the written or spoken word fanned the flame of nationality among downtrodden peoples! The story is the same from land to land and age to age. The soul of a nation in bondage is wrapped around its patriotic literature. Generation after generation of Bohemians, Finns or Poles have drunk at the national fount of poem and song. Within the peasant's thatched home as in the city abode, the well-worn volume, pregnant with past glory, becomes the beacon of hope. It lights the darkness of oppression's heaviest hours. For men of feeling, destiny will ever be hailed in the word that stirs. The harvest reaped by Cavour was of Dante's sowing.

In the bitter linguistic struggles waged in Europe two gratifying facts are discernible. The dominance of the majority by an intellectually gifted minority prevails in every country and age. Furthermore, the survival of oppressed minorities in the midst of oppressing majorities appears to be general. The one is the reward of competence; the other is the triumph of right over might. Both are victories of the human will. Both have been purchased by dint of hard struggle. Humanity is the better for them.

Neither has conquest always been able to introduce a new language. The widening sphere of Roman influence carried the original dialect of the capital to the confines of the world. But it is unlikely that Latin was spoken in the Nubian provinces or other outlying districts to a greater degree than English is spoken in India today. It was only the language of the dominant element and the one in which official transactions were recorded. As a rule the oldest language of a country is spoken by its peasants. The tillers of the soil usually represent the oldest stratum in the population of a region. The principle holds in territories which have borne the brunt of successive invasions. It is the same in Macedonia, Poland or Transylvania. On the other hand, the land-owning class is generally recruited from among past invaders.

The value of language as a national asset was shown in France during the trying days of war when the very existence of the country was at stake. Respect for the mother-tongue is deeply immured in every Frenchman's heart. In no other country does the feeling reach the same pitch. The French educational system provides ample facilities for the early initiation of students to the beauties of their vernacular. The clear and connected thought for which French writing stands pre-eminent, its capacity for expressing the most subtle shades of meaning, are largely results of literary discipline.

A perusal of war-time literature cannot sufficiently indicate the part played by French language in periods of stress. One must preferably have had the privilege of acquaintance with correspondence exchanged between relatives and intimates. Patriotism pours unfaltering from the artless lines never intended for strangers' eyes. It is as if the crowded consciousness of French nationality found constant release through its language. Every observant foreigner in France has been struck by this fact. In some instances where perception was more than usually attentive we find, as in E. Wharton's "Fighting France," that:

" It is not too much to say that the French are at this moment drawing a part of their national strength from their language. The piety with which they have cherished and cultivated it has made it a precious instrument in their hands. It can say so beautifully what they feel that they find strength and renovation in using it; and the word once uttered is passed on, and carries the same help to others. Countless instances of such happy expression could be cited by any one who has lived the last year (1915) in France. On the bodies of young soldiers have been found letters of farewell to their parents that made one think of some heroic Elizabethan verse; and the mothers robbed of these sons have sent them an answering cry of courage."

One of the most remarkable instances of the influence of poetry on national destiny is found in Serbian nationality, which has been cast altogether in the mold of the country's epic ballads or "pjesmes." Although primarily inspired by the valorous deeds of legendary heroes, these indigenous compositions describe Serbian life and nature with extraordinary verisimilitude and beauty. They are national in a significant sense, not merely because the very soul of the Serbian people is displayed in their lines, but also because they have perpetuated Serbian history and language. The purity of the Serbian tongue, its freedom from alien words, no less than the maintenance of historical continuity in Serbia are due, in a large measure, to the wandering of native minstrels—the guzlars—who went to and fro reciting or singing the wonderful exploits of their noted countrymen. Their unconscious, though passionate insistence provided the Serbian with the only schooling in national sentiment which he has undergone for generations beginning with half-mythical times. However slow, the method was effective, for it prevented atrophy of national hopes. Without this influence the Serbians would probably have degenerated into a people listless and inert to the call of nationality. The very name of Serbia might never have been recorded in modern history.

The guzlars were therefore peddlers of nationality. The most convincing evidence of their vital contribution to the formation of the modern Serbian state is found during the five hundred years in which the Turk's benumbing rule was felt in the land. Marko Kraljevitch, the popular hero-knight, feudal lord and outlaw, according as occasion demanded, embodies Serbian resistance and Serbian revolt against Moslem invaders. The stirring accents in which tales of his deep attachment to Serbia were recounted awakened exultant delight in the heart and brain of listeners and inspired them to the hope of liberation from the hated yoke. Serbia was prepared for the day of national independence by means of this slow and century-long propaganda.

Replete with the glow and color of Serbian lands, the pjesme voices Serbia's national aspirations once more in the storm and stress of new afflictions. Its accents ring so true that the geographer, in search of Serbian boundaries, tries in vain to discover a surer guide to delimitation. For Serbia extends as far as her folk-songs are heard. From the Adriatic to the western walls of Balkan ranges, from Croatia to Macedonia, the guzlar's ballad is the symbol of national solidarity. His tunes live within the heart and upon the lips of every Serbian. The pjesme may therefore be fittingly considered the measure and index of a nationality whose fiber it has stirred. To make Serbian territory coincide with the regional extension of the pjesme implies defining of the Serbian national area. And Serbia is only one among many countries to which this method of delimitation is applicable.

In Finland, nationality is embodied in the heartening lines of the "Kalevala," that Iliad of the north which takes its coloring from nature with no less delightful sensitiveness than the Homeric masterpiece. The lines of the poem define this Finnish epic as:

> Songs of ancient wit and wisdom,
> Legends they that once were taken
>
> . . . . . .
>
> From the pastures of the Northland,
> From the meads of Kalevala.
>
> . . . . . .

In this poem the beauty and color of Finland's inland seas and the bleakness of surrounding plains are painted in bold strokes and with loving effusiveness. The Finn finds in its lines a reminder of the scenes among which he has been reared and the link which binds him to his past and to his land. As a mosaic of national life pieced together by patriotism the Kalevala occupies a unique position among literary productions of northern countries. Even a note of Asiatic melancholy pervades its verses as if to recall the share of Asia in the formation of Finnish national life.

The lyrics and songs collected in the Kalevala were brought together in the beginning of the nineteenth century at a critical period of Finnish history when national feeling had sunk to its lowest ebb. Swedes and Russians vied with one another in their efforts to denationalize Finland and bring the peninsula within the sphere of their respective influence. No sooner was the Kalevala published, however, than Finnish nationality asserted itself with renewed vigor. Today after the lapse of almost a century since this revival, Finland's spirit of national independence is diffused more widely than ever among its people. Such was the influence of a literary echo of their land.

Among the peoples of Turkey, nationality and literature become largely expressions of religious feeling. It could not be otherwise in a country in which creed is the only medium of intellectual progress. The oppressed native found refuge from the tyranny of his Turkish masters in his church. His natural yearning for a higher life found solace only within the sanctuaries of his faith. All the education he received was obtained in schools attached to the churches.

But to unravel the hopeless confusion which, at first glance, seems to permeate human groupings in Turkey is, in the main, a problem of geography. The region consists of a mountainous core and a series of marginal lowlands. Its elevated area is a link in the central belt of mountains which extends uninterruptedly from Asia into Europe. This long chain of uplifts is the original seat of an important race of highlanders collectively known as *Homo alpinus*.[2] As far as is ascertainable to date, the mountaineers of Turkey have all the anatomical characteristics pertaining to this branch of the human family. Their religion and language may differ but the physical type remains unchanged. Basing themselves on this relation, anthropologists have assumed that Asiatic Turkey is the brood-home of a sub-species of *Homo*

---

[2] J. L. Myres: The Alpine Races in Europe, *Geogr. Journ.*, Vol. 28, 1906, No. 6, pp. 537-553.

alpinus which is gradually acquiring recognition as a primordial Armenoid element.[3] This type exists in its greatest purity today among the Mohammedan dissenters of the Anatolian table-land as well as among the Druzes and Maronites of Syria.

By geographical position, Asiatic Turkey is the junction of land thoroughfares which trend from south to north as well as from east to west. Its aboriginal population came inevitably into contact with the races whose migrations are known to have begun about 4,000 B.C. A second group of peoples is thus obtained in which the old strain is considerably modified. Armenians, Turks, upland Greeks, Jacobites, Nestorians and most of the Kurds represent this mixed element. A third group consists of lowlanders who never made the ascent of Turkish mountains and consequently carry no traces of Hittite ancestry. Maritime Greek populations and Arabs fall under this classification.

In the main we see that the mountain bears in its central part a homogeneous and coherent people. Distance from the core has slight effect upon the physical characteristics of the mountaineers, as long as they do not forsake the upland for the lowland. Their ideas, however, undergo modifications which can be interpreted as concessions to the views of more powerful peoples with whom contact is established. Customs, however, generally remain unchanged even if they have to be maintained in secrecy.

Nevertheless, relief alone cannot account for the variety of peoples and religions in Asiatic Turkey. The easternmost fringe of Christianity emerging sporadically out of an ocean of Mohammedanism discloses, by the variety of its discordant elements, the extent to which distance from Constantinople, the religious capital of the eastern church, had weakened the power of ecclesiastical authority. Armenians, Nestorians, Chaldeans, Jacobites and Maronites, one and all heretics in the eyes of Orthodox prelates, were merely independent thinkers who relied on the remoteness of their native districts in order to protest, without peril to themselves, against the innovations of Byzantine

---

[3] F. von Luschan: The Early Inhabitants of Western Asia, *Ann. Rept. Smithsonian Inst.* for 1914, p. 577.

theologians, or to stand firm on the basis of the rites and doctrines of early Christianity.

From the social standpoint the eastern half of Asiatic Turkey deserves investigation as the seat of an immemorial conflict between nomadism and sedentary life. Every stage of the transition between the two conditions may be observed. The feuds which set community against community in Turkey often originate in the divergent interests of nomad and settled inhabitant, and are enforced by economic factors. As an example the Kurds of the Armenian highlands may be mentioned. The perpetuation of nomadism in their case is the result of extensive horse-breeding [4]—their chief source of revenue—which compels them to seek low ground in winter.

Viewed as a whole, Asiatic Turkey has changed from an ideal nursery of hardy men to a land of meeting between races and peoples as well as between their ideals. It may be safely predicted that the future of its inhabitants bids fair to be as intimately affected as their past by the remarkable situation of the country and its physical features. One can only hope, for their sake, that a thorough invasion of highland and lowland by the spirit of the west will not be delayed much longer. This much may be said now, that the establishment of Christian rule in the land would probably be attended by wholesale conversions to Christianity in many so-called Mohammedan communities, where observance of Islamic rites has been dictated by policy, rather than by faith.

In dealing with the varied influences which engage attention in a study of linguistic areas the student is frequently compelled to pause before the importance of economic relations. Inspection of a map of Europe suggests strikingly that zones of linguistic contact were destined by their very location to become meeting-places for men speaking different languages. They correspond to the areas of circulation defined by Ratzel.[5] The confusion of

---

[4] D. G. Hogarth: The Nearer East, New York, 1902, pp. 198-199.

[5] F. Ratzel: Politische Geographie, 2nd ed., Munich, 1903. Cf. Chap. 16, " Der Verkehr als Raumbewältiger," pp. 447-534.

languages on their site is in almost every instance the result of human intercourse determined by economic causes. Necessity, far more than the thought of lucre, compels men to resort to intercourse with strangers. In Belgium, after the Norman conquest, the burghers of Flanders were able to draw on English markets for the wool which they converted into the cloth that gave their country fame in the fairs of Picardy and Champagne.[6] We have here a typical example of Ratzel's "Stapelländern" or "transit regions."

In very small localities the spread of language brought about by economic changes has occasionally come under the scrutiny of modern observers. At Grimault, in the ancient land of Burgundy, the deterioration of the local patois due to intensive working of quarries between 1860 and 1880 has been studied by E. Blin.[7] Laborers from remote districts were attracted by the prospect of work. Some intermarried with the natives. The influx of the foreign element was followed by the replacement of the locality's vernacular by French.

In west-central Europe the line of traffic along the Rhine at the end of the twelfth century ran from Cologne to Bruges along the divide between French and Flemish. Lorraine, a region of depression between the Archean piles of the Ardennes and Vosges, invited access from east and west and was known to historians as a Gallo-Romanic market place of considerable importance.[8]

In our time the river trade between Holland and Germany along the Rhine has caused expansion of Dutch into German territory as far as Wesel and Crefeld. The intruding language, however, yields to German wherever the latter is present.[9] Prevalence of French in parts of Switzerland is generally ascribed to travel through certain Alpine passes.[10] The area of

[6] R. Blanchard: La Flandre, Paris, 1906.

[7] Bull. Com. Trav. Hist. et Scien., Sec. Géogr., Vol. 29, 1914, p. xli.

[8] J. Vidal de la Blache: Étude sur la Vallée Lorraine de la Meuse, Paris, 1908, pp. 165-180.

[9] Cf. inset on pp. 63-64, Andree's Handatlas, 6th ed., 1915.

[10] J. Brunhes: La Géographie humaine, Paris, 1912, pp. 598-599.

human circulation between Lake Constance and Lake Geneva has endowed Switzerland with 35 different dialects of German, 16 of French, 8 of Italian and 5 of Romansh.[11] The penetration of German into the Trentino has already been explained. In Austria the entire valley of the Danube has provided continental trade with one of its most important avenues. Attention is called elsewhere to the Balkan peninsula as an intercontinental highway. In a word, language always followed in the wake of trade and Babel-like confusion prevailed along channels wherein men and their marketable commodities flowed.

This retrospect also leads to the conclusion that the influence of physical features in the formation of European nationalities has been exerted with maximum intensity in the early periods of their history. This was at the time when man's adaptation to environment was largely blind and unconditioned by his own will. Freedom from this physical thralldom is attained only through man's practical knowledge of human necessities and a sound vision of the welfare of his descendants. Manifestations of nature can then be made subservient to the human will. In this regard historians may eventually be induced to divide their favorite study into two main periods characterized respectively by man's submission to, or his intelligent control of, environment. A proper understanding of this conception may contribute to the establishment of frontiers with a view to eliminating conflicts due to relics of national or historical incompatibility.

The development of modern boundaries should be regarded as a process originating in barriers first provided by nature and subsequently elaborated by the human will for its purposes. Gradually however natural features of the land lose value as national boundaries. This is the result of man's progress, of the development of railways or wireless stations. It is the removal of natural obstacles; the conquest of distance by speed. All these advances tend to promote intercourse. They are opening the vista of a day when an international boundary will

[11] L. W. Lyde: The Continent of Europe, London, 1913, p. 383.

have no greater importance in world affairs than the limiting line of a city plot.

National frontiers, at best, become established by virtue of historical accidents. At given times and in order to promote fellowship among nations it becomes necessary to define the areas over which certain principles of political jurisdiction are recognized as valid by a given body of men. A national frontier in the strictest sense of the term cannot, therefore, be limited by the surface feature which has shaped its development. It has generally outgrown this phase of its extension together with the constantly increasing range of activity of the peoples it once inclosed. Factors of an ethnological, economic or linguistic nature must, therefore, be considered. Then only will the new delimitation be entitled to be qualified as natural.

The preëminence of the linguistic factor set forth in these pages may be illustrated concisely by the accepted recognition of the "langue d'oïl" as the national language of France by all Frenchmen of the present day, although this would have been impossible five centuries ago. Adoption of the linguistic criterion in boundary delimitation becomes, therefore, a mere matter of expediency. Its worth is not due to any assumed abstract value of language. It is merely a practical manner of settling divergences regarding national ownership of border territories. It is of value because the guiding consideration in boundary delimitation or revision is to eliminate future sources of conflict.

The European war is no exception to the fact that almost every conflict of magnitude has been due, in part, to ill-adjusted frontier lines. Slight regard for national aspirations seems to have prevailed in the delimitations determined upon by the signatory powers of every important treaty. The seed of ulterior fighting was thus sown, for one of the main features of modern history is the growth of national feeling as a dominating force in human affairs.

With Europe rid of Napoleon, the treaty of Vienna was framed by his allied foes in 1815 for the purpose of recasting the political map. No heed was paid, however, to the legitimate desire of smaller European nations to rule themselves. An instance of some of the gross blunders committed then was the merging of Belgium and Holland into one nationality in spite of the protests of their representatives. Feelings of the bitterest nature between Belgians and Dutch engendered by this act ultimately forced a war between the two countries in 1830. It was only after their separation that the enmity of the two peoples gave way to cordial relations. Subsequent history has shown that these two nations have often been of greater help to each other while retaining separate political entity than under forced union. In Italy also the progress made towards union by Italian-speaking peoples was checked by this treaty and the country split once more into a number of small independent states. The assignation of Lombardy and Venetia to Austria led eventually to the war of 1859.

In contrast with these cases, Germany's rise to power with unprecedented rapidity in the history of the world is a striking instance of the splendid development attainable within boundaries peopled by inhabitants of the same speech. With language and an efficient army in control Prussia only needed a leader to direct the gravitation of other German-speaking states within its own orbit. Bismarck stepped in, the right man at the right time. In 1864 he hurled the Prussian fighting machine against Denmark and wrenched the provinces of Schleswig-Holstein from that country. Two years later he turned on Austria and imposed Prussian leadership on the German-speaking world. These warlike moves gave Prussia the ascendency in the North German Confederation. Only the states of southern Germany were now needed to form the German Empire his patriotic mind had conceived. To enlist their sympathies he found it necessary to strike at France. His task was accomplished when a united Germany annexed Alsace-Lorraine.

Bismarck's work was flawless as long as he added Germans to the empire of his creation. He erred grievously, however, in including a small number of Frenchmen with Alsace-Lorraine. Had linguistic boundaries been respected at the treaty of Frankfort, and the French districts of the conquered provinces left to France, it is safe to say that Franco-German relations would not have been marked by the lack of cordiality which has characterized them since 1871. From whatever standpoint the subject be approached, the inclusion of a handful of Frenchmen within German territory was neither politic nor economic. Today Germans may well ask themselves whether the move was desirable.

The task of uniting all Germans under a single scepter was not completed by Bismarck. Ten million Germans are still subjects of the Austrian Emperor. But Austria as a political unit stands on exceedingly shaky foundations. This is due to the inclusion within its boundaries of 10 million Hungarians, 20 million Slavs and several million peoples of Romance speech. As a result, Austria is likely to be split into a number of independent states. Should this dissolution come about, the natural desire of Germans is to witness the crumbling of Austria's pieces into Germany's lap. The union of all German-speaking inhabitants of Europe into a single nation would then become an accomplished fact.

Considered from the broad standpoint of human migrations England, France and Italy may be regarded as understudies in the drama staged on the old continent. The star performers are Russia and Germany, and the issue is between these two nations. The grouping of European nations with Russia is a mere result of Germany's preponderant strength. The end of the conflict will necessarily witness the recasting of alliances along with changes of frontier lines.

For at the bottom of it all the fight is between Slav and Teuton. It is a grim and unrelenting struggle for existence that is shaping itself into one of the world's fiercest racial contests. The Slavic peoples are steadily pressing in from the east though not with the barbarity which characterized their earlier onslaughts. It is the turn of Russians, Poles, Bohemians, Slovenes, Serbians and Croats, slowly to crowd on the descendants of the blue-eyed flaxen-haired barbarians, representing Germanic peoples.

This Slavonic westerly push has always been blocked by the

leading power in the west. France opposed it in the Napoleonic period. Great Britain checked it in the latter half of the nineteenth century. Today it is Germany's turn to stand the brunt of its pressure. As matters stand both Germany and Russia are vigorous, young and fast-growing. The two peoples have taken root on adjacent land like two sturdy oaks. They are now in the stage at which the soil's nourishment at the border suffices only for one. The weaker must wither. The Teuton is expanding eastward, the Slav is spreading westward. Their main clashing-zone happens to be the Balkan peninsula. The ceaseless agitation in this area and its menace to the world's peace is a consequence of the antagonism between the Pan-Slavic Colossus and the Pan-German Titan.

Germany's expansion is a natural phenomenon. The country is overpopulated. It must expand. The sea is a barrier to its westerly expansion. The north is uninviting. The south is being drained of its resources by active and intelligent inhabitants. The "Drang nach Osten" of German Imperialism is therefore inevitable. The line of least resistance points to the east, where fertile territory awaits development.

Little wonder, then, that the attention of Germany's far-seeing statesmen has been directed toward oriental countries, whose wealth of natural resources and genial climate combine to render them ideally attractive. The verdant vales and forest-clad mountains of Serbia, Greece and Bulgaria abound with raw material needed for Germany's increasing industries. Beyond the narrow watercourse, intervening between Europe and Asia, at the Dardanelles and Bosporus lies Asia Minor, a land marvelously rich in minerals and susceptible of great agricultural development. Farther east the exceedingly fertile Mesopotamian valley, once the granary of the civilized world, stretches between the western Euphrates and Tigris, and bids fair to provide humanity anew with vast supplies of cereals.

This is the vision which has floated alluringly before the minds of German and Austrian statesmen, working hand in hand, Austria paving the way in the Balkans, Germany forcing herself successfully in the control of Asia Minor, which today is a German colony in all but name. By their joint efforts, the Teuton brothers have laid the foundation of an empire whose northern shore is washed by the Baltic and whose southern boundary may extend to the Persian Gulf. The great obstacle to this scheme of German expansion is constituted by the neighborhood of Russia and the predominance of the Slavic element in the population of the Balkan peninsula. Montenegrins, Serbians, Macedonians and even Bulgarians dread annexation by Germany.

At the end of the Balkan wars, Russia had scored heavily against Germany. An enlarged Serbia had been constituted directly in the path of Teutonic advance. In addition to this Slavic victory, every Balkan country had been strengthened considerably by the new delimitation of their frontiers. For the first time in their history, Greeks, Bulgarians and Serbians found that their national border could be made to coincide with their linguistic boundary. This national sifting is by no means complete in the Balkan peninsula. But there is no question that notable progress in the recognition of patriotic aspirations was made as soon as the region was rid of its Turkish masters.

With the history of the past hundred years in mind, statesmen engaged in the task of framing peace treaties may well heed the lessons taught by political geography. They might conclude then that greater possibilities of enduring peace exist whenever the delimitation of new frontiers is undertaken with a view to segregating linguistic areas within separate national borders. Commerce and industry will overcome ultimately these barriers and pave the way to friendly international intercourse. These are the lines along which intelligent statecraft will earn its reputation in the future.

The practical value of linguistic frontiers as national boundaries is due to their geographical growth. They are natural because they are the result of human intercourse based largely on economic needs. Having developed naturally, they correspond to national aspirations. Such being the case, the task of frontier

delimitation can be made to assume a scientific form. Only in
the case of uninhabited or sparsely populated regions will an
artificial boundary—say, of the straight line type—prove adequate. But in tenanted portions of the earth's surface where
human wills and desires come into play the problem cannot be
dismissed so lightly. The ordinary laws of science must then be
applied. This, after all, merely implies drawing on the stock of
common sense accumulated by the human race in the course of
its development. The clear duty of statesmen engaged in a
revision of boundaries is to put the varied interests at stake into
harmony with the facts of nature as they are revealed by geography. This is possible because the science deals with the surface of the earth considered as the field of man's activity. Its
data can be drawn upon just as successfully as the engineer
draws upon the energy of a waterfall or a ton of coal. Sound-
ness and permanency of the labor of delimitation can thus be
insured.

The preceding remarks should not be considered as implying
that a mountain, or a river, or even the sea are to be arbitrarily
regarded as frontiers. Lines of water-parting deserve particular
mention as having provided satisfactory national borders in history. But in boundaries each case should be treated upon its
own merits. There was a time when, in Cowper's words:

> Mountains interposed
> Make enemies of nations who had else
> Like kindred drops been mingled into one.

And yet the passes of the Alps refute the poet's statement.
Their uniting function eventually overcame their estranging
power. The easterly spread of French language over the Vosges
concurs in the same trend of testimony. The imposing mass of
the Urals is no more of a parting than are the Appalachians.
To be pertinent, it will be necessary, in each instance, to consider the complex operations of natural laws and the process of
fusing and building up of nationality brought about by their
agency.

The value of mountains in the scheme of useful boundary demarcation has been attested in the European war. Towns and villages sheltered behind rocky uplifts have suffered relatively little from the devastation which has marked the struggle in lowlands and plains. The fact is true for the Vosges mountains, the Trentino uplands and the Carpathian region. Although fighting of an exceedingly bitter character was maintained in each of these areas, the loss in property was never extreme. This is one of the many instances where land configuration lends itself advantageously to delimitation work. The need of trustworthy geographical information in partitioning and dividing up territory is obvious. Upon this basis only can boundary revision be satisfactorily pursued.

The long borderland of the French language which marks the northern and eastern boundary of French lands from the English Channel to the Mediterranean, lies unruffled by political agitation in its southeastern stretch, where Italian and French become interchangeable languages. Modifications in this section of the political frontier hardly need be considered. Their occurrence, if any, will probably come as peaceful adjustments dictated by economic reasons. To the north, however, the line has a history tainted by deeds of violence. In this stretch it forms the divide between two civilizations, the French and the German. These, although having flourished side by side, are distinctly opposed in spirit and method. Here, beginning north of the Swiss border, frontier changes appear inevitable.

In the Vosges uplift, certain facts of geographical import have direct bearing on the international boundary problem. The very occurrence of a mountain in this zone of secular conflict has a significance of its own. Aggression has generally made its way up the steep slope and, since the treaty of Frankfort of 1871, strategic advantages lie on the German side. Moreover the crest line shows French linguistic predominance.

In Lorraine, the steady expansion of French over German territory reveals the assimilative capacity of French civilization. France, unable to send forth colonists because of her lack of numbers, nevertheless contains within herself by virtue of superior civilization the ability to absorb the foreigner. Of this, evidence is to be found in the Alsatian's sympathy for France no less than in the unanimous verdict of impartial foreigners. Belgium's unhesitating rally to the French cause in the present war was also the spontaneous response to the greater cultural appeal emanating from France. The fact is attested by history since the earliest times, for much of the civilization of Germanic peoples has invariably taken its source in the inspiring ideals of the wonderfully endowed inhabitants of French territory.

Upon this historical basis, the intermediate zone between French and German languages might be converted into a number of buffer-states which, from the Alps to the North Sea, would represent the borderland of the central mountain zone and the northern plain. Switzerland, Alsace-Lorraine, Luxemburg and Belgium have been weak spots of European diplomacy on account of geographical circumstances. A just appreciation of this fact alone can provide against a continuance of past weakness.

Whatever the result of the present war, boundary rectifications from the easternmost wedge of Switzerland to the head of the Adriatic may be expected. They were the subject of negotiations between Austria and Italy prior to the latter country's entry into the war in 1915. Austria at that time proposed to cede to Italy a portion of the Trentino or "Süd-Tirol" as it is illogically called by the Germans. The territory which Austria was willing to abandon to prevent Italy from joining the Allies coincided roughly with the extension of Italian language north of the Italian frontier. Italian demands presented then were based, however, upon strategic necessities as well as linguistic considerations. Italy therefore outlined a frontier much nearer to the Adriatic watershed.

The Italian claims may be summarized as follows:[12] From Switzerland the present boundary line is to be maintained to Mount Cevedale, whence it is to strike east to Illmenspitze and

---

[12] D. W. Freshfield: The Southern Frontiers of Austria, *Geogr. Journ.*, Vol. 46, 1915, pp. 414-436.

thence northeast to Klausen passing through Gargazon. From
Klausen the line leads to the south until latitude 46° 30′ is
reached, after which it resumes its easterly course, passes
through Tofana and reaches the old boundary at about 4 miles
northeast of Cortina d'Ampezzo. The population of the last-
named district, formerly Ladin, is now Italian. This boundary

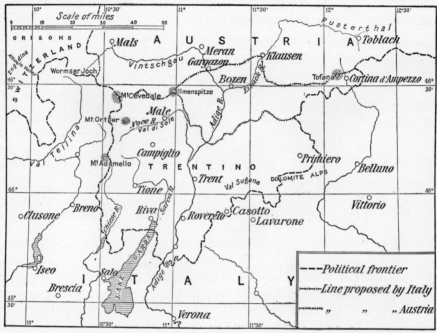

FIG. 67—Sketch map showing proposed changes in the Austro-Italian frontier
according to Austrian and Italian views.

revision will give political validity to the Italian Alps, a region
which is geographically Italian.

Through this line the transfer of the command of the passes
to Italy would become an accomplished fact. It would mean that
the entrance to the Vintschgau, the valley of the Upper Adige
and of the gorge of the Eisack at Klausen with the issue of the
Brenner and Pustherthal railways would be controlled by Italy.
Moreover the frontier has the merit of being identical with the
old bishopric boundary maintained from 1106 A.D. to the Reformation. The flaw, if any, in such an eventual settlement might
be found in the fact that the Botzen district, although econom-

ically Italian, is Teutonic in speech and feeling. The rest of the population in the Trentino favors annexation to Italy.

The Austrian offer to Italy diverges from the Italian project at Illmenspitze [13] and strikes south, carefully avoiding abandonment of territory of German speech to Italy. In doing this, however, it leaves some of the Italian-speaking northeastern districts of the Noce valley in Austrian territory. All the mountain outlets which open into the Adige valley are retained by Austria. This from the Italian standpoint is inadmissible, as it would leave the southern country exposed to aggression from the north. On the basis of the Austrian census for 1910 the changes in population consequent upon such a boundary revision are as follows:

	Italians and Ladins	Germans
In territory offered by Austria	366,837	13,892
In territory retained by Austria	18,863	511,222

In case the Italian claim is granted the following changes will result:

	Italians and Ladins	Germans
In new Italian territory	371,477	74,000
In territory retained by Austria	14,229	440,805

A margin of coastland along the eastern Adriatic is mainly Serbian in nationality though Italian in culture. It was once the nest of pirates who terrorized the Adriatic and Mediterranean. We catch historical glimpses of their retreats to the admirable shelters teeming along the coastland which skirts the Dalmatian mountains. The fringe of long islands deployed like a protecting screen enabled their vessels to evade capture. This feature of the region still exercises its influence, for a strong naval power in control of such a base might easily dominate the Mediterranean lane of traffic between east and west. The political fate of the eastern shores of the Adriatic cannot therefore be sundered from their geographical aspect.

[13] R. von Pfaundler: Österreichisch-italienische Grenzfragen, *Pet. Mitt.*, Vol. 61, 1915, pp. 217-223.

The Italians have been exhibited elsewhere in these pages as a vanishing minority throughout this Dalmatian coast. We are in the presence of Serbians, disguised under various appellations, among which the most familiar are Croatians, Slavonians, Bosnians, Herzegovinians, Montenegrins, Dalmatians and Illyrians. All these elements were susceptible of being strongly knit into a single nationality. The inclusion of a sympathizing, though numerically small, Slovene group could only introduce wholesome competition among them.

Nationalism in this region was awakened by French achievements and influences at the time of its conquest by Napoleon's armies. The French provinces of Illyria, which included Slovene territory on the north and extended as far south as Montenegro, were converted in 1816 into a kingdom of the same name which survived, up to 1846, as part of the Austrian Empire. The taste of political independence acquired by southern Slavs in that interval of time never lost its savor. Schemes for the formation of an independent Jugoslavia were naturally thrown into sharper relief through the medium of linguistic unity.

Such a south Slavic political entity must necessarily be identified with Serbia. Its extent is admirably defined by geographical, ethnographical and linguistic lines all of which coincide, thereby pointing irrefutably to national unity. The Drave, Morava, Drina and Lim rivers, with the Adriatic Sea, encircle this genuine Serbian area. It comprises the entire system of parallel ranges which form the mountainous rearland of the Adriatic. Because of its arduous character the region was never thoroughly mastered by foreigners. Invaders established themselves in force only along the sections of international highways which cross the land. The rest remained accessible to the Serbian natives only.

The defining of an independent Hungary presents little confusion if approached from the main highway of geography. Agreement between the land and its inhabitants appears to exist here, for the Magyar is, in the first place, a lowlander accustomed to live within the precincts of a fertile plain. He has always shunned the mountain and is rarely to be met above the 600-foot contour. As soon as the hills to the north of the vast field of his birth are attained he disappears, leaving a few officials to represent him. Slovak, Rumanian and Ruthenian hillmen then come upon the scene. On the western side, west of the Raab, the heights drained by the river are peopled by Germans and, in spite of a complex boundary zone, a convenient line of demarcation could be drawn upon the basis of elevation. Southward the old-time utility of the Drave as the dividing line between Croat and Hungarian remains unimpaired to this day. In the east, however, around the confluence of this river with the Danube and towards the Theiss valley the swamp lands have repelled the ease-loving Hungarian as effectively as the mountains to the east and north. The Serb, less particular in his choice of residence, advanced northward as far as the swampy land extends. In this section any physical map contains the data for a territorial division.

With regard to Transylvania, conditions may be summarized as follows: the region is scantily populated, valleys constituting centers of human habitation almost exclusively. The inhabitants are overwhelmingly Rumanians.[14] The dominating Hungarian element inhabits isolated communities in their midst. This separation of the rival peoples is of the utmost interest in boundary revision, for which it provides a reliable geographical basis. Wallis has ingeniously shown[15] that a line separating the majority of Hungarians from Rumanians can be obtained by taking language as a guide and that this is possible because there exists no mixing of peoples in the eastern borderland of Hungarian language. In reality, throughout Hungary the only element that has insinuated itself in the midst of Hungarian, Rumanian or Slav populations is the German. This element is generally absorbed except where present in large numbers. The Magyar, however, has never mingled with his neighbors. One is

---

[14] B. C. Wallis: Distribution of Nationalities in Hungary, *Geogr. Journ.*, Vol. 52, 1916, No. 3, pp. 177-189.
[15] Loc. cit.

almost led to seek the reason for his aloofness in his Asiatic origin.

Poland also has its natural place in the European political system. The majority of Poles live in Russian Poland. Out of a total of over 20,000,000 Poles about 12,000,000 are found in the "governments" or administrative districts created by Russia in the sections of Poland within Russia's boundaries. These districts are ten in number and adjoin each other. Geographically they form a unit—the westernmost appendage of the vast united Russian territory which aggregates between one-sixth or one-seventh of the total land surface of the world. Detachment of this Polish section from Russia and its creation into part of an autonomous Poland is practicable without serious loss to Russian unity. Slavic solidarity would in fact be consolidated if Poland were constituted a sovereign state.

To Germany, however, an autonomous Poland which would encompass the million Poles living in the Kaiser's empire implies abandonment of a territory which reaches far into the heart of the country. The Polish strip ends less than a hundred miles east of Berlin. The province of Posen, a considerable portion of Silesia, a narrow strip of West Prussia reaching the Baltic west of Danzig and the Masurian Lakes district are peopled by Poles. Furthermore, and this is of capital importance in German eyes, East Prussia which is German by language and tradition, as well as Prussian to the core, would become isolated from the main mass of the German-speaking people. It is improbable that such a cession of territory will take place as long as Germany has the power to prevent it. It need only be remembered that the first partition of Poland was engineered by Frederick the Great merely to join East Prussia to the rest of his kingdom. Against this last fact, however, the imperative necessity for an independent Poland to obtain an outlet on the Baltic will always prevail in anti-German circles.

Nature therefore points to the existence of a real German menace to Polish autonomy. It is needless to minimize the significance of the points at issue. Prussia, the dominant state in the German nation, will never consent to the impairment of her territorial unity by the surrender of her Polish sections. On the other hand the reconstruction of Poland must be complete if the creation of a Balkanic state of affairs west of the Gulf of Danzig is to be avoided. A partial reunion of Polish-speaking groups under an autonomous government would be the prelude to irredentist questions. This however is precisely what an enlightened world is seeking to prevent.

In reality the German nation would be the gainer by the creation of a reunited Polish state. No better barrier to Russia's westerly advance in Europe could be devised. Conversely Teutonic encroachments on Slavic territory—bound as they inevitably are to be attended by bloodshed—would be effectively arrested. A buffer state between Russia and Germany is the safest guarantee of peace between the two nations. All the inextricable tangles in which Europe has been involved by Polish problems can be unraveled by the restoration of Polish national entity. The problem requires solution for the sake of the peace of the world.

The problems arising along the remaining linguistic boundaries have been exhibited in earlier chapters and require but little mention here. In Schleswig an extension of Denmark's political frontier as far south as the Danish language prevails would be welcomed as the harbinger of lasting harmony between Danes and Germans. The historical frontier between the Danish duchy and Holstein could be utilized to advantage in this change. In this, as in other cases, the principles of geography, modified by national aspirations and economic needs, must in the last resort be recognized as practical and applicable. Bohemia, which has been shown to be splendidly laid off on a physical map, deserves political independence because it is endowed with geographic individuality. This method of solving the problems which for centuries have burdened Europe with strife would, like the splitting of Austria into national fragments, mark an improvement in the lot of a notable proportion of the population of Europe. New impetus would be granted to the development of national sentiment. Humanity owes much to the free play of this feeling. The claims of world brotherhood have received greater attention through its existence. The energies of submerged nationalities have hitherto been absorbed by the struggle for survival. Relief from this stress will be accompanied by respect for alien rights instead of hatred of the oppressor.

Throughout the nineteenth century, as well as in the beginning of the twentieth, reconstruction of nationalities was effected on a linguistic basis. The part played by language during that period is of tantamount importance to the religious feeling which formerly caused many a destructive war. Practically all the wars of the last hundred years are the outcome of three great constructive movements which led to the unification of Germany and of Italy as well as to the disentanglement of Balkan nationalities. These were outward and visible signs of the progress of democratic ideals. The Congress of Vienna failed to provide Europe with political stability because popular claims were ignored during the deliberations. At present, inhabitants of linguistic areas under alien rule are clamoring for the right to govern themselves. The carrying out of plebiscites under international supervision can often be relied upon to satisfy their aspirations and serve as a guide to frontier rearrangements.

All told, the growing coincidence of linguistic and political boundaries must be regarded as a normal development. It is a form of order evolved out of the chaos characterizing the origin of human institutions. The delimitation of international frontiers is as necessary as the determination of administrative boundaries or city lines. Human organization requires it and there is no reason why it should not be undertaken with fair regard to the wishes and feelings of all affected. For nations, like individuals, are at their best only when they are free, that is to say when the mastery of their destiny is in their own hands.

APPENDIX A

GERMAN SETTLEMENTS IN RUSSIA

COLONIES of Germans in Russia are found mainly in the Baltic provinces and around the banks of the Volga. According to the census of 1897 the German residents of the governments of Livonia, Kurland, Esthonia, and St. Petersburg numbered 229,084. The majority of this northern element is distributed along the shores of the Gulf of Riga.

The banks of the Volga were first colonized by Germans in 1763 after a proclamation issued by Empress Catherine II inviting foreigners to settle on either side of the river in the environs of Saratoff and Samara and as far as Tzaritzin. The distress that followed the Seven Years' War in Germany determined a number of families of the afflicted provinces to seek a better lot on Russian soil. By the year 1768 there had been founded 102 German settlements containing a total population of 27,000 inhabitants.[1] The newcomers had to face considerable hardships. Many of them were neither farmers nor peasants. Their endurance was taxed by the rigor of the climate. Insecurity of life and property prevailed as badly as in their devastated motherland. In 1774 rebel bands led by Jemelian Pontgatcheff wrought havoc and ruin in the new districts. Two years later hordes of Kirghiz nomads laid waste the land again and carried off a number of the emigrants as slaves. This state of affairs lasted until the last decades of the nineteenth century. The Tatar raiders were attracted mainly by the cattle of the colonists. The value of horses, camels and cattle stolen between 1875 and 1882 is estimated at 330,000 rubles.[2]

It is estimated that fully five million rubles were spent by the Russian government to plant these foreign colonies. But no onerous terms were imposed on the settlers. A head tax of three rubles constituted their only pecuniary obligation to the state. Furthermore, a liberal administration was provided for their settlements. Each village was ruled by an assembly recruited from among its inhabitants.

Unfortunately for the development of these communities the Russian system of collective ownership known as the "mir" was instituted. Under this form of tenure all land becomes the property of the village. Each male inhabitant is temporarily entitled to a share of the whole area and an exchange of plots is made every ten years. Each village then receives a new fraction and fresh lots are apportioned to those who have come of

---

[1] P. Clerget: Les Colonies Allemandes de la Volga, *La Géogr.*, Feb. 1909.
[2] H. Pokorny: Die Deutschen an der Volga, *Deutsche Erde*, 1908, No. 4, pp. 138-144.

age during the decade. This method of ownership does not lead to development and generally retards rather than promotes agricultural progress.

Furthermore the land is none too fertile. Uncertainty therefore is today the common lot of many of the descendants of the old German settlers. Many prefer to engage in trade rather than in agriculture. The natural increase of the population has brought a certain amount of congestion which has resulted in emigration. Effort is made by German missionary societies to induce these Russian Germans to return to the land of their fathers. The Russian government on the other hand provides them with ample facilities and inducements to settle in Siberia. The region around Tomsk contains a number of villages built up by this emigration. Many however prefer to emigrate to the United States where they find a happier lot. Settlements composed entirely of Volga Germans exist in Wisconsin.

The old German settlers had held steadfastly to their religion. Their descendants have also clung to the faith of their fathers, thus creating a totally separate community in the midst of Orthodox Russia. Their earliest schools had been founded as annexes of their churches and education had been a great factor in the maintenance of language and religion. In 1891 the use of Russian was rendered obligatory in all educational institutions of the Empire. Nevertheless this measure cannot be said to have contributed to weaken the German character of the communities. From Germany itself manifestations of interest towards these faraway centers of German custom have always been keen. Neither has support been lacking.

According to recent statistics the Germans inhabiting the banks of the Volga number close to half a million, distributed equally on both banks of the great inland river. The ethnic type of these Germans has been maintained with remarkable purity and their language contains obsolete forms dating from the eighteenth century. The names of the largest communities and the number of their inhabitants are as follows:

Saratoff	12,500
Norka	13,416
Frank	11,700
Grimm or Lesnoi Karamish	10,761
Baltzer Katharinenstadt or Baronsk	10,134

APPENDIX B

THE BALKAN STATES BEFORE AND AFTER THE WARS OF 1912-13[1]

AREAS (*in square miles*)

State	Former area	New area	Percentage of Increase or Decrease
Montenegro	3,506	5,600	+60%
Albania	—	10,900	—
Serbia	18,650	33,600	+80%
Rumania	50,720	54,300	+ 7%
Bulgaria	37,201	43,300	+16%
Greece	24,966	46,600	+87%
Turkey in Europe	65,370	9,700	—85%

POPULATION

State	Prior to War	After the War
Montenegro	285,000	500,000
Albania	—	900,000
Serbia	2,960,000	4,300,000
Rumania	7,250,000	7,400,000
Bulgaria	4,340,000	4,800,000
Greece	2,670,000	4,600,000
Turkey in Europe	6,130,000	1,600,000

[1] Joerg, W. L. G.: The New Boundaries of the Balkan States and their Significance, *Bull. of Amer. Geogr. Soc.*, Vol. 45, 1913, p. 819.

APPENDIX C

CLASSIFICATION OF LANGUAGES SPOKEN IN EUROPE

Group	Branches	Languages
A. CELTIC		1. Gaelic
		a. Irish
		b. Highland Scotch
		c. Manx
		2. Cymric
		a. Welsh
		b. Low Breton
B. ROMANIC		1. French
		2. Italian
		3. Spanish
		4. Provençal
		5. Portuguese
		6. Romansh or Churwaelsh
		7. Rumanian
C. GERMANIC	Scandinavian	1. Swedish
		2. Danish
		3. Icelandic
	Germanic	1. High German
		2. Low German
		3. Dutch, including Flemish
		4. Frisian
		5. English
D. SLAVIC	Western	1. Polish
		2. Bohemian
		3. Wend
	Eastern	1. Russian, including Ruthenian
		2. Bulgarian
		3. Serbian, including Croatian
E. LETTIC		1. Lettish
		2. Lithuanian
F. HELLENIC		Greek
G. ILLYRIC		Albanian
H. INDIC		Gipsy or Romany

In addition to the above the following non-Indo-European languages are spoken in Europe:

Family	Group	Branch	Language
TURANIAN	FINNIC	Tchudic	1. Finnic
			2. Esthonian
			3. Tchud
			4. Lapp
			5. Voth
			6. Livonian
		Permian	1. Votiak
			2. Sirian
			3. Permiak
		Volgaic	1. Tchuvash
			2. Mordoin
			3. Cheremiss
		Ugric	1. Hungarian
			2. Samoyed
	TATARIC		Turkish
CAUCASIAN			1. Lesghian
			2. Circassian
BASQUE			Basque or Euskara

APPENDIX D

A SELECTED BIBLIOGRAPHY

Aitoff, D. Peuples et langues de la Russie. *Ann. de Géogr.,* Vol. 15, 1909, pp. 92-5.

André, L. *See* Bourgeois, E.

Andree, R. Nationalitätsverhältnisse und Sprachgrenze in Böhmen. *Ver. Erdk.,* Leipzig, 1869, pp. 51-88.

Andree, R. Die Grenzen der niederdeutschen Sprache. *Globus,* Vol. 59, 1891, pp. 29-31, 41-43.

Andree, R. Die Völkergrenzen in Frankreich. *Globus,* Vol. 36, 1879, pp. 6-10, 25-29.

Andree, R. Das Sprachgebiet der Lausitzer Wenden. 1550-1872. *Pet. Mitt.,* 1873, map 17.

Andrié, A. Geschichte des Fürstentums Montenegro. Vienna, 1853.

Annuaire International de Statistique, I: État de la Population (Europe). *Office Permanent de l'Institut International de Statistique.* The Hague, 1916.

Ascoli, G. I. Saggi ladini. *Archivio glottologico italiano.* Rome, 1873.

Auerbach, B. Les Races et les Nationalités en Autriche-Hongrie. Paris, 1898.

Auerbach, B. La Germanisation de la Pologne Prussienne. La loi d'expropriation. *Rev. Politique et Parlementaire,* Vol. 57, juillet 1908, pp. 109-125.

Babelon, E. La grande Question d'Occident. Le Rhin dans l'histoire, Vols. 1 and 2, Paris, 1915.

Bain, R. N. Scandinavia, A Political History of Denmark, Norway and Sweden, 1513-1900. Cambridge, 1905.

Balkan Wars, Causes and Conduct of the, Report of the International Commission to inquire into the. *Carnegie Endowment for International Peace,* Publ. No. 4, Washington, 1914.

Baragiola, A. La Casa Villereccia delle colonie tedesche del gruppo Carnico. Sappada, Sauris e Timau con raffronti delle zone contermini italiana ed austriaca Carnia, Cadore, Zoldano, Agordino, Carintia e Tirolo. Peregrazioni folkloriche. Padua, 1915.

Barker, J. Ellis. The Foundations of Germany. London, 1916.

Battisti, C. Il Trentino. Novara, 1915.

Beauvois, E. La nationalité du Slesvig. Paris, 1864.

Bernhard, L. Das polnische Gemeinwesen im preussischen Staat. Die Polenfrage, Leipzig, 1910.

Bidermann, W. Die Nationalitäten in Tirol und die wechselnden Schicksale ihrer Verbreitung. *Forsch. z. deuts. Landes- und Volkskunde.* Vol. 1.

Bielenstein, A. J. G. Die Grenzen des lettischen Volksstammes und der lettischen Sprache. Petrograd, 1892.

Blanchard, R. La Flandre. Paris, 1906.

Blocher, E., u. E. Garraux. Die deutschen Ortsnamenformen der Westschweiz. *Deutsche Erde,* Vol. 5, 1906, p. 170.

Block, M. L'Ile de France. (Les pays autours de Paris.) Paris, 1913.

Boeckh, R. Die Sprachgrenze in Belgien. *Zeits. für allgemeine Erdkunde*, Berlin, Vol. 3, 1882, pp. 80-97.

Bonmariage, A. La Russie d'Europe. Brussels, 1903.

Boué, A. Ethnographische Karte des Osmanischen Reichs, 1: 3,800,000. Gotha, 1847 and 1855.

Boulger, Demetrius C. A History of Belgium. 2 vols. London, 1902-1909.

Bourgeois, E., et André, L. Les sources de l'histoire de France XVIIme siècle (1610-1715), Vol. 1. Geógraphie et histoire générale. Paris, 1913.

Bourgoing, P. de. Les guerres d'idiome et de nationalité. Paris, 1849.

Bourlier, L. Les Tchéques et la Bohème contemporaine. Paris, 1897.

Bowley, A. L. The Nature and Purpose of the Measurement of Social Phenomena. London, 1915.

Braemer, K. Nationalität und Sprache im Königreiche Belgien. *Forsch. z. deuts. Landes- und Volkskunde.* Vol. 2, 1887.

Brancoff, D. M. La Macédoine et sa population Chrétienne. Paris, 1905.

Brilliant, O. Roumania. New York, 1915.

Bringuier, O., et De Tourloulon, Ch. Étude sur la limite géographique de la langue d'oc et de la langue d'oïl. Paris, 1876.

Brunhes, J. La Géographie humaine. Paris, 1912.

Bürchner, L. Die neue griechisch-albanische Grenze in Nordepirus. *Pet. Mitt.*, Vol. 61, 1915, pp. 68-69.

Burileanu. Romîni din trumghiul Vallona-Ardenita-Berat. *Bull. Soc. Geogr. Romấnă*, Vol. 27, 1906, pp. 39-63.

Cambridge Modern History, Vol. XI, The Growth of Nationalities. Cambridge, 1909.

Chamberlain, H. S. The Foundations of the XIXth Century. London, 1915.

Chantre, E. Les Kurdes, esquisse historique et ethnographique. *Bull. Soc. Anthropol.*, Lyon, 1897.

Charriaut, H. La Belgique Moderne. Paris, 1910. (Chap. III, La situation respective des langues.)

Cherubim, C. Flüsse als Grenzen von Staaten und Nationen in Mitteleuropa. Halle, 1897.

Chervin, A. L'Autriche et la Hongrie de demain. Paris, 1915.

Choroszewski, W. Mapa jezykowa i wyznaniowa Galicji. Lemberg, 1911.

Clare, C. L. The Brenner Pass. London, 1912.

Clerget, P. La Suisse au XXme siècle. Paris, 1908.

Clerget, P. Le Peuplement de la Suisse. *Bull. Soc. Roy. Belge de Géogr.*, Vol. 30, 1906, pp. 73-97.

Colleoni, C. Cima Dodici. Vicenza, 1910.

Coussange, Jacques. La Scandinavie, le nationalisme scandinave. Paris, 1914.

Cromer, Earl. Political and Literary Essays. London, 1916.

Cumont, F. Comment la Belgique fut romanisée. Brussels, 1914.

Cunningham, W. Western Civilization in its Economic Aspects. Vols. 1 and 2. Cambridge, 1913.

Curzon, Lord. Frontiers—The Romanes Lecture. Oxford, 1907.

Cust, R. N. Linguistic and Oriental Essays. London, 1891.

Cvijić, J. L'annexion de la Bosnie et la Question Serbe. Paris, 1909.

Cvijić, J.   Remarques sur l'ethnographie de la Macédoine.   *Ann. de Géogr.*, Vol. 15, 1906.

Dascovici, N.   La Question du Bosphore et des Dardanelles.   Geneva, 1915.

De Backer, L.   La Langue flamande en France.   Ghent, 1893.

Dedijer, Jevto.   La Transhumance dans les pays dinariques.   *Ann. de Géogr.*, Vol. 26, 1916, pp. 347-365.

De Gourmont, R.   La Belgique Littéraire.   Paris, 1916.

De Launay, L.   La Bulgarie d'hier et de demain.   Paris, 1912.

De Lucchi, G.   Trentino e Tirolo.   *Bull. No. 16, Ministero d. Affari Esteri*, Rome, 1915.

Demartean.   Le Flamand, le Wallon, etc., Liége, 1889.

De Martonne, E.   La Valachie.   Paris, 1902.

De Martonne, E.   Recherches sur la Distribution Géographique de la population en Valachie.   *Bull. Soc. Geogr. Rom.*, Vol. 23, 1902.   La Roumanie et son rôle dans l'Europe Orientale.   *La Geógr.*, Vol. 30, 1914-1915.

Denecke, T.   Belgien und Nordfrankreich.   Hamburg, 1915.

De Romanet, le Vicomte.   Les Provinces de la France.   Paris, 1913.

De Tourloulon, Ch., et Bringuier, O.   Étude sur la limite géographique de la langue d'oc et de la langue d'oïl.   Paris, 1876.

Diamandy, V.   Statistica comunelor românesti din Turcia.   *Bull. Soc. Geogr. Rom.*, Vol. 25, 1904, pp. 136-147.

Drachmann, P.   The Industrial Development and Commercial Policies of the Three Scandinavian Countries.   Oxford, 1915.

Ensor, R. C. K.   Belgium.   New York, 1915.

Erdeljanović, J.   Broj Srba i Khrvata.   Belgrade, 1911.

Evans, A.   The Adriatic Slavs and the Overland Route to Constantinople.   *Geogr. Journ.*, Vol. 47, 1916, pp. 241-265.

Eversley, Lord.   The Partition of Poland.   New York, 1915.

Fayle, C. E.   The Great Settlement.   London, 1915.

Fedortchouk, Y.   Memorandum on the Ukrainian Question in its National Aspect.   London, 1914.

Flodströf, I.   Till fràgan om rasskillnader inom Sverifes befolkning.   *Ymer*, 1915, pp. 213-266.

Forbes, Nevill.   The Balkans, a History of Bulgaria, Serbia, Greece, Rumania, Turkey.   ·By Nevill Forbes, Arnold J. Toynbee, D. Mitrany, D. G. Hogarth.   Oxford, 1915.

Franchi, A.   Città Sorelle.   Milan, 1916.

Freeman, E. A.   The Historical Geography of Europe.   London, 1903.   Historical Essays.   London, 1871.

Freshfield, D. W.   The Southern Frontiers of Austria.   *Geogr. Journ.*, Dec. 1915.

Friederichsen, Prof. Dr. Max.   Die Grenzmarken des Europäischen Russlands.   Hamburg, 1915.

Galanti, A.   I Tedeschi Sul versante meridionale delle Alpi.   Rome, 1885.

Garnier, Ch.   Note sur la répartition des langues dans les Alpes occidentales.   *Rev. de Géogr.*, Vol. 40, 1897, pp. 6-12.

Gasselin, L.   La Question du Schleswig-Holstein.   Paris, 1909.

Gayda, V.   Modern Austria, Her Racial and Social Problems.   New York, 1915.

Geiser, Alfred.   Deutsches Reich u. Volk.   Munich, 1910.

Gerland, G.   Atlas der Völkerkunde.   Gotha.

Gibert, F.   Les pays d'Albanie et leur histoire.   Paris, 1914.

Gillieron et Edmont.   Atlas Linguistique de la France.   Paris.

Gjerset, K.   History of the Norwegian People.   New York, 1915.

Gonzaga, C. V. A.   La questione delle Lingue in Austria.   *Boll. del Ministro degli Affari Esteri.*   Rome, 1900.

Grant, M.   The Passing of the Great Race.   New York, 1916.

Gröber, G.   Grundriss der Romanischen Philologie.   Strassburg, 1904-1906.

Guérard, Albert Léon.   French Civilization in the Nineteenth Century.   New York, 1914.

Guizot, M.   Histoire de la Civilisation en Europe.   Paris, 1866.

Guttry, A.   Die Polen und der Weltkrieg.   Munich, 1915.

Guyot, Y.   The Causes and Consequences of the War.   London, 1916.

Guyot, Y.   La Province Rhénane et la Westphalie.   Paris, 1915.

Hanotaux, G.   Contemporary France.   Vols. 1-4.   New York.

Hansen, R.   Die Sprachgrenzen in Schleswig.   *Globus,* Vol. 61, 1892, pp. 376-380.

Hayes, C.   A Political and Social History of Modern Europe.   Vols. 1 and 2.   New York, 1916.

Heinz, Wilhelm.   Das Ansiedlungsgebiet des Vereines Südmark.   *Deutsche Erde,* 1914-1915, pp. 110-131.

Henry, R.   La frontière linguistique en Alsace-Lorraine.   *Les Marches de l'Est,* 1911-1912, pp. 60-71.

Hertslet, E.   The Map of Europe by Treaty.   London, 1875.

Hill, N.   Poland and the Polish Question.   London, 1915.

Hills, Major E. H.   The Geography of International Frontiers.   *Geogr. Journ.,* Vol. 28, 1906, p. 145.

Himly.   Formation territoriale des États de l'Europe centrale.   Vols. 1 and 2.   Paris, 1894.

Hodgkin, T.   Italy and her Invaders.   Vols. 1-8.   Oxford, 1880-1899.

Hogarth, D. G.   The Balkans, a History of Bulgaria, Serbia, Greece, Rumania, Turkey.   By Nevill Forbes, Arnold J. Toynbee, D. Mitrany, D. G. Hogarth.   Oxford, 1915.

Holdrich, T. H.   Political Frontiers and Boundary Making.   London, 1916.

Howe, E. S.   A Thousand Years of Russian History.   Philadelphia, 1915.

Hunfalvy, P.   Die Ungern oder Magyaren.   Vienna, 1881.

Huntington, E.   Palestine and its Transformation.   New York, 1911.

Iorga, N.   Histoire des Roumains de Transylvanie et de Hongrie.   Bucarest, 1915.   Histoire des états balcaniques à l'époque moderne.   Bucarest, 1914.

Italian Green Book, The.   London, 1915.

Jalla, J.   Les Vallées vaudoises sous le règne de Charles Emanuel.   1° jusqu'à l'Édit de Nantes et au Traité de Vervins, 1580-1598.   Torre Pellice, 1916.

Jansen, C., u. Samwer, K.   Schleswig-Holsteins Befreiung.   Wiesbaden, 1897.

Jastrow, Jr., Morris.   The Civilization of Babylonia and Assyria.   Philadelphia, 1915.

Jessen, F. de.   La Question du Sleswig.   1906.

Joerg, W. L. G.   The New Boundaries of the Balkan States and their Significance.   *Bull. Am. Geogr. Soc.,* Vol. 45, 1913, pp. 819-830.

Jonquière, A. de la.   Histoire de l'Empire Ottoman.   Paris, 1914.

Jorgenson.   La Question dano-allemande.   Copenhagen, 1900.

Kalken, F. V. Histoire du Royaume des Pays-Bas et de la Révolution Belge de 1830. Brussels, 1914.

Keane, A. H. Man, Past and Present. Cambridge, 1899.

Kluchevsky, V. O. A History of Russia. Translated by C. J. Hogarth. New York, 1911.

Koch, C. G. de. Histoire abrégée des Traités de Paix entre les Puissances de l'Europe depuis la Paix de Westphalie. Brussels, 1837.

Krehbiel, E. B. Nationalism, War and Society. New York, 1916.

Kurth, G. La Frontière linguistique en Belgique et dans le Nord de la France. Mém. couronnés. *Acad. R. Sci. Lettres et Beaux-Arts de Belgique,* Vol. 48, Brussels, 1895-1898.

Kurth, G. La nationalité belge. Brussels, 1913.

Lambrecht, N. Preussische Wallonie. Essen a. Ruhr, 1909.

Lamy, Étienne. La France du Levant. Paris, 1900.

Langenbeck, R. Die Burgundische Pforte. *Pet. Mitt.,* Vol. 61, 1915, pp. 49-55.

Larmeroux, J. L'Autriche-Hongrie au Congrès de Berlin, 1878. Paris, 1915.

Latham, R. G. Nationalities of Europe. London, 1863.

Lavisse, E., et Rambaud, A. Histoire générale du IVme siècle jusqu'à nos jours. Paris, 1896.

Lazar, V. Die Südrumänen der Turkei und der angrenzenden Länder. Bucarest, 1910.

Leaf, W. Troy, a Study in Homeric Geography. London, 1912.

Leclercq, Jules. La Finlande aux mille Lacs. Paris, 1914.

Lefeuvre-Méaulle, H. La Grèce économique et financière. Paris, 1916.

Lefèvre, A. Germains et Slaves. Paris, 1903.

Lessiak, Dr. Primus. Zwei deutsche Sprachinseln in Friaul: Bladen und die Jahre. *Deutsche Erde,* 1914-1915, pp. 110-131.

Lethbridge, Alan. The New Russia. New York, 1916.

Lippmann, W. Stakes of Diplomacy. New York, 1915.

Löffler, E. Dänemarks Natur und Volk. Copenhagen, 1905.

Longnon, A. Origines et formation de la Nationalité française. Paris.

Louis-Jarau, G. L'Albanie Inconnue. Paris, 1913.

Lowell, A. L. Governments and Parties in Continental Europe. Cambridge, 1915.

Lyde, L. W. The Continent of Europe. London, 1913. Some Frontiers of To-morrow, an Aspiration for Europe. London, 1915.

MacDonnell, J. de C. Belgium, Her Kings, Kingdom and People. London, 1914.

Maranelli, Carlo. Dizionario Geografico dell' alto del Trentino, della Venezia Giulia e della Dalmazia. Bari, 1915.

Marriott, J. A. R., and Roberston, C. G. The Evolution of Prussia: the Making of an Empire. Oxford, 1915.

Massart, J. Belgians under the German Eagle. London, 1916.

Mavor, James. An Economic History of Russia. New York, 1916.

May, G. Le Traité de Francfort. Paris, 1910.

Mazere, N. Harta etnografica a Transilvaniei. 1:340,000. Iasi, 1909. Supliment la harta Transilvaniei. Iasi, 1909.

Meillet, A. Le Problème de la Parenté des Langues. Bologna, 1914.

Meillet, A. De la Légitimité de la Linguistique Historique. Bologna, 1913.

Meillet, A. Introduction à l'Étude Comparative des Langues Indo-Européennes. Paris, 1915.

Meillet, A.   Les Langues et les Nationalités.   *Scientia.*   Sept. 1915.

Mellor, E. W.   The Wendish Baltic Ports of the Hanseatic League.   *Journ. Manchester Geogr. Soc.,* Vol. 19, 1903, pp. 125-150.

Menant, J.   Les Yézidis.   Paris, 1892.

Meyer, C.   Geschichte des Landes Posen.   Posen, 1881.

Mitrany, D.   The Balkans, a History of Bulgaria, Serbia, Greece, Rumania, Turkey.   By Nevill Forbes, Arnold J. Toynbee, D. Mitrany, D. G. Hogarth.   Oxford, 1915.

Morf, H.   Deutsche und Romanen in der Schweiz.   Zürich, 1901.

Morgan, J. de.   Les Premières Civilisations.   Paris, 1909.

Moysset, H.   La Politique de la Prusse et les Polonais.   *Rev. des Deux Mondes,* Vol. 48, 1908, pp. 108-138; and pp. 519-550.

Müller, M.   Biographies of Words and the Home of the Aryas.   London, 1888.

Nabert, H.   Verbreitung der Deutschen in Europa.   1 : 925,000.   Glogau.

Newbigin, M. I.   Geographical Aspects of Balkan Problems in their Relation to the Great European War.   London, 1915.

Newbigin, M. I.   Italy and the Adriatic.   *The Scot. Geogr. Mag.,* Oct. 1916, pp. 466-477.

Niederle, L.   La Race Slave.   Paris, 1911.   Slovanský Svet.   Prague, 1910.

Nitsch, C.   Dialectology of Polish Languages.   Polish Encyclopædia, Vol. 3.   Cracow, 1915.

Norges Land og Folk, topografisk statistik beskrevet.   Christiania, 1898-1915.

Oestreich, Karl.   Die Bevölkerung von Makedonien.   *Sonderabdruck aus der Geographischen Zeitschrift.*

Osborne, H. F.   Men of the Old Stone Age.   New York, 1916.

Otlet, Paul.   Les Problèmes internationaux et la Guerre.   Paris, 1916.

Pais, E.   Ancient Italy.   Chicago, 1908.

Partsch, J.   Schlesien.   Breslau, 1896.

Pernice, A.   Origine ed evoluzione storica delle Nazioni balcaniche.   Milan, 1915.

Perrier, E.   France et Allemagne.   Paris, 1915.

Petrovich, W. M.   Serbia: Her People, History and Aspirations.   London, 1915.

Pfaundler, R. von.   Oesterreichisch-Italienische Grenzfragen.   *Pet. Mitt.,* June 1915.

Pfister, Ch.   La limite de la langue française et de la langue allemande en Alsace-Lorraine.   Considérations historiques.   *Bull. Soc. Géogr. de l'Est,* Vol. 12, 1890.

Phillips, W. A.   Poland.   New York, 1916.

Pirenne, H.   Belgian Democracy: Its Early History.   Manchester, 1915.

Pirenne, H.   Bibliographie de l'histoire de Belgique.   Brussels, 1902.

Pirenne, H.   Histoire de Belgique.   Vols. 1-4.   Brussels, 1900-1911.

Pittard, E.   Les Peuples de la Péninsula des Balkans.   *Rev. Gen. des Sciences,* 1915, pp. 665-675.

Pittard, E.   Dans la Dobrodja.   Geneva, 1902.

Plazanet, Gal.   Essai d'une Carte des Patois du Midi.   *Rev. Soc. Géogr. Comm.,* Vol. 39, Bordeaux, 1913.

Prontuario dei nomi locali dell' Alto Adige.   *Mem. Real. Soc. Geogr. Italiana,* Vol. 15, Part I, Rome, 1916.

Rambaud, A.   Histoire de la Russie depuis les origines jusqu'à nos jours.   Paris, 1914.

Ranke, L.   Weltgeschichte.   Leipsig, 1881-1888.

Ratzel, F. Politische Geographie. Munich, 1903.

Rauchberg, H. Sprachenkarte von Böhmen. Vienna, 1905.

Reade, A. Finland and the Finns. New York, 1915.

Revelli, P. L'Adriatico e il dominio del Mediterraneo Orientale. *Riv. Geogr. Ital.*, Feb.-March 1916, pp. 91-113.

Reyman, E. J. Die Weichsel als Wasserstrasse. Warsaw, 1912.

Reynard, L. Histoire Générale de l'influence française en Allemagne. Paris, 1915.

Richardson, R. The Ethnology of Austria-Hungary. *Scot. Geogr. Mag.*, Vol. 22, 1906, pp. 1-9.

Rieden, J. Das Schwäbische Bauernhaus. *Deut. Alpenzeitung,* Nov. 1915.

Rignano, E. Les Facteurs de la Guerre et le Problème de la Paix. *Scientia.* Vol. 18, 1915, pp. 1-47.

Ripley, W. Z. The Races of Europe. New York, 1899.

Robertson, C. G. *See* Marriott.

Roquette-Buisson (de). Du principe des nationalités. Paris, 1895.

Rosen, Dr. H. Die ethnographischen Verhältnisse in den baltischen Provinzen und in Litauen. *Pet. Mitt.*, 1915, pp. 329-333.

Rosendal, G. Snderjylland. 11 Kort. Odense, 1912.

Rose, J. H. The Future of Europe. *Scientia,* Vol. 19, 1916, pp. 1-11.

Rosi, M. Storia politica d'Europa dopo la pace di Vienna. Milan, 1914-1916.

Sach, L. Das Herzogtum Schleswig-Holstein in seiner ethnographischen und nationalen Entwicklung. Halle, 1896.

Samassa, P. Deutsche u. Windische in Südösterreich. *Deutsche Erde,* Vol. 2, 1903, pp. 39-41.

Sands, B. The Ukraine. London, 1914.

Saxen, R. Répartition des langues. *Fennia,* Vol. 30, 1910-1911. Atlas de Finlande, Carte No. 46. Helsingfors, 1911.

Schlesinger. Das Deutsch-böhmische Sprachgebiet nach der letzten Volkszählung. Vienna, 1894.

Schlüter, O. Die Siedelungen in nordöstlicher Thüringen. Berlin, 1903.

Schneller. Deutsche und Romanen in Südtirol u. Venetien. *Pet. Mitt.*, 1877, pp. 365-385.

Schrader, F., F. Prudent et E. Anthoine. Atlas de Géographie Moderne. Paris, 1908.

Semple, E. C. Influences of Geographic Environment. New York, 1911.

Sergi, G. Europa—L'origine dei popoli europei e loro relazioni coi popoli d'Africa, d'Asia e d'Oceania. Rome, 1908.

Seymour, C. The Diplomatic Background of the War 1870-1914. New Haven, 1916.

Shedd, Wm. A. The Syrians of Persia and Turkey. *Bull. Amer. Geogr. Soc.*, Vol. 35, 1903.

Sirianu, R. La Question de Transylvanie et l'Unité Politique Roumaine. Paris, 1916.

Smirnov, J. Les Populations Finnoises des Bassins de la Volga et de la Kama. Paris, 1898.

Songeon, R. P. Guérin. Histoire de la Bulgarie. Paris, 1913.

Stade, Paul. Das Deutschtum gegenüber den Polen in Ost- und Westpreussen nach den Sprachzählungen von 1861, 1890 und 1900. Berlin, 1908.

Statistique de la Belgique. Recensement général de 1910, Vol. 2 (1912), Vol. 3 (1913), Brussels.

Stephen, H. M. Nationality and History. *The Amer. Hist. Rev.*, Jan. 1916.

Stourdza, A. La Terre et la Race Roumaines. Paris, 1904. La Roumanie et les Roumains. Paris, 1910.

Supan, A. Die Bevölkerung der Erde: Europa. *Ergänzungsh.* No. 163 zu *Pet. Mitt.*, Gotha, 1909.

Switzerland. Atlas graphique et statistique de la Suisse. Département Fédéral de l'Intérieur. Berne, 1914.

Sybel, H. von. Die Begründung des deutschen Reiches durch Wilhelm I. Oldenbourg, 1895.

Sykes, M. The Caliph's Last Heritage: a Short History of the Turkish Empire. London, 1915.

Sykes, P. M. A History of Persia. London, 1915.

Szinnyei, J. Finnisch-ugrische Sprachwissenschaft. 1910.

Tabbé, P. La Vivante Roumanie. Paris, 1913.

Talko-Hryncewicz, J. Polacy Królestwa Polskiego w świetle dotychczasowych badau. *B. int. Ac. Sc. Cracovie, Classe des Sc. math. et nat., B. Sc. nat.*, 1912, pp. 574-584.

Teutsch, F. Die Art der Ansiedelung der Siebengürger Sachsen. *Forsch. z. deuts. Landes- u. Volkskunde*, Vol. 9, 1896, pp. 1-22.

This, G. Die deutsch-französische Sprachgrenze in Lothringen. *Beiträge z. Landes- und Volkskunde von Elsass-Lothringen*, Vol. 1, Strassburg, 1887;—Die deutsch-französische Sprachgrenze in Elsass, *Ibid.*, 1888.

Touchard, G. Les langues parlées en Belgique. *Le Mouv. Géogr.*, 1913, pp. 226-229.

Toynbee, Arnold J. The Balkans, a History of Bulgaria, Serbia, Greece, Rumania, Turkey. By Nevill Forbes, Arnold J. Toynbee, D. Mitrany, D. G. Hogarth. Oxford, 1915.

Troïnitsky, N. Premier recensement général de population de l'Empire de la Russie 1897. Petrograd, 1905.

Tsanoff, R. A. Bulgaria's Rôle in the Balkans. *Journ. of Race Development*, Jan. 1915.

Vallaux, Camille. Le Sol et l'État, Géographie Sociale. Paris, 1911.

Van der Essen, L. A Short History of Belgium. Chicago, 1915.

Veress, A. Acta et Epistolae Relationum Transylvaniae Hungariaeque cum Moldavia et Valachia. Vienna, 1915.

Vidal de la Blache, P. États et Nations de l'Europe. Paris, 1889.

Vidal de la Blache, P. Évolution de la population en Alsace-Lorraine et dans les départements limitrophes. *Ann. de Géogr.*, Vol. 25, 1916, pp. 97-115.

Vidal de la Blache, P. La France, Tableau géographique. Paris, 1908.

Vinogradoff, Paul. Self-Government in Russia. New York, 1916.

Wace, A. J. B., and Thompson, M. S. The Nomads of the Balkans. London, 1914.

Wallis, B. C. Distribution of Nationalities in Hungary. *Geogr. Journ.*, Vol. 47, 1916, pp. 177-189.

Ward, A. W. Germany: 1815-1890, Vol. 1. 1815-1852. Cambridge, 1916.

Warker, Nikolaus. Die deutschen Orts- und Gewässernamen der belgischen Provinz Luxemburg. *Deutsche Erde*, Vol. 8, 1909, pp. 99-104.

Waultrin, M. R. Le rapprochement Dano-Allemand et la question du Schleswig. *Ann. Sc. Pol.*, 1903.

Weigand. Linguistischer Atlas. Leipzig, 1909.

Weill, G. L'Alsace Française de 1789 à 1870. Paris, 1916.

Whitney, W. D. Language and the Study of Language. New York, 1867.

Whitney, W. D. Oriental and Linguistic Studies. New York, 1873.

Wichdorff, H. V. Masuren. Berlin, 1915.

Wiklund, K. B. Språken i Finland, 1880-1900. *Ymer,* 1905, pp. 132-149.

Wissocq, E. de. L'âme Flamande. *Bull. Soc. Normande de Géographie,* 1912, pp. 97-135.

Witte, Hans. Das deutsche Sprachgebiet Lothringens und seine Wandelungen von der Feststellung der Sprachgrenze bis zum Ausgang des 16. Jahrhunderts. *Forsch. z. deuts. Landes- und Volkskunde,* Vol. 8, 1894.—Zur Geschichte des Deutschtums im Elsass und im Vogesengebiet, *Ibid.,* Vol. 19, 1897.

Witte, H. Wendische Bevölkerungsreste in Mecklenburg. *Forsch. z. deuts. Landes- und Volkskunde,* Vol. 16, 1905, p. 124.

Woods, H. C. Communications in the Balkans. *Geogr. Journ.,* Vol. 47, 1916, pp. 265-293.

Wutte, M. Das Deutschtum im Österreichischen Küstenland. *Deutsche Erde,* Vol. 8, 1909, pp. 202, 229.

Xénopol, A. D. Les Roumains au Moyen-Âge. Paris, 1885. Histoire des Roumains de la Dacie Trajane. Paris, 1896.

Zaborowski, S. Les Peuples aryens d'Asie et d'Europe. Paris, 1908.

Zemmrich, J. Deutschen und Slawen in den österreichischen Südetenländern. *Deutsche Erde,* Vol. 2, 1903, pp. 1-4.

Zemmrich, J. Sprachgrenze und Deutschtum in Böhmen. Brunswick, 1902.

Zimmerli, J. Die deutsch-französische Sprachgrenze in der Schweiz; I. Teil, Die Schweiz. *Forsch. z. deuts. Landes- und Volkskunde,* Vol. 8, 1894.

Zimmerli, J. Die deutsch-französische Sprachgrenze in der Schweiz; I. Teil, Die Sprachgrenze im Jura. Basel, 1891. II. Teil, Die Sprachgrenze im Mittellande, in den Freiburger, Waadtländer und Berner Alpen, *Ibid.,* 1895. III. Teil, Die Sprachgrenze im Wallis, *Ibid.,* 1899.

Zsigmond, B. A Magyar Szentkorona országainak néprajzi iskolai fali Térképe. 1:600,000. Budapest, 1909.

APPENDIX E

KEY TO PLACE NAMES

Aa, river, lat. 51°, Pl. I.

Abanj, town, lat. 48° 50', Fig. 48.

Abbateggio, town, lat. 42° 14', Fig. 33.

Abruzzi, province, lat. 42°, Fig. 33.

Abullonia, lake, south of Moudania, lat. 40° 12', Pl. VII.

Acquaviva, town, lat. 40° 53', Fig. 33.

Ada Bazar, town, lat. 40° 45', Pl. VII.

Adalia, town and bay, lat. 36° 53', Pl. V.

Adana, town, lat. 37°, Pl. V.

Aden, gulf of, lat. 12° 46'. See inset map: "Extension of the Hejaz line toward Mecca." Pl. V.

Adige, valley, lat. 45° 40', Figs. 30, 67.

Adrianople, town, lat. 41° 41', Fig. 47.

Adriatic, sea, Pl. IX. See also Figs. 47, 48.

Ægean, sea, Pl. V.

Agaro, district, lat. 46° 15', Fig. 22.

Aidin, town, lat. 37° 48', Pl. V.

Aire, town, lat. 50° 38', Pl. I.

Ala, town, lat. 45° 50', Fig. 30.

Alagna, village, lat. 45° 52', Fig. 22.

Aland, isds., lat. 60° 15', Pl. IX.

Albania, state, lat. 41°, Fig. 53.

Albula, river, lat. 46° 40', Fig. 67.

Aleppo, town, lat. 36° 10', Pl. V, VI, VII.

Alexandretta, town, lat. 36° 35', Pl. V, VI, VII.

Alghero, town, lat. 40° 40', Fig. 43.

Allenstein, town, lat. 53° 45', Fig. 38.

Alpes-Maritimes, dept., lat. 43° 45', Fig. 22.

Alsace, province, lat. 48° 50', Pl. II, IX.

Amasia, town, lat. 40° 39', Pl. VII.

Anderlecht (Brussels), lat. 50° 51', Fig. 14.

Andermatten, village (Italian: La Chiesa), lat. 46° 20', Fig. 22.

Andreasfalva, town, lat. 47° 50', Fig. 44.

Angeln, mts., 54° 35', Fig. 35.

Angora, town, lat. 39° 56', Pl. V, VII.

Anniviers, valley, lat. 46° 15', Fig. 18.

Antigorio, val., lat. 46° 10', Fig. 22.

Antioch, town, lat. 36° 10', Pl. VII.

Antivari, town, lat. 42° 8', Fig. 53.

Aosta, town, lat. 45° 44', Pl. IX, Fig. 22.

Aquitaine, region, lat. 44° 50', Fig. 3.

Arad, town, lat. 46° 13', Fig. 48.

Arax, river, lat. 39° 27', Pl. VII.

Arghana, town, lat. 38° 25', Pl. V.

Argyrocastro, district, lat. 40° 7', Fig. 53.

Arlon, town, lat. 49° 42', Pl. I.

Armenia, province, Pl. VII, VIII.

Armentières, town, lat. 50° 43', Pl. I.

Armorica, region, lat. 48° 10', Fig. 3.

Arnfels, town, lat. 46° 42', Fig. 31.

Arnsberg, town, lat. 51° 24', Fig. 7.

Arta, river, lat. 39° 20', Fig. 53.

Asiago, town, lat. 45° 52', Fig. 30.

Aspropotamos, river, lat. 39° 22', Fig. 53.

Astico, river, lat. 45° 40', Fig. 25.

Augsburg, town, lat. 48° 52', Pl. IX, Fig. 30.

Augustow, town, lat. 53° 30', Fig. 38.

Baden, grand duchy, lat. 48° 30', Fig. 7.

Bagdad, town, lat. 33° 21', Pl. V.

Balearic, isds., lat. 39°, Fig. 43.

Banat, province, lat. 45° 53', Fig. 38.

Bären Kopf, mt., lat. 47° 47', Pl. II.

Bars, town, lat. 48° 15', Fig. 48.

Basra, town, lat. 30° 30', Pl. V.

Bautzen, town, lat. 51° 11', Fig. 41.

Bavaria, kingdom, lat. 49°, Fig. 7.

Beaulard, town, lat. 45° 3', Fig. 21.

Becherek, town, lat. 45° 27', Fig. 48.

Beirut, town, lat. 33° 54', Pl. V.

Belcamen, town, lat. 40° 40', Fig. 53.

Belfort, town, lat. 47° 38', Pl. II, Fig. 18.

Belgrade, town, lat. 44° 47', Pl. IX.

Belluno, town, lat. 46° 8', Fig. 67.

Benkovac, town, lat. 44° 2', Fig. 48.

Berane, town, lat. 42° 47', Fig. 53.

Berat, town, lat. 40° 43', Fig. 53.

Bereg, town, lat. 47°, Fig. 38.

Beskid, mts., lat. 49° 30', Pl. IV.

Bessarabia, province, lat. 47° 20', Pl. III.

Bévéra, valley, lat. 43° 50', Fig. 22.

Bielostok, town, lat. 53° 10', Pl. IV.

Bielsk, town, lat. 52° 50', Pl. IV.

Bienne, town, lat. 47° 9', Fig. 18.

Birnbaum, town, lat. 52° 37′, Pl. IV.

Bistritza, valley, lat. 40° 30′, Fig. 53.

Black Drin, river, lat. 42°, Fig. 53.

Black Forest, mountain region, lat. 48° 20′, Fig. 7.

Blatza, town, lat. 40° 31′, Fig. 53.

Böhmerwald, mt., lat. 49° 0′, Fig. 48.

Bohtan, river, lat. 38°, Pl. VII.

Boitsfort, town, lat. 50° 48′, Fig. 14.

Bolchen, town, lat. 49° 10′, Pl. II.

Boli, town, lat. 40° 45′, Pl. V.

Bolzano, (Bozen), town, lat. 46° 30′, Figs. 30, 67.

Bomst, town, lat. 52° 12′, Pl. IV.

Bosnia, province, lat. 44° 20′, Fig. 48.

Bothnia, gulf, lat. 62°, Fig. 38.

Botzen, (Bozen), town, lat. 46° 30′, Figs. 30, 67.

Boulogne, town, lat. 50° 43′, Pl. I.

Bousson, town, lat. 44° 55′, Fig. 21.

Boyana, river, lat. 41° 52′, Fig. 53.

Brandenburg, province, lat. 52° 26′, Fig. 7.

Branjevo, town, lat. 44° 40′, Fig. 48.

Bredizza, town, lat. 41° 50′, Fig. 53.

Brenner, pass, lat. 47° 3′, Fig. 30.

Brenta, river, lat. 45° 26′, Fig. 25.

Breslau, town, lat. 51° 6′, Pl. IV.

Bressanone, town, see Brixen.

Briançon, town, lat. 44° 50′, Fig. 21.

Brieg, town, lat. 50° 50′, Pl. IV.

Brittany, province, lat. 48° 20′, Fig. 3.

Brixen, town, lat. 46° 41′, Fig. 30.

Bromberg, town, lat. 53° 7′, Pl. IV.

Broye, river, lat. 46° 45′, Fig. 18.

Bruche, river, lat. 48° 30′, Pl. II.

Bruneco, town, lat. 46° 51′, Fig. 30.

Brusa, town, lat. 40° 11′, Pl. V.

Brux, town, lat. 50° 33′, Fig. 48.

Buccari, bay, lat. 45° 18′, Fig. 48.

Budapest, lat. 47° 29′, Pl. IX.

Bukovina, province, lat. 48° 0′, Fig. 44.

Bukschoja, town, lat. 47° 37′, Fig. 44.

Burgundian lands, (see Burgundy), lat. 47°, Fig. 3.

Busi, is., lat. 43° 8′, Fig. 48.

Cairo, city, lat. 30° 2′, Pl. V.

Calliano, town, lat. 45° 56′, Fig. 30.

Canza, village, lat. 46° 25′, Fig. 22.

Carinthia, lat. 47°, Pl. III.

Carniola, province, lat. 45° 58′, Fig. 48. Pl. III.

Carpathian Mts., lat. 48° 30′, Pl. IV.

Cascanditella, town, lat. 42° 16′, Fig. 33.

Casotto, town, lat. 45° 53′, Fig. 67.

Cattaro, town, lat. 42° 23′, Fig. 48.

Caucasus, region, lat. 44°, Fig. 38.

Cazza, is., lat. 42° 55′, Fig. 48.

Cesane, town, lat. 44° 57′, Fig. 21.

Cevedale, mt., lat. 46° 29′, Fig. 67.

Chalcydic peninsula, lat. 40° 25′, Fig. 53.

Champlas du Col, town, lat. 44° 56′, Fig. 21.

Chanak, town, lat. 40° 9′, Pl. VI.

Charmoille, town, lat. 47° 20′, Fig. 18.

Chernikov, city, lat. 51° 29′, Fig. 38.

Chorlu, river, lat. 41° 12′, Fig. 47.

Cilician Gate, lat. 37° 30′, Pl. VII., see inset: "Western Asia showing direction of Main Mountain Ranges."

Clabecq, lat. 50° 40′, Fig. 14.

Clavières, town, lat. 44° 55′, Figs. 21, 22.

Clementi, pass, lat. 42° 30′, Fig. 53.

Collecroce, town, lat. 41° 45′, Fig. 33.

Colmar, town, lat. 48° 6′, Pl. II.

Cologne, town, lat. 50° 56′, Pl. IX.

Constantinople, city, lat. 41°, Pl. VII.

Corfu, is., lat. 39° 37′, Fig. 53, Pl. V, VI.

Cormons, town, lat. 45° 57′, Fig. 31.

Cortina d'Ampezzo, pass, lat. 46° 31′, Fig. 67.

Courtaron, town, lat. 47° 28′, Fig. 18.

Cracow, town, lat. 50° 4′, Pl. IV.

Crasna, lat. 48° 2′, Fig. 44.

Crefeld, town, lat. 51° 21′, Pl. IX.

Cremnitza, river, lat. 40°, Fig. 53.

Crete, is., lat. 35° 15′, Pl. V.

Croatia, province, lat. 45° 40′, Fig. 48.

Cupello, town, lat. 42° 5′, Fig. 33.

Curzola, is., lat. 43°, Fig. 48.

Czernowitz, town, lat. 48° 17′, Fig. 44.

Dalmatia, province, lat. 44°, Fig. 48.

Damascus, city, lat. 33° 30′, Pl. V, VII.

Dangli, mts., lat. 40° 30′, Fig. 53.

Danzig, town, lat. 54° 35′, Pl. IV.

Dedeagatch, town, lat. 40° 55′, Fig. 47.

Delémont, town, lat. 47° 25′, Fig. 18.

Delvino, town, lat. 40°, Fig. 53.

Demir-Hissar, district, lat. 41° 12′, Fig. 53.

Dent d'Hérens, mt., lat. 45° 59′, Fig. 22.

Deutsche-Oth, town, lat. 49° 28′, Pl. II.

Devinska Novaves, town, lat. 48° 18′, Fig. 48.

Devoli, river, lat. 40° 55′, Fig. 53.

Diex, town, lat. 46° 48′, Fig. 31.

Dinaric Alps, mts., lat. 44°, Fig. 48.

Dineir, town, lat. 38° 5′, Pl. V.

Dirschen, (Dirschau or Terzew), lat. 54° 9′, Pl. IV.

Dnieper, river, lat. 49°, Fig. 38.

Dobrac, town, lat. 46° 45′, Fig. 31.

Dobrudja, province, lat. 44° 20′, Fig. 47.

Dodecanesia, isds., lat. 36°, Pl. V.

Doire Baltée, river, lat. 45° 15′, Fig. 22.

Doire Ripaire, river, lat. 45° 10′, Figs. 21, 22.

Doliano, town, lat. 40° 2′, Fig. 53.

Dolomite Alps, mts., lat. 46° 25′, Fig. 67.

Domodossola, town, lat. 46° 8′, Fig. 22.

Don, river, lat. 47° 30′, Fig. 38.

Dorpat, town, lat. 58° 17′, Fig. 38.

Dortmund, town, lat. 51° 31′, Fig. 7.

Douane, town, lat. 47° 10′, Fig. 18.

Drama, basin, lat. 41°' 6′, Fig. 47.

Drave, river, lat. 45° 50′, Fig. 48.

Drin, river, lat. 41° 50′, Fig. 53.

Drinissa, river, lat. 42° 12′, Fig. 53.

Drino, gulf, lat. 41° 50′, Fig. 53.

Dugopolje, town, lat. 45° 10′, Fig. 48.

Duino, town, lat. 45° 50′, Fig. 31.

Duisburg, town, lat. 51° 26′, Fig. 7.

Dukla, town, lat. 49° 26′, Pl. IV.

Dulcigno, town, lat. 41° 54′, Fig. 53.

Dunkirk, town, lat. 51° 7′, Pl. I.

Durazzo, cape and town, lat. 41° 18′, Fig. 53.

Düsseldorf, town, lat. 51° 13′, Fig. 7.

Dux, town, lat. 50° 47′, Fig. 48.

East Prussia, province, lat. 34°, Pl. IV.

Eisack, valley, lat. 46° 30′, Fig. 67.

Eisenau, town, lat. 47° 38′, Fig. 44.

Elbassan, town, lat. 41° 6′, Fig. 53.

Elbe, river, lat. 53°, Pl. IX.

Emscher, valley, lat. 51° 30′, Fig. 7.

Enego, town, lat. 45° 57′, Fig. 25.

Engadine, district, lat. 46° 40′, Fig. 67.

Epirus, province, lat. 40°, Fig. 53.

Erzerum, town, lat. 39° 57′, Pl. VIII.

Erzgebirge, mt., lat. 50° 30′, Fig. 48.

Erzingian, town, lat. 39° 38′, Pl. V.

Eskishehir, town, lat. 39° 44′, Pl. V.

Esthonia, province, lat. 59° 15′, Fig. 38.

Esztergom or Gran-Esztergom, comitat, lat. 47° 47′, Fig. 48.

Etsch, river, lat. 46° 16′, Fig. 30.

Etterbeck, (Brussels), Fig. 14.

Euphrates, river, lat. 37° 50′, Pl. VIII.

Fellin, town, lat. 58°, Fig. 38.

Fenils, town, lat. 44° 59′, Fig. 21.

Fersina, town, lat. 46° 8′, Fig. 30.

Filiates, town, lat. 39° 42′, Fig. 53.

Fiume, town, lat. 45° 19′, Fig. 48.

Fleims, valley, lat. 46° 20′, Fig. 30.

Flensborg, town, lat. 54° 46′, Fig. 35.

Florina, town, lat. 40° 50′, Fig. 53.

Fogaras, town, lat. 45° 47′, Pl. III.

Foppiano, town, lat. 46° 20′, Fig. 22.

Formazza, valley, lat. 46° 15′, Fig. 22.

Franconia, district, lat. 50°, Fig. 7.

Frasheri, town, lat. 40° 25′, Fig. 53.

Freudenthal, town, lat. 47° 45′, Fig. 44.

Fribourg, town, lat. 46° 48′, Fig. 18.

Friuli, district, (see area of Friulian language), lat. 46° 18′, Fig. 43.

Fruttwald, or Canza, village, lat. 46° 25′, Fig. 22.

Frydland, town, lat. 49° 45′, Fig. 48.

Fünfkirchen, town, lat. 46° 6′, Pl. III.

Galicia, province, lat. 48° 50′, Fig. 44.

Gallio, town, lat. 45° 52′, Fig. 25.

Gallipoli, peninsula, lat. 40° 25′, Fig. 47.

Gargazon, town, lat. 46° 36′, Fig. 67.

Gazza, town, lat. 45° 50′, Fig. 30.

Geala, town, lat. 41° 13′, Fig. 53.

Gediz, river, lat. 38° 36′, Pl. VII.

Ghemlick, (Cius), town, lat. 40° 30′, Pl. VII.

Ghison, river, lat. 44° 54′, Figs. 21, 22.

Gléresse, town, lat. 47° 8′, Fig. 18.

Gömö, district, lat. 49°, Fig. 48.

Gopes, town, lat. 41° 13′, Fig. 53.

Gornia Bistrica, town, lat. 46° 30′, Fig. 31.

Gottschee, town, lat. 45° 38′, Fig. 31.

Gradena, basin, see Grödenthal.

Gradisca, town, lat. 45° 15′, Fig. 31.

Gramala, bay, lat. 40° 15′, Fig. 53.

Grammos, mts., lat. 40° 25′, Fig. 53.

Gramosta, town, lat. 40° 23′, Fig. 53.

Grand Paradis Peak, lat. 45° 30′, Fig. 22.

Gran-Esztergom, town, lat. 47° 47′, Fig. 48.

Graudenz, town, lat. 53° 25′, Pl. IV.

Gressoney, lat. 45° 50′, Fig. 22.

Greutschach, town, lat. 46° 51′, Fig. 31.

Grevena, village, lat. 40° 9′, Fig. 53.

Gries, pass, lat. 46° 30′, Fig. 22.

Griffen, town, lat. 46° 50′, Fig. 31.

Grisons, canton, lat. 46° 42', Fig. 67.
Grödenthal, valley, lat. 46° 37', Fig. 30.
Grodno, town, lat. 53° 41', Fig. 38.
Grybow, town, lat. 49° 40', Pl. IV.
Guevgueli, town, lat. 41° 13', Fig. 53.
Gurk, town, lat. 46° 55', Fig. 31.
Gusinye, district, lat. 42° 35', Fig. 53.

Hadikfalva, town, lat. 47° 55', Fig. 44.
Halluin, town, lat. 50° 47', Pl. I.
Hama, town, lat. 35° 13', Pl. V.
Hamburg, city, lat. 53° 33', Pl. IX.
Harput, town, lat. 38° 40', Pl. V.
Havel, river, lat. 52° 43', Fig. 7.
Hazebrouck, town, lat. 50° 44', Pl. I.
Helsingfors, town, lat. 60° 10', Pl. IX.
Hermannstadt, town, lat. 45° 46', Pl. III.
Herzegovina, province, lat. 43° 20', Fig. 48.
Hesse, grand duchy, lat. 51°, Fig. 7.
Hochkönigsberg, mt., lat. 48° 15', Pl. II.
Hodeida, town, lat. 14° 40', Pl. V. See inset: "Extension of the Hejaz line toward Mecca."
Hoeylaert, town, lat. 50° 49', Fig. 14.
Homs, town, lat. 34° 46', Pl. V.
Hont, comitat, lat. 48° 30', Fig. 48.
Huta, town, lat. 48° 22', Fig. 48.

Ile de France, province, lat. 48° 50', Fig. 3.
Ill, river, lat. 48° 25', Pl. II.
Illmenspitze, mt., lat. 46° 28', Fig. 67.
Illyria, province, lat. 46° 15', Fig. 48.
Ilmen, lake, lat. 58° 15', Fig. 38.
Imotski, town, lat. 43° 25', Fig. 48.
Ipek, town, lat. 42° 34', Fig. 53.
Iran, plateau, lat. 32°, Pl. VII. See inset: "Western Asia showing direction of Main Mountain Ranges."
Isargo, river, see Eisack.
Iser, mt., lat. 50° 50', Fig. 48.
Ishtip, town, lat. 41° 45', Fig. 53.
Isnik (Nicaea), town, lat. 40° 40', Pl. VII.
Isonzo, river, lat. 46°, Fig. 31.
Issime, town, lat. 45° 40', Fig. 22.
Istensegitz, town, lat. 47° 52', Fig. 44.
Istria, province, lat. 45° 20', Fig. 32.
Ixelles, (Brussels), Fig. 14.

Jablunka, pass, lat. 49° 34', Pl. IV.
Jaffa, town, lat. 32° 4', Pl. V.
Jakobeny, town, lat. 47° 30', Fig. 44.
Jeihun, river, lat. 37° 30', Pl. VII.

Jerablus, town, lat. 36° 30', Pl. V.
Jerusalem, city, lat. 31° 47', Pl. V.
Jette, town, lat. 50° 51', Fig. 14.
Jevizlik, town, lat. 40° 48°, Pl. VII.
Jidda, town, lat. 21°, Pl. V. See inset: "Extension of the Hejaz line toward Mecca."
Johanisburg, town, lat. 53° 37', Fig. 38.
Julian Alps, mts., lat. 46° 10', Fig. 31.
Jumaya, town, lat. 42°, Fig. 53.
Jura, mts., lat. 46° 50', Fig. 3.

Kailar, town, lat. 40° 29', Fig. 53.
Kalamas, river, lat. 39° 35', Fig. 53.
Kalarites, town, lat. 39° 40', Fig. 53.
Kamienec, town, lat. 48° 40', Fig. 44.
Kanin, mt., lat. 46° 24', Fig. 31.
Karaferia, town, lat. 40° 36', Fig. 53.
Kassaba, town, lat. 38° 8', Pl. V.
Kastamuni, town, lat. 41° 23', Pl. V.
Kastoria, lake, lat. 40° 34', Fig. 53.
Katerynoslav, town, lat. 48° 28', Fig. 38.
Kavalla, town, lat. 41°, Fig. 47.
Kelkid, river, lat. 40° 20', Pl. VII.
Kerepes, town, lat. 47° 35', Fig. 48.
Kharkov, town, lat. 50°, Fig. 38.
Kherson, town, lat. 46° 39', Fig. 38.
Kholm, town, lat. 51° 39', Fig. 38.
Khursk, town, lat. 51° 56', Fig. 38.
Kiev, town, lat. 50° 27', Fig. 38.
Kimara, town, lat. 40° 10', Fig. 53.
Kiri, river, lat. 41° 55', Fig. 53.
Kirlibaba, town, lat. 47° 40', Fig. 44.
Kizil, river, lat. 41°, Pl. VII.
Klagenfurth, town, lat. 46° 37', Fig. 48.
Klausen, town, lat. 46° 39', Fig. 67.
Kliasma, river, lat. 56° 19', Fig. 38.
Klimutz, town, lat. 47° 58', Fig. 44.
Klissura, town, see Vlakho-Klissura.
Knin, town, lat. 44° 3', Fig. 48.
Kockana, town, lat. 40° 20', Fig. 53.
Koekelberg, (Brussels), Fig. 14.
Konia, town, lat. 37° 51', Pl. VII.
Koritza, town, lat. 40° 15', Fig. 53.
Kostenberg, town, lat. 46° 45', Fig. 31.
Kottbus, town, lat. 51° 34', Fig. 41.
Kovno, town, lat. 55°, Fig. 38.
Koweit, town, lat. 29° 30', Pl. VI.
Krajste, valley, lat. 42° 41', Fig. 53.
Krasnostaw, town, lat. 50° 59', Pl. IV.
Kremnitz, town, lat. 48° 42', Fig. 48.
Krushevo, town, lat. 41° 25', Fig. 53.
Kuban, province, lat. 45°, Fig. 38.
Kukush, town, lat. 40° 59', Fig. 53.

Pilsen, town, lat. 49° 45', Fig. 48.

Pindus, mts., lat. 39° 45', Fig. 53.

Pirot, town, lat. 43° 10', Fig. 53.

Pisuderi, town, lat. 40° 45', Fig. 53.

Pressburg, town, lat. 48° 10', Pl. III.

Priepet, river and marshes, lat. 52° 10', Pl. IX.

Prizrend, town, lat. 42° 8', Fig. 53.

Progno, river, lat. 45° 30', Fig. 30.

Prokleita, mts., lat. 42° 25', Fig. 53.

Provence, province, lat. 43° 50', Fig. 3.

Pruth, river, lat. 47°, Pl. III.

Puglia, province, lat. 41°, Fig. 43.

Pusterthal, valley, lat. 46° 44', Fig. 67.

Raab, river, lat. 47° 25', Fig. 48.

Raab, town, lat. 47° 41', Pl. III.

Radgona, town, lat. 46° 40', Fig. 31.

Radkersburg, town, lat. 46° 42', Fig. 31.

Radymno, town, lat. 49° 58', Pl. IV.

Ragusa, town, lat. 42° 37', Fig. 48.

Ras el ain, town, lat. 36° 50', Pl. V.

Rayak, town, lat. 33° 30', Pl. V.

Razlog, town, lat. 41° 51', Fig. 53.

Red Sea, lat. 20°, Pl. V. *See* inset: "Extension of the Hejaz line toward Mecca."

Reichenberg, town, lat. 50° 47', Fig. 48.

Renz, town, lat. 54° 43', Fig. 35.

Resia, town, lat. 46° 30', Fig. 31.

Reval, town, lat. 59° 27', Pl. IX.

Rhenish Prussia, province, lat. 50° 30', Fig. 7.

Rhine, river, lat. 48°, Pl. II.

Rhine Herne, canal, lat. 51° 28', Fig. 7.

Rhodes, is., (the largest of the Dodecanesia group), lat. 36° 23', Pl. V.

Rhode-Saint-Genèse, town, lat. 50° 49', Fig. 14.

Rhodope, mts., lat. 42°, Fig. 47.

Rhone, river, lat. 45°, Fig. 3.

Rhone Valley, lat. 45°, Fig. 3.

Ribeauvillé or Rappoltsweiler, town, lat. 48° 12', Pl. II.

Rienza, river, lat. 46° 50', Fig. 30.

Riga, gulf, lat. 57° 30', Pl. IX.

Rilo, town, lat. 42° 9', Fig. 53.

Rima S. Giuseppe, village, lat. 45° 54', Fig. 22.

Roana, town, lat. 45° 51', Fig. 25.

Roanne, town, lat. 46° 2', Fig. 6.

Rochemolles, town, lat. 45° 8', Fig. 21.

Rodoni, cape, lat. 41° 34', Fig. 53.

Rodosto, town, lat. 41°, Fig. 47.

Rokytince, town, lat. 49° 22', Fig. 48.

Rosa, mt., lat. 45° 56', Fig. 22.

Roshai, town, lat. 42° 49', Fig. 53.

Rotzo, town, lat. 45° 50', Fig. 25.

Rovereto, town, lat. 45° 53', Fig. 30.

Roya, river, lat. 43° 54', Fig. 22.

Rudolfthal, town, lat. 45° 15', Fig. 48.

Rymanow, town, lat. 49° 35', Pl. IV.

Saar, river, lat. 49° 35', Pl. II.

Saaz, town, lat. 50° 21', Fig. 48.

St. Andrea, is., lat. 43° 2', Fig. 48.

St. Bernard, mt., lat. 45° 51', Fig. 18.

Saint-Gilles, town, (Brussels), Fig. 14.

St. Gotthard, town, lat. 46° 58', Fig. 31.

Saint-Hermagoras, town, lat. 46° 43', Fig. 31.

Saint-Josse-ten-Noode, town, (Brussels), Fig. 14.

St. Omer, town, lat. 50° 45', Pl. I.

St. Pancrace, town, lat. 46° 48', Fig. 31.

Sakaria, river, lat. 40°, Pl. VII.

Sakaria, valley, lat. 40°, Pl. VII.

Salbertrand, town, lat. 45° 6', Fig. 21.

Salecchio, town, lat. 46° 20', Fig. 22.

Salerno, town, lat. 40° 40', Fig. 43.

Salonica, town, lat. 40° 38', Pl. IX and Fig. 47.

Samarra, town, lat. 34° 10', Pl. V.

Sampeyre, town, lat. 44° 35', Fig. 22.

Samsun, town, lat. 41° 18', Pl. VIII.

San, river, lat. 50° 34', Pl. IV.

Sana'a, town, lat. 15°, Pl. V. *See* inset: "Extension of the Hejaz line toward Mecca."

San Felice Slavo, town, lat. 41° 54', Fig. 33.

San Giacomo di Lusiana, town, lat. 45° 30', Fig. 25.

San Giovanni Teatino, town, lat. 42° 24', Fig. 33.

San Juan, point, (Gulf of Drino), lat. 41° 45', Fig. 53.

San Juan de Medua, town, lat. 41° 55', Fig. 53.

San Martino di Perrero, town, lat. 44° 56', Fig. 21.

San Michele, (German: Pommat), village, lat. 46° 20', Fig. 21.

Sanok, town, lat. 49° 34', Pl. IV.

San Pietro Brazza, town, lat. 43° 19', Fig. 48.

Santi-Quaranta, (Preveza), town, lat. 39° 49', Fig. 53.

INDEX

Aasen, Ivar, 99
Abruzzi, 88
Adalia, Gulf of, 251, 256-257
Adige, 84
Adige valley, 70, 74
Adriatic, control, 83-84; eastern coast, 337-338; piracy, 86, 87; problem, 199-201; Serbia and, 180
Adriatic coast and German language, 68
Adriatic provinces, 76
Ægean, 174, 175, 247-248, 274
Aidin railway, 250, 251, 255
Albanach, 192
Albania, 84, 163, 164, 180, 181, 187, 189, 193-201; Greek boundary, 197; importance, 199; national feeling and boundaries, 194, 195; **religion, 201**
Albanian, 87, 90, 163, 165, 192
Albanians, 175, 192-201
Alemanni, 44
Aleppo, 224, 225, 259, 261, 264
Alexandretta, 244, 261
Alexandria, 233, 234
Alghero, 64
Allevis, 285
Alpes-Maritimes, 64
Alpine race, xiv, 4, 5, 6, 19, 38, 40, 41, 323-324
Alps, 42, 333
Alsace, 38-49; Lower and Higher, 41
Alsace-Lorraine, 329-330, 334-335; linguistic boundary between French and German, 35-49
Alsatians, 40, 41, 46, 47
Amanus, 259, 260
America, discovery of, 233, 235
Anatolia, 225, 247, 248, 266, 271, 275, 276, 284; Turks in, 281
"Ange," 36
Anglo-Saxon, 13
Ansariyehs, 298-299
Ansiedelunggesetz, 127
Antioch, 297, 298
Aosta, 60
Aptals, 289
Arabia, 238; British influence, 240-241; France and, 266

Arabic, 225, 230; in Turkish, 280
Arabs, 307-308
Aram, 302
Aramaic, 302, 306
Arameans, 302-303
Argana, 261, 266
Argyrocastro, 197, 199
Arlon, 22
Armenia, 224, 244, 254, 266; etymology, 291
Armenian, Persian words in, 272
Armenians, 272, 289-294
Armenoids, 271, 273, 285, 324
Armorica, 56
Arnaut, 194
Aromunes, 163
Aryan, Albanian, 192; Armenians, 291, 292; early home, 7; Lithuanians, 104, 105; vagueness of term, 8
Ashkenazim, 301
Asia Minor, 175, 225, 228-229, 269, 270; geography, 252; Greeks in, 273-278; highway character, 249; Mohammedan dissenters, 285-289; Mohammedan immigrants, 282-284; peoples and villages, non-Turkish, table, 308-309; resources, 253-255; Turks in, 278-282. *See also* Turkey
Asiatic trade with Europe, 233-236
Asiatics in Europe, 174-176
Assassins, 298
Athens, 248
Augustus, 64
Austria, 95, 330; as protector of Europe, 82; census returns, character, 76; Dalmatia, 87; foreign policy, 80; Italian frontier claims (with sketch-map), 335-337; Jewish capitalists, 125; Lombardo-Venetia, 74; Poles in, 130; sketch-map showing Slavs and their languages, 183; Slovene in, map, 81
Austria-Hungary, 155, 156; Adriatic provinces, 76; Italians in, 66; nationality, 83; Polish provinces, table, 138; population and weakness, 80-82; Serbians in, 181-182

367